J. D. SALINGER

J. D. SALINGER

A LIFE

—⚬—

Kenneth Slawenski

Random House
NEW YORK

Copyright © 2010 by Kenneth Slawenski

Published in the United States by Random House, an imprint of
The Random House Publishing Group, a division of
Random House, Inc., New York.

RANDOM HOUSE and colophon are registered trademarks of
Random House, Inc.

This work was originally published in the United Kingdom as
J. D. Salinger: A Life Raised High by Pomona Books,
West Yorkshire, England, in 2010. Published by arrangement with
Pomona, England Ltd.

ISBN 978-1-4000-6951-4

Printed in the United States of America on acid-free paper

www.atrandom.com

4 6 8 9 7 5 3

Book design by Liz Cosgrove

To
my mother

Contents

Introduction

Since I have maintained a website devoted to the life and works of J. D. Salinger, it has grown extensively over time and receives a healthy amount of traffic but rarely generates more than a handful of e-mails per day. So you can imagine my surprise when I checked the mail on Thursday, January 28, 2010, and found not three or four messages shouting to be opened but fifty-seven. They were left unopened, too, for hours until I had gathered up the courage to confront them. By glancing at the e-mail on top of the heap, I knew exactly what had happened and how I would always remember that day. The news stared me down from my inbox through the starkest, most ugly of headers. It read: Rest In Peace J.D. Salinger. It should have read: Quicksand.

A few words of explanation are probably in order here. For nearly as long as I had been running the Salinger site, I had been chipping away at this book, determined to one day deliver a true and fair and unsentimental account of Salinger's life justly infused with appreciation for his works. After seven years, I had finally completed that task. In fact, I had sent in the final draft of my final chapter only a week before. For seven years, then, I had been completely immersed in Salinger: in his writings, his philosophy, and the smallest details of his life. Salinger had become my constant companion. And now he was gone.

Though I could perhaps push aside my e-mails for a time, I felt I could not ignore my website. My last post was now three weeks old, a message of congratulations to the author on his ninety-first birthday, complete with warm wishes for a long life that suddenly seemed obscene. Attempting to address Salinger's death, I searched my mind for a tribute I knew I should have already prepared but had been unable to even consider. Impossibly, I fumbled for a sentiment that would match the man. Not an epitaph. I remembered Holden Caulfield's disgust at all the phonies laying flowers on Allie's grave until it began to rain and their priorities suddenly shifted. Salinger himself did not believe in death, and I knew that. What I needed to offer was a salute, a call to gratitude rather than sorrow. What Salinger deserved was an affirmation, and I requested that others join me in presenting it.

I still doubt the quality of my delivery. It pales in the face of countless eloquent memorials Salinger has received since. But it is honest and heartfelt. It is not mourning for the dead. It is an invitation to salute. A salute not to the memory but to the essence of J. D. Salinger, and I offer it here again to anyone who wishes to honor the author now or at any time in the years to come:

> Read. Explore, whether for the first time or twentieth, *The Catcher in the Rye*. Read *Nine Stories, Franny and Zooey, Raise High the Roof Beam and Seymour*. Re-experience Salinger's works in tribute to the author who is so deeply embedded within them. Salinger the man may be gone—and for that the world is an emptier place—but he will always live within the pages he created, and through his art remain as vital today and tomorrow as when he walked the boulevards of New York and strolled the woods of New Hampshire.

Kenneth Slawenski
March 2010

J. D. SALINGER

1. Sonny

The Great War had changed everything. As 1919 dawned, people awoke to a fresh new world, one filled with promise but uncertainty. Old ways of life, beliefs and assumptions unchallenged for decades, were now called into question or swept away. The guns had fallen silent only weeks before. The Old World now lay in ruins. In its place stood a new nation poised to assume the mantle of leadership. No place in that land was more anxious or more ready than the city of New York.

It was the first day of the first year of peace when Miriam Jillich Salinger gave birth to a son. His sister, Doris, had been born six years before. In the years since Doris's birth, Miriam had suffered a series of miscarriages.

This child too was almost lost. So it was with a mixture of joy and relief that Miriam and Solomon Salinger welcomed their son into the world. They named him Jerome David, but from the very first day, they called him Sonny.

Sonny was born into a middle-class Jewish family that was both unconventional and ambitious. The Salinger line reached back to the village of Sudargas, a tiny Jewish settlement (shtetl) situated on the

Polish-Lithuanian border of the Russian Empire, a village where, records show, the family had lived at least since 1831. But the Salingers
were not given to tradition or nostalgia. By the time Sonny was born,
their link to that world had nearly evaporated. Sonny's father was ro-
bust and motivated, determined to go his own way in life. Typical of
the sons of immigrants, he had resolved to free himself of any connection with the world of his parents' birth, a place he considered backward. Unknown to Solomon at the time, his rebellion was actually a
family tradition. The Salingers had gone their own way for generations, seldom looking back and growing increasingly prosperous with
each step. As Sonny would one day reflect, his ancestors had an amazing penchant "for diving from immense heights into small containers
of water"—and hitting their mark every time.[1]

Hyman Joseph Salinger, Sonny's great-grandfather, had moved
from Sudargas to the more prosperous town of Taurage in order to
marry into a prominent family. Through his writings, J. D. Salinger
later immortalized his great-grandfather as the clown Zozo, honoring him as the family patriarch and confiding that he felt his great-
grandfather's spirit always watched over him. Hyman Joseph remained
in Russia all his life and died nine years before the birth of his great-
grandson. Salinger knew of him only through a photograph, an image
that offered a glimpse into another world. It depicted an elderly peasant brimming with nobility, erect in his long black gown and flowing
white beard, and sporting a tremendous nose—a feature that Salinger
confessed made him shudder with apprehension.[2]

Sonny's grandfather Simon F. Salinger was also ambitious. In 1881,
a year of famine (though not in Taurage itself), he left home and family and immigrated to the United States. Soon after arriving in America, Simon married Fannie Copland, also a Lithuanian immigrant, at
Wilkes-Barre, Pennsylvania. The couple then moved to Cleveland,
Ohio, where they found an apartment in one of the city's many immigrant neighborhoods and where, on March 16, 1887, Fannie gave
birth to Sonny's father, Solomon, the second of five surviving children.[3]

By 1893, the Salingers were living in Louisville, Kentucky, where
Simon attended medical school. His religious training in Russia served
him well, enabling him to practice as a rabbi in order to finance his education.[4] Upon obtaining his medical degree, Simon left the pulpit

and, after a brief return to Pennsylvania, moved the family to its final destination in the center of Chicago, where he set up a general practice not far from Cook County Hospital.[5] Sonny knew his grandfather well, as do readers of *The Catcher in the Rye*. Dr. Salinger often traveled to New York to visit his son and was the basis of Holden Caulfield's grandfather, the endearing man who would embarrass Holden by reading all the street signs aloud while riding on the bus. Simon Salinger died in 1960, just short of his hundredth birthday.

. . .

In the opening lines of *The Catcher in the Rye,* Holden Caulfield refuses to share his parents' past with the reader, deriding any recount of "how they were occupied and all before they had me, and all that David Copperfield kind of crap." "My parents," he explains, "would have about two hemorrhages apiece if I told anything pretty personal about them." This apparent elusiveness on the part of Holden's parents was imported directly from the attitudes of Salinger's own mother and father. Sol and Miriam rarely spoke of past events, especially to their children, and their attitude created an air of secrecy that permeated the Salinger household and caused Doris and Sonny to grow into intensely private people.

The Salingers' insistence upon privacy also led to rumors. Over the years, Miriam and Sol's story has been repeatedly embellished. This began in 1963, when the literary critic Warren French repeated a claim in a *Life* magazine article that Miriam had been Scotch-Irish. In time, the term "Scotch-Irish" transformed itself into the assertion that Salinger's mother had actually been born in County Cork, Ireland. This led in turn to what is perhaps the most commonly repeated story told about Salinger's mother and father: that Miriam's parents, supposedly Irish Catholic, were so adamantly opposed to her marriage to Sol, because he was Jewish, that they gave the couple little choice but to elope. And, upon learning of their daughter's defiance, they never spoke a word to her again.

None of this has any basis in fact, yet by the time of her death in 2001, even Salinger's sister, Doris, had been persuaded that her mother had been born in Ireland and that she and Sonny had been purposely denied a relationship with their grandparents.

The circumstances surrounding Miriam's family and her marriage to Sol were quite painful enough without embroidery through rumor. However, Salinger's parents exacerbated that pain by attempting to conceal their past from their children. In doing so, they not only invited fictitious versions of their history but confused their children too. By attempting to restrain Doris's and Sonny's natural curiosity, Miriam and Sol actually gave credence to a fabricated past that remained with them all their lives.

Sonny's mother was born Marie Jillich on May 11, 1891, in the small midwestern town of Atlantic, Iowa.[6] Her parents, Nellie and George Lester Jillich, Jr., were twenty and twenty-four, respectively, at the time of her birth, and records show that she was the second of six surviving children.[7] Marie's grandparents George Lester Jillich, Sr., and Mary Jane Bennett had been the first Jillichs to settle in Iowa. The grandson of German immigrants, George, Sr., had moved from Massachusetts to Ohio, where he met and married his wife. He served briefly with the 192nd Ohio Regiment during the Civil War, and after he returned home in 1865, Mary Jane gave birth to Marie's father. George, Sr., eventually established himself as a successful grain merchant and by 1891 was in firm position as head of the Jillich clan, with his sons George, Jr., and Frank following him into the trade.

Although Marie later maintained that her mother, Nellie McMahon, had been born in Kansas City in 1871, the daughter of Irish immigrants, four sets of federal census records (1900, 1910, 1920, and 1930) suggest that she is more likely to have come from Iowa. Family tradition has it that Marie met Solomon early in 1910 at a county fair near the Jillich family farm (an unlikely location since no such farm existed). The manager of a Chicago movie theater, Solomon, who was called "Sollie" by his family and "Sol" by his friends, was six feet tall with a whiff of big-city sophistication. Just seventeen, Marie was an arresting beauty, with fair skin and long red hair that contrasted with Sol's olive complexion. Their romance was immediate and intense, and Sol was determined to marry Marie from the start.

A rapid series of events, some of them heartbreaking, would occur that year, culminating in Marie's marriage to Sol in the spring of 1910. While the Salingers had steadily improved their position since Simon's arrival, the Jillichs had suddenly encountered difficulties. Marie's father had died the previous year.[8] Unable to keep the family afloat, her mother had taken the youngest of the children and relocated to Michigan, where she later remarried. Marie did not move with her mother, because of her age and her relationship with Sol. Her swift romance and marriage to Solomon therefore proved to be providential, especially when, by the time of Sonny's birth in 1919, her mother, Nellie, had also died.[9] The loss of both parents was possibly enough to make Marie reluctant to discuss them even with her own children. Rather than cling to the past, she devoted herself completely to a new life with her new husband. Left with only the Salingers now as family, she sought their acceptance by embracing Judaism and changing her name to Miriam, after the sister of Moses.

Simon and Fannie thought that Marie, with her milky-fair skin and auburn hair, looked like "a little Irisher."[10] In a city with thousands of eligible Jewish girls, they never dreamed that Sollie would bring home a red-haired Gentile from Iowa, but they accepted Miriam as their new daughter-in-law, and she soon moved into their Chicago home.

Miriam joined Sol working at the movie theater, where she sold tickets and concessions. Despite their efforts, the theater was unsuccessful and was forced to close, sending the new bridegroom in search of employment. He soon found a position working for J. S. Hoffman & Company, an importer of European cheeses and meats that went by the brand name Hofco. After the disappointment with the theater, Sol swore never to fail at business again and applied himself to his new company duties with devotion. This dedication paid off, and after Doris's birth in December 1912, he was promoted to general manager of Hoffman's New York division, becoming, as he coolly declared, the "manager of a cheese factory."[11]

Sol's new position required the Salingers to move to New York City, where they settled into a comfortable apartment at 500 West 113th Street, close to Columbia University and the Cathedral of Saint John the Divine. Although Sol was now in the business of vending a series of hams—distinctly the most unkosher of foods—along with his cheeses, he had managed to continue the Salinger custom of advancing beyond the previous generation, an accomplishment of which he was extraordinarily proud. But business became his life, and by the time of his thirtieth birthday in 1917, his hair had gone completely "iron grey."[12]

. . .

Until he was thirteen, Sonny attended public school on the Upper West Side. This is a class photo of Salinger and his schoolmates on the steps of P.S. 166, circa 1929.

The 1920s were years of unparalleled prosperity, and no place shone brighter than New York City. It was the economic, cultural, and intellectual capital of the Americas, perhaps even of the world. Its values were beamed across the continent through radio and absorbed by millions through publications. Its streets held sway over the economic vitality of nations, and its advertising and markets determined the desires and tastes of a generation. In this opportune place and time, the Salingers thrived.

Between Sonny's birth in 1919 and 1928, Sol and Miriam moved the family three times, always to a more affluent Manhattan neighborhood. When Sonny was born, they were living at 3681 Broadway, in an apartment located in North Harlem. Before year's end, they had moved back to their original New York neighborhood, into a residence at 511 West 113th Street. A more ambitious move came in 1928, when the family rented an apartment just a few blocks from Central Park at 215 West 82nd Street. This home came complete with servants' quarters, and Sol and Miriam quickly hired a live-in maid, an Englishwoman named Jennie Burnett. Sonny grew up in a world of increasing comfort, insulated by his parents' indulgence and their growing social status.

In the 1920s, religion and nationality became increasingly important the higher one climbed the social ladder. In New York especially, pedigree and Protestantism were the hallmarks of respectability. As the Salingers advanced upward and downtown, they shifted increasingly into an atmosphere of intolerance that would prove uncomfortable.

In reaction, they raised Sonny and Doris with a mixture of lukewarm religious and ethnic traditions. They never forced their children to go to church or synagogue, and the family celebrated both Christmas and Passover. Later in life, Salinger would craft most of his characters with similar backgrounds. Both the Glass and Tannenbaum families would easily acknowledge their half-Christian, half-Jewish heritage, and Holden Caulfield would comment that his father had been "a Catholic once, [but had] quit."

Miriam adored her son. Perhaps because his birth was a difficult one or in response to feeling abandoned during her own youth, she indulged him. Sonny could do no wrong. This put Solomon in the precarious position of attempting to discipline him while trying not to invoke the wrath of his wife, which could be considerable. By most accounts, when a crisis arose in the family, it was usually Miriam's judgment that prevailed, leaving Sonny largely unrestrained.

Salinger blossomed under his mother's attention and he was close to her all her life, even dedicating *The Catcher in the Rye* "To My Mother." She always believed that her son was destined for greatness, a belief he came to share. Consequently, they had a rare bond of understanding. Well into adulthood, Salinger and his mother exchanged gossipy letters, and he reveled in telling her acerbic stories of the people that he knew. Even during the war, Miriam enjoyed cutting articles out of movie-star magazines and sending them to her son, complete with her own comments scribbled in the margins. Salinger spent hours on the front line reading the clippings his mother had sent him, all the while dreaming of Hollywood and home. Reinforcing each other in these ways, Miriam and Jerome shared a sense of humor and closeness that unified them, often to the exclusion of others. Because his mother understood him so well and believed in his talent completely, he came to expect the same reaction from others and had little patience or consideration for those who might doubt him or not share his point of view.

Among the doubters was Salinger's father. As he rose in status, Sol came to identify with the world of his neighbors, for the most part wealthy businessmen and stockbrokers, and allowed his heritage as the son of Jewish immigrants to recede discreetly into the background. In 1920, when he described himself as the manager of a "cheese factory" to census takers, he admitted that his parents had been born in Russia. By 1930, he presented his situation differently, informing record takers that he worked in produce as a commission merchant and his parents had been born in Ohio. Solomon clearly saw nothing wrong in blending in as a route to success. Though some might regard this as evidence of a talent for fiction that his son would soon inherit, Sol came to represent the very values that his son scorned, traits that Salinger's future characters would condemn as phoniness, concession, and greed.

Worse still, Sol never seemed to understand his son's aspirations and wondered why Sonny could not be more practical. When Salinger, at an early age, expressed a desire to become an actor, Sol balked at the idea in spite of his wife's tacit approval. Then, when he later announced his intention to become a writer, Sol scoffed again. Not surprisingly, Salinger grew up considering his father shortsighted and insensitive, and their relationship was strained. Years later, Sonny's best friend, Herb Kauffman, would recall having dinner at the Salinger home as a teenager when Sonny and Sol began to fight: "Sol just didn't want his son to be a writer," he observed, adding that Jerome often treated his father unfairly.

Perhaps upon Sol's insistence, Sonny was sent away every summer to Camp Wigwam, located far from New York City, deep within the woods of Maine. Yet if Sol hoped that Sonny's camp experience would teach him conformity, he was mistaken. Founded in 1910, Camp Wigwam was a model of diversity that placed strong and equal emphasis on both athletics and the creative arts. Sonny flourished in this atmosphere. Camp records show that he excelled in sports and other group activities, but he was especially drawn to the camp's theatrical program. In 1930, at the age of eleven, Jerome (Salinger was called both "Sonny" and "Jerome" at camp) took part in a number of camp plays, starring in two, and was named "Favorite Camp Actor."[13] This distinction resulted in a fascination with the theater that would last for years. Salinger also stood out physically. He was taller than the other children, and the camp's 1930 group photo shows him looming over the rest, with his shirt playfully torn to resemble Tarzan's.

Basking in this attention, Salinger enjoyed Camp Wigwam, and the memories of his childhood summers in the woods always remained happy and vivid. Later in life, they would inspire him to seek refuge in similar surroundings and to return there through his stories, sending his characters off to camp one after another.*

. . .

In 1930, the Great Depression gripped America. New York City was no longer a place of opportunity. Gleaming scenes of commerce and optimism were replaced by breadlines and despair. If Sol and Miriam's march into high society the decade before had been remarkable, it now became astonishing. Defying the tide of poverty that permeated the city, the Salingers continued to increase their wealth and improve their social status. In 1932, they made what would prove to be their final move: across Central Park to the grand Upper East Side. Sol moved his family into a plush apartment in the Carnegie Hill district at 1133 Park Avenue at 91st Street. In a city of contrasting neighborhoods, where location was a defining factor of self-worth, the Salingers' new home was the epitome of success. Affluent and comfortable, the prestigious building was within sight of Central Park and within easy walking distance of the park zoo and the Metropolitan Museum of Art. The Salingers were so proud of their new home that for many years they

---

*Almost a century after its founding, Camp Wigwam is still in operation, practically unchanged from the time that Salinger enrolled there. It still sports the same infirmary where Seymour Glass developed a crush on a nurse in "Hapworth 16, 1924." It also continues the policy of "spending money" from home that Holden Caulfield so bitterly complained of in "The Ocean Full of Bowling Balls."

1133 Park Avenue. Salinger was raised in this apartment building on Manhattan's affluent Upper East Side from the time he was thirteen and enjoyed its comforts until age twenty-eight. The basis of the Glass family home in *Franny and Zooey*, it remained the Salinger family home until his parents' death in 1974. (Ben Steinberg)

used personalized stationery whose letterhead excluded the family name but included the Park Avenue address.

Until the Salingers' move to 1133, Sonny had attended public schools on the West Side. But the sons of successful Park Avenue businessmen did not attend public school. Instead, they were given a private education, usually at a prestigious boarding school far from home. The Salingers wanted something similar for their own son but were unwilling to have him move away, so they opted to send him to school on the familiar West Side, enrolling him at the McBurney School on West 63rd Street.

Enrollment at McBurney was certainly a step up from public education, but it was a far cry from the impressive prep schools attended by the Salingers' new neighbors. Even more striking, the school was run by the adjacent YMCA, meaning that Sonny, who was thirteen at the time, went directly from his Bar Mitzvah to the Young Men's Christian Association.

At McBurney, Sonny strengthened his growing interest in drama by performing in two school plays. He was also captain of the school fencing team, whose equipment he later claimed to have lost on the subway.

He began to write too and contributed to the school newspaper, *The McBurnian*. Academically, he appeared distracted and bored by his classes, and spent days gazing out of the window over Central Park and visiting the nearby Museum of Natural History. As a result, his grades were barely passing and put him close to the bottom of his class. During the 1932–1933 school year, he earned a 66 in algebra, a 77 in biology, an 80 in English, and a 66 in Latin. The 1933–1934 year was worse: a 72 in English, a 68 in geometry, a 70 in German, and a 71 in Latin.[14] In a public school, Sonny could have gotten away with these scores, but in a private school, where grade point average translated into funding, his performance was unacceptable. Despite his attending the Manhasset School during the summer in an attempt to boost his average, the McBurney administration requested that he not return for the 1934 enrollment.

Sonny's expulsion from McBurney also severed his link to the YMCA, which would prove to be his last childhood connection to a formal religious organization. As their parents advanced socially, Sonny and Doris's upbringing grew increasingly secular until, by the mid-1930s, the family had abandoned all displays of religious affiliation. When Doris married in May 1935 in a ceremony that took place in the Salinger living room, the wedding was officiated by neither rabbi nor priest but by the famous humanist reformer Dr. John Lovejoy Elliott, the leader of the New York Society for Ethical Culture.

· · ·

In September 1934, Sonny was almost sixteen. His parents sensed that their son was at a crossroads. Reluctantly, they saw he needed a more disciplined atmosphere than he could find at home. With an overly indulgent mother and a father reined in by his wife's intensity, it became apparent that Sonny should go away to boarding school. Sonny himself wanted to study acting, but Sol refused: with the Depression still looming, no son of his would become an actor. Sonny would attend a military boarding school instead.

It is easy to imagine Sol sending Sonny away as a kind of punishment for being dismissed from McBurney. However, there is every indication that the Salingers chose the Valley Forge Military Academy together, as a family. It is also likely that Sonny agreed to enroll at Valley Forge without the protestations or sullenness that we might associate with the character of Holden Caulfield. The logic behind this conclusion is simple: Miriam would never have forced her son to do anything against his wishes, and Sol dared not defy Miriam.

After contacting the academy, Sol chose not to accompany his son to the registration interview. His failure to attend has been cited as evidence of a deteriorating relationship between father and son; but there was another, more disturbing reason for Sol's absence. The Depression had a chilling effect on the position of Jews in America. The 1930s were a time of anti-Semitism in the United States, as elsewhere. Many Americans blamed the economic collapse on greedy bankers and looked upon the Jews, many of whom were prominent in the field, with resentment. This animosity ran deep, and Jews were marginalized or excluded from society on many levels. Education was no exception. Most universities and private schools applied quotas designed to keep Jewish enrollment to a minimum. Sol was undoubtedly aware of this policy. When the day came for Sonny's interview at Valley Forge, Sol stayed at home. He sent his wife, with her fair complexion and auburn hair, instead. There is nothing to indicate that Sol ever attempted to deny his religion. But on this occasion he chose not to subject himself to scrutiny that might jeopardize his son's chances. Throughout their troubled relationship, nothing would speak as loudly of the love Sol had for his son than his absence on that day.

When Sonny, his sister, and his mother arrived at Valley Forge on Tuesday, September 18, they were on their best behavior. With enrollment scheduled for the following Saturday, it was important that they make a good impression, especially since McBurney had sent Salinger's records to the academy along with a short evaluation of the candidate that called his attention "fuzzy" and ranked him fifteenth in a class of eighteen. McBurney had measured Sonny's IQ at 111, commenting that although his ability was plentiful, he did not know the word "industry." He was, the report concluded, "Hard hit by adolescence his last semester with us" (*sic*). Fortunately, Valley Forge was still a young school in competition with wealthier and more fashionable academies.

Whether the applicant was "fuzzy" or not, it was reluctant to turn away a paying recruit, and Sonny's application was accepted. Two days later, from his office in Manhattan's Franklin Street, the relieved Sol Salinger sent the academy the $50 registration fee along with a note thanking the interviewer for his courtesy. Bearing in mind the McBurney report, he also assured the school official, Chaplin Waldemar Ivan Rutan, in a letter dated September 20, 1934, that "Jerome will conduct himself properly and . . . you will find his school spirit excellent."

. . .

When Jerome entered Valley Forge in 1934, he joined the ranks of 350 cadets in the school's regimen of discipline, military service, and strict routine. Cadets were roused from bed at 6 A.M. to begin a day of formations, classes, speeches, and endless marching. Activities were communal and followed a firm schedule. Cadets slept in shared rooms, ate together in the dining hall, and were required to attend church services on Sundays. Taps were blown at 10 P.M. sharp, bringing an end to the day. All these rituals were strictly supervised and enveloped in a military atmosphere that stressed duty, honor, and obedience. Infractions of the rules were dealt with harshly; and there were many rules at Valley Forge. A cadet's personal items were to be arranged according to regulation. His uniform was to be worn at all times and kept immaculate. Stepping off academy grounds without permission was a serious offense. Females were forbidden on campus. Smoking was tolerated only with written permission from a cadet's parents and was forbidden in dorms.

Having enjoyed a life being spoiled by his mother, refusing to apply himself to his studies, and flouting the few rules ever imposed on him, entering this world of unbending military discipline came as a great shock to Jerome. What made the transition even more difficult was the fact that many of the cadets at Valley Forge did not like him. Salinger was a thin, lanky teen (school photographs picture him awkwardly awash in his dress uniform, always in the back row) with what some students considered a snobbish New York attitude. Other cadets resented him for entering Valley Forge two years later than most and avoiding freshman hazing. Alone, and lacking the support of his family for the first time, Sonny sought refuge in sarcasm and feigned aloofness, attitudes that did not make him popular.

Salinger quickly adapted. He discarded his nickname of Sonny and refused to be called Jerome. Now known only as Jerry Salinger, he began to display a biting wit that drew a handful of cadets to his side, some of whom would become the most devoted of friends. A number of older cadets, including William Faison and Herbert Kauffman, remained attached to Salinger long after graduation. Both of Salinger's roommates, Cadets Richard Gonder and William Dix, became close friends. Decades later, Salinger remembered Dix as being "the best and the kindest,"[15] while Gonder recalled his exploits with Salinger happily, describing Jerry as "condescending but loving."[16]

It is clear that Salinger used Valley Forge as the basis of Holden Caulfield's prep school when he wrote *The Catcher in the Rye,* and readers have sought to uncover Holden's personality within young Salinger ever since. Derisive of the phoniness of the schools they attended and of the "stuffed shirts" who drove the routine, Jerry and Holden shared many attributes. Like Holden, Salinger enjoyed breaking the rules, even if it was just to sneak off campus for a few hours or smoke in his dormitory. Both boys were fond of mimicry, dry humor, and wisecracks. Yet, for every Holden-like quality that Salinger displayed at Valley Forge, he also exhibited a characteristic very unlike his later creation.

On occasion, Salinger was invited to his English instructor's home for afternoon tea, meetings that doubtless inspired Holden's visit to Professor Spencer in *The Catcher in the Rye* but certainly never involved being subjected to lectures on life or essays on the Egyptians.

There actually was a cadet named Ackley enrolled at Valley Forge at the same time as Salinger. Long after the publication of the novel, Ackley's best friend rose vehemently to his defense, angrily asserting that his pal was nothing like the character in the book.

The unfortunate character of James Castle also appears to be based upon fact. Salinger's classmates reported that a cadet fell to his death from an academy window just before Salinger's enrollment. Apparently there was some question as to how he had fallen, and the tragedy instantly became a campus legend.

Colonel Baker, Valley Forge's founder, and his equivalent, Mr. Thurmer, Pencey's headmaster, were similar to each other in many ways. Both were avid fund-raisers and constructed a kind of Potemkin village for the cadet families on Sundays. Overstarched and bedecked in military finery, Colonel Baker would have been an easy target for Jerry's scathing mockery. Yet, years later, Salinger turned to Baker on a number of occasions for help and advice, and it was Baker's endorsement of Salinger's character that often outshone the opinions of others.

Salinger did well at Valley Forge. Whatever his inward rebellion against the authority of the place, it did indeed provide the discipline necessary for him to apply himself. His grades improved markedly. He developed a small circle of close friends. He became involved in campus activities, including intramural sports and, uncharacteristically, the glee club. The clubs and organizations that Salinger joined at Valley Forge would serve him well in future years. The French Club, the Non-Commissioned Officers' Club, Plebe Detail (an officer cadet group), the Aviation Club, and his two years' service in the Reserve Officers' Training Corps would all contribute to his military service during the Second World War and, although the author would be loath to admit it, perhaps helped him survive those years.

Although Salinger fulfilled all the requirements expected of a cadet,* his true interests lay in drama and literature. Apart from the activities required of him, Salinger joined two campus organizations whose significance eclipsed all the others: the drama club, Mask and Spur, and the academy yearbook, *Crossed Sabres*.

After his performances in plays at McBurney had won him the grudging admiration of the otherwise hostile faculty, acting had fallen into Salinger's comfort zone and he was keen to continue performing once exiled to Valley Forge. So, though he may have joined most other clubs out of obligation, he joined Mask and Spur out of conviction. None of the club's eighteen other budding actors was more talented than Jerry, and he took part in every play they performed. Popular or not, everyone agreed that Salinger was a natural. One classmate recalled that even offstage, "he always talked in a pretentious manner as if he were reciting something out of Shakespeare." Academy yearbooks contain prominent photos of the obviously delighted Salinger in full costume, gleefully miming for the camera.

Salinger often said that he became a writer at Valley Forge. Friends recalled him scribbling under the covers by flashlight long after taps.

---

*In the spring of 1936, Salinger's conformity to both the ethos and the curriculum of the academy was rewarded when he was promoted to cadet colonel just in time for graduation.

JEROME DAVID SALINGER
CORPORAL   "B" COMPANY
January 1, 1919   New York, N. Y.

Activities

Private, '34; Intramural Athletics; Mask
and Spur, '34, '35; Glee Club, '34, '35;
Plebe Detail, '35; Aviation Club; French
Club; Non-Commissioned Officers' Club;
Literary Editor, 1936 CROSSED SABRES.

NINETY-SIX

Cadet Corporal Salinger in 1936, in his yearbook photo from Valley Forge Military
Academy. Salinger used his own boarding school as the inspiration for Holden Caulfield's
Pencey Prep when writing *The Catcher in the Rye*. Unlike Holden, Salinger excelled at
Valley Forge. (Valley Forge Military Academy)

He was the literary editor of the yearbook both years that he attended
and is featured in them prominently. It is actually hard to turn a page
in either the 1935 or 1936 *Crossed Sabres* without coming across Jerry
Salinger. He is pictured with almost every club, with every play, and
even with the yearbook staff itself. His 1936 photo is large, taking up
half a page. One suspects that Jerry also had a hand in the layout of the
yearbook, which could almost pass for a pictorial supplement to *The
Catcher in the Rye*. There are photos of the chapel, cheering crowds at
the football game, and even a young man upon a leaping horse. But
Salinger's greatest contribution to *Crossed Sabres* was his writing. His
voice can be heard on nearly every page: ironical, observant, and good-
naturedly witty. When casting predictions on his classmates in a section called "Class Prophecy," Salinger foresaw one cadet "playing strip
poker with Mahatmi Ghandi" (*sic*), while he himself was to write a
great play.[17]

. . .

When Salinger graduated from Valley Forge in 1936 after two constructive years, he seemed to have found his way. Whatever his apprehension upon entering the school, he had explored his talents to a degree that would have been improbable in New York. Through all his precociousness and bite, it seems that Jerry recognized his affection for the place. Through *Crossed Sabres,* he left the school a gift upon his graduation that truly represented the spirit he had brought there, one of both genuine warmth and veiled sarcasm. Salinger wrote the class song of 1936, and it is still sung at Valley Forge to this day:

> Hide not thy tears on this last day.
> Your sorrow has no shame:
> To march no more midst lines of gray,
> No longer play the game.
> Four years have passed in joyful ways.
> Wouldst stay these old times dear?
> Then cherish now these fleeting days
> The few while you are here.
>
> The last parade, our hearts sink low:
> Before us we survey—
> Cadets to be, where we are now
> And soon will come their day.
> Though distant now, yet not so far,
> Their years are but a few.
> Aye, soon they'll know why misty are
> Our eyes at last review.
>
> The lights are dimmed, the bugle sounds
> The notes we'll ne'er forget.
> And now a group of smiling lads:
> We part with much regret.
> Goodbyes are said, we march ahead
> Success we go to find.
> Our forms are gone from Valley Forge
> Our hearts are left behind.

. . .

In the autumn of 1936, Salinger enrolled in New York University at Washington Square, where he attempted to pursue a bachelor of arts degree. Washington Square, located in Greenwich Village, put Salinger back at home on Park Avenue and in the same atmosphere that he had been sent to Valley Forge to avoid. Away from the discipline of the military academy, he quickly drifted back into boredom and distraction.

At first glance, Washington Square appears to be an ideal setting for Salinger. Avant-garde in tastes and trends, this main branch of NYU was renowned for its melding of academic and artistic spirits. By all accounts, Salinger should have excelled there—and perhaps that was his intention. But the bohemian atmosphere of the Village campus may well have served as a diversion, rather than as an opportunity for Salinger to apply his talents. Situated in a nucleus of theaters, movie houses, and cafés, the college's surroundings may have proved a lure far more irresistible to Salinger than the classroom. Of the classes in which he enrolled, it is uncertain just how many he actually attended. When he received his midterm grades during his second semester, it became clear that he was not going to pass, and he abruptly left the college.

After Salinger dropped out of New York University, his father attempted to give him direction. A practical man, Sol hoped to involve Jerry in the cheese and meat import business that had treated him so well. Jerry, of course, was in no way inclined to follow in his father's footsteps, so Sol half sweetened, half disguised the offer. After informing his son that his "formal education was formally over."[18] Sol "unelaborately"* presented him with the opportunity to travel to Europe under the guise of refining his French and German. Hoping that his son would develop an interest in the import business along the way, Sol arranged for him to travel to Poland and Austria as translator for a Hofco business partner, in all likelihood a ham exporter named Oskar Robinson, one of the richest men in Poland and known throughout Europe as "the King of Bacon." Salinger agreed. In reality, the choice

---

*Salinger's inference here is that his father had never mentioned that he would be traveling to Poland, a detail that would have given Salinger pause for thought.

was not his to make. Whatever options he had once had in the matter had been extinguished by his failing grades. So, in early April 1937, Salinger set out for Europe where he would spend the next year.

After brief stops in London and Paris, he traveled to Vienna. There he spent ten months living in the city's Jewish quarter with a family that he quickly came to adore and with whose daughter he experienced his first serious romance. We know little of Salinger's Austrian "family," only that he idealized them to the extent that they would be symbols of purity and integrity for the rest of his life. Salinger would often look back upon them with increasing idealism, comparing life with his own family to the domestic bliss he encountered in Vienna. To Ernest Hemingway he later recalled memories of the innocent beauty of the family's daughter. When gripped by despondency after the war, he returned to Austria in vain to seek her out. In 1947, he immortalized her and her family in his story "A Girl I Knew."

While Salinger was pursuing his Austrian romance, his Polish sponsor, Oskar Robinson, died of a heart attack in a Vienna casino, reportedly while winning at the roulette table, and Salinger was sent north to the Polish town of Bydgoszcz, where he stayed in a guest apartment of Robinson's meatpacking factory and experienced the more basic side of his father's import business.* This included getting up before dawn and toiling with peasants in the city slaughterhouse. Each morning, Salinger would trudge off to butcher pigs destined for the American market as "canned picnic hams." He was accompanied by the head "slaughter master," who enjoyed shooting his gun into lightbulbs, over the heads of squealing swine, and at birds that dared cross his path. It quickly dawned on Jerry that whatever the life of a meat exporter might involve, pigs held sway over much of it. If Salinger learned anything in Poland, it was that he was not suited for his father's line of work.

In 1944, Salinger maintained that, in an attempt to apprentice him to the family business, his parents had "dragged [him] off" to "slaughter pigs" in Poland.[19] In 1951, the *New Yorker* editor William Maxwell concluded that although Salinger hated his father's attempted solution

---

*Poland is proud of its connection with Salinger. Plans are under way in Bydgoszcz to honor him with an annual Salinger festival and to place a statue at the site where he worked, which is now a shopping center. According to the *Krakow Post* newspaper, a design was chosen in 2009 featuring a sculpture of Salinger standing in a patch of living rye.

to his problems, "there is no experience, agreeable or otherwise, that isn't valuable to a writer of fiction."[20] Furthermore, it is impossible to view Salinger's year in Europe outside the context of the times. The atmosphere of menace so pervasive in Austria and Poland while Salinger was living there certainly had a profound effect upon the aspiring young writer and would stain even his fondest memories of those places with connecting sorrows.

Salinger's stay occurred at a crucial moment in history. In 1938, Europe was spiraling headlong toward the Second World War. During the months he lived in Vienna, Austrian Nazis were bullying their way to power and Nazi thugs released from prison regardless of their offense freely terrorized the streets of Vienna. Passersby suspected of Jewish descent were forced to scrub the gutters to the mocking jeers of spectators, while Jewish homes and businesses were ransacked by marauding gangs. Witnessing this nightmare, Salinger's feelings of personal peril were outweighed by his fears for his adopted Vienna family. He himself could leave this dangerous place, but his hosts had nowhere to go. Before Salinger returned home to New York, German forces had entered Vienna and Austria had ceased to exist as a nation. By 1945, every member of Salinger's Austrian family had been murdered in the Holocaust.

Arriving in Poland, Salinger entered a nation as tense as Austria had been perilous. Surrounded by enemies, Poland was cloaked in a feeling of unease that he could not help but sense after what he had witnessed in Austria. Few of those whom Salinger knew while slaughtering pigs would survive the next few years.

On March 9, 1938, Salinger boarded the *Ile de France* at Southampton to return to the United States. Secure once again in his parents' Park Avenue apartment, far from the tensions of Europe, he was happy to be home. Maxwell's later observation, though, contained more than an element of truth. Salinger's life might not have been affected by Europe the way that his father had hoped, he may not have returned any less aimless than when he left, but after living among those whose lives were so vastly different from his own, lives that were a constant struggle or in constant peril, he learned to appreciate people with whom he would previously have had little in common. In future years, when Salinger would fight in Germany during the Second

World War, this rearrangement of attitudes was especially evident. While living in Europe during 1937–1938, Salinger came to embrace German culture, the German language, and the German people, and he learned to distinguish between Germans worthy of admiration and the Nazis among them.

. . .

That autumn, Salinger enrolled at Ursinus College, situated in rural Pennsylvania not far from Valley Forge Military Academy. Apart from its familiar location, the college was an unlikely destination for Salinger. Ursinus was sponsored by the German Reformed Church, and many of Salinger's schoolmates were from a Pennsylvania Dutch background. Students at Ursinus had to wear name tags and exchange greetings when approaching each other on campus. A small, isolated place, Ursinus was a world away from Salinger's complex upbringing on the Upper East Side of Manhattan.

The effect of a privileged Jewish boy from New York being in this small college enclave must have been extraordinary. While many of Salinger's Ursinus classmates later claimed to barely remember him, others recalled him with sullen resentment. These were usually Salinger's male classmates. Those who had the fondest memories of Jerry were invariably women (which might explain the glowering attitude of Ursinus's male students). By the time Salinger began classes at Ursinus, he was almost twenty and had developed into a handsome young man with a mischievous smile. Six feet two and with a slim build, he stood out in a crowd. His fingers were long, if nicotine-stained and nail-bitten. His complexion was olive-toned and his hair almost black. His most memorable attribute, though, appears to have been his eyes, which were deep, penetrating, and dark. All this added up to an almost exotic look for Ursinus in 1938, and the women loved it. Forty-seven years later, one Ursinus alumna recalled:

> Jerry was not an easily forgettable character. He was a handsome, suave and sophisticated New Yorker in a black Chesterfield coat . . . we had never seen anything quite like it. We were enchanted by his biting and acerbic humor. . . . Most of the girls were mad about him at once.[21]

Besides beguiling the women, Salinger pursued his other interests with a newfound enthusiasm. Of the eight courses in which he was enrolled, four were related to language and writing: English literature, French, and two different English composition courses. Joining the college newspaper, *The Ursinus Weekly,* he soon had his own column. Initially called "Musings of a Social Soph: The Skipped Diploma," it was not long before the name was changed to "J.D.S.'s The Skipped Diploma." These articles consisted of Jerry's comments on a variety of campus topics ranging from glib blurbs about college life to long and invariably sarcastic theater reviews. Already, he was routinely criticizing novels for being "phony."

On one occasion, he took a swipe at the author Margaret Mitchell: "For Hollywood's sake, it would be well for the authoress of 'Gone With the Wind' to rewrite same, giving Miss Scarlett O'Hara either one slightly crossed eye, one bucked tooth, or one size-nine shoe."[22] In another "Book Dept." review, he was similarly dismissive of his later friend Ernest Hemingway: "Hemingway has completed his first full-length play. We hope it is worthy of him. Ernest, we feel, has underworked and overdrooled ever since 'The Sun Also Rises,' 'The Killers,' and 'Farewell to Arms.' "

"The Skipped Diploma" was certainly nothing approaching literature, but nevertheless was his first writing in public print and is still read by admirers—although often with a combination of disappointment and forgiveness. If there is anything in "The Skipped Diploma" that remotely connects with Salinger's own situation, or at least with his decision to attend Ursinus, it is contained in one of his first commentaries, entitled "Story" and dated October 10, 1938: "Once there was a young man who was tired of trying to grow a moustache. This same young man did not want to go to work for his Daddykin—or any other unreasonable man. So the young man went back to college."

Willing to work for "Daddykin" or not, Salinger remained at Ursinus for only one semester before returning home to New York. Although his grades at Ursinus were not good, he enjoyed the experience immensely and spoke highly of the college and his time there. However, he had found a definite direction in his life: the desire to become a professional writer. It was a decision that required confidence and conviction and one that would also require support from others.

After leaving Ursinus, Salinger did not seek parental approval for the path he had decided to take. Instead, he simply announced his intention to become a writer, presenting them with a fait accompli. His mother, of course, supported him fully, but Sol was less enthusiastic. In 1938, the United States was barely crawling out of the Great Depression. Sol had spent the past nine years successfully protecting his family from the poverty and desperation that surrounded them. He had watched brilliant businessmen crumble under the uncertainty of those years and knew that life offered no guarantees. To Sol, Sonny's decision seemed foolhardy and dangerous. If a rift existed between father and son, it certainly grew wider now. Later in life, Salinger would still find it difficult to forgive his father for what he perceived to be his lack of vision and confidence.

Salinger found support from a source more objective than his parents. At Valley Forge, he had befriended an older cadet from Staten Island named William Faison. About the time of Salinger's graduation, Faison introduced him to his older sister, Elizabeth Murray, who had recently returned from living in Scotland with her husband and ten-year-old daughter. Aged about thirty, refined, well educated, and much traveled, Murray delighted Salinger, who soon grew to respect her opinion above all others. In turn, Elizabeth supported Jerry completely. In 1938, they became frequent companions, spending long nights in the restaurants and cafés of Greenwich Village, where they discussed literature and Salinger's ambitions. He read his stories to her, and she offered suggestions. On Elizabeth's advice, Salinger began to read the writings of F. Scott Fitzgerald. He found in Fitzgerald not only an author to emulate but also a kindred soul. Elizabeth Murray entered Salinger's life when he most needed encouragement, and he owed her a massive debt of gratitude. They would remain friends and confidants for years to come. As 1938 came to a close, Salinger had made the firm decision to become a professional writer. As a compromise with his parents, only one of whom supported his ambition, he agreed to go back to school yet again, to study writing.

2. Ambition

Salinger enrolled at Columbia University in January 1939. He signed up for a short-story writing class taught by Whit Burnett, who was also the editor of *Story* magazine, and a poetry class with the poet-playwright Charles Hanson Towne. Although he had decided to write for a living, Salinger was still unsure of his specific genre. Through his interest in acting, he envisioned himself carving out screenplays, but he was also interested in writing short stories. So, in an attempt to make a decision, he enrolled in both classes, taught by well-known professionals very different from each other in approach and style.

Whit Burnett was a risk taker. He and his then-wife, Martha Foley, had founded *Story* magazine in Vienna in 1931, during the depths of the Depression. In 1933, the couple moved the operation to New York City, establishing its offices on Fourth Avenue. Under Burnett's guidance, *Story* devoted itself to presenting the works of promising young writers, most of whom had been turned away by more conventional and popular magazines. Burnett's aesthetic instincts were very reliable, and he eventually introduced the world to such authors as Tennessee Williams, Norman Mailer, and Truman Capote. With only a modest circulation of 21,000 in 1939 and always struggling to make ends meet, *Story* was well respected in literary circles and considered cutting edge for its time.

In contrast to Burnett, Charles Hanson Towne was the epitome of convention. Sixty-one years old when Salinger entered his class, Towne was distinguished in nearly every area of literary undertaking. Professionally, he had been an editor and had successfully led a number of popular magazines, among them *Cosmopolitan, McClure's,* and *Harper's Bazaar.* Despite his editorial duties, Towne still found time to work on his own writing. The terms "prolific" and "diverse" do not begin to cover the extent of his production. He wrote numerous plays, novels, song lyrics, and even an etiquette manual. Towne's greatest love, though, was poetry. His poems, like his other endeavors, were successful because they matched readers' expectations. His poetry always rhymed and used the flowery phrases that contemporary readers anticipated. A typical example of Towne's style is his 1919 poem "Of One Self-Slain":

> When he went blundering back to God,
> His songs half written, his work half done,
> Who knows what paths his bruised feet trod,
> What hills of peace or pain he won?
>
> I hope God smiled and took his hand,
> And said, "Poor truant, passionate fool!
> Life's book is hard to understand:
> Why couldst thou not remain at school?"

Exactly what Salinger hoped to learn from such verse is unclear, but it is likely that he was drawn to Towne because of his fame as a playwright and not his reputation as a poet. Towne, however, had chosen to teach poetry at Columbia, forcing Salinger to study an art form in which he had never expressed any serious interest.

Salinger's enrollment at Columbia was his third attempt at college in as many years, and the stakes were now high. At Ursinus, he had boasted to classmates that he would one day write the Great American Novel. He had even challenged his parents with the demand that he be allowed to attend writing classes in order to fulfill his potential. Yet once the semester began, Salinger was as listless and unfocused as ever. In Burnett's class, he rarely volunteered, and he produced next to nothing. Instead, as Burnett would often remind Salinger, he spent his time sitting in the back row, gazing out of the window.[1]

In contrast to his apathetic performance in Burnett's sessions, Salinger was more conscientious in his poetry class. He doubtless felt that he had more in common with Charles Hanson Towne than with Whit Burnett. Towne had been more successful as a writer than Burnett, and his interests in acting and playwriting matched Salinger's own. In Towne's class, Salinger developed a genuine interest in poetry, attempting verse that revealed a simmering contempt for upper-class pretensions. Though his short-story assignments have disappeared, a sample of his Columbia poetry still survives. Among the collected papers of Charles Hanson Towne are a number of assignments written by his Columbia students in 1939, including one by "Jerry Salinger" entitled "Early Fall in Central Park," which begins, "Slobber and swarm, you condemned brown leaves . . ."[2]

At the end of his first semester at Columbia, Salinger was rewarded in recognition of his attentiveness, if not his talent, with a copy of Towne's 1937 poetry book, *An April Song*. It is probable that each of Towne's other nine poetry students also received a copy. Salinger's was inscribed:

To Jerome Salinger,
for his unfailing attention in the Spring Course, 1939,
at Columbia University,
from Charles Hanson Towne, New York, May 24: 1939.

At Columbia, something profound happened to Salinger that drew him out of his complacency. The event did not occur in Towne's poetry class, as Jerry might have expected. It happened in Burnett's class; and although the event was a subtle one, it changed Salinger forever. One day, Whit Burnett decided to read William Faulkner's "That Evening Sun Go Down" aloud to his pupils. Burnett read the story in an impassive voice: "You got your Faulkner straight, without any middlemen between," Salinger remembered. "Not once . . . did Burnett come between the author and his beloved silent reader."[3] The exercise taught Salinger the boundaries of good authorship and respect for the

Jerry in 1939, in a photo taken by his friend Dorothy Nollman while he was on break from Columbia University. Within a year, Salinger's first short story would be published and his career launched. (Dorothy Nollman/Peter Imbres)

reader. Throughout his career, he would remember Burnett's lesson and strive to write from the background, to never interfere with the reader and the story, submerging his own ego to allow direct participation between the reader and the character.

According to Salinger, Burnett often arrived late to class and left early, but he taught with humility and effectiveness. He had a passion for short stories that pervaded the classroom, and his love of the art form was itself the greatest teacher. Introducing his students to authors of all statuses and styles, he presented each story absent of opinion, teaching his students not only the importance of good writing but also a reverence for good reading.

So in the end it was Whit Burnett's inspiration that took hold. As a result, Salinger finally applied himself to his studies. He also began to write outside the classroom, at home and on his own. After drifting through his first semester staring out of the window and shooting wisecracks to the student sitting next to him, Salinger reenrolled in Burnett's class and gave it another try.

In September, Jerry took his place in Burnett's Monday-night class, again sitting quietly in the back row, disguising the fact that something inside him had changed and that that something was chipping away at the cocky, sarcastic attitude he had sported throughout his school years. In a letter to Burnett that November, Salinger declared his repentance, admitting that he had been lazy and too wrapped up in his own ego.[4] Serious at last, in a moment that required a certain courage, he approached his professor with an assortment of his own writings. Flipping through the pages, Burnett was astonished to discover the serious talent buried within the indifferent young man in the back row. "Several stories seemed to come from his typewriter at once," he recalled years later, still in amazement, "and most of these were later published."[5]

By semester's end, Whit Burnett had become Salinger's mentor, a near–father figure whom Jerry looked to for advice and approval. Salinger fell over his own feet in the effort to please him. His contemporary letters portray him as very much the wide-eyed kid and flow with admissions of ignorance and an abundance of saccharine. Such was his gratitude for Burnett's attentions that on one occasion he actually assured the editor that he would do anything for him—short of committing murder.[6]

By late 1939, Salinger had finished a short story entitled "The Young Folks," and he presented it to Burnett for review. Burnett liked it so much that he suggested Salinger submit it to *Collier's,* a popular magazine featuring short stories sandwiched between noisy advertisements. *Collier's, The Saturday Evening Post, Harper's,* and a variety of women's magazines were commonly known as "the slicks," and were the established venue for short stories in the 1930s and 1940s.*

On the morning of November 21, Salinger, with manuscript in

---

*The nickname refers to the slick (glossy) paper normally used for the pages of these magazines. The term was used derisorily by many of the literary-minded, suggesting that the content was shallow or glib.

hand, traveled downtown to the offices of *Collier's* and delivered his story personally. The magazine rejected it, as Salinger had suspected it would.[7] This, however, was Jerry's first experience of the rough-and-tumble of professional writing, and he stoically recognized its value.

His student's lesson with the slicks now complete, Burnett asked for "The Young Folks" back and took it to Story Press. There it sat for weeks while he debated with himself whether to publish it in *Story* magazine. For Salinger, to whom Burnett had made no promises, the wait must have seemed like an eternity.

Whit Burnett did not coddle Salinger. He did not discover a literary genius sitting in the back row of his Monday class and deliver him to instant fame. Rather, he forced Jerry to work for his own success. As a mentor, Burnett may well have had every intention to publish his pupil, but as a teacher, he first demanded that his student exhaust other options. Only when "The Young Folks" had been rejected by a magazine other than his did Burnett come to the rescue and retrieve the story.

Shortly after his twenty-first birthday, in January 1940, Salinger received word from *Story* that "The Young Folks" had been accepted and would be published in a forthcoming edition. He wrote to Whit Burnett that he was "thrilled," and also somewhat relieved. "Thank God," he imagined his old classmates responding, "he certainly talked about it enough!"[8] Elevated by the achievement and anxious to strike out on his own as a professional writer, Salinger decided not to reenroll at Columbia. His schooldays were over.

Now convinced that he had embarked on a bright path of literary triumphs, Salinger treated "The Young Folks" like a newborn child. On February 5, *Story* magazine informed him that it would send out cards announcing the story's publication and the author's emergence onto the literary stage. Salinger gladly provided names of recipients for the cards and in return received an advance copy of the issue.

Salinger said that each day spent waiting for the issue's publication felt like Christmas Eve. Restlessly, he planned on going away to celebrate, but his parents went instead, leaving Jerry home alone to spend his days playing records, drinking beer, moving his typewriter from room to room, and reading aloud to the empty apartment.[9] Distracted by his excitement, it was not until February 24, almost six weeks after "The Young Folks" had been accepted, that Salinger remembered to properly thank the magazine for the opportunity. Burnett's reaction to Jerry's enthusiasm was almost paternal. He told Salinger that he hoped the story's presentation would meet well with his "discriminating eye" and invited him to the annual Writers Club dinner in May. Salinger happily accepted.[10]

The spring edition of *Story* magazine finally introduced the world to the writings of J. D. Salinger. Within its red-and-white cover rested his five-page story, for which the author was belatedly paid all of $25. The story satirized characters very much like himself and the people that he knew: upper-class college students obsessed with the petty details of their own shallow lives. It was characteristic of its time and heavily influenced by the writing style of F. Scott Fitzgerald.

"The Young Folks" is mainly a dialogue between two young people who meet at a party, an unpopular girl named Edna Phillips and William Jameson Junior, a nail-biting scotch drinker reminiscent of Salinger himself. Much of their conversation is strained as Edna desperately attempts to retain Jameson's attention; he is plainly distracted by a vacuous blonde holding court in the next room.

Like many of his future characters, the young misfits chain-smoke for entertainment, allowing Salinger to produce the story's central prop: a rhinestone-encrusted cigarette case from which Edna smokes the last of her cigarettes. When Jameson finally extracts himself from Edna's company, she wends her way upstairs and into an empty set of rooms off limits to her and the other young guests. Twenty minutes pass before Edna returns. Across the room sits an attractive blonde enjoying the company of a handful of young men. One of them clutches a scotch in one hand and bites the nails of the other. Edna then opens her small black case studded with rhinestones and containing about a dozen cigarettes. Removing one, she calls to the other partygoers to change the music. Edna Phillips wants to dance.

. . .

As the Great Depression persisted, people loved to read about the fortunate lives of the rich. But rather than depicting affluent young lives as enviable, "The Young Folks" shone a stark spotlight on the unglamorous truths of upper-class society. It exposed the emptiness and unromantic realities of their pampered existence: the characters of Salinger's first story are dull and brittle, with their trivial social skills having long ago eclipsed any hint of introspection or empathy.

When Salinger's euphoria over "The Young Folks" began to fade, he discovered that he was unable to sell another story. For eight months, he submitted one attempt after another to various magazines, receiving only rejection slips in reply. Outwardly, he feigned stoicism, claiming to recognize the value of the process and reporting to Whit Burnett that he was finally oriented to his new career. Inwardly, he was growing despondent and reconsidering becoming an actor or playwright.

In March 1940, Salinger submitted another attempt to Burnett called "The Survivors," which he may have begun the previous year. The work confirmed Salinger's talent, but Burnett found its ending ambiguous and returned it to be revised. The following month, Salinger presented the editor with another story, a tense dialogue piece entitled "Go See Eddie" about a beautiful but self-centered femme fatale who devastates the lives of those around her to save herself from boredom. Burnett rejected this attempt too, but he did so gently, explaining that though he personally liked the piece, the magazine was unable to "fit it in," a common excuse at Story Press.[11] On April 16, he sent a letter to Salinger suggesting that the story be submitted to *Esquire* instead and enclosed a personal referral to be forwarded to *Esquire* editor Arnold Gingrich. Salinger masked his disappointment with an upbeat response on the next day, expressing gratitude to Burnett for his personal approval of the story. "That is satisfaction enough almost," he declared ambiguously; but as he wrote those words, "Go See Eddie" was already on its way to *Esquire* with Burnett's endorsement.[12] A few weeks later, Salinger's optimism began to wane. *Esquire* had turned down "Go See Eddie," and it seems apparent that other attempts had suffered a similar fate.

That May, however, Harold Ober Associates, one of the most prestigious literary agencies on Madison Avenue, agreed to represent Salinger. The agency designated Dorothy Olding, an agent who had joined Ober two years before, to market Salinger's work. Just turned thirty, Olding had already distinguished herself and could count Pearl S. Buck and Agatha Christie among her clients. But it was not Olding herself who impressed Salinger. Harold Ober Associates was the literary agency of his idol, F. Scott Fitzgerald. Yet, if Jerry expected that his new agent would ensure that his stories were sold to magazines, he was mistaken. Shortly after signing to Ober, he wrote of having a story at *Harper's Bazaar* awaiting publication. No Salinger story would appear in *Harper's* until 1949, and no other reference to this piece can be found. Another unnamed piece was submitted to Whit Burnett in August. That story too was turned down.

Salinger could at least assuage his doubts with the knowledge that Scott Fitzgerald had suffered a similar period of rejection. In fact, Salinger would have needed only to walk a block in order to gaze up at the apartment where Fitzgerald had sat brooding over his own inability to sell his work. For when Fitzgerald had first moved to Manhattan, just six weeks after Salinger's birth, he had settled at 1395 Lexington Avenue at 92nd Street, around the corner from where Salinger now lived on Park Avenue.

With Ober seemingly unable to promote his stories, Salinger grew anxious and spoke again of becoming a playwright. He talked about rewriting "The Young Folks" for the theater and taking the lead role himself. For a while, he tried his hand at writing radio scripts and briefly collaborated on a radio program being produced by Story Press.[13] By and large, he had little success at scriptwriting and seriously considered giving up writing altogether.[14] "I wondered if I was a has-been at twenty-one," he grieved.

In the late summer of 1940, Salinger embarked on a monthlong trip to New England and Canada, where he contemplated the direction of his life. The solitude and surroundings seem to have had a restorative effect, and he began writing a long story about people sitting in the lobby of a hotel. Writing to Burnett from Quebec, he reported happily that "This place is full of stories." As his enthusiasm gained force, Salinger began to realize that he was destined to be a short-story writer first and foremost, and for the rest of his life, whenever his creativity fell barren, he sought to re-create the effects of his stay in Canada.

When Salinger returned, his optimism was stronger than ever, but events dented his confidence. On September 4, *Story* rejected another submission. On the same day, Salinger completed the hotel piece that he had begun in Canada and sent it to Jacques Chambrun, an obscure agent whom Burnett had introduced to him the previous March.[15] According to Salinger, he instructed Chambrun to submit the attempt to *The Saturday Evening Post*.[16] No further mention was made of this story (or of Chambrun, for that matter), and it was certainly rejected in turn. Undaunted, Salinger retrieved his old story "The Survivors" from what he described as his "bottom draw" and rewrote it. He sent it again to *Story* along with a sheepish note apologizing for its lack of quality. As he had suspected, Burnett turned the piece down yet again, and this story too has disappeared.

Despite these setbacks, Jerry retained his poise. Far from being discouraged, in September he announced to Whit Burnett and Elizabeth Murray his plans to write an autobiographical novel, "something new," he promised.[17] Exactly what was so compelling about his life that people would pay to read about it was unclear, but Burnett was enthusiastic about the notion. After his rather tepid reaction to Jerry's recent works, the magnitude of his interest should have been puzzling, but Salinger was young and naive, even though he might have thought otherwise. If he thought, however, that the lure of a novel would make his other stories more attractive to the editor, he was mistaken. Burnett's interest quickly turned into insistence, and though the rejections from *Story* continued undiminished, they were now accompanied by demands for a novel.

· · ·

Jerry Salinger, while having a strong sense of destiny, had periods of deep doubt, evident in self-deprecating comments that sometimes expressed genuine discouragement. Yet Salinger either possessed or developed a remarkable professional tenacity that remained with him throughout his career. He never allowed self-doubt to dilute his ambition. Few traits could have been more valuable.

When considering Salinger's career, especially during the early years, it is important to distinguish between ambition and confidence. Certainly, Salinger had abundant self-confidence, but on the occasions when his confidence ran dry, it was ambition that kept him going. In 1940, his ambition was directed toward recognition and literary success. In years to come, the goal of his ambition would change, but the instinct itself would never desert him.

There is an additional explanation for Salinger's sustained composure at this time: his story "Go See Eddie" had finally been accepted for publication. Although not picked up by any of the high-profile magazines, its eventual acceptance must have come as vindication to the author.

As 1940 came to a close, "Go See Eddie" was published in the University of Kansas *City Review,* an academic magazine with a limited circulation. Meanwhile, Salinger began sketching the outline of a novel that would one day become *The Catcher in the Rye.*

At the same time as "Go See Eddie" was published and Salinger's confidence was restored, F. Scott Fitzgerald died in Hollywood, at the age of forty-four.

. . .

In 1941, Salinger established himself as an author on the rise, a writer both insightful and marketable.* The challenge presented was one of direction: during the year, Salinger would produce two distinctly different types of story, one commercial and the other increasingly calling the reader to self-examination. As the year wore on and his maturity and reputation grew, Salinger was progressively torn between the two.

No contrast portrays the paradox better than the opening and closing episodes of 1941, the first of frivolous distraction and the last of impending war. Bolstered by the sale of "Go See Eddie" but cash-strapped and in need of employment, at the beginning of 1941, Salinger and his best friend, Herb Kauffman, took positions on the entertainment staff of the SS *Kungsholm,* a lavish Art Deco cruise ship operated by the Swedish American Line.[18]

On February 15, the liner slipped away from the cold port of New York, bound for a nineteen-day Caribbean journey with stops at Puerto Rico, Cuba, Venezuela, and Panama. Along with travelers seeking tropical comforts and respite from thoughts of war, Jerry Salinger set out to enjoy a long working vacation, romancing girls and relaxing with his friend in the sunshine.

As a member of the entertainment staff, Salinger acted in plays, accompanied the daughters of rich passengers to dances, and spent his days organizing and playing deck sports. A photo of Salinger aboard the *Kungsholm* shows him happy, flawlessly dressed and groomed, the

---

*The year, however, was not without its rejections. In June, Dorothy Olding submitted his story "Lunch for Three," which had previously been declined by *The New Yorker,* to *Story,* where it was again rejected.

very picture of congeniality. He loved his time aboard the *Kungsholm*. Later, when his mind sought flight from darker realities, he would always remember the voyage, recalling the sunny beaches of Puerto Rico and the moonlit harbor of Havana.

The time spent aboard the *Kungsholm* would prove to be a twilight of innocence, not only for the young author but also for the nation. The Second World War had begun in Europe more than a year earlier, and though the United States was resisting being drawn into the conflict, the war cast a shadow over every aspect of American life. In immediate response to the German invasion of France in 1940, Congress had enacted the Selective Service Act, establishing the first peacetime draft in American history.

Even aboard the *Kungsholm*, the war was a constant topic of conversation, and Salinger left the ship on March 6 having correctly gauged the popular appetite for positive short stories about the military. Recognizing his opportunity to appeal to high-paying commercial magazines, he immediately penned "The Hang of It," a short, conventional story about the virtues of army life. Designed to appeal to the expectations of the wider reading public, the story abandoned Salinger's previous attempts at exposing the frailties of upper-class youths and contained no hint of psychological depth. A simple story with a fashionable O. Henry ending, "The Hang of It" was intended to make readers smile and designed to sell.

Almost in imitation of the story's military characters, or perhaps in emulation of Scott Fitzgerald, who had joined the service twenty-three years before, Salinger, upon completing "The Hang of It," attempted to enlist in the army and fulfill a desire that he had expressed in the summer of 1940. He saw himself, somewhat naively, writing his novel as a soldier.

Since Salinger had never displayed any overt patriotism in the past, this desire may appear baffling. One can only speculate that he found it increasingly difficult to write while still living with his parents. In light of his age and ambitions, his position was certainly not a good one: "The Young Folks" had earned $25, and even if Salinger managed to sell a story every month, he clearly could not afford to strike out on his own.

Considering his relationship with his mother, who was unwilling to let go of her son, it is unlikely that the Salingers would have set him up with an apartment, even had he asked. It was perhaps this motivation, more than any feelings regarding the war in Europe, which led to his desire to join the military. Amazing in hindsight was his notion that army life would afford him the leisure time necessary to construct a novel.

Much to his shock, when Salinger arrived at the army enlistment center, he was turned down. His recruitment physical revealed a mild heart irregularity of which he had been unaware.[19] At that time, the U.S. military sorted potential recruits by categorizing them between 1-A and 4-F, from totally fit to completely unqualified to serve. Salinger's heart condition resulted in his classification as 1-B—not a serious health threat but enough to prohibit his recruitment. Salinger was bitter at the verdict. In 1948, he would vividly recall that hurt through the character of Franklin in "Just Before the War with the Eskimos" as well as through numerous characters who would suffer the consequences of "some kind of heart trouble."[20]

Although the army had turned away the author, it eagerly accepted his story. In both 1942 and 1943, "The Hang of It" was included in *The Kit Book for Soldiers, Sailors and Marines,* a story and cartoon collection intended to accompany servicemen into the field. Consequently, "The Hang of It" was Salinger's first appearance in book form and was carried into battle by countless soldiers.

. . .

Before appearing in *The Kit Book,* "The Hang of It" was published in *Collier's,* where it was given a full-page illustrated spread on July 12. On one level, Salinger recognized it as an embarrassment and advised friends to avoid the story. On another, however—that of ambition and professional advancement—he accepted his *Collier's* debut as a triumph. In the days before television, when reading was the prime source of light entertainment, *Collier's* was one of a handful of America's most popular magazines that afforded its contributors immediate exposure on a national scale. And it paid well. So, though Salinger was dissatisfied with the story's lack of serious content, he was thrilled by the rewards of its commercial value. Besides, he rationalized, once he had established himself with the more popular venues, they would come round to accepting his more incisive and riskier works.[21]

The summer of 1941 produced the perfect scenario for Salinger to exploit this newfound recognition when he left for vacation with his old Valley Forge friend William Faison, the younger brother of Elizabeth Murray. Together, they spent the summer at Murray's home in the wealthy New Jersey shore town of Brielle. Murray, whom Salinger had nicknamed his "Golden Girl," was proud of his recent success and anxious to show him off to her friends, a social circle that included the parents of the most elite of the debutante set. In July 1941, then, Salinger found himself among a collection of young women so rich and beautiful that they were the constant subject of newspaper gossip columns—the type of girls he had so scathingly described in his writings. Among them were the inseparable trio of Carol Marcus, who was dating the author William Saroyan; Gloria Vanderbilt, the famous "poor little rich girl"; and Oona O'Neill, the daughter of the playwright Eugene O'Neill.

Vivacious and captivating, Oona O'Neill was someone whose beauty was often described as "haunting" and "mysterious." Adding to her appeal, her father was America's foremost playwright, a connection that certainly elevated her status in Salinger's eyes. Yet though most descriptions raved about her looks, few ascribed to Oona any depth of character. She appeared to be a shallow, self-preoccupied rich girl. Some blamed her father. Eugene O'Neill had abandoned the family when Oona was barely two years old and had ignored her since, leaving her with an attention-craving personality and a frivolity exacerbated by her companions, Marcus and Vanderbilt. Elizabeth Murray's daughter perhaps put it best when describing young Oona: "She was a blank," Murray recalled, "but she was stunning in her beauty."[22] O'Neill was exactly the kind of girl whom Salinger had long claimed to despise. Perhaps, in some unfathomable way, that is why he fell so deeply in love with her.

To Salinger's relief, Oona returned his interest, initially perhaps on account of his friendship with Whit Burnett, with whom her father had a working relationship. (Oona missed her father so much that she kept a scrapbook of him, reportedly so that she would not forget what he looked like.) Age sixteen, six years younger than her new admirer, she was possibly also intrigued by his relative maturity and his status as a published writer. From his comments and letters, it is clear that Salinger was under no illusions regarding her lack of depth—or the uneven nature of their relationship. "Little Oona," Salinger grieved, was "hopelessly in love with little Oona."[23] Nevertheless, his feelings toward her were steadfast, and when they returned to New York, they began a romance that would affect the author for years to come.

In August, Salinger was back in New York but not at home on Park Avenue. Perhaps finding it difficult to work in his parents' apartment, he holed up for two weeks in the Beekman Tower Hotel on East 49th Street, a short distance from Rockefeller Center. Although Salinger reported that his time at the Beekman had been unproductive, it resulted in a short story that he referred to as "The Lovely Dead Girl at Table Six" but that we know today as "Slight Rebellion off Madison," Salinger's first Caulfield story and a section of the novel he had been working on for the past year.[24]

After leaving the Beekman, Salinger sent the story to his agents at Ober Associates, where it received a lukewarm response. "A little slow," they noted, "but nice atmosphere and kid's viewpoint."[25]

By May 1941, Salinger had also completed what would be his next published work, "The Heart of a Broken Story." Few readers recognized the work as an attempt to satirize the stories being promoted by commercial magazines. It was a witty piece that parodied not only the recipe for short romances but the gangster movies popular at the time. The story also has a bleak and serious underside that displays the dilemma in which Salinger currently found himself: whether to strive for quality or salability. The tale begins as a typical boy-meets-girl story. Its main characters, Justin Horgenschlag and Shirley Lester, board the same Third Avenue bus on their way to work. Horgenschlag falls in love with Shirley at first sight and becomes frantic to go out with her. At this point, Salinger interrupts the narrative, explaining to the reader that he cannot continue the account as planned (intended— he points out—for *Collier's*). The characters are simply too ordinary for the plot he has envisioned, and he cannot seem to get them "together properly."[26] After leading readers through a series of humorous scenarios that take the luckless Horgenschlag to prison, Salinger decides to abandon the whole idea of constructing a romance. Reality is back: Shirley and Horgenschlag never speak a word to each other, and the story ends as they disembark the Third Avenue bus and resume their separate lives, loveless and mundane.

In "The Heart of a Broken Story," Salinger begins his refusal to create his characters artificially, declining to force them to be romantic

or heroic. By satisfying neither commercial nor "serious" requirements, the story challenges readers to make their own decisions. Is
"The Heart of a Broken Story" actually "The Story of a Broken Heart"?
Will they continue to accept the happy fluff being peddled by the popular magazines or begin to demand less cheerful but more believable
alternatives? The author's decision is plain. If readers of "The Heart of
a Broken Story" expect a happy ending, they will be sorely disappointed.

. . .

"The Heart of a Broken Story" was published in September 1941, not
in *Collier's,* as Salinger had expected, but in *Esquire,* an edgier publication geared mainly to men. For all the story's humor, its skeptical conclusion demonstrated that Salinger was unwilling to abandon serious
literature. Yet, at the same time, he recognized that he needed to support himself. So he made a conscious decision to separate his writings
between those containing introspection and nuance and the more marketable works that could earn him a quick, easy buck.

Salinger often poked fun at his commercial stories, such as "The
Hang of It," lacking in quality but easily sold to popular magazines.
However, there was one magazine whose recognition Salinger desired
above all others and to which he refused to submit minor stories, regardless of the outcome. That magazine was *The New Yorker,* the most
respected and financially rewarding literary venue to which an author
could aspire.

Now a professional writer, Salinger became increasingly uneasy.
Somehow, his daily life did not measure up to his achievements and
there was little he could point to in proof that he had actually "made
it." He was still living at home with his parents, a situation that was becoming increasingly intolerable. His romance with Oona O'Neill was
incomplete and conducted largely at her discretion. And he was dissatisfied with the circulation and presentation of his stories, the best of
which had been reined in by their limited distribution while his least
significant had gained the greatest exposure. Salinger saw *The New
Yorker* as a solution to all his problems. If he could persuade it to publish another of his more incisive, quality stories, he would attain the respectability that he felt he deserved, impress Oona O'Neill, and begin
to alter his daily situation.

By the time "The Heart of a Broken Story" was published, Salinger had completed his darkest work yet, "The Long Debut of Lois Taggett." The tale of a debutante and her long, strange process of coming out, this bleak story once again revolves around upper-class young people. In it Salinger equates fashionable trends with phoniness and a lack of values. Throughout the story, Lois struggles to deal with the harshness of reality while inching toward some level of compassion. Before she can let go of pretense, she must first deal with a psychotic husband, a loveless second marriage, and her child's crib death.

Despite the story's many oddities (Lois's husband, for example, suffers from a bizarre allergy to colored socks), Salinger was convinced it would allow him to break through onto the pages of *The New Yorker*.[27] As soon as it was completed, he instructed Dorothy Olding to submit it to the magazine.

. . .

By late 1941, Salinger was producing stories in rapid succession, each an experiment designed to both find his own writing style and distinguish what was salable to various magazines. To his disappointment, "The Long Debut of Lois Taggett" was rejected by *The New Yorker*, and Salinger sent it on to *Mademoiselle*, indicating a definite decline in ambition.[28] In fact, in 1941, *The New Yorker* rejected not only "Lois Taggett" but seven Salinger stories in all. "The Hang of It" had been returned by March, "The Heart of a Broken Story" by July, and "The Long Debut of Lois Taggett" before summer's end. In addition, stories such as "The Fisherman," "Monologue for a Watery Highball," and "I Went to School with Adolph Hitler" not only were rejected by the magazine but are now lost.[29] Salinger, who was probably desperate for any form of affirmation after this string of defeats, actually found encouragement in one of these dismissals. While declining to publish another now-lost story called "Lunch for Three," *New Yorker* editor John Mosher sent a note to Dorothy Olding giving it positive personal feedback. "There is certainly something quite brisk and bright about this piece," he wrote. The magazine, however, was searching for short stories of a more conventional nature.[30]

Meanwhile, Salinger's personal life was proving as thorny as his professional. After returning from the Jersey shore, he managed several dates with Oona O'Neill in Manhattan, where she was attending the Brearley School, close to Salinger's home. Catering to Oona's flamboyant tastes, he paraded down Fifth Avenue with her, dined at fine restaurants he could barely afford, and spent evenings sipping cocktails at the glamorous Stork Club, where they socialized with movie stars and high-society celebrities in an atmosphere that must have made Salinger cringe. He was, he confessed to Elizabeth Murray, simply "crazy about her." Yet by October, Salinger was seeing less and less of O'Neill and was increasingly forced to sustain the romance through letters.[31]

The chill in Salinger's relationship with Oona O'Neill added urgency to his need to be published by *The New Yorker*. Perhaps such a high-profile success would command Oona's attention and place him closer to the preening personalities she had so admired at the Stork Club.

In October 1941, Salinger received the news that *The New Yorker* had accepted one of his submissions, the portion of his novel he had reworked at the Beekman Tower Hotel and delivered to his agent in August. He had renamed the story "Slight Rebellion off Madison" and described it as "a sad little comedy about a prep school boy on Christmas vacation."[32] It was a spiritually autobiographical piece, he admitted, starring a discontented young New Yorker named Holden Morrisey Caulfield. (Salinger spelled Morrisey with one "s," unlike the more usual Morrissey.)

To coincide with the story's Christmas setting, *The New Yorker* planned to publish it in its December issue. Salinger was ecstatic, believing he had finally won the recognition he so frantically craved. When he received the news, he was completing a piece entitled "Mrs. Hincher," which he described as a horror story, adding that it would be his first and last.* He would now concentrate on stories about Holden Caulfield instead. "Slight Rebellion" had unlocked a path to creativity that would alter his life.

---

*An incomplete version of this story resides at the University of Texas, Austin. It relates the tale of a woman who believes she is her own child. In what is perhaps the most bizarre Salinger story known, Mrs. Hincher's husband bursts into his wife's room to find her curled up in a crib, convinced she is a baby. Salinger renamed this piece "Paula" upon its completion and sold it to *Stag* magazine, where it stalled. The story went unpublished, and in 1961, *Stag* reported that it had gone missing from its files.

The first of nine stories featuring the Caulfield family, "Slight Rebellion" supplied the avenue along which Salinger's career would move until it culminated in *The Catcher in the Rye*. Proclaiming his upcoming *New Yorker* debut to Elizabeth Murray, Salinger bragged that the magazine had requested he write more stories about Holden Caulfield. Salinger said that he did indeed have another Caulfield story ready for submission but, still testing the waters, decided to submit a different story instead.[33]

"Slight Rebellion" would prove to have a long history that would deliver both pain and triumph. Salinger reworked it several times and even changed its title. Still struggling with the piece in 1943, he would refer to it in sarcastic frustration as "Are You Banging Your Head Against the Wall?" Unfortunately, whatever Salinger had hoped to accomplish with "Slight Rebellion," at least artistically, evaded him. Despite his near obsession with the story, he was never completely happy with it.[34] It is the first story in which he appears to examine his own character more deeply. His previous sketches had been directed toward the shortcomings of others, but in "Slight Rebellion" he aligns himself so closely with Holden Caulfield as to cast his own spirit within the main character. Rather than keeping personal issues at arm's length, he now graduated to embracing them as a means of bonding with his characters and readers alike, presenting qualities all the more human because they are his own.

Home from Pencey Prep on Christmas vacation, Holden Caulfield takes his girlfriend, Sally Hayes, on a date, first to the theater and then ice skating at Rockefeller Center. At the skating rink, Holden begins to drink and offers a tirade on the things he claims to hate: his school, theaters, newsreels, and the Madison Avenue bus. In an effort to avoid convention, Holden asks Sally to run away to New England with him. "We'll live somewhere with a brook and stuff," he tells her. ". . . Then, later on, we'll get married or something." When Sally refuses, Holden goes to a bar to get drunk and then sulks in the bathroom, where he encounters the barroom piano player. "Why don't you go home, kid?" the piano player asks. "Not me," Holden mutters. "Not me."[35]

Encountering "Slight Rebellion off Madison," present-day readers are sometimes tempted to dismiss it as an unpolished chapter of *The Catcher in the Rye*. Although the story contains characters and events familiar to readers of the novel, its tone and feel are foreign to it. The Holden Caulfield of *Catcher* and the Holden Caulfield of "Slight Rebellion" are driven by different motivations, a difference that changes not only the story's characters but also its primary message. Stylistically, "Slight Rebellion" is stiff and its characters purposely deadpan. Its Holden Caulfield is distant, with a third-person voice far removed from the reader. Produced at a time when Salinger's writing wavered between the thoughtful and the commercial, it stands somewhere in between and has as much in common with "The Young Folks" as with *The Catcher in the Rye.*

The driving force of the story is Holden's pronouncements on the things he claims to hate, a scotch-drenched litany later repeated in the novel but whose vehemence and self-derision are stronger in the short story. In "Slight Rebellion," Holden appears as a typical well-heeled teenager doing the ordinary things any upper-middle-class boy might do. Salinger emphasizes the point by noting that girls often thought they saw him shopping in the city when in fact it was someone else. Yet, beneath his conventional facade, Holden seethes with discontent and longs to escape the world in which he feels entrapped.

By portraying Holden's dissatisfaction and rebellion against what is expected of him, Salinger reveals the tumult that often simmers beneath the surface of individuals in real life. Like the later Holden of *Catcher,* the Holden of "Slight Rebellion" is torn in opposite directions, one of fulfilling expectations and one of rebellion. In the predictable world of Sally Hayes, there is nothing more commonplace than trimming the tree at Christmas. Although Holden protests against conformity, he is repeatedly drawn to Sally's request that he help her trim the tree. He is attracted to the ritual as a comfort, despite its conventionality. At the same time as disdaining ordinary life, he is still desperate to be accepted into it.

The end of the story contains a neat ironic twist when we find Holden cold and drunk, waiting for the very Madison Avenue bus he loathes so much. If this story contains any autobiographical comment, it is to be found within this final scene, where Holden so clearly yearns for the very things he claims to hate. Containing an element of self-derision, "Slight Rebellion" portrays an individual trapped by the limitations of his own experience. Holden, like his creator, might scorn the mundane, but that is all he knows. In fact, that is what has come to define him. Sally Hayes, a character who resembles Oona O'Neill, is presented as being shallow and concerned only with fashionable traditions. She is comfortable. Holden, on the other hand, is too introspective and complex to accept the world without question. The sadness of the story's ending lies in our realization that Holden Caulfield has become the very thing he despises. While hating the bus, a symbol of normality, he is still dependent upon it.

Though Salinger may have devoted his writing to exposing and parodying the emptiness of upper-class Manhattan society, it was the only world he knew. It had helped mold him and, despite the most scathing of insights, he had become part of it.

So "Slight Rebellion" was a confession, an explanation of the frustration Salinger was experiencing in his own life at the time. Just as he felt torn between professional directions, he discovered a similar contradiction in his personal life. While Holden Caulfield decries the falseness of trendy society, his creator was sitting in the Stork Club, entertaining a life of pretension and craving the very things he reviled in print.

3. Indecision

On December 7, 1941, the Japanese bombed Pearl Harbor and the United States found itself at war. Four days later, Jerry Salinger sat at his desk on Park Avenue, attempting to absorb the feelings of outrage and patriotism that swept over him.[1] As throngs of men rushed to enlist, he was overcome by frustration. Desperate to contribute to the war effort, he complained to Whit Burnett that his 1-B classification left him feeling helpless, a sorrow tempered by the expectation that "Slight Rebellion" would be appearing in the next issue of *The New Yorker*.[2]

Two days later, the U.S. government commandeered the SS *Kungsholm*. Pressed into military service as a troop transport, the luxury liner saw its stylish furniture stripped from its cabins and discarded onto its pier. Salinger's beloved story suffered a similar fate. After reevaluating the popular mood following the attack on Pearl Harbor, *The New Yorker* decided to cut "Slight Rebellion" from its next issue and suspend it indefinitely. The nation was no longer anxious to read the frivolous whining of dissatisfied upper-crust youths.

When Salinger received the news about "Slight Rebellion," he was crestfallen. But he was also stubborn and immediately instructed Dorothy Olding to submit "The Long Debut of Lois Taggett" to *Story*. Then, ignoring the slight by *The New Yorker*, he sent it a new piece, one about "an obese boy and his sisters."[3] That attempt may have been "The Kissless Life of Reilly," a story that Salinger referred to in a January 2 letter. *The New Yorker* rejected it (as did *Story* magazine). Despite its hesitation on "Slight Rebellion," it claimed to have expected a story about Holden Caulfield instead. Returning the submission, *New Yorker* editor William Maxwell noted to Dorothy Olding, "it would have worked out better for us if Mr. Salinger had not strained so for cleverness."[4]

Salinger, though, was now more determined than ever to break onto the pages of *The New Yorker*. He became increasingly compliant and finally submitted the Holden Caulfield story that *The New Yorker* had demanded—a sequel to "Slight Rebellion" called "Holden on the Bus."[5] The story was rejected. This time, *The New Yorker* faulted its Holden character for having "no sense of decorum or when to be silent," an ironic pronouncement, as both submissions have since disappeared.[6]

Jerry now found himself in an embarrassing position and was perhaps fearful of Oona O'Neill's reaction. The world had become obsessed with the war effort, and people could speak of little else. Radio, movies, newspapers, and magazines fed the frenzy. While almost everyone he knew had enlisted for service, he remained in his parents' apartment, at the age of twenty-three, barred from fulfilling his obligation at a time of war by a minor heart condition. To make matters worse, his chosen profession was selling him short. After he had told everyone about the imminent publication of "Slight Rebellion off Madison," *The New Yorker* gave no indication of ever releasing it.

With no one else to turn to, he petitioned Valley Forge founder Colonel Milton G. Baker, pleading for intervention.[7] The appeal proved unnecessary when the army relaxed its classification standards and Salinger soon found himself deemed suitable for service. In April 1942, his draft notice arrived.

Jerry completed the questionnaire with relish: his official enlistment records are peppered with his unique sense of humor. Under "civilian occupation," Salinger claimed to be a carpenter of railway cars. When asked to declare the extent of his education, he admitted only to "grammar school."[8] Regardless of his draft board high jinks, he was relieved to begin military service.

Yet, with reality sinking in that he was now leaving home, perhaps to fight a war rather than to write novels, Salinger began to review his motives. His first enlistment attempt had been an effort to draw him away from home and been driven mainly by frustration, while his feelings after Pearl Harbor had been largely patriotic. Facing his parents' anguish over seeing their son leave for war, Salinger encountered a conflict of responsibilities. To say that he was torn about joining the army would be an overstatement. Perhaps to his own surprise, he discovered a bond with home and family that he had never expressed before. Having previously sought to distance himself, he began to develop an appreciation for the simple things that bind family members together and to contemplate the common yet complex dynamics of family structures.

There also arose within Salinger a fear that he might be leaving a world to which he would not return. Not simply fear of death but fear of a world yet again swept away, the world of home and the world of simple beauty. Something within Salinger, even at this early date, perceived a world that was quickly losing its innocence.

"The Last and Best of the Peter Pans" is a story in which Salinger examines his own mixed response to induction into the army and leaving home. At the same time, he establishes the family of Holden Caulfield as a kind of surrogate for his own. "The Last and Best of the Peter Pans" was never published and remains in the archives of Story Press, which were donated to Princeton University in 1965. It is an intensely personal work that examines what was arguably Salinger's closest relationship: that with his mother. "The Last and Best of the Peter Pans" remains the deepest insight into the strong character of Miriam Salinger, her protective bond with her son, and his conflicting feelings regarding it.

Salinger aligns himself completely with the narrator of "Peter Pans," Holden's older brother, Vincent Caulfield. Although mentioned, Holden does not appear in the story. Instead, "The Last and Best of the Peter Pans" is largely a dialogue between Vincent and his mother, Mary Moriarity. Vincent begins by describing his mother's enveloping personality and striking red hair. One day he discovers that she has intercepted his draft board questionnaire from the mail and hidden it in a kitchen drawer. Enraged, Vincent confronts her. A long argument ensues between them over the questionnaire and the army. Mary defends her actions, protesting that Vincent would not be happy in the service. In an attempt to emphasize the joys of home and the dangers of war, she calls Vincent's attention to his little sister, Phoebe, playing outside in her new blue coat. Vincent is pierced with love, but he forces himself to turn away. When Vincent averts his eyes from his sister, Mary reminds her son of the death of his younger brother, Kenneth. Vincent feels guilty about Kenneth's death, and Mary comes across as manipulative and determined: "She looked slightly afraid to approach the subject; but she came equipped, as always, to get there," Vincent tells us.[9] In the last paragraph, Vincent, now suffering a confusion of emotions, accuses his mother of a number of unwitting hypocrisies, of asking a blind man for the time or a lame man to catch a child crawling off a cliff. Retreating to his room, perhaps recognizing his mother's unwillingness to sacrifice another son so soon after Kenneth's death, Vincent dubs her "the last and best of the Peter Pans," seeking not longevity for herself but life for her children. Still Vincent refuses to address his conflicting emotions, though it is clear by the end that he will go off to war. In future stories, Vincent Caulfield will become a symbol of emotional reticence, entrapped by his pain.

. . .

Private Jerome David Salinger, Army Service Number 32325200, reported for active duty at Fort Dix, New Jersey, on April 27, 1942.[10] From Fort Dix, he was immediately assigned to A Company of the 1st Signal Corps Battalion, located at Fort Monmouth, New Jersey. The Signal Corps was responsible for communications duties ranging from the development of radar to the deployment of carrier pigeons, and it valued technical ability above all else, skills sorely lacking in their new conscript. Fort Monmouth's location, near Sandy Hook and the Jersey shore, was ideal for Salinger. It allowed him easy access to home while on leave and was a short drive from the town of Point Pleasant, where Oona O'Neill had a house with her mother.

Fort Monmouth is surrounded by marshy inlets, creeks, and patches of woods. Although uninviting, its geography provides a selection of training environments that make it especially practical for the military. When Salinger arrived there, it was undergoing wartime ex-

pansion, with construction at every turn. The atmosphere was one of
organized tumult as the camp pulsated with the ebb and flow of departing units and new recruits. While additional wooden barracks were
being built to accommodate new troops, Salinger spent his nights in
one of dozens of the large identical tents that faced the central parade
ground. There he was cramped together with other soldiers from
across the nation. Complaining that the men in his tent were "always
eating oranges or listening to quiz programs," he found it impossible
to write.[11]

The present-day concept of J. D. Salinger makes it difficult to imagine him happy in the army. Salinger is synonymous with a kind of rebellion that, along with his indulged Park Avenue sophistication,
would seem to make him out of place in military barracks. The philosophy of army life, too, appears opposed to that of the author, whose
solitude and individuality have come to define him. Yet Salinger had a
tendency to orderliness, a trait that drove him in search of meaning behind ostensibly arbitrary events. Moreover, despite his youthful reputation for apathy, he had developed a discipline and tenacity as a writer
that translated well into a soldier's life of duty and drive.

The army would eventually have a profound effect upon Salinger's
work. Cast adrift in a cauldron of social realities, among soldiers from
the Deep South and ex–tenement dwellers from impoverished inner
cities, he was forced to adjust his attitude to people. His view of humanity shifted with every new individual he encountered, which had a
substantial effect upon his literary sensitivities. Due to his Valley Forge
education, he was more comfortable with military routine than most
and began to develop friendships with people he would not have engaged with in civilian life.

Salinger's initial comfort in the army had a cooling effect upon his
writing career. Soon after his arrival at boot camp, Salinger told Whit
Burnett that although he missed his "little typewriter terribly," he was
actually looking forward to taking a short break from writing. He
would write little during 1942. Instead, he turned his energies toward
advancing his position in the military and becoming a commissioned
officer.

Salinger's sudden switch from writer to soldier caused the first in a
series of subtle rifts with Burnett. Citing his military education and
ROTC service, Salinger felt it natural that he be commissioned as an

officer rather than remain a private, and in June he applied for acceptance into the Officer Candidate School. To help secure a commission, Salinger requested letters of recommendation from Burnett and Valley Forge headmaster Colonel Baker. Baker's response was enthusiastic:

> I am of the opinion that he possesses all of the traits and character which will qualify him as an outstanding officer in the army. Private Salinger has a very attractive personality, is mentally keen, has above-average athletic ability, is a diligent worker and thoroughly loyal and dependable. . . . I believe he would be a genuine credit to the country.[12]

In contrast, Burnett's recommendation was more tentative:

> I have known Jerry Salinger, who has taken work under me at Columbia University, for three years, and he is a person of imagination, intelligence, and capable of quick and decisive action. He is a responsible individual and it seems he would be a credit to an officer's rank if he sets his mind in that direction.[13]

If Salinger recognized the ambiguity in Burnett's last line, he did not let on; perhaps he understood the editor's reluctance. In the same letter in which Salinger requested support, he admitted to having stopped writing since his induction. Burnett's halfhearted endorsement came along with a note to the effect that he had received "The Long Debut of Lois Taggett" and liked it very much. Burnett appeared to be playing a subtle game of carrots and sticks, to keep Salinger in the writers' ring.

"Lois Taggett" was accepted for publication by *Story,* rescuing it from oblivion and pleasing Salinger. But Salinger had been denied enrollment by the OCS, which pleased Burnett. If Salinger blamed his editor at all for the OCS rejection, the feelings were veiled. Writing to Burnett on July 12, Salinger thanked him "for letters, acceptances, and Burnettery in general" but concluded by announcing that he had been accepted into the Army Aviation Cadets. This military advancement would require a transfer far away from New Jersey, from weekends on Park Avenue and the offices of Story Press.

Summer's end found Salinger aboard a troop train heading into the

Deep South. He switched trains in Waycross, Georgia, a thousand miles from Fort Monmouth, and traveled west, through the town of Valdosta, until he reached his final stop, the U.S. Army Air Forces base in Bainbridge, Georgia, home for the next nine months.

In many ways Bainbridge resembled Fort Monmouth. At Bainbridge, the clamor of construction was replaced by the constant noise of aircraft. Giant water towers cast long shadows over the camp. The barracks were wooden but ramshackle and roofed with sticky black tar paper. Even though the base had been built on a swamp, the air at Bainbridge was thick with dust and hot close to the point of suffocation. To escape, soldiers took their leave across the river into downtown Bainbridge, the seat of Decatur County. Downtown was a drowsy place, complete with a town square, ornate courthouse, and Confederate war monument. It even boasted a lacy gazebo. The town might have appeared quaint to those passing through, a throwback to a bygone era, but to Salinger it was exile to Saint Helena. Decades later, when asked to recall the place, he would quip, "Bainbridge wasn't exactly Tara."[14]

Salinger complained to Burnett that the base was the kind of place in which Faulkner and Caldwell "could have a literary picnic" but one that a boy from New York longed to leave. For the first time, Salinger appeared to have suffered homesickness, lamenting that he would rather be north "about a thousand miles." Bainbridge, however, would provide Salinger with an opportunity similar to the one he had found at Valley Forge. Its mundane routine gave him time to write, and he was prolific there. The length of time that he spent in Georgia provided stability and the leisure to scrutinize others in depth, perhaps for the first time. This, too, would show itself in his writing. He even found romance in the sleepy town across the river.

Salinger had been promoted to an instructor in the Officers, First Sergeants, and Instructors of the Signal Corps. Bainbridge was home to the U.S. Army Air Corps Basic Flying School, where he was to teach. Although he had pursued the appointment after being turned down by the Officer Candidate School, Salinger was mildly surprised when it actually came. He was not mechanically inclined but still found himself teaching others the workings of an airplane.

While he spent his days instructing recruits and training pilots, he found his nights free and returned to writing. Although he had written little since being drafted, his army experience caused him to reconsider his work. Changes in environment and new friendships with soldiers from diverse backgrounds provided fresh creative insights. He had been anxious to publish "The Long Debut of Lois Taggett" since its completion the previous year, but when it finally appeared in the September–October issue of *Story,* he claimed that he now found it "boring."[15]

Burnett was relieved by Salinger's return to writing, but he still feared losing his prime prospect to military life and pressured him to produce more. He also approached Dorothy Olding on a number of occasions, requesting that she "sound him out about a book." "I am very much interested in Salinger's turning his hand to a novel," Burnett wrote, "if he is not too busy."[16]

Although both Burnett and Olding were keen to see Salinger continue working on the Holden Caulfield book, Salinger was unable to offer them the reassurance they sought. In late 1942, he informed both that though he had again taken up writing, his army duties prevented him from resuming the novel; that would require much more time than he had available. If the opportunity presented itself in the future, he promised, he would consider continuing the book.[17] In fact, once Salinger had settled at Bainbridge, he began to write vigorously. When he replied to Burnett and Olding regarding the novel, he was working on at least four separate short stories.

In September, when he was still experiencing regret and homesickness after arriving at Bainbridge, Salinger's thoughts turned to Oona O'Neill. He wrote to Oona, perhaps on his first night in Georgia, telling her that he now realized how much he loved and missed her. This was the first of many letters that he would send her from Bainbridge. Small novellas in their own right (some were fifteen pages long) and written almost daily, Salinger's love letters were crammed with both romance and irony. Oona was flattered and intrigued by the letters and showed them off to her friends, especially Carol Marcus and Gloria Vanderbilt. Their feelings about both Salinger and his correspondence appear to have been split. This "Jerry" boy of Oona's, they deduced, seemed to have two personalities: sentimental and cheeky.

Truman Capote related Oona's friends' reactions to Salinger's letters in his unfinished novel *Answered Prayers.* According to Capote's gossipy account, Carol Marcus considered them "sort of love-letter essays, very tender, tenderer than God. Which is a bit too tender." None of this would have bothered Salinger, who thought Marcus and Vanderbilt strange and dull.

Carol Marcus's engagement to William Saroyan—an author Salinger admired—was almost ruined by Salinger's letters (and by her own audacity). Saroyan had recently been drafted into the service, putting Carol into the unenviable position of having to write to a famous author in order to maintain their relationship. As Marcus put it, "I told Oona I was afraid that if I wrote to Bill, he'd find out what an idiot I was, and decide not to marry me, so she marked the clever passages in her letters from Jerry and let me copy them, as my own, in my letters to Bill."[18] Once reunited with Saroyan, Marcus was distraught to learn that he was unsure about whether to marry her. His opinion of Carol had changed after reading all those "lousy glib letters" she had sent. Marcus frantically admitted to the deception and, after gaining his forgiveness, married Saroyan in February 1943.*

Working on a number of stories, Salinger was eager to retain his public profile. Seeking a swift commercial release to accomplish this, he remixed an old recipe assured of success and submitted it to *Collier's,* the same bastion of high-profile kitsch that he had so bitterly complained about only months before. On December 12, 1942, *Collier's* published "Personal Notes of an Infantryman." It is plain that Salinger released "Infantryman" purely because it was expedient to do so. "Infantryman" is constructed using the same simple formula as "The Hang of It" and is essentially the same story. The fact that both pieces were picked up by *Collier's* was not surprising. Salinger was gradually learning which magazines liked what kind of writing. Like "The Hang of It," "Personal Notes of an Infantryman" employs a neatly predictable O. Henry ending and is imbued with patriotism and a warmth toward the military.

Despite the similarities between "The Hang of It" and "Personal Notes of an Infantryman," the two narratives left different footprints on Salinger's career. When "The Hang of It" was published by *Collier's* in July 1941, Salinger was thrilled at what he viewed as a breakthrough. It was this story that he used to impress Oona O'Neill. In

---

*Carol Marcus actually married Saroyan twice, in 1943 and again in 1951. In 1959, she married the actor Walter Matthau. Marcus was an inspiration for Holly Golightly, the lead character of Truman Capote's *Breakfast at Tiffany's.* She died in July 2003.

contrast, "Infantryman" was deployed by Salinger only as literary filler, to plug the gap between his period of literary inaction and the completion of more discerning works. It was certainly not a story that Salinger bragged about. Nor could he attract Oona's attention as easily with this story as he had with "The Hang of It." In any case, Oona was now in Los Angeles, where her mother, Agnes Boulton, was hoping to build her daughter into a movie star.

. . .

Salinger began 1943 by producing a series of commercial stories designed to reproduce the easy sale of "Infantryman" to *Collier's* and better pieces targeted at *The New Yorker*.[19] He even began to think of selling his work to Hollywood, where he might impress and be closer to Oona after the war.

Salinger's turn to commercialism in early 1943 is unsurprising. He found it easy to produce such works, which was attractive considering the amount of time now consumed by his army duties. The "slicks" also paid well, and his correspondence throughout 1943 demonstrates a certain eagerness to make money.

In the months straddling 1942 and 1943, Salinger also submitted two satirical stories to *The New Yorker*. The first, entitled "Men Without Hemingway," lampooned the grandiose war novels he supposed would result from the conflict. Another, awkwardly named "Over the Sea Let's Go, Twentieth Century Fox," was a spoof on the propaganda films being spewed out by Hollywood.[20] *The New Yorker* returned them both. By February, Salinger had also sent *The New Yorker* a short story called "The Broken Children," which he considered his best work since entering the service.[21] In the end, "The Broken Children" was rejected not only by *The New Yorker* but by *Story* as well. The rejections mean that none of these stories has survived.

Understandably, Salinger became increasingly bitter toward *The New Yorker* over the course of 1943. It had been almost two years since the magazine had accepted "Slight Rebellion off Madison," and Salinger now began to doubt that he would ever see the story in print. *The New Yorker*, he claimed, was interested only in its own clique of (as he put it) "little Hemingways."[22] Feeling excluded and frustrated, he turned to other magazines.

In April, his agent sold "The Varioni Brothers" to *The Saturday*

Evening Post, the same magazine that had given Scott Fitzgerald his break. With its striking Norman Rockwell covers, the *Post* had developed into the quintessential American magazine of the 1940s. A notch above *Collier's* in popularity and respectability, its national circulation of four million allowed it to pay handsomely for Salinger's work. None of this, though, prevented him from mocking the magazine or belittling the stories it purchased from him.

Salinger's tendency to ridicule his own works is something of a mystery when considering "The Varioni Brothers." He apologized profusely for this story, explaining its lack of quality with the excuse that it had been written with Hollywood in mind.* However, his explanation appears to be somewhat insincere. Beneath an admittedly movie-styled surface, "The Varioni Brothers" examines the power of success to destroy true inspiration and contains an unmistakable analysis of the author himself, a sophisticated parable that Hollywood would certainly not have understood.

"The Varioni Brothers" follows the lives of two brothers, a musician in pursuit of success and a writer in pursuit of quality. The musician overpowers his weaker, more sensitive brother with his ambition for fame and forces him to abandon a novel that he has been writing on the back of matchbooks and instead write lyrics for his songs. The songs become hits, and the brothers are catapulted to wealth and renown. What is transparent while reading "The Varioni Brothers" is that both brothers are based upon Salinger himself. In order to give the Varioni brothers life, the author splits himself between two facets of his own personality and the two diverse professional roads open to him. Salinger created Joe Varioni as a writer, teaching English at a small college while working on his book. Joe's writing is serious, if in disarray, and Salinger elevates it to the level of "art" in this story. Joe's influential professor, a Burnett-like academic, goes as far as to call him a "poet." Joe Varioni is so much the dedicated writer that Salinger longed to be that it is surprising not to encounter him submitting works to *The New Yorker.* On the other hand, Joe's brother, though talented, only cares about fame and fortune. He does not write music as art but as a product, a fact verbalized in his lament that he "cannot

---

*Salinger not only excused the quality of "The Varioni Brothers" to Burnett—a professional confession—but also derided the story to his closest personal friends and secretly ridiculed those who spoke highly of the work.

hear the music" he creates.[23] He is lazy, pushy, and sometimes wicked. In case it's not clear enough, Salinger even names this brother "Sonny," after his youthful self. If *Collier's* had had a music department, Sonny Varioni would have been camped out on its doorstep.

"The Varioni Brothers" is a kitschy kind of morality play, and Sonny's greed inevitably destroys his brother. One night, during a celebrity-studded party thrown for them, Joe is gunned down by a gangster who mistakes him for Sonny. At the time, Joe was uncharacteristically at the piano, playing a song called "I Want to Hear the Music." Here again, Salinger's message is clear. He expresses his fear that his own commercial success will suffocate his creative purity. Unlike in "The Heart of a Broken Story," there is no longer any ambiguity: "The Varioni Brothers" displays commercialism as pure evil and Salinger's own immature attraction to it as equivalent to death.

. . .

Salinger had not intended that "The Varioni Brothers" should reach the public through the pages of the *Post* or of any other magazine. Although much of his writing, including *The Catcher in the Rye,* professes disdain for motion pictures, Jerry always adored the movies and longed to see his name on the silver screen. Before "The Varioni Brothers" was purchased by the *Post,* Salinger had given it, along with several other pieces, to the well-known literary agent Max Wilkinson. Wilkinson had taken the story to Hollywood and tried selling it to the studios.[24] Hollywood showed some interest, but the attention was short-lived and the prospect, along with Salinger's association with Wilkinson, soon faded. Ultimately, his attempted foray into the movies resulted only in a number of stories purposely diluted for Hollywood, something he later acknowledged with embarrassment.[25]

If Salinger's efforts to sell his works to Hollywood seemed to conflict with his writings, it was perhaps an act of disguised desperation. Since Oona O'Neill had moved to Los Angeles in the autumn of 1942, their relationship had rapidly disintegrated. Despite numerous lengthy letters to Oona, he had heard little from her since she had left New York. By early January, he was beginning to read gossip columns linking his girlfriend with the legendary actor Charlie Chaplin.

O'Neill had indeed become involved with Chaplin. When she and her mother arrived in California, Chaplin was casting a movie called

Shadow and Substance, and Oona, who by now had had a few quick acting lessons, auditioned for the lead role. Chaplin never made the film and Oona's career as a Hollywood star never left the station, but she pursued Chaplin despite the fact that he was thirty-six years her senior. Chaplin was notoriously attracted to younger women, and he succumbed to O'Neill's advances. Their romance became a media sensation. At the same time Chaplin was embroiled in a scandal, accused of fathering the child of Joan Barry, an actress whose own youth (she was thirty-one years younger than he) added to the outrage. The resulting paternity suit consumed much of 1943 and provided a sensational backdrop for his romance with O'Neill. When the media learned of the affair, Chaplin was painted as a moral degenerate and "un-American." There was a successful crusade to boycott his movies.*

Oona's breakup with Salinger and her union with Chaplin were the great romantic tragedy of Jerry's life. And there was no escaping the subject: the front pages of newspapers carried photos of Chaplin being fingerprinted in connection with his paternity suit and accompanying articles accused the actor of entrapping the young, "innocent" daughter of America's favorite playwright in a diabolical act of "white slavery." This man had stolen Jerry's "little girl," the one he had idealized and hoped to marry.[26] The episode was also publicly humiliating for Salinger. Everyone knew how he felt about O'Neill. The same army buddies to whom he had proudly displayed Oona's picture now looked at him with sympathetic eyes.

Despite these events, Salinger's pride and tenacity prevented him from indulging in any public lamentation. Instead, he either ignored the situation or feigned stoic indifference. In a January 11 letter to Elizabeth Murray, who knew every detail of the romance, Salinger already claimed to have lost his passion for O'Neill, affecting a kind of romantic amnesia. As for the breakup itself, rather than finding fault with O'Neill or Chaplin, Salinger blamed Oona's mother.[27] In fact, apart from complaints about incessant but minor health problems (allergic reactions and constant toothache) and his shifting moods,

---

*The controversy haunted Chaplin for years after returning to his native England. In 1956, the Crown considered Chaplin for knighthood. According to the British Foreign Office, the 1943 paternity suit (which Chaplin lost, although later blood tests proved he was not the father) and his relationship with Oona O'Neill were cited among the reasons the honor was deferred. He was finally knighted in 1975.

Salinger avoided revealing any sense of resentment. It was not until July that he would finally admit to loathing Chaplin.[28]

Salinger's reluctance to admit his hurt helps explain what are otherwise perplexing sections of a story written at Bainbridge entitled "Death of a Dogface." Although it is a commercial story, penned with the intention of being sold to *Collier's* or the *Post,* it is nevertheless interesting in the light of what Salinger was living through at the time and speaks powerfully of Salinger's feelings about the army, war, and love.

The tale is of the unsightly but sensitive Sergeant Burke, who takes a new recruit named Philly Burns under his wing and gives him desperately needed confidence. The story makes it clear that Salinger was developing a growing sense of solidarity with his fellow soldiers. But when the sergeant dies at the end, saving lives during the attack at Pearl Harbor, Salinger condemns him to a bloody, lonely, and inglorious death—in sharp contrast to most stories of the day. "Death of a Dogface" also contains a section that, with unintentional irony, appears to relate directly to Salinger's own life. Sergeant Burke takes Philly to see Charlie Chaplin's movie *The Great Dictator,* knowing that the girl he secretly loves will be in the theater. Readers of the day probably thought little of the peripheral references to Chaplin. Yet, in the light of Salinger's personal life, their blasé, near-sympathetic nature is striking.

> "What's the matter, Mr. Burke? Don't you like Charlie Chaplin none?" . . .
> Burke says, "He's all right. Only I don't like no funny-looking little guys always getting chased by big guys. Never getting no girl, like. For keeps, like."[29]

However, far from "never getting no girl," on June 16, 1943, Charlie Chaplin married Oona O'Neill. They remained together until Chaplin died in 1977 and had eight children.*

---

*Few believed the marriage would last. Salinger himself wrote a letter mocking the couple on their wedding night and sent out copies to friends. Eugene O'Neill was so appalled by the union that he never spoke to his daughter again. His fury was such that his will stipulated that she receive nothing of his inheritance. In 1954, after Chaplin fled America, Oona renounced her U.S. citizenship in favor of her husband's. After Chaplin's death in 1977, friends say, Oona became a lost soul. She died in 1991.

. . .

While in the service, Salinger developed the ability to counter misfortune by redirecting his energies. When rejected by love, he sought another romance or threw himself into writing. When frustrated by writing, he immersed himself in army duties. Denied military promotion, he became even more determined. The drive of his ambition left him no time to adequately deal with painful events. The same strength that allowed him to transfer his energies prevented him from properly managing his own insecurities, hurt, or feelings of loss. For this reason, Salinger's words, whether spoken or written, often denied, or at least evaded, many of the feelings engendered by events. During the uneasy year of 1943, Salinger's letters were rife with such evasion. His correspondence displayed a tendency to acknowledge major issues almost by subterfuge, subtly injecting a topic into the page and quickly exiting the subject. As a result, many of his 1943 letters to Whit Burnett and Herb Kauffman, while not willfully deceptive, are misleading and give an incomplete rendition of the year's events and his true state of mind. This same tendency carried over from his personal correspondence into his professional work. He speaks of it in his 1959 story "Seymour—an Introduction" when he warns, "the thing to listen for, every time, with a public confessor, is what he's not confessing to."[30]

The year 1943 contained three major examples of the elusive nature of Salinger's "confession." First, there was his refusal to recognize the events regarding Oona. The few times he did address the issue, he denied romantic feelings that he had professed with passion only months before.[31] The second was his awkward apology for "The Varioni Brothers," a story he was secretly fond of that contained an inner message far more personal than he ever acknowledged. The third was perhaps the best example of the hit-and-run nature of Salinger's writings: the Georgia Peach.

That spring, ignoring his failed romance with Oona O'Neill, Salinger wrote repeatedly of his continued desire to marry, citing a renewed courtship with an old girlfriend from New York who attended Finch Junior College. Nothing more is known of the Finch girl, and Salinger's reluctance to use the telephone appears to have ended the relationship. However, that June, just as Oona was being married to Chaplin, Salinger told Whit Burnett that his continued bachelorhood was the result of distraction rather than Oona's desertion, insisting that his work and persistent roving eye prevented him from settling down. As an example, he painted a scenario of walking into the post exchange on base at Bainbridge and immediately falling for the girl working there.[32] He presented the scene hypothetically to disguise the truth. Reading Salinger's rendition, it was unlikely that the editor could have realized that the event had in fact occurred. Here, as in many of his stories, it was the quietest of Salinger's passages, the one easily overlooked, that contained the true message.

Laurene Powell was seventeen when she first met Private Salinger in the autumn of 1942. She worked at the post exchange of the Bainbridge Army Air Forces Base and was a striking, intelligent young woman. Her family still recalls her being an authentic "Georgia Peach," an old-fashioned southern belle. Born and bred in Bainbridge, Laurene undoubtedly found the sudden wartime influx of soldiers appealing. For a young woman who had spent her life in a sleepy southern town, sudden exposure to all these men must have been an eye-opening experience. Laurene was attracted by Salinger's good looks and New York sophistication, and he by her beauty and "unbounded depths."[33] Despite Salinger's frequent distractions and the attentions of Laurene's numerous admirers, the relationship lasted for at least six months.

For Salinger, the timing could not have been better. Life with Laurene certainly softened the blow during the months of Oona O'Neill's rejection. It might well explain his declared loss of affection for O'Neill in a January letter to Elizabeth Murray. And it gave him a path along which to channel his romantic energies. Laurene recalls that Salinger proposed marriage to her. Whether such a proposal was ever actually made or not remains an open question, but the timing of her recollection does coincide with Salinger's letters expressing his intention to marry. He was certainly serious enough about the relationship to bring his mother and sister down from New York to meet her.*

Whatever the true depth of feeling, the association was good for

---

*Details such as this lend the story added veracity. Southern etiquette at the time required a girl to be introduced to her suitor's father. Sol's absence in this account, together with Miriam's and (especially) Doris's presence, are elements typical of the Salinger family that Laurene would not have understood.

both parties. Laurene's mother, Cleata, however, instantly wary of this slick boy from New York, was less thrilled by the romance. One evening in early spring 1943, Laurene and Jerry stood in the living room of the Powells' Bainbridge home. Peeking through the dining room doors was Cleata, lying in wait, watching the couple's reflection in a mirror. According to Laurene, when Salinger bent over to kiss her, "the door flew open, Mama came rushing out and demanded he leave the house, and not see me again." Jerry, seldom one for confrontation, quickly fled, and Laurene ran sobbing to her room. The romance ended there. By May, the Georgia Peach was engaged to a more acceptable New Yorker, a lieutenant in the Air Corps whom Salinger knew and disliked.

Salinger himself either remained perplexed by the relationship's sudden termination or was reluctant to recount its details. His feelings of bewilderment or reticence were expressed in his unpublished 1944 short story "Two Lonely Men," which takes place at Bainbridge. In another example of Salinger slipping a personal episode into a story and fleeing before he is forced to explain it, the narrator of "Two Lonely Men" describes the main character's life at the army base with a clear reference to Laurene Powell:

> sometimes—in the beginning, anyway—he dated a good-looking brunette who worked at the Post Exchange; but something happened there—I'm not sure what. . . .[34]

After the breakup, *The Saturday Evening Post* published three Salinger stories between February and July 1944. These were written (or at least started) while he was stationed at Bainbridge. A fourth story was published in March 1945.

After Laurene had begged her mother for months for permission to read the *Post* pieces, Cleata finally agreed and Laurene obtained one of them. The memory of it remains strong because she saw herself in the story's character. The story that she read is most likely "Both Parties Concerned," which Salinger originally entitled "Wake Me When It Thunders." If so, it not only gives us an image of Laurene as a sensitive young woman but might also explain a drastic redirection in Salinger's writing. The character of Ruthie is the first completely sympathetic woman found in Salinger's literature. If readers have anyone to thank for Salinger's sudden sensitivity toward his stories' female characters, it could well be Laurene Powell.

"Both Parties Concerned" is the story of a young couple grappling to cope with responsibilities brought on by marriage and parenthood. Modern readers are likely to be distracted by a series of clichés, but to 1940s readers, it was a timely and intimate mirror of contemporary life. Billy and Ruthie Vullmer are new parents who admit to marrying too young and against the wishes of Ruthie's mother. Despite the new circumstances, Billy is determined to retain an adolescent lifestyle, taking Ruthie out every night to a rural nightclub called Jake's. In contrast, and apparently unnoticed by Billy, marriage and motherhood have matured Ruthie past her husband. She would rather spend a quiet night at home with Billy and the baby than dancing and drinking at a roadhouse. The clash of priorities results in an argument, and Billy returns from work one evening to find that Ruthie has packed her bags, taken the baby, and gone back to her mother. In a scene reminiscent of Holden Caulfield in the Wicker Bar, Billy reacts by sulking with a bottle of bourbon and pretending that he is Sam, the piano player from *Casablanca*. Much to her mother's annoyance, Ruthie and the baby return to Billy. The experience has shown him how selfish he has been and taught him to appreciate his wife and her tenderness. As a signal to the reader that Billy has finally grown up and accepted his responsibility as a husband, he tells Ruthie to wake him up if it thunders during the night and she becomes frightened. When the thunder begins that night, Billy awakes to find Ruthie gone from the bed, an excellent example of Salinger disguising a major point with subtlety. Searching for his wife, Billy is surprised to discover her in the kitchen. He had expected to find her in the closet—her usual hiding spot—cringing in fear of the storm. If we did not think Billy a heedless husband before, we certainly do now. What kind of husband would sleep through a storm while his wife cowered in a closet? How many times had fear forced the sensitive Ruthie in search of a protection she did not find at her husband's side? The episode is an important one, amplifying Billy's lack of responsibility and Ruthie's sensitive nature.[35]

When published in February 1944, the story was popular. It contained characters who were immediately recognizable. Everyone who read it could directly identify with Billy and Ruthie or knew people just like them. America had been at war for almost two years. Millions of men had been called away from home and family. Their wives and girl-friends lived in terror that they would never return. Many men struggled to recall their wives' faces. Some had never laid eyes upon their own children. And they read "Both Parties Concerned" not only with recognition but also with envy. They not only related to the story's characters but longed to be in their places, knowing exactly what they would do if they were.

Billy and Ruthie were created as simple characters, but their simplicity adds to their believability. Their reactions to events are common-place, leading to a certain intimacy between characters and readers. Perhaps the most successful portion of the story is when Billy finds Ruthie's letter explaining why she has left. In his depression, Billy reads the letter over and over again, until he has memorized it not only forward but also backward. It is a foolish act, but one all the more poignant for being so easily related to by the reader. Billy reciting Ruthie's letter backward reaches deep into his psyche and somehow grants legitimacy to similar moments in our own lives. Salinger's ability to transmit self-image to the reader in this way is what gives his writing life.

. . .

In late May 1943 Salinger was transferred from Bainbridge to the Army Air Forces Classification Center at Nashville, Tennessee, the first in a series of reassignments and relocations over the next eight months. At the Classification Center, he underwent a series of tests to determine whether he should be a pilot, bombardier, or navigator. Salinger, though, was despondent over these choices and reapplied to the Officer Candidate School. This time he was accepted, but, as weeks passed without further word, his relief soon turned to frustration. He traveled to Washington, D.C., in an attempt to persuade officials there to intercede for him. He wrote again to Colonel Baker at Valley Forge, begging him to pressure the OCS for a commission. When his Nashville tests came back, Salinger was promoted to acting first sergeant, but that only annoyed him further. He had done everything possible to secure a commission and had now come to the end of his options. "I want to be an officer so bad," he lamented, "and they just won't let me."[36]

At Nashville, Salinger became depressed. His frustration over his assignment and rank swiftly led to a general bitterness with army life. He hated being a mere noncommissioned officer and found that his mundane responsibilities were sapping his energy.[37] Most of all, he was lonely.

At Bainbridge, which he missed, he'd had a handful of close friends. In Nashville, he had no one. He claimed to like the soldiers at Nashville but felt removed from them. Increasingly weary and cynical, he began to feel removed even from himself. He wanted to go home.[38]

In July, Salinger was again transferred, this time to Patterson Field in Fairfield, Ohio, where he was designated staff sergeant and put in charge of a ditch-digging operation. Needless to say, the appointment did little to lighten his gloom. When not dragging himself through paperwork, he spent his days barking orders at recruits and trying to instill if not fear, at least compliance. This forced him to assume a false menace and to conceal his literary bent from his soldiers: they would have been less likely to obey such a person.

After drilling recruits during the day, Salinger spent his nights quietly writing. At Nashville, he attempted a bizarre fiction entitled "Paris" about a Frenchman who kidnaps Adolf Hitler by sealing him into a trunk, a plotline no publisher would touch.[39] But excited over the appearance of "The Varioni Brothers" in *The Saturday Evening Post* on July 17, he immediately sent them two more stories, both rejected and now lost. One was entitled "Rex Passard on the Planet Mars," which Salinger sent to *Story* after its rejection by the *Post,* to similar effect. The other, "Bitsy," was among Salinger's favorites. He described it as being about a girl who reached for people's hands under tables, but Salinger's story descriptions were often incomplete and sometimes misleading. After the *Post* rejected "Bitsy," it too was sent off to *Story,* which declined it because of its depiction of an alcoholic.

As the year developed, the scope of Salinger's literary interests began to broaden. Seeking solitude when on leave, he often traveled to nearby Dayton, cloistering himself in the Hotel Gibbons, where, in a shift toward literature more complex than that of his fellow authors Ring Lardner and Sherwood Anderson, he turned to the works of Fyodor Dostoyevsky and Leo Tolstoy.

Foremost in Salinger's mind, though, was his own novel. After constructing a number of stories about Holden Caulfield, he wavered between either tying them together in one complete work or presenting them as a collection of separate short stories. By the summer of 1943, Salinger seems to have made a decision. "I know the boy I'm writing about so well," he declared to Burnett. "He deserves to be a novel." Burnett was more than pleased by the decision.

Salinger's renewed commitment to serious writing after the earlier stories of 1943 is best demonstrated by "Elaine," which he probably began in the early summer. Salinger attempted to write the story commercially enough for publication in the *Post* but soon found himself agonizing over each line and constantly redrawing its details. Once he had completed "Elaine," he rightly recognized it as his finest work to date and became possessive of it. The story represents a further stage in Salinger's exploration of innocence and was undoubtedly influenced by his new nighttime friends, the great Russian authors.

"Elaine" is the story of a beautiful girl slightly slow on the uptake who is set adrift in a world anxious to consume her. Good-natured, sweet, and trusting, Elaine Cooney is so intellectually challenged that she requires more than nine years to complete eighth grade. After her graduation, she is sent out into the adult world, where her only anchors are her mother and grandmother, guardians too distracted by their own escape into the fantasy of movies to notice Elaine's shortcomings or the impending dangers around her. Instead, they are obsessed by a continual pilgrimage from one movie theater to another. At one of these cinemas, Elaine meets an usher called Teddy who escorts the unsuspecting girl to the beach where he duly takes advantage of her. A month later, they are married. The wedding reception is marred by an argument between Elaine's new mother-in-law and Mrs. Cooney. Elaine's mother and grandmother suddenly realize their love for the new bride and, feeling unable to live without her, whisk her away from the clutches of Teddy and his guests.[40]

What elevates "Elaine" above Salinger's previous stories is the suggestion that Elaine cannot now return to a world of innocent illusion; once she has been defiled, her purity begins to fade. We also suspect that her mother's sudden rush of emotion is not strong enough for Elaine's needs and will soon be submerged by her own Hollywood fantasies, leaving Elaine once again stranded in a world that will complete the decay that Teddy has set in motion.

However, Elaine too might find solace in the fantasy world of movies; and the narrator appears to support allowing Elaine her own

An Air Corps photo taken in 1943 while Salinger, between boot camp and combat, was assigned to the Public Relations Department of the Air Service Command. A year later he would be fighting in Europe.

reality in view of her limitations, just as we grant children their individual reality in light of their innocence.

. . .

The same literary pursuits that Sergeant Salinger attempted to conceal from his ditch-digging troops rose to save him from the mundane duties he had begun to loathe. After stumbling upon "The Varioni Brothers" in *The Saturday Evening Post* and "The Hang of It" in *The Kit Book for Soldiers, Sailors and Marines,* his superiors at Fairfield assigned him to write for the Public Relations Department of the Air Service Command, to serve in what Salinger described to Burnett in July 1943 as "a huge, stupid office with lots of typewriters." Though it was not the commission that he longed for, he was at least agreeable to the position. If writing publicity pieces for the Air Corps did not appeal to him, working behind a typewriter certainly did.

When not writing press releases at ASC headquarters in Dayton, Salinger found himself traveling to places such as Washington, D.C., and New York. In September, he was scheduled to fly with a photographer from *Life* magazine to a nearly barren region of Canada, where he was to write an ASC publicity piece for *Collier's*.[41] But Salinger's career in public relations came to an abrupt end and the Canada trip was canceled.[42]

As early as July, the government had begun an investigation to determine Salinger's political reliability. Agents visited McBurney and Valley Forge to gather information. Salinger himself had invited the investigation by applying for a position with the Counter Intelligence Corps. The War Department sent out an inquiry to Whit Burnett and others:

> Subject: Jerome David Salinger
> Will you be kind enough to inform this office of your opinion of this person's discretion, character, integrity and loyalty to this country and its institutions? Have you any information that he is a member of any organization which advocated the overthrow of our constitutional form of government, is there any reason to question his loyalty to the United States?
>
> James H. Gardner,
Captain, Air Corps[43]

When Salinger was informed of the contents of Captain Gardner's letter, he must have been amused.* Discretion and loyalty were the very qualities that the army had begun to erase from him. In the eighteen months since his conscription, it had been unable to recognize his talents. Instead, he had been bounced from one position and place to

---

*Salinger would remember the inquisitive Gardner. Within a year, his name was applied to the unfortunate lead character of "The Magic Foxhole."

the next. Frustration over his slow advancement had caused him to forsake his military aspirations and direct his ambition back to writing. Now, after delivering what Salinger viewed as disappointments and insults, the army was finally beginning to pay attention.

It was not Salinger's talents as an author that it was focusing on. Nor was it his military education or previous service. Rather, the army was attracted to his knowledge of languages, particularly German and French. It was also drawn to the fact that he had spent a year in territories now occupied by the Germans and had witnessed the advent of Anschluss (political union) with Austria. After Salinger's year and a half of military service, the army had finally found a place for him, not as a commissioned officer or in public relations but as an agent for the Counter Intelligence Corps.

CIC agents were in essence spies for the army, but not spies in the traditional sense. In years past they had been infiltrated into army units to monitor the patriotic reliability of domestic troops. The outbreak of the Second World War had changed their purpose completely. By the end of 1943, the long-anticipated Allied invasion of occupied Europe was drawing near. Each regiment involved was to be assigned a contingent of two CIC agents responsible for communicating with the native population and weeding out any Nazi offenders who might be hiding among them. As an agent, Salinger would be embedded into an army unit for the duration of the war and, besides fighting side by side with these soldiers, was expected to use his talents to increase the safety of their advance by arresting and investigating elements of the population that might pose a threat.

In preparation for his new assignment, Salinger was relocated to Fort Holabird, Maryland, an army base on the outskirts of Baltimore.* There he was reclassified as a corporal and began counterintelligence training. Reporting his transfer to Burnett on October 3, he confided that he was finally bound overseas for the invasion of Europe. Still, it was Burnett he sought to comfort: "I haven't forgotten the book," he reassured him.[44]

---

*Fort Holabird was also the army depot for jeeps ready to go overseas and contained thousands of jeeps at any given time. It was here that Salinger fell in love with the jeep, his vehicle of choice until very old age.

After nearly two years of preparation, the approaching reality of war caused Salinger to react in the way that had become usual for him: by writing. "Last Day of the Last Furlough" represents a defining moment both in Salinger's career and in his life. Initially, he was unsure of the quality of "Furlough" and was uncharacteristically neutral about it.[45] At the time he had no way of knowing the impact it would have upon his future writings. Indeed, when Salinger wrote "Furlough," he was not certain there would be a future at all. Ian Hamilton interpreted "Last Day of the Last Furlough" as Salinger's letter home to his family in the event of his being killed in action. The result is a moving story laden with significance.

It is the third Caulfield story and expands upon themes and emotional conflicts that first appeared in "The Last and Best of the Peter Pans." In many ways, it is a continuation of that story and the second installment of a series that follows Vincent Caulfield and his friend Technical Sergeant John "Babe" Gladwaller throughout the war. Although Vincent Caulfield plays a major role in the story, Babe is the character in whom Salinger appears to invest part of his own self. The story's first line identifies Babe by his army serial number of 32325200, Salinger's own.

Trying to strike as many notes as possible, Salinger divided "Furlough" into five scenes, each delivering its own message. The first scene depicts Babe caught between youth and adulthood, a twenty-four-year-old soldier temporarily surrounded by the props of his childhood. The story opens with Babe at home from the army on furlough, in his room surrounded by books. Like the author himself, Babe has been reading Dostoyevsky and Tolstoy, Fitzgerald and Lardner. Babe's mother, meanwhile, who has just presented her son with chocolate cake and milk, sits quietly in a corner, studying his face with love. In the second scene, Babe meets his little sister Mattie in front of her school with his sled, another article of his youth. This is a short scene, made up of seemingly insignificant events. Yet Salinger had developed the ability to imbue the ordinary with deeper meaning and the scene actually speaks of responsibility, compromise, and the strength derived from human connection. Babe wants to take his sister down Spring Street on the sled because the incline is best there, but Mattie is afraid. She sees Spring Street as a dangerous place where only older, foul-mouthed boys dare sled. Babe tries to calm her. "It's all right when you're with me," he comforts her. As they mount the sled at the top of Spring Street, Mattie grips Babe tightly from behind. Babe feels her shaking and feels bad about it. He tells her that they can choose another, safer street to slide down instead. But Mattie puts her trust in her older brother and wants to go down Spring Street for his sake. She trusts him because he has taken responsibility. Her trust, in turn, gives Babe the strength to offer compromise.

Salinger's message in this scene is in stark contrast to the childhood memories expressed in T. S. Eliot's 1922 poem *The Waste Land*. Eliot set his sled scene at a time similar to Salinger's, on the cusp of world war, representing not only a final ritual of childhood innocence but also an impending descent into the abyss. Eliot's sled ride is a cry for a lost and irretrievable world. In contrast, Salinger's version is empowering. Mattie's confidence in her brother creates a synergy, structuring a connection that overcomes fear. It is a hopeful, if unsure, scene. As it was written at an uncertain time, Salinger had no assurance that the ride would not be as final an act as Eliot's, but he imbued the scene with a strength that Eliot did not, suggesting that, with Spring Street now conquered, there would be more sled rides after the war.

The third scene of "Furlough" depicts the arrival of Babe's friend Vincent Caulfield and speaks of friendship and potential loss. This is the scene perhaps most closely identified with Salinger himself as he calls upon both characters to express his own feelings: Babe his emotions regarding the army and leaving home, Vincent his professional persona and his foreboding over the war's possible impact upon his writing. Although Babe is clearly the chosen vessel of Salinger's message, Caulfield still enjoys many of the author's personal characteristics. He is described as charming, somber, and possessing a sharp wit, not unlike Salinger himself. We also learn through this scene that Vincent is an author, albeit a writer of soap operas. At twenty-nine, Vincent Caulfield is clearly an older-brother figure, and much of this scene is a dialogue about friendship and the camaraderie among soldiers.

The scene's most famous section refers to Vincent's nineteen-year-old brother, Holden. Vincent tells Babe that Holden has been reported missing in action. He refers to it a number of times, becoming increasingly preoccupied with his brother's disappearance. Vincent's references to Holden are brief and are not repeated outside this scene, but Salinger will later delve deeper into Vincent's thoughts on this loss in "This Sandwich Has No Mayonnaise."

The fourth scene is Salinger's statement on war. The main characters are seated around the dinner table, where a discussion occurs between Babe and his veteran father. Mr. Gladwaller begins to reminisce about his experiences in the First World War, but Babe interrupts him, criticizing the glorification of war and the nostalgia that propels it, and drawing attention to the effect that glamorizing war has had upon history. It is a lofty speech, and Babe pronounces it self-consciously. Its sentiment contrasts with Salinger's own acceptance of all things military while an eager private only a year before. At the end of his speech, Babe vows never to speak of the war after it has ended:

> "I believe . . . that it's the moral duty of all the men who have fought and will fight in this war to keep our mouths shut, once it's over, never again to mention it in any way. It's time we let the dead die in vain. It's never worked the other way, God knows."[46]

It is a famous quote, representing a kind of oath, one that Salinger himself never broke. The final scene of "Last Day of the Last Furlough" has become a familiar one. It depicts a moment of contemplation, an event bordering on revelation, which takes place at the bedside of a child. It is late at night, and Babe cannot sleep. He sits alone in his room thinking of his sister, Mattie. To himself, he recites an appeal for the little sister he may never see again. The passage is an exquisite monologue cautioning little Mattie of the fleeting nature of childhood. Embedded within it is a prayer that she will retain the virtues of her youth as she grows. A strong sense of Babe's nostalgia for his own childhood is detected as he whispers his prayer for Mattie. "Try to live up to the best that's in you," he implores, speaking as much to himself as to his sister. This is the last night before Babe goes overseas. He needs to look at his sister just one more time. He craves one last connection with her beauty and the remnants of his own innocence, virtues he fears he must leave behind. He sneaks into Mattie's room and kisses her. Then he speaks an oath to himself that reminds us of

Holden at the edge of the cliff, ready to prevent the descent of way-ward innocence. It is, despite its gentleness, a rationalization of war when Babe vows to protect his sister with his gun. But this oath is also a definition of "home" as a spiritual place found through his sister. As Babe gently caresses Mattie and her innocence, he also reestablishes a connection with his own childhood and attains a level of purity he as-sumed had long since deserted him. In future stories, this connection will be a profound one. In "Furlough," it is tempered by a sense of re-sponsibility and uncertainty that he will ever see home again.

"Last Day of the Last Furlough" is, among other things, a resigned declaration of Salinger's willingness to do his duty in combat. Through "Furlough" he acknowledged his responsibility to protect those he cherished. Yet knowledge of the author is not necessary to appreciate the story, for "Furlough" faithfully depicts sentiments and anxieties felt by soldiers about to go to war. When published in July 1944 in *The Saturday Evening Post,* "Last Day of the Last Furlough" was remark-ably successful.

If present-day readers struggle to appreciate the circumstances that made "Furlough" attractive to readers in 1944, they can nevertheless understand the insights it provides into Salinger's later works. Like most of the Caulfield stories, "Furlough" points to *The Catcher in the Rye* in both characters and themes. It may also refer directly to the novel when Vincent mentions that Holden is missing in action. En-veloping "Furlough" is Salinger's fear that he might soon die in battle. Likely to be called overseas at any moment, he wrote this story as if it were his last. And had he died in Europe, Holden Caulfield would have died with him.

The greatest similarity between "Furlough" and *Catcher* appears at the end of both works and centers on the recognition of beauty and the preservation of innocence. The image of Babe in the act of emo-tional release at the bedside of his little sister inevitably reminds us of Holden beside Phoebe's bed, confiding his dream of being the catcher in the rye. And while it will be years before we hear Holden's confes-sion, his voice is clearly heard in Babe's prayer for Mattie's innocence:

> "You're going to be smart when you grow up. But if you can't
> be smart and a swell girl, too, then I don't want to see you grow
> up. Be a swell girl, Mat."

When Babe exhorts Mattie to be a "swell" girl, he of course means "genuine." It's the opposite of Holden Caulfield's "phony," and Salinger has already elevated the concept to a higher state of being, to a truth his characters must strive for and jealously maintain. Because he has already defined the concept of "home" through connection with Mattie's childlike innocence, it gives double meaning to his desire to return home. "It would," Babe says at the end of the story, "be swell to come back."[47]

The implications of "Furlough" are straightforward but powerful. Babe's capacity, in the face of death, to recognize the beauty of his sister's innocence suggests that in a callous, superficial society that glorifies war, it is beauty that offers hope and gives life meaning.

Completed at Fairfield by October, under the lingering misery of Salinger's Nashville-induced depression and in reaction to the uncertainty of impending combat, the story is notably void of negativity. Salinger's own ability to confirm the beauty of life from beneath the apprehension and despondency he was suffering is testimony not only to his personal perseverance, but also to the evolution of his literary ideas. These ideas were not only being offered to readers; in this story, Salinger was plainly using writing as therapy and as a means to soothe his fears. Through "Last Day of the Last Furlough," Salinger's work developed from a genre that presented mainly observation to one that provided hope.

4. Displacement

On January 1, 1944, at Fort Holabird, Salinger celebrated his twenty-fifth birthday. Initially, he had expected to be stationed there for about six weeks, but three months had passed while he awaited deployment overseas. Preparations for the invasion of occupied Europe were under way, and Holabird was thick with rumors that it would be launched the following spring.[1]

While awaiting departure, Salinger studied for the Counter Intelligence Corps and continued to write. Uncertain as to his fate in Europe, he focused on his career, producing a large number of submissions and receiving a large quantity of rejections. Between October 1943 and the beginning of February 1944, *Story* magazine alone declined five such attempts, and as *Story* had become Salinger's vehicle of last resort, the total number of rejections can easily be doubled.

Story's dismissals were doubtless valid, but some responses were perhaps callous under the circumstances. Rebuffs were characteristically brief. Many bordered on sarcasm. On December 9, 1943, shortly after election day, Whit Burnett informed Harold Ober, for instance, that Salinger's latest submission "did not quite get [his] vote." When turning down "What Got into Curtis in the Woodshed?" a short time later, Burnett was openly scornful. "A goofy kid is taken on a fishing trip," he wrote. "I see nothing here."[2]

Nearly all these rejections contained demands for Salinger's novel: "I don't think the times are quite right to work it into the magazine. I am very much interested in a book-length project" or "Thank you for letting us see this new one by Salinger, but . . . I am still hoping to see something of a more extended form from him."[3] Still another claimed, "I like this one of Salinger's very much, but I have accepted one very much the same . . . and am looking forward to a novel from him some day."[4]

In fairness, Burnett was a businessman first and a mentor second. In the five years of their friendship, Salinger had contributed just two stories to the magazine, and Burnett owed him nothing. It is difficult to judge whether Burnett was right to refuse publication since all five stories rejected by him during the winter of 1943–1944, including the intriguingly entitled submission about Curtis, are now lost.

Amid these disappointments, Salinger managed to score his greatest professional triumph to date. During the second week of January, Dorothy Olding informed him that she had sold three short stories to *The Saturday Evening Post*. Stuart Rose, the magazine's editor, had purchased "Death of a Dogface," "Wake Me When It Thunders," and "Last Day of the Last Furlough" for a substantial sum. Elated and certainly relieved, Salinger quickly informed Burnett. After sheepishly reminding the editor that he would soon be overseas, Salinger announced his *Post* sales with an enthusiasm bordering on rapture. "My God," he exclaimed, "the millions of people who'll read them. Can you imagine?"[5]

Whether Salinger felt vindicated by the sales and was gloating or was just overexcited is a matter of interpretation. Either way, Burnett could not have helped feeling a sting over the news of Salinger's new patron. After *Story* had sent out a flood of rejection notices, the *Post* had bought not one but three Salinger pieces, for considerably more than the $25 per piece paid by *Story*. To make matters worse, one of the stories that now belonged to the *Post* mentioned Holden Caulfield, the subject of the novel that Burnett longed to get his hands on.

Salinger's professional position actually lay somewhere between his *Story* and *Post* experiences. Soon after his confident note to Burnett, Salinger sent a similar message to Wolcott Gibbs, who was filling in for Gus Lobrano as *The New Yorker*'s fiction editor. After boasting about his *Post* triumphs and advising the magazine to broaden its concept of fiction, Salinger notified Gibbs that his agent was sending "Elaine" for approval. This story would come with a stipulation: it was not to be touched in any way. If *The New Yorker* wanted to publish "Elaine," it would have to leave it intact. Not a single word was to be altered, edited, or removed.[6]

To Gibbs, the message appeared brazen, while Salinger thought he was being magnanimous. He was still angry about *The New Yorker*'s 1941 reversal on "Slight Rebellion off Madison." Deepening the insult, the magazine had contacted him during the summer of 1943 and again offered to release the story in its next Christmas edition. But it now claimed it was too long and portions would have to be cut. Salinger had been incensed but resigned to the alteration.[7] Yet, when the December *New Yorker* hit the stands, "Slight Rebellion" was still missing from its pages. Emboldened by his *Post* success and confident about the quality of his story "Elaine," Salinger felt free to present *The New Yorker* with conditions before allowing it to feature his work. Derisive of such demands, *The New Yorker* sought to chastise Salinger for his impudence. When "Elaine" arrived at Gibbs's office a week later, it was swiftly rejected. The editor, William Maxwell, broke the news to Dorothy Olding in no uncertain terms: "this J.D. Salinger," Maxwell wrote, "just doesn't seem quite right for us."[8]

By the time "Elaine" was on its way to *The New Yorker*, Salinger was en route to Europe. On Tuesday, January 18, he boarded the USS *George Washington*, a troop transport heading for England, where he would complete his counterintelligence training in preparation for the invasion. When the day of embarkation finally arrived, Salinger felt calmer than he had expected. The transport ship was also conveniently docked in New York, allowing him the opportunity to re-create the quiet farewell of Babe Gladwaller with his own family. And just as Babe had done in "Last Day of the Last Furlough," Salinger sought to avoid the emotions of a public send-off and forbade his family, especially his mother, to see him off at the dock. As he marched in formation to the ship, he suddenly caught sight of his mother. She was scurrying along-side him, ducking behind lampposts and trying her best to remain un-seen.[9] Once on board, Salinger settled into his bunk while the soldiers around him joked and laughed to camouflage their nerves.

. . .

Salinger cannot have been surprised that his mother had defied his in-structions and come to see him off. His actual departure gave rise to emotions that he could not have anticipated when writing "Furlough," and he sought to acknowledge his emotions in another story about a soldier's final farewell. He began this next work perhaps even aboard ship, a short story called "Once a Week Won't Kill You," about a sol-dier leaving for the service and his concern for an aunt. In this story too, there would be no noisy send-off, no showy parade or marching band to usher away young men about to die. It would, though, be laced with nostalgia for a world Salinger was already beginning to miss and feared he might never see again.

On January 29, 1944, the *George Washington* docked at Liverpool, where he joined tens of thousands of American troops in preparation for the incursion into occupied Europe. Traveling directly on to Lon-don, he was formally embedded into the 12th Infantry Regiment of the 4th Infantry Division as counterintelligence officer and staff ser-geant, making the unit Salinger's home until the end of the war.

From February 1944, all of Salinger's correspondence passed through military censors, thus muddying the specifics of his actions while in En-gland. We know from his letters that he spent time in Tiverton, the Devon town where the 4th Infantry had its headquarters, and in Der-byshire and London, attending CIC training courses. As the invasion drew nearer, he participated in amphibious landing exercises on the south coast at Slapton Sands, between Plymouth and Dartmouth, and on the north coast at Woolacombe Bay, sites chosen by the Allied High Command because they resembled the French coastline.

Tiverton was a town very similar to the one described in his 1950 story "For Esmé—with Love and Squalor." It was small and charming and had a population of about 10,000 before its own invasion by American servicemen. Set among the hills of Devon, Tiverton is a quaint place with narrow cobblestone streets that meander along the contours of the land. They were streets that Salinger loved to stroll in his spare time, often stepping into a pub for a drink or slipping into a church during choir practice.

The 4th Infantry had taken over a number of large buildings in and around Tiverton. Division headquarters was located at Collipriest House, a large estate just outside town, and it was here that Salinger collected his mail, reported for assignments, and, as in "For Esmé," attended "rather specialized pre-Invasion training" courses.[10] These courses instructed Salinger in combat espionage, sabotage, and subversion, and how to deliver security lectures to the troops, search captured towns, and interrogate both civilians and enemy troops in occupied territory.

The image of J. D. Salinger wandering the streets of Tiverton in pensive solitude illustrates the contemplative mood that absorbed him while he was stationed in England. During the months he trained for the invasion, Salinger began to reevaluate his attitude toward both his writing and his life.[11]

But the army had changed him. Since his induction, he had become rougher, less refined than in his youth. His personal letters displayed a coarseness that would have made his mother blush. And he began to drink. By the time he was stationed in England, his letters began to allude to problems with alcohol. He admitted that his sarcasm, once loosened by drink, became especially acerbic and created conflicts with his fellow soldiers. In England he tried to limit his drinking; and when he did drink, he tried his best not to inflame others.[12]

He claimed to have made a number of conscious resolutions to be calmer and kinder in future, not only to others but also to his characters. When he felt vulnerable, his instinct had always been to turn to sarcasm and aloofness. In his present situation, crowded together with nervous soldiers uncertain of the future, that instinct worked against him and he learned the benefits of displays of tolerance and camaraderie. Still, there is no reason to believe that Salinger's self-assessment was not sincere. On a daily basis, Salinger came into contact with British soldiers and civilians whose lives had been ravaged by war. Only the coldest of men would not have undergone an examination of his life and attitudes.

Psychological changes in reaction to war are the basis of a story that Salinger wrote in England and titled "The Children's Echelon."[13] No matter how much he worked the story, he remained unsure of its quality. Many of his attempts while in England were failures, both aesthetically and in publishing terms, and this story was possibly his least successful. It was inspired by Ring Lardner's "I Can't Breathe," which had been written as a series of diary entries. Salinger initially disliked the format. So, when he began his own version, he wrote it in the third person. Dissatisfied, he returned to the story and rewrote it, this time in a style dangerously similar to Lardner's. When completed, the work ran to twenty-six pages and 6,000 words, by far the longest story he had written.

The diary installments follow the life of Bernice Herndon, an immature eighteen-year-old desperate to appear grown up to the outside world. With the war escalating in the background, she calculatingly changes her opinion about everything she mentions: her friends, her family, and the war itself. But the changes are superficial. Believing herself immune to the fate of her friends, whose husbands die in combat as the story progresses, Bernice secretly marries an unattractive army private named Royce Dittenhauer, largely to make herself feel mature.

The veiled stagnancy of Bernice's outlook is displayed in the story's most interesting scene. Strolling through Central Park and commenting on how "lovely" everything is, Bernice settles down at the carousel to watch the "darling" children. There, her eye is caught by a little boy riding the carousel and wearing a blue suit and beanie. This section is so evocative of the later one in *The Catcher in the Rye* that, at first glance, they appear to be replicas. Yet although the settings are the same, Bernice Herndon is the very opposite of Holden Caulfield. Unlike Holden, whose accepting anticipation of children tumbling from the carousel in his own scene signifies genuine change, Bernice almost screams out loud when the boy nearly falls off his horse.[14]

When "The Children's Echelon" appeared before Burnett for approval, it met with the most scathing critique ever suffered by a Salinger work. Burnett himself summarized the story as being about a "dumb girl in love with the same kind of guy," adding that it was "somewhat trivial, but not bad." Someone else at *Story* added that no one would believe that a girl could possibly be that dumb. The magazine's final pronouncement was scorching, declaring that "In these times it would be a waste of paper to print the story."[15]

The story survives only through its submission by 1946 to a collection of Salinger works which was itself never published. "The Children's Echelon" does not end there. In 1947, Salinger drew upon it liberally to write "A Girl in 1941 with No Waist at All," rearranging its parts as sparingly as Bernice Herndon rearranged her outlook.

. . .

While Salinger was preparing for D-Day, his *Saturday Evening Post* stories began to hit the stands. It took weeks for copies to reach him, but when they did, he was shocked by what he saw. The names of two stories had been changed. On February 20, "Wake Me When It Thunders" was issued as "Both Parties Concerned," and on April 15, "Death of a Dogface" was published as "Soft-Boiled Sergeant." Salinger felt betrayed and used, believing the *Post* had taken advantage of his being overseas to alter his work without permission. As he flipped through the pages containing his stories, he was further incensed by what he found around them. Garishly colored advertisements overwhelmed them on all sides. Stories he had intended to ignite reflection were shouted down by movie-star endorsements and ads for Calox Tooth Powder. Salinger was furious. He swore never again to deal with the slicks, regardless of how much they paid. "Let us be broke and obscure," he pouted.[16]

The *Post*'s actions reinforced Salinger's opinion that he had done the right thing in instructing *The New Yorker* not to alter a word of "Elaine" and perhaps helped soothe his disappointment over its rejection of that story. He also must have felt relief knowing that "Elaine" was now in the hands of Whit Burnett, who had received it on April 14.[17] Burnett, at least, would never alter his work without consultation. Nevertheless, this experience, after the fiasco of "Slight Rebellion," only furthered his distrust of editors and their motives.

Salinger tried not to let his irritation with the *Post* affect his new attitude of being warmer and kinder. He donated $200 to what Burnett later identified as "the encouragement of other writers" by bestowing it on a short-story contest run by *Story* magazine. Thrilled by Salinger's generosity and hoping to view it as a precedent, Burnett noted in the magazine that Salinger was the only author ever to have made such a contribution.

This same unselfish spirit found its way into Salinger's work. His stories had long dealt with average moments, the depth of their meaning found within simple acts. By 1944, Salinger was specializing in creating characters ennobled by small, seemingly insignificant deeds. Through characters such as Babe Gladwaller and Sergeant Burke, Salinger took the common traits and simple acts of loyalty, friendship, and duty that he now found all around him and elevated them in celebration of the potential for dignity in everyone. For Salinger in 1944, the acknowledgment of nobility within simple acts became a conscious philosophy, and it became a force in his work.[18]

It was never Salinger's assertion that people were noble by default. In his earliest stories, some of his characters are flawed beyond redemption. But in those works, Salinger rarely gave his protagonists the means by which to elevate themselves. Only after joining the military did he allow them occasions to which they could rise, or not. Now he began to test their moral fiber against a military backdrop, giving them the opportunity for quiet heroism or callous deceit. In the tradition of the medieval morality play, Salinger portrayed both outcomes as examples to his reader. A character who becomes heroic is an inspiration, but one who becomes corrupted is a lesson.

"Two Lonely Men" opens with a comic description of an Air Corps base very much like Bainbridge. An unnamed narrator tells the story of two misfit soldiers, Master Sergeant Charles Maydee and Captain Huggins, whose friendship grows over nightly games of gin rummy at the base. Throughout the story, the narrator relays a number of details that are seemingly insignificant but nonetheless create a sense of unease in the reader's mind. Maydee goes home to San Francisco on furlough and spends his time alone. While he is still on leave, Huggins shows up in the city but only sends him a postcard. Evidently, he is too busy visiting friends to see his rummy partner. Back at base, Huggins and Maydee play a rummy tournament with a fifth of scotch as the prize. Huggins, who possesses the scotch, loses the contest but doesn't forfeit the bottle, and the episode is never mentioned again. The turning point of the story occurs when Huggins, prompted by Maydee, sets his wife up at a nearby hotel. Maydee is never invited to meet his friend's wife. Instead, Huggins stops going to the Ground School and now sees little of his friend. The card games end, and Maydee is again alone and miserable. One night, while Maydee is reading at the Ground School, Huggins appears, distraught and incoherent. Something has happened with his wife. She is having an affair with a pilot and has asked Huggins for a divorce in order to marry her lover. Maydee some-how finds a way to repair his friend's marriage and return his confi-dence. But he must meet alone with Huggins's wife for a week and a half in order to do it. As the story ends, Maydee enters the barracks very drunk and announces to the narrator that he has applied for trans-fer overseas. When asked why, Maydee despondently replies that he cannot stand the sight of Huggins.[19] Of course, Huggins has been duped by his friend. Retrospect reveals the story littered with clues—those slight, only marginally disturbing details left unanswered or un-explained. No pilot had ever fallen in love with Huggins's wife; the culprit had been Maydee all along. Desperate to preserve their friend-ship, he sought to have Huggins split with his wife or, perhaps worse and posing as a pilot, engaged Huggins's wife in an affair.

At first glance, Salinger appears to punish these two men severely for their shortcomings, Huggins for his selfishness and Maydee for his treachery. Yet, as the story closes, the two men are no worse off than they were at its beginning. Huggins is still a fool, cuckolded by a woman who remains untrustworthy. Maydee is still a scoundrel and has learned nothing of the lessons that true friendship can offer. Both are as lonely in the end as they were at the start. And that's the result of their sins. Both men were granted the opportunity to advance their compassion through the bond they had formed. It was the small steps they refused to take that led to their eventual downfall: the fulfillment of a promise, a sincere invitation, a visit to a friend. In short, Maydee and Huggins simply refused to do the right thing. In "Two Lonely Men," Salinger points to these small omissions as breeding the treach-ery that would be their ruin. Maydee and Huggins were not "ordinary heroes"—not because it was not in their nature but because they chose not to be. When the occasion to grasp heroism arose, they succumbed to ego and let it slip away.

. . .

On the morning of April 28, a catastrophe occurred at Slapton Sands, where a full-dress rehearsal of the D-Day landing was scheduled to take place in a maneuver dubbed Operation Tiger (similar exercises were held all over the British Isles). Salinger found himself crowded aboard a naval convoy in Lyme Bay, waiting his turn to practice storming the beach. Seeking to condition the troops to the fury of artillery fire, the operation's commanders had decided to explode live ammunition from the vessels, and the soldiers themselves were equipped with live rounds.

The maneuver attracted the attention of German torpedo boats, which scrambled to attack the flotilla. Laden with fuel and jammed with thousands of troops, the vessels were particularly vulnerable and, once struck, exploded into fireballs. The result was carnage, and 749 soldiers lost their lives; their bodies either pulled from the English Channel or washed out to sea.*

The army quickly raced to cover up the incident and swore everyone who had been there to secrecy. Salinger never spoke of the experience.

Beyond being sworn to secrecy himself, Salinger was charged with ensuring the silence of other soldiers. With the disaster at Slapton Sands, the role of the CIC agents reverted to its original purpose of keeping watch over fellow American troops. On the morning of April 28, CIC agents were dispatched to each hospital receiving the casualties of Operation Tiger and ordered to prevent any discussion between wounded troops and hospital staff. As doctors and nurses scrambled to save lives in imposed silence, CIC agents loomed menacingly in the background, their rifles cocked and bayoneted.[20]

This was a terrible position for Salinger, one that defied the feelings of solidarity he had come to embrace. It was also a situation that would last until D-Day. With the invasion merely weeks away, all troops involved were gathered into camouflaged marshaling areas on the south Devon coast, which had been emptied of civilians. Cordoned off from contact with the outside world, the troops were closely guarded by members of the Counter Intelligence Corps, who were now responsible for reporting any hint of treason.[21]

. . .

From the first week of September 1940, Whit Burnett had pushed Salinger to write the novel that would ultimately become *The Catcher in the Rye*. Salinger's response was immediate and reassuring: he would

---

*No one was officially held responsible for events at Slapton Sands, but the admiral in charge took his own life and some argue that responsibility must be borne by the RAF Coastal Command, for failing to protect the flotilla, and by its commander in chief, William Douglas.

write the novel while in the army. Since Salinger's induction, Burnett had become increasingly impatient for him to complete the work or at least to make substantial progress.

Salinger had given Burnett ample reason to be protective of the project, stating in a number of letters that Story Press and the novel were in a sense betrothed. Salinger had claimed to be writing the book for Burnett, repeatedly assuring him that it would belong as much to Story Press as to the author himself. In the meantime, Story Press had entered into a partnership with the wealthier Lippincott Press for the production of books at a rate that Story Press alone could not afford. The agreement was ideal for both companies: Story Press, with its connections to innovative and well-known authors, would supply the talent, and Lippincott would supply the capital. With Lippincott's backing, Burnett now sought a writer who could produce a best seller to extend *Story*'s wealth and reputation. He believed that Salinger could produce that novel.

Burnett had reason to be nervous, though. Salinger was a short-story writer who was uncomfortable writing longer pieces. Accustomed to writing stories of about twelve pages, he had struggled with "The Children's Echelon" partly because it ran to more than twenty-five pages. He even blamed that story's failure on its length.[22]

Aware of this tendency, Burnett worried about Salinger's commitment to producing a novel. And Salinger offered no firm assurances. Attempting to overcome his difficulties with length, he had chosen to construct the novel by writing it in segments—as a series of short stories that could be strung together into a book. By March 1944, he had completed six chapters written in this manner, none of which Burnett had seen. Armed with material that could be presented either way, Salinger now vacillated between completing the novel and releasing its chapters as separate short stories. With D-Day approaching and Salinger's anxiety increasing, Burnett sought a way to prevent the release of the stories and preserve the book project.

On April 14, Burnett approached Salinger with a proposal to publish a collection of his short stories as an anthology. He suggested that the book be named after Salinger's first story, "The Young Folks," and be divided into three parts, with "the first third of the book [being] stories of young people on the eve of the war, the middle third in and around the army, and then one or two stories at the close of the war."[23]

This would conveniently crowd out any contributions narrated by Holden Caulfield. Having offered this option, Burnett warned Salinger that if the collection failed, it could ruin the author's career. But Burnett made his personal opinion plain: "If, on the other hand, it goes over," he coyly reflected, "it will bridge the gap until your novel is completed."[24]

Salinger's response was cautious. He said that the idea of a short-story anthology frightened him. He claimed to be modest about the quality of his work and said he realized the implications if the project failed. He was relatively unknown, and to risk having his first book flop could be professional suicide. But he did not reject the idea either. Instead, he listed eight stories that he felt might be included in the collection.* If Burnett had sent him mixed messages when offering to publish the anthology, Salinger was equally ambiguous. More certain were Salinger's remarks regarding the Holden Caulfield novel. He warned Burnett that he had suspended work on the book but assured him that the six Holden Caulfield stories he had written were all in his possession and that his agent had none of them. "I need them," he declared.[25]

Among the six Holden Caulfield stories (or chapters, depending on Salinger's mood) in his possession in April 1944 was the story "I'm Crazy." The history of this piece is particularly interesting. Salinger would use it in 1944 as an indicator to test Burnett's commitment to the now-proposed *Young Folks* anthology. The following year, he submitted the story to *Collier's*, which published it in its December 1945 issue. Eventually, however, the story appeared in its intended position, incorporated into *The Catcher in the Rye* as the chapters in which Holden visits Mr. Spencer and leaves Pencey Prep. Since much of "I'm Crazy" appears in *The Catcher in the Rye* with minor alterations, its plot is familiar to many readers. Yet the story was written six years before the novel was published, offering fascinating contrasts and insights into the evolution of the book. Also, because this story falls between Holden's first account in "Slight Rebellion off Madison" and his final testimony in *The Catcher in the Rye*, it should be recognized as sharing

*The eight stories Salinger listed as being his best to date were "The Young Folks," "The Long Debut of Lois Taggett," "Elaine," "Last Day of the Last Furlough," "Death of a Dogface" ("Soft-Boiled Sergeant" in the *Post*), "Wake Me When It Thunders" ("Both Parties Concerned" in the *Post*), "Once a Week Won't Kill You," and "Bitsy."

elements of both, with a climax resembling that of its predecessor, "Last Day of the Last Furlough."

In "Madison," Salinger used a remote third-person narrative to tell Holden's tale. "I'm Crazy" employs a first-person account through the voice of Holden Caulfield and is far more intimate than Salinger's first attempt. However, the story is not relayed as a stream of consciousness, and the voice of Holden in "I'm Crazy" is not the same as it will be in *Catcher*. Though far more intimate than the self-conscious exchange of "Madison," it is still not completely spontaneous. The narration of "I'm Crazy" is more deliberate and certain than it is in *Catcher*. In some instances, it is also more precise and poetic.

Stylistic differences aside, the major distinction between "I'm Crazy" and *The Catcher in the Rye* is in their endings. In *Catcher*, the climax comes at the Central Park carousel, but in "I'm Crazy," it comes at the bedside of Holden's little sister, much as it did for Babe Gladwaller. After accepting the chastisement of his parents—an event we never witness in *Catcher*—Holden slips into his sisters' room while they are asleep. There he pauses briefly at Phoebe's bedside. But it is another sister, Viola, who makes her sole appearance in this story, who draws Holden's attention and becomes the source of his enlightenment. Viola is sleeping in her crib with her Donald Duck toy. She has recently taken a strange liking to cocktail olives (which she calls "ovvels"), and Holden has brought her some. He lines them up on the railing of Viola's crib. "One of them fell on the floor," he tells us. "I picked it up, felt dust on it, and put it in my jacket pocket. Then I left the room."[26] This is a tiny act involving common and unremarkable elements, but it can also be interpreted as symbolic: Holden's withholding of the soiled olive represents his desire to protect the purity of his little sister, a sign of his appreciation of Viola's innocence. It is an appreciation that he attains at the same time that he surrenders the rights to his own. Returning to his room, Holden speaks to the reader of compromise. He seals the story with a definitive statement that the later novel lacks: "I knew everybody was right and I was wrong," he concludes with resignation.

The fourth of Salinger's Caulfield stories, "I'm Crazy" expounds upon themes first tackled in "Last Day of the Last Furlough." "I'm Crazy" goes beyond "Furlough" and Babe's appreciation of beauty. Added to Holden's experience is an almost spiritual unity with his sister that the "Furlough" scene lacks. In that scene, Babe explained at length the reasons for his connection with Mattie, as if the reader needed to be convinced. In "I'm Crazy," there is no explanation because none is needed. Readers instinctively feel the connection between Holden and Viola without the need for persuasion. Here Salinger displays a gift for connecting his characters directly to the reader, an aspect that will prove fundamental to the success of *The Catcher in the Rye*.

"I'm Crazy" is tender, authentic, and even sensitive in its ending, but it lacks the spiritual force of *Catcher* that makes the novel so compelling. Holden's acknowledgment of beauty at Viola's crib side is gentle, yet profound; but it falls short of revelation. The bond that will connect Holden to Phoebe and Allie in *The Catcher in the Rye*, and will join closely so many of Salinger's future characters, has yet to develop fully. Before it does, it will require a spiritual transformation and revelation within the author himself.

5. Hell

Tyger! Tyger! burning bright,
In the forests of the night;
What immortal hand or eye,
Could frame thy fearful symmetry?
. . .
When the stars threw down their spears,
And water'd heaven with their tears;
Did he smile his work to see?
Did he who made the Lamb make thee?

—William Blake, "The Tyger"

Tuesday, June 6, 1944, was the turning point of Salinger's life. It is difficult to overstate the impact of D-Day and the eleven months of continuous combat that followed. The war, its horrors, agonies, and lessons, would brand itself upon every aspect of Salinger's personality and reverberate through his writings. Salinger frequently mentioned his landing at Normandy, but he never spoke of the details, "as if," his daughter later recalled, "I understood the implications, the unspoken."[1] This "unspoken" element has hindered researchers for decades.

Salinger's reluctance to recount events, combined with the secretive nature of his wartime intelligence duties—which could have drawn him to unknown locations at any time—has tempted biographers to treat his war years clinically, to cite impersonal statistics and place-names before hurrying to periods more substantially documented. Even without Salinger's firsthand account, it is better to draw on the testimony of those around him who may have shared his experiences than to diminish them out of convenience.

By the end of May 1944, the Allies had amassed an invasion force incomparable in human history. They divided this force into three groups, each assigned a letter designating their projected landing point. Salinger's 4th Infantry Division was appointed as Task Force U— for Utah Beach—and was made up of three infantry regiments, the 8th, 12th, and 22nd, joined on D-Day by the 359th and 70th Tank Battalions. These units were themselves divided into twelve convoys for the cross-Channel voyage and were to storm the beach in waves.

Salinger spent days confined on board his troopship, docked most likely in the port of Brixham in Devon, awaiting departure for Normandy. Each day brought fresh rumors of imminent departure, only to prove false as favorable launching conditions slipped away. With little to do but anticipate what was to come, the wait was excruciating. Finally, on the night of June 5, the men were given a steak dinner—a sign, perhaps, of building up the soldiers' physical resources—and Salinger's ship slipped out of port and headed for the coast of France. Together with the dread of what lay across the Channel, the soldiers of the 4th carried the memory of Operation Tiger and feared attack from the moment of departure. Twelve miles from the Normandy shore, the transport's engines fell silent, and its troops, who could now hear the distant rumble of artillery shells, anxiously waited for sunrise and the call to battle.

When the order came, Salinger crammed into a landing craft along with thirty other soldiers. Thrown about by violent waves, they were dwarfed by their setting. Around them, immense warships discharged guns that set the morning sky ablaze and consumed the air with blasts of thunder. As their craft inched forward, the men could see artillery fire hitting the sand, sending up showers of debris. Slowly, the transport sputtered to a stop and a smoke screen was sent up to signal the assault. Some of the men whispered prayers. Some cried. But most were silent. Suddenly, the vessel's landing ramp crashed open into the surf and they waded into the water and headed for the beach.

As part of the 4th Counter Intelligence Corps Detachment, Salinger was to land on Utah Beach with the first wave, at 6:30 A.M., but an eyewitness report has him landing during the second wave, about ten minutes later.[2] The timing was fortunate. The Channel's currents had thrown the landing off 2,000 yards to the south, allowing Salinger to avoid the most heavily concentrated German defenses. There were also fewer land mines in this sector, and engineers quickly removed those they found. Within an hour of landing at Normandy, Salinger was moving inland along an underdefended causeway and heading west, where he would eventually connect with the 12th Infantry Regiment.

The 12th had not been so lucky. Although it had landed five hours later, it had encountered obstacles that Salinger had not. Just beyond the beach, the Germans had deliberately flooded a vast marshland, up to two miles wide, and had concentrated their firepower on the only open causeway. The 12th had been forced to abandon the causeway and wade through waist-high drainage water while under constant threat from enemy guns. In many spots, the ground dropped abruptly and soldiers suddenly found themselves submerged. It took the 12th Regiment three hours to cross the flooded marsh, and its members would for the rest of their lives remain terrified by the experience.[3] By the end of the day, the unit had pushed nearly five miles into occupied territory when they were stopped at the village of Beuzeville-au-Plain.* There they encountered the now-infamous Norman hedgerow, a feature of the land their training had neglected. Called bocage by the French, the growth was insurmountable and blinded the regiment to the Germans within the village. Rather than engage an unseen enemy, the men decided to dig in beside the hedgerows. They spent a long, sleepless night—afraid to fire, afraid to smoke, afraid to speak. For members of the 12th, "the longest day" was not yet over. Instead, it had ushered in a living hell that would be Salinger's quarters for the next eleven months. Somehow (and he must have realized this on that

*Of all the troops to storm Utah Beach on D-Day, none penetrated farther into enemy territory than the 12th Infantry Regiment.

very first night), he would have to find the strength to survive and emerge with his soul intact.

For decades to come, J. D. Salinger would count among his most treasured belongings a small casket, a container protecting some of the most cherished articles he possessed: five battle stars and the Presidential Unit Citation for valor.[4] Although an intelligence agent, once upon the field of battle, he was forced to become a leader of men, responsible for the safety and actions of squadrons and platoons. The lives of his fellow soldiers depended upon the orders he gave, and he met that responsibility with an unflinching sense of duty.

Unlike many soldiers who had been impatient for the invasion, Salinger was far from naïve about war. In stories like "Soft-Boiled Sergeant" and "Last Day of the Last Furlough," he had already expressed disgust with the false idealism applied to combat and attempted to explain that war was a bloody, inglorious affair. But no amount of insight into the ugliness of war, whether provided by logic or by personal contact with those who had experienced it, could have fully prepared him for what was to come.

At dawn on June 7, it became clear to the men of the 12th that the Germans had concentrated at a point just west of Beuzeville-au-Plain. Hedgerows or not, this pocket blocked their advance and would have to be dealt with. At 6 A.M., they engaged the German forces, who, shocked by the assault, eventually abandoned their positions. The regiment then pushed north in pursuit of the retreating Germans.

Salinger and his division were designated to fight their way north and take the port city of Cherbourg. Without control of the port, supplies and men could not be discharged to the extent needed to support the Allied invasion. If Cherbourg was not taken, the entire operation would be in danger of collapse. Yet it would take far longer for the 12th to accomplish its primary missions. After advancing five miles on D-Day, they continued to advance at rapid speed, unaware that they would soon be measuring their progress not in miles but in yards.

All three regiments of the 4th Infantry Division (the 4th, 8th, and 22nd) had pursued the enemy to a line running roughly 8,000 yards across the Cotentin Peninsula. Along this line the Germans had constructed a series of gun batteries. Here, they halted their retreat and turned to face their hunters. The 12th suddenly found itself in a terrible position between an enemy strongpoint at the village of Émondeville and the guns of the fortress of Azeville.[5] Wedged into this position with no room to maneuver, the regiment experienced its first true taste of combat.

Bombarded constantly by mortar fire from Émondeville and the heavy guns of Azeville, the 12th fought for two days and nights. Recognizing the severity of their situation, division commanders called upon all surrounding regiments to focus on the Azeville fortress and relieve the 12th's flank, allowing it to concentrate on Émondeville, where the regiment was outnumbered two to one and pinned down under heavy bombardment. There it had assaulted the German position, gaining only a few feet at terrible cost. After scrambling to collect the dead and wounded, it stormed the position yet again, gaining only a small plot of dirt at the price of more human lives. Time after time that day, the 12th Regiment hurled itself against the enemy until the Germans silently withdrew and Émondeville was taken.[6] When the assault was finally over, the magnitude of the slaughter became evident. The 12th had lost 300 men. They had sacrificed one in ten of their own to take a village whose entire population numbered fewer than 100. Salinger's whereabouts during the battle are uncertain, but the experience scorched itself into the psyches of the men with whom he served.

It was not until June 11 that the regiment reached its initial D-Day objective northeast of Montebourg. Energized by its success at Émondeville, the 12th Regiment pushed forward at an amazing speed. As it turned out, it moved too quickly. It was now a mile ahead of the rest of the division and in danger of being cut off. With Montebourg in its sights, it was ordered to withdraw until the 8th Regiment could catch up. As it did so, regrouped German forces who had retreated from the gun batteries replaced the regiment around the town, occupying the very area it had just vacated.[7] It has since been estimated that Montebourg was held by no more than 200 Germans, a fraction of the force that assaulted it. Their superior position enabled them to hold off both the 12th and 8th regiments for more than a week. With soldiers of the 12th in the forefront, the division finally retook the town on the night of June 19, after struggling to regain ground it had occupied and intended to hold eight days before.

On June 12, Sergeant Salinger scrawled a three-sentence postcard to Whit Burnett whose very construction evoked the trauma he was experiencing. After assuring the editor that he was okay, Salinger wrote that, under the circumstances, he was "too busy to go on with the book right now."[8] The note is difficult to decipher as a result of poor handwriting. Written only six days after D-Day, it may indicate that he was rushed while writing it, still traumatized over his experiences.

The Germans now withdrew to Cherbourg, their last line of defense. Their backs were to the sea. Well fortified and ringed with strong defensive positions, Cherbourg became a formidable fortress. The capture of Montebourg had opened the way to Cherbourg for the Allies, who now began to encircle the city. It took five days for them to inch their way into the garrisoned port. Although Cherbourg was shelled to near desolation, numerous demands for its surrender went ignored. With nowhere to retreat to, the Germans were compelled to fight on. What ensued was urban warfare—fighting street by street and house by house, where Salinger learned to fear the hidden eyes of enemy snipers. It was not until the night of June 25 that he and his regiment entered what was left of the city, unchallenged. The devastation there was tremendous, but the port was secured and with it the Allied invasion of occupied Europe.[9]

The battle for Cherbourg was emblematic of the initiative consistently taken by the 12th Regiment. Throughout the Normandy campaign, Salinger's men were at the forefront of the action. At Émondeville, adjoining forces had to be called in to support them. After being pounded at Émondeville, they hunted down the fleeing Germans to the village of Joganville, where they exacted a ferocious revenge. At Montebourg, they had impatiently pulled ahead of the rest of the division, coming dangerously close to the fortified city itself. On being ordered to withdraw and set up defensive positions instead, they insisted upon retaking the position they had advanced to the day before. An appraisal of the 12th Regiment's actions during June 1944 appears to be as much a study of collective emotion as of tactics. The same troops that had hesitantly dug in beside the hedgerows of Beuzeville-au-Plain on the night of June 6 could be found aggressively thrusting themselves against the enemy on the ninth, following the bloodbath at Émondeville. Battles such as Émondeville had a galvanizing effect upon the 12th Regiment, and Salinger was no exception. The slaughter there had been their baptism by fire. It served to give them purpose and solidified them as a brotherhood. Salinger did not fight to liberate France or to preserve democracy. Like all soldiers of his regiment, he fought with the purest sense of devotion, not for the army but for the boy next to him.

During campaigns such as the siege of Cherbourg, Salinger's counterintelligence duties were pushed to their limits. It was his job to interrogate both locals and captured enemy in order to gather any information that could be helpful to division command. As the Cherbourg battle progressed and it became clear to the Germans that they were defeated, they began to surrender in large numbers. The 12th Regiment alone took 700 prisoners on June 24, followed by 800 the next day. Salinger had to decide whom to interrogate and how to interpret what information he gathered. It was an enormous undertaking and one that had to be accomplished while trying to keep himself alive.

On July 1, the regiment was ordered from Cherbourg south to Gourbesville, near Utah Beach and Beuzeville-au-Plain. There the exhausted men were finally granted three days' rest. This was Salinger's first break from combat in twenty-six days and his first opportunity to properly bathe and change his clothes. The division took this time to assess the situation: of the 3,080 members of Salinger's regiment who had landed with him on June 6, only 1,130 remained. The sense of loss that these numbers represent is made even worse when one discovers that they were typical for the unit throughout the conflict. Of all the American regiments to serve in Europe during the Second World War, Salinger's unit suffered the highest rate of casualties.*

. . .

On June 9, while Salinger was at Normandy, "Elaine" was accepted by *Story* magazine for the "usual fee of twenty-five dollars."[10] On the same day, in a letter to Harold Ober, Whit Burnett also reconsidered his offer to publish the *Young Folks* anthology, preferring to wait for Salinger's novel instead.[11] With survival a daily challenge, one might assume that short-story collections and payments of $25 now meant little to Salinger, but throughout this time, his ambition remained undiminished.

---

*During June 1944 alone, the 12th Infantry Regiment lost 76 percent of its officers and 63 percent of its enlisted men.

Dorothy Olding wrote immediately to Salinger about Burnett's change of mind. Salinger addressed the issue from Cherbourg on June 28, two days after the city was taken. His reaction was acquiescent and calm. He stated that he understood Burnett's reluctance to publish the collection, assuring him that he would continue the Holden Caulfield novel after the war. He believed that, given the opportunity, he could make short work of the project and complete it within six months.[12]

Burnett was no doubt relieved to receive such a response, but there were reasons for Salinger's tone that the editor could never have grasped. Since D-Day, Salinger's persona had taken on a childlike quality of wonder and gratitude that was in stark contrast to his cynicism during previous years. He poked fun at his frayed nerves, describing himself as jumping headlong into ditches at the slightest sound of an explosion. He admitted that he was scared; and of his combat experiences he could write nothing. They were beyond words. In June 1944, Sergeant Salinger was happy just to be alive, but the *Young Folks* episode would not be forgotten.

With the fall of Cherbourg, Normandy was secured for the Allies. Into the city's port poured thousands of fresh troops and countless tons of supplies, all heading south along country roads that soon became congested with crawling tanks and swarms of soldiers. The challenge that now faced the army was to break out of Normandy and sweep into the heart of Europe.

Amid the fields at the base of the Cotentin Peninsula, the city of Saint-Lô rose up like a dream, an ancient citadel that now blocked the Allies' exit from Normandy much as Montebourg had stood in the way of Cherbourg. And like Montebourg, Saint-Lô would have to be taken, regardless of the cost. The fight for Saint-Lô was painstakingly slow and bloody. The city lay in a region perfect for guerrilla warfare. The landscape was dominated by a patchwork of fields divided by hedgerows, the same unrelenting growth that had confounded Salinger and his men the night of D-Day. These obstacles encircled Saint-Lô like a labyrinth of earthen valleys, with foliage so intertwined with the ground that it drew the earth upward, creating natural ramparts. Cutting through them proved impossible. Worse still, they hid the unit from air cover, making the soldiers vulnerable to "friendly" bombs and fire, and prevented the passage of tanks.

Within this maze of growth and fields, the 4th Infantry Division was forced into hand-to-hand combat. Every field held its own battle. After stepping over bodies, soldiers would find themselves in another field looking exactly like the last. For the 12th, the first troops to enter this insanity, it was Émondeville on a grand scale.

What is now known as "the Battle of the Hedgerows" was a bitter discouragement for American troops. The common soldiers had expected to sweep from Normandy into open France and quickly rout the Germans. Instead, they encountered stiff resistance and circumstances of which their superiors had been unaware. The sight of thousands of Allied tanks being unloaded at Cherbourg had rallied them. The signal to open the campaign on Saint-Lô and the carpet bombing of the city and its outskirts had given them confidence in their strength. But they soon found themselves in a medieval brawl, their airpower and tanks useless. When Saint-Lô was finally taken on July 18, nothing was left of the city. It became known as "the Capital of Ruins."

Salinger dealt with the terror of constant battle and proximity to death by disconnecting himself from it. Many people process horror in this way, as a necessity of survival. They become cold to the actuality of occurrences, submerging them rather than dealing with them on the spot. Salinger was aware that he was experiencing this kind of disconnection. Writing home, he said that he could remember events and single moments in time since landing in Normandy but was unable to recall the feelings of fear and panic that had accompanied them. For the time being, at least, he felt it was better that way.[13]

Salinger most likely spent the next two weeks advancing through the countryside south of Saint-Lô, helping mop up pockets of resistance and combing French towns along the way. Tiny villages such as Villedieu-les-Poêles, Brécey, and Mortain had suddenly become vital centers of communication and were converged upon by counterintelligence agents ordered to secure local rail, radio, and telegraph stations for the Allies.

Salinger may actually have been stationed just outside Mortain when the neighboring 30th Infantry Division met with especially fierce resistance from what appeared to be a German Panzer division. By the morning of August 7, it became clear that the opposing division had now become four, and had been joined by infantry. The 30th was alone, facing an all-out counteroffensive ordered by Hitler himself. The adjacent 12th Infantry Regiment was quickly attached to the 30th Infantry Division and rushed to the scene, where it again found itself under attack on two fronts against numerically superior forces.* This was the battle now known as "Bloody Mortain," and accounts portray Salinger's unit in a state of frenzy, firing wildly at an enemy determined to crush it.[14] Salvation arrived in the form of fighter-bombers that blackened the skies over Mortain for five days, bombarding the German lines as they had at Saint-Lô and ending the battle of Bloody Mortain.

After their defeat at Mortain, the Germans were in full retreat from France. The 4th Infantry Division spearheaded the race toward Paris, with the 12th Regiment in the lead. At first, the American command had decided to avoid the capital altogether. After the carnage of Normandy and the breakout, they feared the Germans would defend it to the last man. But to the French, delivering the city from Nazi occupation was a matter of honor; and they successfully campaigned for American help. As the 12th Regiment neared Paris, events occurred that would save many lives. Sensing liberation at hand, on August 18, the citizens of Paris called a general strike. As the day progressed, the strikers threw up barricades and by the next day had begun to battle with the Germans. On August 24, the 12th Infantry Regiment, together with the Free French 2nd Armored Division, took up positions south of the city.

As the Americans had feared, Hitler ordered Paris to be defended to the last man or else be completely destroyed. At this critical moment, deliverance came from the most unlikely quarter. General Dietrich von Choltitz, the military governor of Paris, defied Hitler and refused to defend or destroy the city. (Hitler is said to have telephoned Choltitz, demanding, "Is Paris burning?") At noon on August 25, 1944, Choltitz surrendered the city to the French along with 17,000 German soldiers.

As the Germans were surrendering Paris, Salinger and the 12th were already in the city, the first American troops to enter the capital.[15]

---

*The 12th remained attached to the 30th Infantry Division until August 13, when it was certain the danger had passed.

Some German snipers were still active, but, as Salinger observed, the Parisians did not seem to care. In jubilation, they thronged the boulevards to greet their liberators.

Salinger's description of the liberation of Paris is filled with delight. As he drove down the boulevards in his jeep, he was mobbed by joyful crowds. Women dressed in their finest held their babies up to be kissed or rushed to be kissed themselves. Men hurried to offer gifts of wine. Such offerings struck him as being especially sweet after the bitter experiences of Utah Beach, Saint-Lô, and Cherbourg. It almost gave meaning to the Normandy campaign, he reflected.[16]

The 12th Regiment was ordered to flush out resistance from the city's southeast quadrant to the Hôtel de Ville. Salinger was also designated to seek out Nazi collaborators from among the French. According to John Keenan, Salinger's CIC partner and best friend throughout the war, they had captured such a collaborator when a nearby crowd caught wind of the arrest and descended on them. After wresting the prisoner away from Salinger and Keenan, who were unwilling to shoot into the throng, the crowd beat the man to death. Salinger could do nothing but watch.[17] The event is a bizarre footnote to what was otherwise one of the finest days of Salinger's life. The fact that a human being whom he held in charge was beaten to death before his eyes—without affecting the joy of the day—indicates how much Staff Sergeant Salinger had become accustomed to death by the summer of 1944 and his sense of detachment.

Salinger was in Paris for only a few days, but they were the happiest days he would experience during the war. His recollection of them is contained in a September 9 letter to Whit Burnett that remains the most euphoric he ever wrote.

To the military triumph, Salinger had added his own, more personal, victory: he had spent time with Ernest Hemingway in Paris. Hemingway was serving as a war correspondent for *Collier's* and had reportedly managed to slip into Paris ahead of the liberating armies. Salinger knew this and decided to seek him out. There was no question in Jerry's mind where to find Hemingway. He jumped into his jeep along with Keenan and made straight for the Hôtel Ritz. Hemingway greeted Salinger like an old friend. He claimed to be familiar with Salinger's writings and to have recognized him from his picture in *Es-*

quire. When Hemingway asked if Salinger had any new works on him, Jerry managed to locate a copy of *The Saturday Evening Post* containing "Last Day of the Last Furlough," which had been published that July. Hemingway read the story and was impressed. The two writers talked shop over drinks, to the great relief of Salinger, who had been longing for literary conversation. He was also relieved to find that Hemingway was not at all pretentious or overly macho, as Salinger had feared. Instead, he found him to be gentle and well grounded: overall, a "really good guy."[18]

At first glance, it might appear that Salinger was exploiting the opportunity to bask in the glow of Hemingway's fame. The truth is probably more complex. Salinger, the great setter of stages, was undoubtedly aware of the scene that he had crafted. He had never professed admiration for Hemingway or his work. On the other hand, he did admire Sherwood Anderson and F. Scott Fitzgerald, who, on these very same streets of Paris years before, had taken Hemingway under their wings when he was still a struggling writer. Salinger, therefore, was not so much savoring the company of Ernest Hemingway as he was partaking in the spirits of Anderson and Fitzgerald. Moreover, it is likely that Salinger perceived his time with Hemingway as a generational passing of the torch and that he went to the Hôtel Ritz not to pay homage but to collect what he considered to be his rightful inheritance.

Salinger and Hemingway would continue their relationship for years to come, through at least one additional meeting and an exchange of letters. In his book *J. D. Salinger*, Warren French provides an unverified and fanciful account of the two men meeting. According to French, who was himself wary of the story, Hemingway was explaining to Salinger the superiority of the German Luger over the American .45. To demonstrate his point, he fired his Luger at a nearby chicken and shot off its head. Salinger was horrified. According to French, Salinger later related the incident in "For Esmé—with Love and Squalor," when the character of Clay shoots a cat. Though it is doubtful that the chicken story is true, Salinger derived great personal strength through his relationship with Ernest Hemingway throughout the war and called him by his nickname, "Papa." This admiration did not necessarily transfer to Hemingway's writing, as displayed by

Holden's later condemnation of *A Farewell to Arms* in *The Catcher in the Rye,** but during the war years, Salinger was grateful for Hemingway's friendship and thanked him for providing rare moments of hope.[19]

. . .

By September 1944, Salinger had submitted his short story "I'm Crazy" to Whit Burnett, who must have been appalled to receive it. The first story narrated by Holden Caulfield, it was certainly one of the "six chapters" Salinger had completed for the book promised to Story Press. Burnett knew this and, upon receiving "I'm Crazy" as a separate short story, must have seen his hope for a novel fade before his eyes. Salinger had to be aware that he would have this reaction. He must have known too that Burnett could never publish the story.

There are two possible reasons why Salinger submitted "I'm Crazy" at this time. Unsure that he would survive the war, he may have sought the assurance that Holden would have his say regardless. It is also likely that Salinger presented the story in reaction to Burnett's June reversal on the *Young Folks* anthology. Burnett was not alone in possessing options that could be withdrawn. Salinger was the source of his longed-for Holden Caulfield novel and held complete power over that prospect. His submission of "I'm Crazy," with the implied intention of releasing his novel chapters as individual stories, might force the editor to reconsider publishing the collection.

Burnett was holding "I'm Crazy" when Salinger readdressed the anthology issue in his exuberant letter of September 9. Without this knowledge, Salinger's attitude regarding the collection might appear ambiguous; but the submission of "I'm Crazy," together with the letter's enthusiastic tone and three-page postscript, leaves little doubt that he was asking Burnett to reconsider publishing the collection. War or no war, he said, he was continuing to write, and between April 14

---

*Salinger separated Hemingway's professional persona from his personal one. He told Elizabeth Murray that Hemingway was kind by nature but had been posturing for so many years that it now came naturally to him. Salinger disagreed with the underlying philosophy of Hemingway's work. He said that he hated Hemingway's "overestimation of sheer physical courage, commonly called 'guts,' as a virtue. Probably because I'm short on it myself."

and D-Day had completed six stories.* Even on the front lines, he had begun another three. Of these new stories, Salinger was confident enough to include them in a list to be used if Burnett reconsidered publishing the anthology. Of the stories already completed, the list included "The Long Debut of Lois Taggett," "Elaine," "The Young Folks," "Last Day of the Last Furlough," "Wake Me When It Thunders," "Death of a Dogface," "The Children's Echelon," "Once a Week Won't Kill You," "Boy Standing in Tennessee," "Bitsy," "Two Lonely Men," and "I'm Crazy." Of the three unfinished stories, Salinger had titled only "The Magic Foxhole." He was unsure whether to name the second story "What Babe Saw" or "Oh-La-La." The third story was not named at all, and he simply called it "Another piece untitled."

Within weeks, Whit Burnett had recommitted to publishing the *Young Folks* anthology. He detained "I'm Crazy" until October 26, by which time Salinger had returned to combat. In a short note sent to Harold Ober announcing *Story*'s acceptance of "Once a Week Won't Kill You," Burnett stated that he was "returning the other story of his which we have been holding. I'M CRAZY."[20] Salinger's second unfinished piece would not be named either "What Babe Saw" or "Oh-La-La" but would be published in 1945 as "A Boy in France." The unnamed story was either "This Sandwich Has No Mayonnaise" or "A Young Man in a Stuffed Shirt," an unpublished war story later rejected by Burnett and since withheld by the author.

. . .

Of all the stories of J. D. Salinger to remain unpublished, perhaps none is finer than "The Magic Foxhole," the first story he wrote while fighting on the front line. Based upon Salinger's own experiences during D-Day and succeeding encounters and the only work in which Salinger depicted active combat, "The Magic Foxhole" is an angry story and a

---

*Later in 1944, Salinger claimed to have written eight stories since arriving overseas in mid-January and three since D-Day. The September 9 account refers only to stories penned since April 14, when Burnett first offered to collect Salinger's stories into a book. This leaves two stories to be written between mid-January and mid-April. If Salinger's account is correct, these stories may be chapters of *The Catcher in the Rye* or are now completely lost. It is also possible that Salinger wrote his lost story "Daughter of the Late, Great Man" at this time.

strong condemnation of war. It is a story that could have been written only by a soldier.*

Its message countered the propaganda common in 1944 with a frankness that could have been interpreted as subversive. After completing "The Magic Foxhole," Salinger predicted that his wartime stories would "not be published for generations."[21] Even had this story slipped past the military censors, it is hard to imagine a publisher with the courage to print it.

"The Magic Foxhole" opens days after D-Day on a slow-moving convoy presumably heading to Cherbourg. It casts the reader as an anonymous hitchhiking GI picked up by the narrator, a soldier named Garrity. Addressing the reader only as "Mac," Garrity eagerly recounts the events of a battle fought by his battalion directly after D-Day. His tale focuses on the company point man, Lewis Gardner, and the experiences that caused him battle fatigue.

Garrity and Gardner's battalion had emerged from storming the beach on D-Day only to encounter a German stronghold. The Germans, who outnumbered them two to one, had entrenched themselves into woods upon a hill. Between the enemy and Gardner's battalion lay a deadly marsh dubbed "The Widow Maker's Swamp." Here, the Germans pinned the men down for two days and nights, while Garrity and Gardner's battalion attempted to take the enemy position. Repeatedly they crawled through the marshland, seeking to reach the Germans, who barraged them with gunfire and mortars. Whenever heavy arms began to explode around them, they scrambled for one of a handful of foxholes, holes that were too far apart to protect all the men. Because Gardner was the company point man, he maintained a position 50 feet in front of the rest and always got a hole to himself. Every foxhole that Gardner occupied held him alone and was therefore seemingly magic.

The situation is futile, and Salinger conveys its hopelessness with the authenticity of a participant. Readers experience the stench of the swamp and have a clear image of the sheer waste of battle. Admiration is inspired and increased with every pointless yet unquestioned assault upon the German defenses. There is no glory in this fight, only the steel determination of its men and the mad scramble to survive.

---

*The byline of "The Magic Foxhole" may indicate Salinger's realization that the story would go unpublished. It is the more vulnerable "Jerry Salinger" rather than the usual, more professional "J. D. Salinger."

As the battle progresses and Gardner seeks refuge within successive foxholes, he begins to see a strange ghostlike soldier wearing glasses and a futuristic helmet. He confides these encounters to Garrity, who at first thinks Gardner insane. After several meetings with the phantom soldier, Gardner learns to his shock that the apparition is his own son, Earl, who is yet to be born. At this point, Gardner begins to unravel. Believing Earl to be participating in some future war, he resolves to kill his son in the hope of preventing the conflict. Upon learning of Gardner's plan, Garrity is alarmed. He decides to jump into a foxhole along with Gardner and knock him out with the butt of his rifle in order to spare his ghost-son. But Garrity is struck in the back by shrapnel and never makes it into the hole with Gardner.

Garrity awakes from his shrapnel wound at a hospital set up on the beach. There he locates Gardner, who has been mentally destroyed. Unwilling to stay on his stretcher, Gardner pitifully clings to a pole stuck in the sand. Salinger's description of his condition contains a quality for which his later *New Yorker* stories will be famous: an ability to transfer multiple messages and emotions through a handful of simple words. Gardner, with death in his eyes, now stands on the beach in his hospital nightshirt, clinging to the pole, "holding on tight, like as if he's at Coney Island on one of those rides where if you don't hold on tight you'll go flying off and get your head cracked open."[22]

A closer, perhaps retrospective examination of Garrity's tale reveals that he is also suffering from battle fatigue, to a lesser degree than his friend. His speech is erratic and hurried, his thought patterns scattered. He has also developed a morbid fascination with suffering, traveling daily to the beach to gaze upon the mangled and limbless soldiers being evacuated. He is not yet as sick as Gardner, but that day is swiftly approaching.

Salinger's criticism of the army is strong in this piece. Apart from condemning the army's crushing of individuality, he calls alarm to the official policy of sending broken men back to the front before they are mentally healed. The story also contains an unspoken yet pervasive depiction of men used as cannon fodder. In "The Magic Foxhole," the army is a cold, faceless entity devoid of compassion, a machine soullessly reusing its parts to the point of disintegration. The admiration for the loyalty and tenacity of the soldiers as individuals is plain, but so is the derision for the military mechanism running

in the background that drives them on regardless of the consequences.

The story's anger is outweighed by a sense of grief, and though
much of Salinger's fury was directed toward the army, his despair was
directed more at the pointlessness of war. This sense of futility is presented through the battle scene but is best conveyed at the story's end.
Garrity seeks out Gardner not to see his condition but to find out
whether he has killed his phantom son. Gardner has not. He allowed
Earl to live because his son "wanted to be here." The line is pregnant
with meaning, and its words have resulted in Gardner's fatigue far
more than the battle or the specter of Earl. Gardner's future son's willingness to be on the field of battle convicts Gardner. After all that he
had witnessed and suffered, what did he do—or not do—in the future
that allowed it to happen again? After his experience at "The Widow
Maker's Swamp," it would have been his duty to teach his son the ter-
rors and uselessness of war. Realizing that that never happens and that
his own failure is to blame for Earl's eagerness "to be here," Gardner
is cast into madness.

Salinger also uses Earl's words to challenge his generation, asking
them to teach their children not the phony glory of war but the cruel
stupidity of it. As Garrity begins to tell a story about a nurse he met on
the beach, readers realize that he himself has already forgotten these
lessons. As the story closes, he calls out to another hitchhiking soldier,
"Hey, buddy! Want a lift? Where are you going?" This is Salinger's
question to us: What will we do to see that war never happens again?
What direction will we take? What path will we teach our own children? In the autumn of 1944, this kind of message was explosive, made
all the more incendiary by the fact that it was written by a staff sergeant
serving on the front.

The most powerful portion of "The Magic Foxhole" is the opening
lines, which describe landing at Normandy on D-Day. The scene un-
folds in silent slow motion and is brilliantly conveyed. There is nothing
on the beach but dead bodies and a solitary living figure—a chaplain
crawling around in the sand, frantically searching for his glasses. As his
transport nears the beach, the narrator watches the surreal scene in
amazement, until the chaplain too is torn to pieces and all motion
stops. Only then is there room for the noise of explosions. This segment is hauntingly moving but above all highly symbolic. It was no ac-

cident that Salinger chose a chaplain to be alone among the dead in the heat of war. It was also no accident that this doomed cleric should be desperate for the clarity of his glasses in the chaos around him. His fate displays the image of someone who believed he held the answer and, when it was needed most, discovered he did not. It is an image of despair and hopelessness—a great wail of anguish. Held within it is a critical moment of advent in Salinger's writing. For the first time, J. D. Salinger asks the question: where is God?

. . .

After the liberation of Paris and the subsequent German retreat, General Dwight D. Eisenhower's chief of staff declared with confidence that "militarily, the war is over." The Allied generals agreed. Even Churchill and Roosevelt expected victory by mid-October. Orders were given to pursue the Germans and hasten their surrender. In the meantime, the post exchange was instructed to stop any delivery of Christmas packages to the troops from home. The war would not last that long.

. . .

The Hürtgen Forest occupies approximately 50 square miles of territory along Germany's border with Belgium and Luxembourg. To unsuspecting eyes the forest appears ancient—something out of a storybook opera—but it is a modern construction, designed by the German High Command to take advantage of every rise and dip of the landscape and to serve as a killing ground for invading armies. Its trees were a hundred feet tall and planted so close together that they blocked out the sunlight. Changes of weather regularly drew in deep fog that obscured surroundings, making it impossible to see just a few feet away. Within the forest hills were pillbox defenses that, covered with foliage, blended in, making them as invisible as they were deadly. Even the trees and forest floor were booby-trapped, strewn with barbed wire and littered with camouflaged land mines called "Bouncing Bettys." In this eerie place, death could come with every footfall, every brush against a stone or touch of a branch.

Parallel to the border and dipping deep into the center of the Hürtgen Forest, the Nazis had constructed a line of barriers and fortifications called the Siegfried Line. The Germans themselves called this barrier the West Wall, and in some places the Siegfried Line actually was a wall, complete with concrete barricades called "dragon's teeth." In other places, the line was less clear, designed as a purposeful illusion of normalcy. Upon crossing the line into the forest, jeeps and tanks became useless on the winding woodland paths and troops disappeared from sight, stripping them of air cover.

To force the Germans' early surrender, Eisenhower sent two armies, the First and the Third, to take the Siegfried Line and cross the Roer and Rhine rivers within Germany. The Roer ran along the edge of the Hürtgen Forest, and American commanders decided that in order to take the river, the forest had to be cleared of all resistance.

Hitler, however, had no intention of surrendering. In fact, the Germans were planning a major counteroffensive that would become the Battle of the Bulge. Hitler's plan was twofold. A series of dams sat within the Hürtgen Forest that controlled the Roer River. He plotted to breach those dams upon the outset of the counteroffensive and flood the U.S. First Army's path into Germany. With the First Army mired down, he could throw all of his strength at the remaining American Third Army. One hundred fresh battalions were sent to man the defenses of the Siegfried Line in and around the Hürtgen Forest. They were ordered to stave off the Allied advance into Germany until the counteroffensive could be organized and to protect the dams so vital to its success.

When Salinger described the liberation of Paris, he was already en route to the German border. Spirits were high as his regiment reached Luxembourg on September 7, and Belgium two days later. They believed that they had left the worst of the war behind them in Normandy. From now on, they would play the role of conquering heroes. Salinger's division was to have the honor of being the first to enter Germany. Once it had crossed into the Third Reich and breached the Siegfried Line, its orders were to sweep away any resistance from the area of the Hürtgen Forest and take up positions to protect the flank of the invading First Army.

With these decisions and in this unwary mood, the stage was set for what would become the blackest months of Salinger's life. Already, during the advance of September, signs began to appear that, while dim annoyances at the time, would prove devastating in the months to come. For instance, one week into the dash to Germany, gasoline became dangerously scarce. Then there was a shortage of cigarettes—a considerable blow to troop morale. Most ominous of all, it rained heavily throughout September and the soldiers soon discovered that their army-issue boots absorbed both water and mud. When a request for overshoes was made, it was ignored. With Salinger's men advancing as quickly as possible and the muddied roads behind them becoming increasingly impassable, they began to outpace their lines of supply. They continued on as the weather grew unusually cold for September, a precursor of what would become the bitterest winter in living memory. Not surprisingly, the same officials who had ordered the suspension of delivery of Christmas packages had given little thought to things such as winter gear or overshoes for the troops.

On September 13, the 12th Infantry Regiment crossed into Germany, entering a heavily wooded country in the shadow of the Schnee Eifel, an imposing ridgeline that hugged the Hürtgen Forest. A landscape of steep valleys and rolling hills, the area had been a favorite skiing destination for Germans before the war. Despite the difficult landscape, the 12th had so far encountered no resistance, as its division commanders had hoped. Unknown to the soldiers, their ammunition supplies were far behind them and they would have been hard pressed to fight for any length of time had they been attacked. Relieved and encouraged by the ease of the advance, division commanders ordered the 12th and 22nd regiments to break through the Siegfried Line.

It was drizzling at 1 P.M. on September 14 when the 4th crossed the Siegfried Line.[23] Taking advantage of a chilly fog that blanketed the woods, Salinger and his comrades scaled the Schnee Eifel and breached the line without encountering a single enemy soldier. Division commanders were encouraged and ordered the 12th to secure the area's major highway so that it could be used by the U.S. First Army in its triumphal march into Germany. The regiment secured a hill overlooking the highway and dug in for the night.

The next morning, the soldiers awoke to a very different scene. The woods that had been empty only a day before were now full of enemy troops. Abandoned pillbox fortifications were manned and firing on their positions, and they found themselves confronted by the 2nd SS Panzer Division. The Germans had not expected the Americans to penetrate the Siegfried Line in the rugged area of the Schnee Eifel and had concentrated their forces in more logical locations. When they had

learned of the advances of the 12th and 22nd regiments, they had
taken immediate action and slipped their forces into place overnight.

The regiment was now entrenched in a quagmire. During the day,
it carried out patrols and tried to clear its area of land mines, all the
while under artillery and sniper fire. At night, the Germans would slip
out of their pillboxes and replace the mines that had been removed. In
the Schnee Eifel, the soldiers of the 12th Regiment fought one engagement after another to hold their sector of the line—a sector made
worthless because they had lost control of the highway.

Deep within the Hürtgen Forest and surrounded by a thin ribbon
of fields and villages lies the Kall River Valley. The valley is actually a
gorge, with steep mountainsides rising up from the river. Along the
top of the gorge runs the Kall Trail, a haphazard dirt track clinging
perilously close to the cliff edge. The valley and the fields around it
were, in essence, a shooting range for the Germans, who sat propped
upon the surrounding hills. On November 2, the Allied command sent
the 28th Infantry Division into the valley to seize the towns whose positions controlled the forest.

At first, the 28th appeared to be surprisingly successful. The division had divided itself between its regiments, with each regiment operating as an independent fighting unit, and managed to take one of the
towns, a portion of the gorge, and a thickly forested plain bordering
the valley. What the 28th did not realize was that the Germans had allowed them to split up in this way and had surrounded each regiment.
Nothing obstructed the Germans from bombarding them at will, both
from their mountain strongholds and from the darkness of the forest
itself.

Unable to move safely in any direction, the 28th Division was
forced to defend impossibly vulnerable positions for two weeks.* In a
desperate effort to relieve them, the Allied command ordered tanks to
be sent down the Kall Trail, ignorant of the fact that it was a morass of
mud and fallen trees. In many places, the road fell away under the
weight of the tanks, sending them plunging into the gorge below.

---

*The 28th Infantry Division consisted of members of the Pennsylvania National Guard
and wore a red keystone, a symbol of the state, as a shoulder patch and was called the Keystone Division. To the Germans, this keystone resembled a bucket. Because so many of the
28th Division died at the Kall Trail, the Germans renamed it the "Bloody Bucket Division,"
a title that has since become a point of pride.

With the failure of the tanks to rescue the 28th, the Allied command called upon the 12th Infantry Regiment, which, on November 6, was attached to the besieged 28th Division and made its way into the Hürtgen bloodbath. Strewn with burned-out tanks and the bodies of the dead, the Kall Trail was a fearsome precursor of the weeks ahead. Yet the regiment dutifully took up its position on the forested plain, relieving the broken remnants of a unit that was at near collapse.

The original plan had been for the 12th Regiment to create and maintain an escape path for the members of the 28th Division who had survived. But once in the forest, leaders of the 28th Division ordered the regiment to divide itself into separate units, and the groups to simultaneously strike out from the forested plain into the Kall River Valley, imposing the same flawed strategy that had doomed the 28th. When officers of the 12th Regiment received the order, they protested, pointing out the folly of splitting up their men. Their objections fell on deaf ears. The 12th, now in segments, advanced unevenly, and its men soon became disoriented. Unable to communicate with one another, entire companies fell to the Germans. Others were lost in the forest for days and, as their supplies depleted, were forced to scavenge food from the bodies of the dead. Outnumbered four to one and short on ammunition, the soldiers were in a desperate situation. "God, it was cold. We were hungry and thirsty," recalled a survivor. "That night we really prayed. In the morning, we found out that God had answered all our prayers. It snowed during the night, and the whole area was covered with fog—perfect for getting out. The supply line was littered with dead. The men that came out with me were so damned tired that they stepped on the bodies. They were too tired to step over them."[24]

Within five days, the 12th Regiment had lost more than 500 men and were ordered to slip away to the rear and reorganize what little was left of them. But there was no "rear." When the exhausted soldiers reached their previous encampments, they found their foxholes occupied by the Germans. The regiment commanders could stand no more. The 12th, depleted beyond repair, was detached from the 28th Infantry Division on November 11. Two days later, there would be nothing left of the 28th, except for a handful of broken and wounded men.

Still the men were not allowed to leave Hürtgen. After the annihilation of the 28th Division, all three regiments of the 4th Infantry Division were called upon to replace them. Despite their weakness and depleted numbers, Salinger and his fellow soldiers were expected to remain in the forest, support their sister regiments, and somehow maintain an offensive.

When Salinger entered the Hürtgen Forest, he crossed the threshold of a nightmare world. The most senseless carnage of World War II on the western front arguably took place at Hürtgen during the winter of 1944. But it was the day-to-day terror of the place that drove men to the brink of despair. Trapped in the gloom of the forest, death could come at any moment and from any direction. Here the enemy was invisible, requiring a constant supply of adrenaline that was impossible to sustain. Madness seeped up through the mud or poured down with the incessant rains.

The slaughter at Hürtgen was so great that the 12th Regiment was kept afloat only by an inadequate influx of replacements. By some unfathomable logic, commanders were required to place orders for troop replacements in advance of the need. As a result, there were never enough troops, increasing the burden on survivors such as Salinger, who had quickly become hardened veterans of war. When replacements did arrive, there was no time to orient them. Years later, one such soldier vividly remembered the brutal but efficient method used by the 12th Regiment to instruct its newest members:

> We were a bunch of raw recruits sent up as replacements and didn't know what we were up against. Walking up to our appointed positions, we had to walk over dead soldiers. I can remember three or four that had been dead for some time. I believe this was an attempt to get us used to seeing such sights.[25]

Even the company camps were dangerous places. Salinger had been taught to hit the ground facedown when being shelled, to avoid horizontally flying debris. At Hürtgen, the Germans employed tree bursts, which exploded well above the soldiers' heads, resulting in a shower of shrapnel and shredded tree limbs that poured down like a thousand spears. Jerry quickly learned to "hug a tree" at the first sound of an explosion and to cover his foxhole with as many tree branches as possible.

Nearly half of the 2,517 casualties suffered by the 12th Infantry Regiment in Hürtgen were due to the elements.[26] Men froze to death in their foxholes or lost limbs to frostbite. The filth of the place was inescapable, and the weather was either drenching wet or burning cold. For more than a month, Salinger and his men were forced to sleep in muddy or frozen holes with no chance to wash or change their clothes. A successful attempt was made to obtain additional blankets, woolen underwear, and overcoats.* But overshoes and sleeping bags were still impossible to secure even though the division had been requesting them since the beginning of September.[27]

The soldiers wore boots that acted like sponges, soaking up the rain, and trench foot decimated the ranks. Salinger was fortunate. He later recalled how he managed to keep his feet dry. His mother had fallen into the habit of knitting him woolen socks. Each week he would receive a package from home, containing yet another pair of socks. Such indulgence might have made him smile in July, but in November, it helped keep him alive.[28]

The great tragedy of Hürtgen was the pointlessness of it all. Why the Allied command so stubbornly insisted upon fighting for this useless piece of ground under such impossible conditions is incomprehensible. The Germans fought to hold the place mainly in order to control the dams, prizes that could have been taken with greater ease by simply going around the forest rather than through it. Even when the significance of the dams finally began to seep into the consciousness of the Allied commanders, they refused to alter their course, electing to seize the small towns controlling the dams by taking the most direct route possible—straight through Hürtgen into the Kall River Valley, where they were completely at the mercy of the Germans.

For these reasons, Hürtgen is viewed by historians as a military failure and a waste of human life. It was among the greatest Allied debacles of the war. Yet great strides were made within the forest by the 4th Infantry Division, measures that later allowed the dams to be wrested away from Hitler, but at a terrible cost. Those gains were almost exclusively due to the valor of the common soldiers. During the long winter of 1944, not a single division commander or staff member set foot upon Hürtgen soil.

The blackness of Hürtgen did permit Salinger a rare glimpse of so-

---

*The regiment was issued greatcoats that absorbed the rain and hampered movement. Most soldiers quickly discarded them, but some later froze to death.

lace. During the battle for the forest, Hemingway was serving as a correspondent and briefly stationed with the 22nd Regiment, just a mile from Salinger's encampment.

One night during a lull in the fighting, Salinger turned to fellow soldier Werner Kleeman, a translator for the 12th Regiment he had befriended while training in England. "Let's go," Salinger urged, "let's go see Hemingway."[29] The two men donned their heaviest coats, gathered together their guns and flashlights, and made their way through the forest. A mile later, they reached Hemingway's quarters, a small cabin lighted by the extraordinary luxury of its own generator.

The visit lasted two or three hours. They drank celebratory champagne from aluminum canteen cups, and Kleeman listened as Salinger and Hemingway talked of literature. It was a singular moment in the forest, one that left Salinger refreshed and Kleeman impressed. When recalling the visit in a letter five months later, Salinger still drew strength from the memory.[30]

Salinger's choice of visiting companion was perhaps an expression of gratitude. Among his commanders in the Hürtgen Forest was an officer Kleeman described as having been "a heavy drinker" and cruel to his troops. This officer ordered Salinger to remain in a frozen foxhole overnight, knowing that Salinger was without proper supplies. When the temperature dropped to dangerous levels, Kleeman became fearful for his friend's life. After sneaking over to find Salinger shivering in the now snow-covered hole, Kleeman secretly delivered two items from Salinger's belongings that helped him survive: a blanket liberated from a hotel after the Battle of Cherbourg and a pair of his mother's ubiquitous woolen socks.

Hürtgen changed Salinger profoundly, but it changed everyone who experienced it in a similar way. Even Hemingway found it difficult to write for years after his experience there. Hemingway openly blamed the forest, but most survivors never spoke of Hürtgen again. Silence was the overwhelming reaction. Yet a recognition of the conditions at Hürtgen and the sufferings that Salinger endured are essential to understanding the depth of his later works. Within the Hürtgen Forest lie the origin of Babe's mournful lament for the 12th Regiment in "The Stranger" and the nightmares suffered by Sergeant X in "For Esmé—with Love and Squalor."

. . .

While Salinger was enduring Hürtgen, "Once a Week Won't Kill You" was published in the November–December issue of *Story*. The appearance of this piece, its plot trivial in comparison to his present circumstances, was tinged with irony. It must have been difficult for Salinger to recall the motivation behind the piece or even the persona who had penned it. Whit Burnett, still delighted about Salinger's $200 contribution to *Story*'s writing contest, wanted to exploit Salinger's donation as well as his presence on the battlefield by including a short biography of the author in the issue. Deep within the Hürtgen Forest, Salinger composed a short autobiographical profile and sent it off to New York.

Initially this sketch appears unremarkable, especially considering when it was written. A placid, humorous self-account, it is still recalled to draw a correlation between Salinger and the character of Holden Caulfield. Salinger speaks of bouncing from one school to another and dropping his marbles in the American Indian Room of the Museum of Natural History. There is perceptible wartime numbness beneath the surface of this piece. In it Salinger admits to an inability, since being in the army, to recall the people and places of home, as if his prewar life were slipping away, with normality becoming increasingly distant and obscure. There is a definite hint of frayed nerves as he explains his life by reciting one dismal event after another. Even at Hürtgen, Salinger assures his readers that he is "still writing whenever [he] can find the time" and whenever he can find "an unoccupied foxhole."[31]

From Hürtgen, Salinger also wrote to Elizabeth Murray. In a letter containing mood shifts between his happy recollections of Paris and the depressing experiences of the forest, he tells Murray that as well as meeting Hemingway, he has been writing as much as possible. He claims to have completed five stories since January and to be in the process of finishing another three. Years later, Salinger's counterintelligence colleagues would remember him as constantly stealing away to write. One recalled a time when they came under heavy fire. Everyone began ducking for cover. Glancing over, the soldiers caught sight of Salinger typing away under a table, his concentration apparently undisturbed by the explosions around him.[32] Such examples demonstrate Salinger's need to write. At Hürtgen, with the memory of his former life slipping away, Salinger used the familiar act of writing to carry him through—as a way to survive.

By the first week of December, all three regiments of the 4th Infantry Division were exhausted. If the 12th Infantry Regiment were ever to be effective in combat again, it would have to be completely rebuilt. On December 5, Salinger and his men received word that they were leaving Hürtgen. Few of the men who had entered the forest a month before had survived. Of the original 3,080 regimental soldiers who went into Hürtgen, only 563 were left. For those soldiers especially, walking out of the forest alive was a victory in itself.

. . .

"A Boy in France" is a quiet tale of the inner workings of a battle-worn soldier in search of a moment's rest in a foxhole. It is the second of three stories that Salinger documented having written while on the front lines during the closing months of 1944.* Although it contains no reference to any Caulfield family member, it mirrors the rhythm and message of *The Catcher in the Rye* and other Caulfield works. Therefore, it should be considered as Salinger's sixth Caulfield story.

While critics have tended to neglect it, "A Boy in France" represents an important stage in the development of Salinger's work. His previous story, "The Magic Foxhole," asked about the existence and nature of God. As if in reply to those questions, "A Boy in France" contains a declaration of conviction, and through this story, faith and authorship become intertwined.

The story takes place in Normandy, where Salinger began writing it, but its content reflects more his experience at Hürtgen, where it was probably completed. Told in a near-stream of consciousness, the narrative is saturated with an authenticity that only an actual soldier could provide. As the story begins, readers sense the rumbling of distant gunfire and the smell of dank, cold earth. Sleeping alone upon this ravaged ground is an exhausted, filthy boy dressed as a soldier. He is the boy in France. He is awakened by terrible thoughts of the day's battle, thoughts "that could not be disremembered."[33] His weary mind attempts to rally him. This is not a safe place, and he must move on. He

---

*"A Boy in France" was reprinted in *The Saturday Evening Post Stories, 1942–1945,* by Random House, 1946, pages 314–320, making it the second Salinger story to appear in book form.

puts on his helmet, collects his bundle, and begins his wandering in search of a place of safety. As he departs, he calls to another soldier, "I'll holler when I get there." But he does not know where he is going.

Finally overcome by weakness, the boy finds a safe place to rest: a foxhole, empty except for a blanket (the recent shroud of a soldier) and the stench of death. With the last of his strength he attempts in vain to "dig out the bad places," and lowers himself into the hole. When lumps of dirt begin to cover him inside the earthen tomb, "he did nothing about it." The boy is bitten on the leg by a red ant. In an attempt to kill the offender, he reencounters the place where he lost an entire fingernail during that day's battle. He places the wounded finger under his blanket and recites a list of wishes that momentarily ends the war and transports him back home, where his fingernail is miraculously reaffixed. There, he recites a poetic chant, vowing to block out the world. A mere notch away from pure poetry, this incantation is among Salinger's most melodious literary moments and imbues this story with a charm paradoxical to its setting.

At this point in his career Salinger began to write serious poetry. Whole sections of "A Boy in France" are restrained from becoming poetry only by form and punctuation. For example, when the boy's refrain is broken up according to its flow, its sentences reveal six verses bound by the refrain of "I'll bolt the door."

When the boy opens his eyes he finds himself still upon the battlefield, alone with his throbbing finger. In despair, he reaches into his pocket, where he has kept a link to home. With eyes pressed close, he slowly reads "the abracadabra" that has always worked before, a breathless account of a movie premiere from a world in which there is no war. But its empty words have lost their magic here and the boy pushes them away. Yet he has kept a more faithful memory, a letter from home tattered by use. He holds it with tenderness and begins to recite it as if it were a prayer.

Readers come to realize that they already know this boy. He is Babe Gladwaller, and the letter is from his little sister, Mattie. Salinger deliberately withholds the soldier's identity until the end of the story. The poignancy and truth of "A Boy in France" lie in the universality of the central character: Babe represents every soldier who was ever lonely and drained by the demands of war.

Mattie begins her letter by telling Babe that she knows he is in

France. She continues by saying that there are few boys now at the beach and that Lester Brogan was killed in the Pacific. Mr. and Mrs. Brogan still go to the beach, she says, but now they sit in silence, never going into the water. Mattie then tells the strange tale of the death of Mr. Ollinger, portraying death as an unseen hand blindly snatching life away from among them. She closes her letter with the wish that Babe will come home soon. It is a predictable statement but one that rejuvenates him. After reading the letter he lifts himself up from the foxhole and shouts, "I'm over here!" to the nearest soldier. Then he whispers to himself, "Please come home soon" and falls blissfully asleep.

The message of this story hinges upon two poems that Babe longs to hear above all else. One is "The Lamb" by William Blake, and the other is "Chartless" by Emily Dickinson. These poems hold similar messages. When read together, they add a powerful statement to this story.

The Lamb

Little Lamb, who made thee?
Does thou know who made thee?
Gave thee life, and bid thee feed,
By the stream and o'er the mead;
Gave thee clothing of delight,
Softest clothing woolly bright;
Gave thee such a tender voice,
Making all the vales rejoice?
Little Lamb, who made thee?
Does thou know who made thee?

Little Lamb, I'll tell thee,
Little Lamb, I'll tell thee.
He is called by thy name,
For He calls himself a Lamb.
He is meek, and he is mild;
He became a little child.
I a child, and thou a lamb,
We are called by His name.
Little Lamb, God bless thee!
Little Lamb, God bless thee!

Chartless

I never saw a moor,
I never saw the sea;
Yet know I how the heather looks,
And what a wave must be.

I never spoke with God,
Nor visited in Heaven;
Yet certain am I of the spot
As if the chart were given.

The first of many stories in which Salinger equates poetry with spirituality, "A Boy in France" represents a major stage in Salinger's spiritual journey. In "The Magic Foxhole," the scene with the chaplain appears to question the existence of God or at least the participation of God in human lives. In "A Boy in France," the existence of God is affirmed, and it is here that Salinger acknowledges his spiritual quest.

That Salinger had a religious experience at this time should come as little surprise. The front lines of battle are often the scene of spiritual awakenings. However, in 1944, his perception of God was still an abstract one built upon ideas already traveled. In "Last Day of the Last Furlough," Babe decided that life was worth living and fighting for because it held beauty. In "France," he realized that it was beauty through which God began to reveal Himself. Within the tomb of his foxhole, Babe sees no mystical apparition, nor is he engulfed by a heavenly light. But he does see God, if only through the beauty of his little sister's innocence, and, upon feeling his own connection with it, knows once again that he is alive.

Fourteen years after Salinger's descent into Hürtgen, he recalled a haiku written by the nineteenth-century Japanese poet Kobayashi Issa:

"The Peony is this big!"
The child's arms
Outstretched

It was enough, maintained Salinger, that Issa had drawn attention to the peony. The remaining obligation lay in the hands of the reader.

"Whether we go to see his fat-faced peony for ourselves is another matter," he wrote. An effort is required because the poet "doesn't police us."[34]

Salinger's reference to Issa's haiku was drawn in correlation to his own writings. The essence of "A Boy in France" must be felt by the heart to be fully experienced, just as only the heart can truly see the peony. The poetry and prose of "A Boy in France" contain great meaning. Babe's news clippings and Mattie's letter offer a message. The story's final lines provide a conclusion. Yet a profound experience is also held within the words of Dickinson and Blake that elevate this story to a spiritual level. Salinger does not police us to this place. Instead, we must go ourselves to incur the experience. In future works, this will be a staple of Salinger's better writings. In the winter of 1944, the full bloom of Salinger's peony was still years away; but its seed was planted then, in the unlikely soil of "Bloody Hürtgen."

. . .

On December 8, Salinger arrived at his new post, an area in Luxembourg described as being "a paradise for weary soldiers."[35] Evidence shows that he was deployed in the area of Echternach, a town across the Sauer River from Germany. For the first time in weeks his unit would sleep on actual beds, eat real food, shower, and change their clothing at will. Some were even promised passes to Belgium or Paris. Most comforting, the new position was chosen because it was quiet, away from the heat of combat, which some believed would break these soldiers.

On December 16, after a short week of relative calm and inactivity, the 12th Infantry Regiment—still far from having been rebuilt—was suddenly engulfed by German forces. At dawn, Echternach and surrounding towns came under artillery fire, destroying the regiment's communications centers and essentially cutting it off from the rest of the division. At 9 A.M., the force of two German infantry regiments—complete and fresh—slammed into the 12th head-on. The troops were stunned. Entire companies were surrounded. Whole platoons were isolated and lost.

This was Hitler's great counteroffensive, the first day of the Battle of the Bulge, initially focused almost exclusively on the 12th Infantry Regiment. While the 12th fought for its existence, both regiments adjacent to the 12th (the 8th and 22nd) reported little or no enemy activity on December 16.[36]

The Battle of the Bulge was the costliest engagement in American military history. For Salinger and his comrades it must have seemed like an extension of Hürtgen. It meant more nights sleeping in the snow. It meant more fighting in the forest—this time the Ardennes. It meant more exhaustion and blood.

The 12th struggled bravely against the odds. In Echternach, E Company was encircled on December 16 and survived only by finding refuge in the ruins of a hat factory. For three days, the company fought the encroaching Germans as other troops from the 12th struggled to relieve them. On December 19, just as Echternach was being overrun by German forces, an armored task force rammed its way into the town to rescue the besieged men. To the surprise of the task force, the leader of E Company refused to leave the hat factory and insisted upon defending it with his remaining soldiers. Cut off from communications, he had received no orders to relinquish his position. Unable to persuade the unit to retreat, the task force stayed with it in the hat factory until nightfall, when they were forced to withdraw to protect their tanks. As they withdrew, they could see enemy soldiers swarming over the factory. The opportunity for E Company to escape had vanished.[37] No one would survive.

The situation was chaotic. The regiment had been sliced into segments, many no larger than platoons of twenty men that were forced to react as independent fighting units. Although Echternach fell briefly to the enemy, the 12th Regiment successfully defended surrounding towns, preventing the Germans from advancing to Luxembourg City and thereby saving the nation.

In the end, Hitler's offensive failed—not because it was ill planned or because the Allies outmaneuvered him but due to attrition. In the winter of 1944, the German army dealt the Allies a blow that nearly toppled them, with Salinger and his regiment receiving the lion's share of the punishment. But the Allies regained the ground they had lost because they had the ability to replace the fallen. The Germans did not. The troops and equipment lost by the Germans in places such as Echternach and the Ardennes doomed the counteroffensive to failure and sealed the fate of the Third Reich.

On December 27, Salinger and his men reentered the shell of what had once been Echternach, where, according to the division report, they predictably "found no sign of any human habitants." Within the town's ruins, Sergeant Salinger at last found the opportunity to write home. His family and friends had not heard from him since December 16, the first day of battle.* Since then, American newspapers had been bursting with news of the counteroffensive and Salinger's friends and family had begun to fear the worst.

During the struggle, Betty Yoder, an old friend of Salinger from Ursinus College, twice telegraphed Whit Burnett, asking for news. On December 31, she wrote, asking for "any information on Jerry Salinger." She knew that he was stationed "near Echternach," she said, and confided that although "He is a very valued friend," he would "scorn [her] for this letter."

Not until January did Miriam Salinger receive word from her son. Upon hearing the news of Salinger's safety from her, Whit Burnett was genuinely relieved and scrawled a memo in response to Yoder: "Salinger well. Letter and photo to his mother dated December 27th also manuscript to his agent."[38]

. . .

The deeds and trials of the 12th Infantry Regiment are more than mere footnotes to the life and work of J. D. Salinger. They are ingrained in his person and in the stories he crafted. Salinger the man and the events of war are as inseparable as the author and the works that he penned. Equally, incidents that happened to the 1st or 2nd Battalion or to C, F, or E Company are not merely examples of what could have occurred in Salinger's life; they are illustrations of what he actually endured. To know anything of the 4th Infantry Division during the Second World War is to realize that horror and bravery were the daily experience of all of its men.

When the Battle of the Bulge ended in January 1945, American troops of the 82nd Airborne Division crossed the border into the Hürtgen Forest, presumably on their way to Berlin. As they passed through the forest and into the Kall River Valley, they were forced to march on foot. The snows had begun to melt, and the mud of the trail

*Salinger was probably oblivious to the opening hours of the Battle of the Bulge when he penned his letter home and may have been with the 1st Battalion, on leave, on December 16 and not called into action until the following day.

made the valley impassable by jeeps. As they marched, the soldiers encountered scenes of horror. The melting snows revealed the corpses of thousands of American soldiers, many lying with arms frozen skyward as if in supplication.

. . .

The pain of loss dominates Salinger's seventh Caulfield story, "This Sandwich Has No Mayonnaise." No documentation exists to confirm exactly when this piece was written. Even after its publication by *Esquire* in October 1945,* no reference to the title can be found in any of the available correspondence of Salinger, Ober Associates, or Story Press. "Mayonnaise" is in all likelihood Salinger's third story written on the battlefield, under construction and yet unnamed in September 1944, and may contain elements of his unpublished 1944 story "A Boy Standing in Tennessee," which has vanished.

As "This Sandwich Has No Mayonnaise" opens, Sergeant Vincent Caulfield is at boot camp in Georgia, sitting aboard a truck along with thirty-three other GIs. It is late evening, and despite a downpour the men are bound for a dance in town. But there is a problem. Only thirty men are allowed to go to the dance, and the group aboard the truck contains four extra. The truck is delayed while the men wait for a lieutenant from Special Services to arrive and resolve the issue. As they wait, the conversation among the men reveals that Vincent is in charge of the group and therefore responsible for excluding the extra men.

In a stream-of-consciousness exploration of loneliness and nostalgia, the narrative concentrates less on what is happening on the truck than on what is going on in Vincent's mind. Vincent's younger brother, Holden, has been reported missing in action in the Pacific and is probably dead. Vincent is traumatized by the news and unable to concentrate on anything else.

While the men on the truck talk about home, where they come from, and what they did before the war, Vincent experiences a series of flashbacks. He sees himself at the 1939 World's Fair with his sister Phoebe as they visit the Bell Telephone exhibit. When they come out, they find Holden standing there. Holden asks Phoebe for her auto-

---

*"This Sandwich Has No Mayonnaise" was reprinted in *The Armchair Esquire, 1958 & 1960* (New York: G. P. Putnam's Sons, 1960), pp. 187–197.

graph, and Phoebe playfully punches him in the stomach, "happy to see him, happy he was her brother."[39] Amid the background conversation on the truck, Vincent's mind keeps leaping back to Holden. He sees him at Pentey Prep,* on the tennis court, and sitting on the porch at Cape Cod. How can Holden possibly be missing? Vincent refuses to believe that he is.

When the lieutenant arrives he is visibly annoyed. When he asks about the situation, Vincent feigns ignorance and pretends to count heads, all the while mentally scoffing at the lieutenant, the other men, and himself. He offers a movie to anyone willing to forgo the dance. Two soldiers skulk off into the night, but Vincent still has two men too many. Finally he makes a decision and orders the last two men to the left to leave the truck. One soldier dismounts and slips off. Vincent waits and finally notices another body emerge. As the figure enters the light, the image of a young boy is revealed. All eyes are fixed upon him as he stands in the drenching downpour. "I was on the list," the boy mutters, almost in tears. Vincent says nothing. In the end it is the lieutenant who orders the boy back into the truck and arranges for an extra girl at the party to match the extra man.

As the story ends, the men are on their way to the dance and Vincent is again lost in his thoughts of Holden. Overwhelmed, he pleads to his missing brother: "Just go up to somebody—and tell them you're Here—not Missing, not dead, not anything but Here."

A major thrust of "This Sandwich Has No Mayonnaise" is Vincent's inability to connect with either himself or those around him. The cause of Caulfield's disconnection is his refusal to take the extra step necessary to change it.

The boy's appearance is the climax of the story. Until that moment, readers are faced with a confusing juxtaposition of dialogue and events occurring simultaneously. Only when the boy emerges from the shadows is the reader's attention drawn to one solitary character. The only moment when the background dialogue ceases is when the reader is focused on the boy standing in the rain. The moment is surreal. Sal-

---

*Holden's boarding school is spelled Pentey in this story, as it is in "I'm Crazy," completed by early 1944. Like *The Catcher in the Rye*, "Slight Rebellion off Madison" spells the school Pencey; but because "Slight Rebellion" is known to have undergone several alterations before its publication in December 1946, it is uncertain what spelling Salinger originally used. As a result, the spelling of Holden's preparatory school cannot be used to determine the age of this story.

inger reinforces the sensation by casting it slowly. After traveling through Vincent's mental snapshots of his young brother, readers are naturally struck by this boy's image. A figure that appears from the darkness, he is vulnerable and distressed, seeking someone to guide him. He is the spirit of Holden Caulfield, a test to his brother. Vincent must take a step to make him complete. He must connect with this boy and recognize his brother within him. He must put his own pain aside and do a simple but symbolic thing: he must give up his spot on the truck.

He reaches out and turns up the boy's collar to protect him from the rain but then remains silent and does nothing. Moments later, the boy is gone from the scene and Vincent, aboard the truck once again, is completely submerged by his loss. He mentally babbles to Holden, telling him to stop whistling, stop wearing his robe to the beach, and sit up straight at the table.

If actually written during the closing months of 1944, during the weeks that encompassed Schnee Eifel and Hürtgen, "Mayonnaise" casts a particular light on its author. Grappling to deal with death, Salinger casts himself as Vincent Caulfield, who, mirroring his creator, remained torn between repressing his feelings and admitting the reality in which he was embroiled.

. . .

On New Year's Day 1945, Jerry Salinger turned twenty-six. Just a year before, he had been at Fort Holabird, awaiting deployment overseas. Now, from his camp in Luxembourg, before him lay the Sauer River and Germany beyond, the same boundary he had crossed three and a half months before on his way into Hürtgen.

On February 4, the 4th Infantry Division crossed the Siegfried Line at precisely the same place it had in September 1944. For most troops, this was a festive occasion, their first time on German soil. But for the few veterans like Salinger who had survived the first crossing, the event was dark with the memory of fallen friends. Haunted by the first incursion's outcome, Salinger reentered Germany wary and bitter. It is not hard to imagine him surrounded by the excitement of new recruits, whose jaunty eagerness must have fallen on his ears as obscenely as the words of Babe's frivolous news clippings.

With the division now largely motorized, its advance through Germany was swift. Making its way to the Rhine, it encountered resistance in towns such as Prüm and Oos, the same places Salinger would have engaged only months before; but it was becoming clear that Germany had lost the war and opposition would not reach the ferocity of Hürtgen. On March 30, Salinger and the 4th Division crossed the Rhine at Worms, from which they advanced southeast through Württemberg and into Bavaria.

Meanwhile, Salinger's professional voice was being heard back home. The March–April issue of *Story* magazine featured "Elaine," his study of unguarded beauty trampled underfoot. On March 31, Babe's exhausted prayer emerged from the trenches as "A Boy in France" was published in *The Saturday Evening Post*.

Throughout the final phase of the war, the 4th Division increasingly turned its attention from combat to the job of occupation. Freed of the daily struggle for survival, Salinger began to employ his counterintelligence training in each town the unit secured. Upon entering a town, he would survey all public buildings, especially those involving communication and transportation. Those would be shut down to prevent anyone from slipping in or sneaking out. To avert communication between the locals and the enemy, radio stations, telegraph centers, and post offices were occupied immediately. Salinger would confiscate their records, review them, and send them to division headquarters for further analysis.

Vital to Salinger's CIC role—and to the safety of the 12th Regiment—was his ability to communicate with the local populations in their own language. It was Salinger, for instance, who, on entering a town, would address its citizens and convey the regiment's rules and regulations to them. He would then screen the inhabitants, interviewing as many as possible in order to gather information and weed out threats to his fellow soldiers: plots of resistance and Nazis concealed within the population.

Perhaps the most interesting aspect of Salinger's intelligence duty was his mandate to arrest suspects and interrogate prisoners. The notion of J. D. Salinger rushing from house to house, seizing villains, and grilling them under naked lightbulbs might appear absurd to us today but that is exactly what happened. By all accounts, he performed his tasks with the same integrity he applied to his writing.[40]

. . .

The archives of Salinger's agent, Harold Ober Associates, contain a document dated April 10, 1945, that lists nineteen possible stories to be included in the proposed *Young Folks* anthology. The list includes all fifteen stories that Salinger himself suggested to Whit Burnett in September 1944 with the exception of "Soft-Boiled Sergeant." In addition, two stories are named that appear for the first time. They are "Daughter of the Late, Great Man" and "The Ocean Full of Bowling Balls."

"Daughter of the Late, Great Man" was never published, but the Ober document describes it as "Daughter of author gets Old Man."* Clearly, this story was about Oona O'Neill and Charlie Chaplin.

The remaining new story, "The Ocean Full of Bowling Balls," was held by Salinger until 1948, at which time he sold it to *Woman's Home Companion*. But the magazine's publisher found it depressing and refused to print it. Salinger then took back the story and, by 1950, had submitted it to *Collier's*. At *Collier's*, it was purchased by Knox Burger, who was the magazine's fiction editor. Unfortunately, the same publisher who had rejected the story at *Woman's Home Companion* was now working at *Collier's* and still objected to the story. By then it was late 1950 or early 1951; *The Catcher in the Rye* was awaiting publication, and Salinger changed his mind about releasing "Ocean." He reimbursed *Collier's* its fee and withdrew the story. "The Ocean Full of Bowling Balls" was never submitted for publication again.

There is a scene in "Seymour—an Introduction" in which Buddy Glass and his brother Seymour are playing marbles. Seymour stands, as Salinger relates, faultlessly "balanced," a smooth, symmetrical marble in hand, looking upon his brother with love. Seymour is about to instruct Buddy on releasing one's will, one's conscious self, in order to find the place of perfect connection.[41] This scene is similar to one that occurs between Kenneth Caulfield and his brother Vincent in "The Ocean Full of Bowling Balls." And though Salinger presents the scene

*Also handwritten at the bottom of this document is what appears to be an outline for the collection. It differs markedly from Burnett's suggestion that the anthology be split up into three sections that revolve around the war. Instead, Ober suggests they be categorized as "I. The Girl, II. The Boy, III. Holden's Story."

with Seymour as an instruction to readers on how to approach his works, those familiar with the "Ocean" tale recognize this parable as being its thrust and primary message.

"The Ocean Full of Bowling Balls" is the seventh of Salinger's Caulfield stories and one of his finest unpublished works. It portrays the last day in the life of Allie Caulfield, who in this story is named Kenneth. In "Ocean," readers witness the arrival of the author's most elevated character form to date. Kenneth Caulfield is Salinger's first enlightened child.

"The Ocean Full of Bowling Balls" takes place on Cape Cod. Vincent Caulfield, who narrates the story, is about eighteen. Also in the house are his parents, who are actors, his brother Kenneth, who is twelve, and his sister, Phoebe, who was born not long before the story takes place. Vincent's brother Holden is away at camp.

Vincent begins his narration with a description of his brother Kenneth. He paints a portrait of a thoughtful, sensitive, and intelligent boy, a child so curious that his shoes turned up as he was always bending down to investigate things on the ground. Vincent describes his brother's red hair, explaining that it was so vibrant as to be seen at a great distance. He relates a time when he was playing golf with Helen Beebers and became aware of his brother watching him from far off.

Kenneth had two great loves: literature and baseball. He married them by filling his lefty first baseman's mitt with lines of poetry that he could read while in the field. Holden has discovered a quote by Robert Browning on Kenneth's mitt, which Vincent relays:

> I would hate that death bandaged my eyes and forbore, and bade me creep past.

One Saturday afternoon in July, Vincent, who is a struggling writer, comes down from his room to the porch of the house where Kenneth is sitting and reading. In a solemn mood, Vincent coaxes his younger brother away from his book and tells him the story he has just written, a short tale titled "The Bowler."

"The Bowler" is a story of a man whose wife will not let him do anything he wanted. He cannot listen to sports on the radio, read cowboy magazines, or indulge any of his interests. The only thing his wife will let him do is go bowling, once a week, on Wednesday nights. So every Wednesday for eight years the man takes his bowling ball down from the closet and goes out. One day the man dies. His wife faithfully visits his grave every Monday to place gladioli on it. On one occasion, she happens to go on a Wednesday. On her husband's grave, she finds fresh violets. Calling the caretaker over, she asks who left the violets. The caretaker tells her that they were left by the same woman who leaves them every Wednesday, probably the dead man's wife. Infuriated, the woman goes home. That night, the neighbors hear the sound of crashing glass. The next morning they see a shiny, new-looking bowling ball sitting on the woman's lawn amid shards of broken windowpane.[42]

Kenneth's reaction to Vincent's story is not what Vincent anticipated. Upset by the ending, he accuses Vincent of taking revenge on a character who is now defenseless. Touched by his brother's sentimentality, Vincent destroys the story.

A child with "heart trouble," Kenneth is portrayed as being spontaneous, determined to live every moment to the full. He convinces his brother to take him to a place called Lassiter's for fresh steamers (clams). During the drive they have a conversation about Vincent's girlfriend, Helen Beebers. Kenneth tells Vincent that he ought to marry Helen as she has exceptional qualities. Among them is her tendency to play checkers without moving her kings from the back row. He asks Vincent about his love for Phoebe and Holden. Kenneth confides that while looking at his baby sister lying in her crib, he actually feels that he is her. He then chides Vincent for being reticent with displays of love.

After eating steamers at Lassiter's, Vincent instinctively feels that they should drive to a spot on the beach that Holden has christened "The Wise Guy Rock," a large, flat slab jutting into the ocean and accessed by a series of jumps from stone to stone. On the rock, they survey the water, which Vincent describes as being calm. There Kenneth reads a letter that he received that day from Holden. The letter is humorous and riddled with spelling errors. In it, he complains that the camp stinks and is full of rats. He then proceeds to expose the phoniness of the camp counselors in a series of amusing yet thoughtful tales.*

Kenneth then picks up a pebble, examining it for flaws. He wonders

*According to Jack Sublette in his 1984 annotated bibliography of J. D. Salinger, *Collier's* fiction editor, Knox Burger, stated in 1948 that "Ocean" "contains the greatest letter home from camp ever composed by man or boy."

aloud what will become of Holden, who cannot seem to compromise—even though he knows that life will go smoother for him if he does. Then Kenneth decides to go for a swim. This is against Vincent's better judgment. The sky grows dark, and the ocean becomes violent. He begins to discourage Kenneth from going into the water but soon feels compelled to allow him. Something inside Vincent realizes that he should not stop his brother, and he restrains himself. After his swim, when Kenneth is almost out of the water, he suddenly falls unconscious. Vincent scoops his body up from the beach and races him home, driving the first mile or so with the brakes on.

When he arrives at the house with Kenneth, Holden is sitting on the porch with his suitcases. He tries to revive his brother but is so clumsy in the attempt that it angers Vincent. They carry Kenneth's body into the house and call a doctor, who arrives shortly after their parents return home from rehearsals. At ten past eight that night, Kenneth dies. The story ends with Vincent explaining his motivation for telling it: he was seeking through narration to put his brother to rest. Kenneth has been with both himself and Holden since his death, haunting them throughout the war. Vincent feels that Kenneth should no longer be "hanging around."

There are two sentences within "The Ocean Full of Bowling Balls" that suggest a growing spiritual dimension to Salinger's work. Short and seemingly insignificant, they acknowledge an awareness of the interconnection of people through love and the power of human connection to transcend death.

Kenneth, in a moment of both disclosure and guidance, asks Vincent, "When you look in that crib they got Phoebe in, are you nuts about her? Don't you feel like you're even her?" Vincent claims that he understands his brother's sentiment, but Kenneth proceeds to lecture him on showing love without restraint. The line hints that Kenneth Caulfield has had an awakening at the crib side of his infant sister. Kenneth speaks not only of love for Phoebe but of the feeling of oneness, of sameness with her. This awareness has taught him the value of expressing love completely, without reservation, a consciousness that Vincent lacks. The experience also allows Kenneth to accept his own death, knowing that he will survive through his siblings. It is an expounded version of the experience that Babe had with Mattie, that the

Holden of "I'm Crazy" had at the crib side of his sister Viola and will have again with Phoebe in *The Catcher in the Rye.*

Kenneth is a symbol of balance. He is a figure of unity between poetry and prose, intellect and spirit, even life and death. When he picks up the pebble on the beach, the narrator tells us that he examined it for its symmetry, hoping to find it without flaws. The scene is a forerunner of Seymour teaching Buddy how to play marbles, not because of the stone but because of the balance and acceptance both scenes represent—the willingness to release in order to truly connect. Kenneth's time on Earth is ebbing away, and he thinks of Holden and Holden's inability to compromise, his lack of balance. When he is gone, Kenneth wonders, what will happen to Holden?

When Kenneth enters the water at "Wise Guy Rock," he knows he is about to die. Vincent tells us that he became triumphant and taunted death for its lack of real power over him. "If I were to die or something, you know what I would do?" Kenneth asks. "I'd stick around," he said. "I'd stick around a while." Salinger reinforces Kenneth's spiritual acceptance of death through Browning's poem much in the same way as he confirmed Babe's faith through the poems of Blake and Dickinson in "A Boy in France." His declaration of "sticking around" is in stark contrast to his brother Holden, who will later live in terror of "disappearing."

Perhaps the relative calm of the race through Germany in early 1945 enabled Salinger to begin dealing with what he had endured since D-Day. "The Ocean Full of Bowling Balls" shows the author grasping for a spiritual recourse to deny the existence of death, or at least its power. What Salinger could not have imagined at the time was that true hell had yet to come and that he stood only at its doorstep.

· · ·

It was Salinger's intelligence duties that delivered the final horrors of the war. Five months before, the Counter Intelligence Corps had compiled and disseminated a confidential report to its agents entitled *The German Concentration Camps.* The document named, described, and located fourteen major camps within greater Germany as well as more than a hundred connected subcamps. CIC officers were instructed that upon entering an area suspected of containing one of these camps, it was their duty to make straightaway for its location, where they were to assess the situation, interrogate the inmates, and file a report with headquarters. In addition, any troops not related to the CIC who encountered such places were to contact the nearest counterintelligence agents.

On April 22, after a surprisingly difficult fight for the town of Rothenberg, the path of Salinger's division brought it into a triangular region approximately 20 miles on each side, situated between the Bavarian cities of Augsburg, Landsberg, and Dachau. This territory held a series of 123 internment camps that together formed the Dachau concentration camp system, places whose stench, according to eyewitnesses, could be smelled 10 miles away. As the 12th Regiment swarmed into the area at the end of April 1945, it inevitably came upon those camps.

On Monday, April 23, Salinger and his regiment were in Aalen and Ellwangen, villages recognized by the United States Holocaust Memorial Museum as having contained a subcamp of Dachau. On April 26, the 12th reported from Horgau, where another Dachau subcamp was located. On April 27, the regiment stood on the west bank of the Lech River across from the city of Augsburg, the site of two more camps.

On April 28, after traveling through Augsburg, Salinger was likely stationed at Bobingen, the site of both division and regimental headquarters, just 12 and 9 miles north of the infamous camps at Landsberg and Kaufering IV.

On April 30, the day Hitler killed himself in Berlin, the 12th Regiment crossed the Amper River at Wildenroth, midway between Landsberg and the main death camp at Dachau. This route brought Salinger's division through the area of Haunstetten, the site of one of the largest subcamps in all of Germany and the location of a huge Messerschmitt factory worked by slave labor.

At the time most of Salinger's fellow soldiers were baffled by what they had discovered. Sensing the war was at a close and convinced that they had already witnessed the worst, the unit was blindsided by the atrocities that now rose up around them. Even the daily regimental reports were unbelieving, slow to acknowledge that they were not freeing ordinary prisoners of war. On April 23, division headquarters noted that "The 12th Infantry Regiment reported the location of an Allied Prisoner of War camp containing approximately 350 prisoners."

Five days later, on April 28, the report recorded that "A French Prisoner of War Inclosure [*sic*] with 60 French soldiers was reported by the
12th Infantry."

A deeper description of the surreal scenes that Salinger was forced
to process can be found in the personal diary of an average soldier, a
member of the 552nd Field Artillery Battalion, which was attached to
the 12th Infantry Regiment during the closing weeks of April 1945.

> When the gates swung open we got our first look at the prison-
> ers. Many of them were Jews. They were wearing black and
> white striped prison suits and round caps. A few had shredded
> blanket rags draped over their shoulders. . . . The prisoners
> struggled to their feet after the gates were opened. They shuf-
> fled weakly out of the compound. They were like skeletons—all
> skin and bones.[43]

In 1992, the 4th Infantry Division was recognized by the U.S.
Army as a liberating unit of Nazi concentration camps, and it is evident
that J. D. Salinger was called upon to take part in the liberation of victims of the Dachau concentration camp system. Like so many who encountered such scenes during the war, Salinger has never spoken
directly of his experiences, and we cannot be certain of exactly what his
intelligence duties demanded of him in these places. The subcamps of
Dachau liberated by Salinger's division were Horgau-Pfersee, Aalen,
Ellwagen, Haunstetten, Turkenfald, and Wolfrathausen.[44]

In Bavaria, Salinger's fragile ties to normalcy were strained to the
point of rending, while at the same time his pockets burned with pages
of *The Catcher in the Rye,* with their scenes of children ice skating
and little girls in soft blue dresses. During that chilly April of 1945,
J. D. Salinger was changed forever, a witness not only to the carnage of
innocents but to the mutilation of everything he cherished and had
clung to for sanity. It was a nightmare that, once entered, created an
indelible pain. "You could live a lifetime," he mourned, "and never
really get the smell of burning flesh out of your nose."[45]

. . .

When the Second World War ended on May 8, 1945, J. D. Salinger
had served in the army for more than three years. Since mid-1943, he

had consistently expressed a longing to return home to New York and
civilian life. Even before entering combat, he claimed to have given up
on finding happiness until after the war and was uncertain how much
of his former life would remain.[46] He had entered the army anxious to
serve, believing the surroundings would afford him the leisure to write
at will. Three years on, he was jaded and bitter over the realities he had
encountered. The scars, both physical and psychological, would remain with him for the rest of his life. Hurling himself for cover, he had
broken his nose, a disfigurement he refused to repair. The sound of explosions had stolen much of his hearing, and by war's end he was par-
tially deaf. Constant combat served to cut him off from his own
feelings and left no time to deal with the horror he had lived through.
As the war began to wane, new atrocities arose to haunt him. Unlike
most of the soldiers he had originally embarked with, from D-Day to
VE Day, he had somehow managed to survive. Throughout the war,
he had conducted himself with professionalism. His service had been
honorable. He had never let his men down, crumbled under pressure,
or failed to deliver in times of need. But by May 8, he had given everything. Now drained, there could be no one more anxious for the discharge due him. The war was over, and it was time to go home.

But Salinger did not go home. On May 10, the U.S. Army established Counter Intelligence Corps Detachment 970 to assist in the Allied occupation and conduct the "denazification" of Germany. Instead
of being discharged, Salinger was reassigned to this detachment for the
next six months and moved, along with other CIC agents, to Weis-
senburg, outside the city of Nuremberg. He had already written home,
warning that his war might continue for some time.[47] It meant that he
was parting company with the 12th Infantry Regiment, which had
been his home for more than a year. Now among strangers, the events
and emotions that combat had held at bay, "those that were not potentially and thankfully void," as Babe had grieved in "A Boy in France,"
"began to trickle back into his mind." When the soldiers of the 12th
were discharged and he was left behind to deal with his memories, he
began to sink into despair.

On May 13, about the time of his reassignment, Salinger wrote to
Elizabeth Murray. The letter shows him dejected, expressing his resentment toward the army and its conduct of the war. He was distraught over the horrors he had lived through and haunted by the dead

whom he had known. His own survival might have been nearly miraculous, but it carried with it a guilt particular to the survivors of war. "It's been a mess Elizabeth," he told Murray. "Wonder if you have any idea."[48]

In times past Salinger had turned to writing to ease his pain and express inner feelings difficult to convey in daily life. During the war, when he found trouble expressing himself through prose, he turned to poetry.

In 1945 alone, he submitted at least fifteen poems to *The New Yorker*—so many that the editors started to complain.[49] Regardless of the method employed, he had always used writing to deal with difficult emotions. It would have been natural for him now to render his feelings and experiences into a war novel. Many who knew him, Whit Burnett not the least among them, expected that he would do exactly this. But they were to be disappointed. After depictions of combat in "The Magic Foxhole" and "A Boy in France," Salinger reverted to observing Babe's oath in "Last Day of the Last Furlough" and chose "never to speak of it again." Yet he did recognize the need for such a novel. In an interview with *Esquire* released that October with "This Sandwich Has No Mayonnaise," he made it clear that he, however, was not ready to author it:

> So far the novels of this war have had too much of the strength, maturity and craftsmanship critics are looking for, and too little of the glorious imperfections which teeter and fall off the best minds. The men who have been in this war deserve some sort of trembling melody rendered without embarrassment or regret. I'll watch out for that book.[50]

. . .

In the summer of 1945, Jerry Salinger's war experiences, extended service, sudden loneliness, and reluctance to express his pain converged upon him with disastrous effect. As the weeks wore on, his depression deepened and his feelings began to immobilize him. He had seen many cases of battle fatigue on the front, what we would now call post-traumatic stress disorder, and recognized the potential menace of his current state of mind. In July he voluntarily checked himself into a general hospital in Nuremberg for treatment.

Most of what we know about Salinger's hospitalization is derived from a July 27 letter he wrote to Ernest Hemingway from the hospital. Addressed to "Poppa," it began by openly confessing that he had been "in an almost constant state of despondency" and wanted to talk to someone professional before it got out of hand. During his stay, the staff had peppered him with questions: What was his childhood like? How was his sex life? Did he like the army? Salinger had given a sarcastic answer to each question—except for the one about the army. That query he had answered with an unambiguous "yes." He had the Holden Caulfield novel in mind when he gave the answer, explaining to Hemingway he was afraid of the impact a psychological discharge might have on how the book would be perceived.

It was a splendid letter, and the wit of Holden Caulfield leapt off its pages. "There are very few arrests left to be made in our section," he writes. "We're now picking up children under ten if their attitudes are snotty." He also claimed that his mother had walked him to school until he was twenty-four, due to the danger of the New York streets. There are also moments of sadness as Salinger conveys his hope of traveling to Vienna to find the family he lived with in 1937. Also apparent is a need for affirmation. At times, his tone is nearly pleading. Will Hemingway please write to him? Can Hemingway possibly find the time to visit him in New York? Is there anything Salinger can do for him? In his fragile state Salinger was reaching out to a friend, one whom he perceived to share both his wartime experiences and his literary commitment. "The talks I had with you here," he told Hemingway, "were the only hopeful minutes of the whole business."[51]

Salinger seems to have suspected that Hemingway was troubled and in need of support. He twice asked if Hemingway was really working on a novel, as if doubting the information. As for himself, Salinger reported having written "a couple more stories," a number of poems, and part of a play about Holden Caulfield. A curious section of the letter is Salinger's news about the *Young Folks* anthology. He told Hemingway that the venture had "collapsed" yet again, and though he claimed not to be bitter about the situation, he then proceeded to describe just how bitter he was.

Perhaps Salinger's most judicious words were reserved for the topic of F. Scott Fitzgerald. As usual, Salinger defended Fitzgerald against the critics, stating that the beauty of Fitzgerald's writings was most applicable to his personal shortcomings. According to Salinger, however, Fitzgerald was about to ruin his novel *The Last Tycoon* when he died, and it was perhaps best that he had never finished it—possibly the harshest criticism of Fitzgerald that Salinger ever delivered.

At the time Salinger entered the hospital, he had already attempted some form of self-therapy by employing the old "abracadabra that had always worked before." In late spring or early summer, he wrote the eighth and last of his Caulfield stories, a work that was published as "The Stranger," in which his alter ego, Babe Gladwaller, returns home after the war, suffering from very much the same symptoms that Salinger was experiencing.

. . .

"The Stranger" is easy to date. On July 27, Salinger told Hemingway that he had completed at least two more stories that he jokingly called "incestuous." There can be little doubt that the reference relates to "The Stranger." Hemingway had read Salinger's first story about Babe and Mattie, and it requires no gift of insight to imagine him poking fun at the degree of closeness between brother and sister.

Narrated in the third person, "The Stranger" contains a memorial to the dead of the 12th Infantry Regiment, who are represented by Vincent Caulfield. It has a redemptive ending comparable in delicacy to that of "A Boy in France," whose message runs parallel to most Caulfield stories by offering hope through the appreciation of beauty through innocence. The story is also a strong forerunner of "For Esmé—with Love and Squalor." Both demonstrate rejuvenation through the power of human connection and offer a similar hope to similar characters under similar circumstances.

It is a sad element of "The Stranger" that Salinger cast it back home in New York. There was probably no other place where he would have rather been when he wrote it. Yet Babe Gladwaller, who is once again the story's main character, is unable to adjust to civilian life after his wartime experiences. This is the same Babe Gladwaller who was broken and battered in France. Since then he has suffered the anguish of the Hürtgen Forest and the Battle of the Bulge. It was at Hürtgen that Babe's friend Vincent Caulfield was killed. And this is the premise of the story. Babe has gone to the apartment of Vincent's former girl-friend, Helen Beebers, to give her a poem written by Vincent and to share the circumstances of Vincent's death. The act is a form of therapy for Babe but one so painful he cannot accomplish it alone. For strength and spiritual direction, he is accompanied by his little sister, Mattie.

When they arrive at Helen's, Babe's eyes are bloodshot and weepy, and he sneezes incessantly. Yet it is his state of mind that most needs healing. Babe's return to New York only amplifies the extent to which he has been altered. Physically, he is home, but his mind is still imprisoned in a place of death. Every common act takes Babe back to the ghosts of dead soldiers, "to the music of the unrecoverable years; the little, unhistorical, pretty good years when all the dead boys in the 12th Regiment had been living and cutting in on other dead boys on lost dance floors: the years when no one who could dance worth a damn had ever heard of Cherbourg or Saint Lo, or Hurtgen Forest or Luxembourg."[52]

When Babe first meets Helen, he is struck by her beauty, but his visit is one of obligation. His duty is to recount the specifics of the death of Vincent Caulfield, to omit nothing or embellish any of its details. Vincent was standing with Babe and a handful of other soldiers in the Hürtgen Forest, warming their hands by a fire, when a mortar suddenly exploded in their midst. Vincent was hit. Taken to the medic tent, he died within three minutes of being struck, without last words but with his eyes wide open.*

It may seem improper for Babe to take his twelve-year-old sister on an excursion whose purpose is to describe a death. Ostensibly, Mattie and Babe are on their way to a matinee, but more directly her presence is necessary to keep Babe grounded. At Babe's side, Mattie is a figure of integrity. Babe needs a physical reminder of her childlike perception in order to stay on target and deliver a complete description of Vincent's death unmodified by adult embellishments.

After exorcizing the ghosts of his memories, Babe and Mattie are presented walking toward Central Park. Babe's telling of Vincent's story has relieved him of a burden, but there remains a gnawing sadness inside him. With the intuition of a child, Mattie asks her brother, "Are you glad to be home?"

---

*The senseless manner of Vincent's death was doubtless the basis of the death of Walt Glass in Salinger's 1948 story "Uncle Wiggily in Connecticut."

"Yes, baby," Babe answers. ". . . Why do you ask me that?" Suddenly the small things of life, previously muted, rise into focus, and Babe enters the beauty of the present moment. When Mattie brags that she can eat with chopsticks, Babe gives a simple but significant reply. "Kiddo," he says, "that's something I'll have to see." The statement is a promise, the first time Babe actually looks forward. Up to this point in the story, all of Babe's thoughts and words have referred to the past.

At the story's conclusion, Mattie does something common to children that Babe finds remarkable because he is seeing it as if for the first time.

She skips from street to curb and back again. About this action, Babe addresses the reader for the only time in the story, asking, "Why was it such a beautiful thing to see?" The answer to Babe's question is the same answer that readers encounter at the end of *The Catcher in the Rye.* Mattie's skipping is beautiful for the same reason that Holden cries at the carousel. After all that Babe has been through, he still retains the ability to recognize beauty and to appreciate innocence. His soul is alive.

. . .

During the Second World War, countless soldiers suffered what is now referred to as post-traumatic stress disorder. But the condition was not accepted in 1945, condemning most soldiers to suffer in silence. After the war, these soldiers were discharged and returned home, where they melted into the population and dealt secretly with their demons.

Unlike many such veterans, Salinger was able to do something about the horror he had witnessed and the effect it had upon him. He eventually rediscovered the power to write. He wrote about and for all of the soldiers who could not find the words themselves. Through his writings, he sought answers to the questions that his service experiences had exposed, questions of life and death, of God, of what we are to each other.

The insight that Holden finds at the Central Park carousel is the same that finally soothed Salinger's reaction to the war. After realizing this, they both fell silent—never to speak of it again. It is, therefore, with J. D. Salinger and the Second World War in mind that we should read Holden's parting words in *The Catcher in the Rye:* "Don't ever tell anybody anything. If you do, you start missing everybody."

All the dead soldiers.

6. Purgatory

After leaving the hospital Salinger sought normality and comfort. If forced to remain in Germany after the war, he was determined to carve out a life that resembled as closely as possible the one he imagined building had he returned home.

Shortly after VE Day, Salinger applied to Counter Intelligence for transfer to Vienna.[1] It was his dream to return to Austria and find the family he had lived with seven years earlier in the hope of reestablishing the bond he had shared with the daughter. As unrealistic as the scenario was, Salinger expressed his intention clearly, ignoring the reality that the war had changed life irrevocably. Counter Intelligence refused Salinger's request, assigning him to the Nuremberg area instead. However, it appears that he traveled to Vienna regardless and sought out his cherished Austrian family.

The details of what Salinger encountered in Vienna are unclear, but he soon returned to Germany. It is likely that the circumstances of his story "A Girl I Knew" mirror actual events. If so, Salinger arrived in Vienna only to learn that every family member had perished in the concentration camps, including the girl with whom he had had his first romance. The enormity of this tragic ending is why "A Girl I Knew" likely recounts fact. Salinger's intense feelings for this family make it inconceivable that he imposed such a fate upon them through fabrication.

Certainly, Salinger returned from Austria shaken. The deaths of these people, whom he idealized, confirmed that every aspect of his former life had been shattered by the war. If any event proved the impossibility of Babe's final wish in "Last Day of the Last Furlough" to return "home" to a place identical to the one he had left, it was Salinger's own return to Vienna. In reaction, he seized the first chance for happiness that became available, even though it ran contrary to his better judgment.

That September, Salinger shocked his family and friends with the announcement that he was getting married. He told them he had met a Frenchwoman named Sylvia and she had spellbound him. Salinger described her as being "very sensitive" and "very fine." This vague description satisfied no one. After writing stories such as "The Children's Echelon," with stern pronouncements against the irresponsibility of wartime marriages, his decision struck home with a thud. Salinger's mother was especially incredulous. She had expected her son home by now. Instead, he was remaining overseas and marrying a foreign woman he barely knew.

By December 1945, Salinger had constructed a new life in Germany. He and Sylvia had married on October 18, in the village of Pappenheim, and had since moved into a pleasant house about 25 miles south of Nuremberg in the town of Gunzenhausen. He had bought himself a new car, a two-seater Škoda. To complete the idyll, the couple was joined by a dog, a black schnauzer that Salinger named Benny. Christmas Day found the new family happy and content, feasting on a giant holiday turkey. He and Sylvia enjoyed taking rides in the new car with Benny riding along "on the running board, pointing out Nazis to arrest."[2] In short, Salinger had built in Germany the happy life being experienced by countless soldiers who had returned home to the United States. It was a life that resembled a postwar, semi-Germanic Norman Rockwell illustration to excess, and it was an illusion. Within a year, the house would be gone, the Škoda sold, and the marriage over.

Salinger kept details about Sylvia a mystery, especially to his family. With his friends, most of whom learned of the marriage through his mother, Salinger was even less forthcoming. They recalled Sylvia as being a psychologist or perhaps an osteopath. Others were even less sure. Salinger himself said that she had been a mail carrier, but that comment was plainly sarcastic.

Sylvia was born Sylvia Louise Welter in Frankfurt am Main, Germany, on April 19, 1919.[3] An ophthalmologist by profession, she spoke four languages and, as a recent university graduate, certainly outstripped her new husband in formal education.* At five feet, five inches, with a milky-light complexion and brown hair and eyes, Sylvia was vibrant and attractive. Salinger would later claim that she had "bewitched" him and held powers—dark and sensual—that cast a spell over him.[4] It seems that the same aura of mysticism that seeped into Salinger's writings also entered his first marriage. He claimed that their bond bordered on telepathic.[5] Certainly, their relationship was highly charged, both sexually and emotionally. But her nationality was an obstacle. In 1945, American service members were forbidden to marry German nationals. So Salinger presented Sylvia with a counterfeit passport as an engagement gift, granting her bogus French citizenship in the process.†

As if his marriage to the enigmatic Sylvia were not shock enough for his family, when he was discharged from the army in November, he chose to remain in Germany. Once again, the decision ran contrary to what he had long professed. After three and a half years away from home—two of those years overseas—he finally had the opportunity to return to New York. It had been his sustaining dream for years, but when it was finally within reach, he ignored it.

Apparently the desire of Babe Gladwaller to return home to the security and love of his family had been replaced by apprehension. Salinger explained to Elizabeth Murray that his perception of life had changed, that he now saw the world as being divided between those who had shared the anguish of war and those who were "too civilian." He admitted having been in the army too long, seen too much, be-

---

*Records show that Sylvia was fluent in German, English, French, and Italian. Her university dissertation paper ("Unmittelbare Kreislaufwirkungen des Apomorphins") is still available in the National Library at Frankfurt am Main. On July 28, 1956, she moved to the United States, eventually marrying a successful automotive engineer and settling in Michigan. She devoted much of her life to her medical practice, which included glaucoma research. Upon the death of her husband in 1988, Sylvia dedicated her remaining years to caring for the elderly and died on July 16, 2007, after being cared for in the same nursing home where she herself had worked.

†Sylvia's "French" passport was found among her belongings upon her death, as were numerous articles about J. D. Salinger and a number of clippings about Joyce Maynard.

come too complete a soldier to return to the comfort of civilian life that he had once craved.[6]

If Salinger felt unready to return home in 1945, he could console himself with the assurance that there was still work to be done in Germany. The government offered lucrative packages to CIC agents who were prepared to continue their activities. Sylvia too was a compelling incentive for him to remain. It was also possible that he had developed a strong emotional interest in the work he was doing. It was important work that might well have appealed to his sense of duty. After the exposure of the Nazi death camps at the end of April and his distress over the murder of his Austrian family, what Salinger had already acknowledged as his "personal war"[7] may have become very personal, indeed. When his official term of service ended, he signed a contract with the Department of Defense and continued serving Detachment 970 as a civilian.

Salinger served with Detachment 970 for almost a year, from its inception in May 1945 until his contract expired in April 1946. During this time he was responsible for locating and arresting war criminals within the American zone of occupation. Agents were guided by "automatic arrest" lists, which included former Nazi leaders, Gestapo troops, military officers, and anyone suspected of war crimes. In the first ten months following the war, Detachment 970 arrested more than 120,000 suspects in Germany alone, 1,700 of them accused of atrocities in connection with the concentration camps, mainly Dachau.[8]

Salinger was part of Team 63, serving in Sector VI, which included the city of Nuremberg. It was here that the International Military Tribunal was established and where top Nazi officials were put on trial in November 1945. It is unclear whether Salinger was connected with the war crimes tribunal, but his assignment to Nuremberg as an interrogator and translator makes this probable. In any case, Salinger reported to the Joint Allied Control Center, which had been established near his home and where an interrogation center was located that held more than 8,000 high-profile members of the Nazi SS.

In addition to cleansing his sector of war criminals and questioning former Gestapo members, Salinger would have been involved in the repatriation of refugees—at least to the degree of distinguishing actual expatriates from Nazis in victims' clothing. The Nuremberg area contained a number of large camps for displaced persons, called DP camps, which housed former prisoners of war, victims of concentration camps, displaced slave laborers, those whose homes had been destroyed, and large numbers of orphans. For such work, Salinger was especially well suited.

Trouble soon erupted in Salinger's marriage. The passion that had drawn the couple together transformed into confrontation. Theirs was a union of extremes. When they were happy, they were ecstatic; but when they disagreed, the aggression became vicious. Both were stubborn and obstinate, and it was not long before they began to clash. Salinger's penchant toward gloomy sarcasm and Sylvia's apparent intractability would prove the couple's undoing.

Around this time, Salinger began to show signs of estrangement, chronically avoiding communication with people he had known for years. An avid letter writer all his life, when he married Sylvia, he suddenly stopped corresponding with family and friends. Apart from infrequent notes to his mother, Salinger's letters home ceased and he habitually ignored those he received. His disregard became an ongoing joke within the Salinger family, but his friends assumed something had happened to him; some even feared he was dead. After sending numerous letters and receiving no reply, one friend was so convinced that Salinger had met a foul end that she contacted his mother in desperation. After Miriam gave the woman the Gunzenhausen address, she wrote expressing her relief, congratulating him on his marriage. Though this letter is available to researchers, Salinger's reply is not, if he answered it at all.

Not all of Salinger's friends were as lucky or so resourceful. In March, Basil Davenport (who was an editor at the Book-of-the-Month Club) finally got in touch after months of effort:

> Well, for God's sake, it's nice to know you're alive at least! You may not believe it, but it's the truth that I was honestly worried about you. . . . I wrote a couple of letters to your military address and got no answer; then I saw a story of yours in *Collier's* and wrote you care of them; then, still not hearing, I found a name that looked like yours in the New York telephone book, and called a number of times to make inquiries.[9]

In April 1946, Salinger's contract with the Counter Intelligence Corps came to an end. After spending a week in Paris, where he obtained immigration papers for Sylvia, the couple proceeded to the port of Brest. There, on April 28, they boarded the USS *Ethan Allen,* a naval vessel bound for New York. On May 10, after four long years of war, Salinger finally arrived home at Park Avenue with Sylvia and Benny.[10]

Exactly how he imagined he could live with his new wife in his parents' apartment is a mystery. Sylvia and Miriam locked horns immediately. Lost in the strangeness of her husband's world and unable to live under Miriam's scornful domination, by mid-July Sylvia had returned to Europe and soon filed for divorce. Benny remained. The very existence of Salinger's first wife quickly became a forbidden subject within the Salinger family, along with Miriam's parents and assorted great-grandfathers. For the rest of his life Salinger would resurrect the subject of Sylvia when he found it convenient, either to mock her severity or to talk of her magnetism. But others were never allowed to broach the subject to him uninvited.

. . .

When Sylvia left for Europe, Salinger judiciously traveled to Florida to avoid the possible gloating of his family. On July 13, while staying at the Sheraton Plaza Hotel in Daytona, he wrote to Elizabeth Murray about the collapse of his marriage. He and Sylvia had made each other miserable, he said, and he was relieved to see the relationship end. He also confessed that he had not written a word in the eight months they were together.

In Florida, he managed to complete his first story since early 1945. He considered the piece unusual and named it "The Male Goodbye." Now lost, some researchers believe it was an early draft of "A Perfect Day for Bananafish." There is another possibility: the University of Texas possesses a six-page typewritten manuscript called "Birthday Boy," written by Salinger shortly after his breakup with Sylvia. Relaying the disintegration of a doomed relationship, "Birthday Boy" may actually be an early draft of "The Male Goodbye."

"Birthday Boy" is set in a hospital, where a young man named Ray*

---

*This is the first of three successive main characters whom Salinger will name Ray. The Ray of "Birthday Boy" will be followed by Ray Kinsella in "A Young Girl in 1941 with No Waist at All" and Raymond Ford in "The Inverted Forest." Each of these characters is portrayed as being alcoholic. This is an interesting trend in Salinger's writings but one whose significance remains obscure.

is visited by his girlfriend, Ethel. It is Ray's twenty-second birthday, a fact of which his father, who had previously visited, had been unaware. Ray is spending the day as we suspect he has for quite some time, in a hospital bed. While most of Ethel and Ray's initial interaction avoids the reason for Ray's hospitalization, it soon becomes apparent that he is undergoing rehabilitation for alcoholism. Ethel attempts to make pleasant small talk and read to Ray at his bedside, but he is uninterested. Ray is the embodiment of cynicism. After feigning sexual interest in Ethel with a playful grope, he pressures her to sneak in "a lousy drop" of liquor by hiding it in a perfume bottle. When Ethel refuses, Ray's true colors emerge and he curses her in front of the doctor, telling her, "If you come back here, I'll kill you."[11]

Ethel is portrayed as sweet and long-suffering, while in contrast Ray is consumed by selfishness. He is abusive, impenitent, and completely controlled by his addiction. Salinger leaves no room for readers to take sides in this story; "Birthday Boy" contains no fat-faced peony. Perhaps it is too late for Ethel, just as it appears to be too late for Ray. As Ethel boards the hospital elevator, it "descended with a draft. Chilling [her] in all the damp spots." Her misery is complete. Having left Ray's room, her stoic cheeriness dissolves and she begins to sob. Yet Ray has not depleted all of the reader's condemnation. Some remains for Ethel. Her refusal to recognize the extent of Ray's disease and to bury the corpse of their relationship earns her a share of scorn. We realize that Ethel and Ray's relationship is doomed. We also realize that Ray's alcoholism has infected him with alienation and a callousness that may be contagious. Ethel's denial of these facts and her insistence upon pursuing her own illusions will be her certain downfall. Readers have no doubt that, despite Ray's warning, she will be back the next day.

"Birthday Boy" is an unusually short story and one that remains unpolished. It offers neither enlightenment nor redemption. It is an expression of sheer sourness, a tart splatter of forlorn rage. However, it is probably dangerous to read its characters as autobiographical. If the figure of Ethel was inspired by Sylvia, the character of Ray must be based upon Salinger. If so, it demonstrates a degree of self-hatred that was uncharacteristic of the author and sympathy toward Sylvia that was unlikely.

The probability is that "Birthday Boy" was never intended to be a great story. After the stress of war and eight months of silence, writing it was accomplishment enough. Plainly, Salinger had difficulty locating his previous literary levels, and for the next year and a half he would struggle to rediscover his touch. Ironically, like Ethel's in "Birthday Boy," Salinger's problem was one of denial. Even though the war still raged within him, he avoided writing about it. Salinger would not develop as an author until he found the strength to engage with the ramifications of war.

. . .

The previous July, Salinger had revealed with some annoyance that his plan to release a short-story collection had collapsed. The circumstances of this disappointment are unclear, but considering the anthology's turbulent history, the episode is not surprising. By December 1945, the book deal was back on track and Burnett had once again recommitted to publishing the collection.

In the months between July and November 1945, Salinger had again pulled out his Caulfield story "I'm Crazy" and submitted it for publication. This time, it was offered to *Collier's*, which accepted it immediately and published the story on December 22, three weeks after renaming and publishing "The Stranger." Salinger's motives for sending "I'm Crazy" to *Collier's* and Burnett's reaction to this can only be guessed at, but it is perhaps more than a coincidence that around the time of the story's acceptance by *Collier's*, the two men renewed their agreement to publish the *Young Folks* anthology. Moreover, the records of Story Press indicate that Salinger had agreed to a new contract by early 1946 and had been paid an advance of $1,000.

The archives of Story Press contain a document listing nineteen stories agreed upon by Salinger and Burnett for possible inclusion in the collection.* Although the Story Press list is dated 1946, it appears to have originated late in 1945, while Salinger was still living in Germany, since it announces that "J. D. Salinger has just had two stories accepted, and one is being marketed by his agent." The two stories can

---

*They are "Daughter of the Late, Great Man," "Elaine," "The Last and Best of the Peter Pans," "Both Parties Concerned," "The Long Debut of Lois Taggett," "Bitsy," "The Young Folks," "I'm Crazy," "A Boy Standing in Tennessee," "Once a Week Won't Kill You," "Last Day of the Last Furlough," "Soft-Boiled Sergeant," "The Children's Echelon," "Two Lonely Men," "A Boy in France," "Young Man in a Stuffed Shirt," "The Magic Foxhole," "Slight Rebellion off Madison," and "The Ocean Full of Bowling Balls."

only be "I'm Crazy" and "The Stranger," both published in *Collier's* in December 1945.

Handwritten at the bottom of this document are plans by Burnett to include promotional blurbs by himself, fellow editors Jesse Stuart of *Collier's,* William Maxwell of *The New Yorker,* and Stuart Rose of *The Saturday Evening Post,* alongside endorsements of Salinger's talents by the authors William Saroyan and Ernest Hemingway. In addition, mention was to be made of Salinger's upcoming novel, which, according to Story Press, was one-third done.

In a letter sent to Salinger in Germany, Whit Burnett finally revealed his intention for the *Young Folks* anthology to fill the gap between Salinger's short stories and his eventual novel—Burnett's actual object of desire. He admitted that the aim of the collection was to create greater interest in Salinger among the reading public and to generate anticipation of the Holden Caulfield book. With Burnett's cards on the table, and the $1,000 advance in hand, Salinger returned to the United States in 1946 assured of the anthology's publication. According to Burnett, the book was a done deal.

Soon after Salinger had returned home (and probably about the same time that his marriage was disintegrating), Burnett invited him to lunch at the Vanderbilt Hotel on Park Avenue and East 34th Street. The editor had bad news. Lippincott Press, which was to finance Salinger's collection, had turned the book down, and Story Press alone was unable to finance the project. Despite Burnett's promises, there would be no *Young Folks* anthology.

Salinger was furious. He felt used, not only by an editor but also by a friend. He never forgave Whit Burnett for what he perceived to be deception. The long and, at times, taxing relationship between the two men ended that afternoon. Salinger became convinced of the treachery of editors everywhere. After his experiences with *The New Yorker* over "Slight Rebellion off Madison" and *The Saturday Evening Post*'s changing his story titles, Burnett's apparent betrayal only reinforced what Salinger had already suspected. He would remain suspicious of editorial methods and motives for the rest of his career.

The dispute also affected Whit Burnett. As late as 1963, the clash remained fresh in his mind and he still sought to reverse the outcome. Even at that late date, he begged Dorothy Olding to clarify the circumstances of the failed book deal to her client. "Despite all our screaming," Burnett claimed, "Lippincott had the final veto . . . and all we could do was take their final judgment." He went on to explain that Story Press "almost broke with Lippincott at the time because they wouldn't take this book."[12] Salinger would have none of it. What made him feel especially foolish at the time was the fact that he had turned down another book offer while holding out for Burnett. In September 1945, he had received an alternative proposal from Don Congdon, who had been his editor at *Collier's* and had since moved to the publishing house of Simon and Schuster. Congdon approached Salinger, anxious to publish a collection of his stories. Salinger liked Congdon and was tempted to sign on to the project but, after hearing from other Simon and Schuster officials, became wary of their tone. "He thought they were a 'smart-ass' publisher," Congdon explained.[13] After his experiences over the *Young Folks* anthology, Salinger admitted not feeling up to the risk at that time.[14]

Angry with Burnett and bitter over the way he had been treated, Salinger committed another in a series of irrational acts. He took what he had completed of the Holden Caulfield novel and submitted it for publication as a ninety-page novella. Information on this is scant, and we know of it only through William Maxwell, who heard the account from Salinger in 1951. Maxwell indicated only that the manuscript had not been presented to *The New Yorker*.[15] Yet it is reasonable to assume that this original form of *The Catcher in the Rye* was submitted to Simon and Schuster. At the time of his fallout with Burnett, Salinger had grown close to Don Congdon. If he wanted to submit the abbreviated version of *Catcher* for publication—with *The New Yorker* and Story Press out of the equation—Congdon, and Simon and Schuster, would have been the logical choice.

Spite was not the sole reason for offering the ninety-page *Catcher*. After working on the novel for six years, he was becoming exasperated with it. Experiencing difficulty writing even the shortest of stories after the war, the prospect of producing a novel now seemed slight. In his interview with *Esquire* the previous October, Salinger had admitted doubts that he was capable of completing the novel. He confessed himself to be a short-story writer rather than a novelist; or, as he had put it, "a dash man and not a miler."[16]

Salinger's judgment soon returned, and he realized how impulsive he had been to send off *Catcher* incomplete. He quickly retracted the manuscript and recommitted himself, at least emotionally, to its completion. But it had been a close call. He also turned once more to short-story writing and in the closing months of 1946 began to resemble the dedicated author he had been before 1945. The outbreak of impulsiveness that had begun with the end of the war and his marriage to Sylvia had come to an end.

. . .

By November 1946, Salinger had finished his first substantial story since writing "The Stranger" a year and a half before. Through it, he sought to turn back the clock to before the war and its disoriented aftermath. "A Young Girl in 1941 with No Waist at All" returns Salinger to the decks of the SS *Kungsholm,* where he had served on the ship's entertainment staff, back in the final carefree moments prior to the Second World War. While Salinger might have used the characters' transition into adulthood as a metaphor for society's own loss of innocence at the onset of war, he preferred to exploit the narrative to correct personal mistakes and romanticize the lost past. He avoided attempting anything original in this story and revised an old plotline, rewriting "The Children's Echelon" with a reverse ending.

Although Salinger strove to write during the day, his nights were spent in Greenwich Village, where he socialized with a group of trendy artist types and joined a small group of poker players, which met each Thursday night at Don Congdon's apartment in lower Manhattan. Salinger recalled the poker group and this period of his life in "Seymour—an Introduction," when Buddy Glass mentions that he "went through a short period . . . when I played a semi-private, strenuous, losing game of turning into a good mixer, a regular guy, and I had people in frequently to play poker."[17]

Besides playing poker and striving to be a "good mixer," Salinger spent considerable time in Greenwich Village's cafés and nightclubs, frequenting bohemian spots such as the Blue Angel and Reuben Bleu, where an assortment of in-vogue intellectuals regularly met to discuss the arts and peruse upcoming talents. A typical night on the town for Salinger began at Renato's Restaurant in the Village for dinner and proceeded a few blocks up to the discreet bar Chumley's. There he and his companions would enjoy drinks, entertainment, and literary conversation.* "He was a most attractive, social being," Congdon recalled, "although he was very private about things, too. We would go out to dinner, go to clubs. Once, we went to hear Billie Holiday."[18]

Unexpectedly single again, Salinger sought to soothe his disappointment by dating as many women as possible. According to a later article in *Time* magazine, Salinger "brought an astonishing collection of girls to the Village" in 1946. He reportedly stationed himself in the drugstore of the Barbizon Hotel, where he successfully "bagged with unobtrusive efficiency" a wide assortment of attractive residents. It is unlikely that Salinger was seeking serious romance so soon after his failed marriage. He rarely dated a girl more than once and was not above employing a playful ruse to get a date. According to *Time,* he actually told one prospective girlfriend that he was a goalie for the Montreal Canadiens.[19]

Another account of Salinger at this time was recorded by the author A. E. Hotchner, who knew him through the Congdon poker group and would occasionally accompany him on his nights out on the town. At the time, Hotchner was a struggling freelance writer and was fascinated by Salinger's intensity, but he found that Jerry always seemed to keep him at arm's length:

> I never felt that he was a friend, he was too remote for friendship, but on a few occasions he invited me along on one of his night-clubbing sprees. . . . On these occasions, we stayed up late drinking beer and enjoying the endless parade of beginning performers, some of whom were destined to have successful careers. In between the acts, Jerry talked, mostly about writing and writers, but sometimes he took on institutions, like the posh schools that had dismissed him, country clubs . . . and so forth.[20]

Remembering Salinger as having "an ego of cast iron," Hotchner was impressed by Salinger's dedication to his craft and struck by his conviction that he was destined for greatness. "He was an original,"

---

*Until its closure in 2007 for indefinite structural repairs, Chumley's remained largely unchanged from when Salinger was a regular customer. Proud of its popularity among famous authors over the decades, the bar's owners festooned the walls with photographs of well-known literary patrons. Salinger's photograph hung next to that of Ring Lardner, one of Salinger's favorite authors.

Hotchner recalled, "and I found his intellectual flailings enormously attractive, peppered as they were with sardonic wit and a myopic sense of humor."

Salinger's reaction to Hotchner was typical. He saw it as his role to instruct Hotchner in the art of writing, despite the fact that he was only a year Hotchner's senior. Salinger's attitude might appear arrogant (and on some level it probably was) but Hotchner credited Salinger with teaching him about writing from the heart. One example he gave is especially interesting. It not only reveals something of Salinger's concept of his own writing but also involves "The Ocean Full of Bowling Balls." Hotchner claimed to have written a story named "An Ocean Full of Bowling Balls" and accused his friend of stealing the title. Though it is doubtful that Salinger would have found such a title irresistible, Hotchner gave no indication that he ever denied the accusation. Instead, Salinger defended himself by comparing the relative merits of the two "Bowling Balls" stories (and another by Hotchner entitled "Candle in the Poolroom Window"). Of Hotchner's pieces, Salinger apparently said, "There's no hidden emotion in these stories. No fire between the words."[21]

Salinger insisted, perhaps condescendingly, that Hotchner was writing of things he knew nothing about and needed to place himself in his stories. "Writing as an art is experience magnified," he declared. It was a criticism that Hemingway would also make of Hotchner and one that Hotchner took to heart. The most interesting aspect of Hotchner's account is the words Salinger chose. He did not advise Hotchner to embed fire "into" his words but rather to place the fire "between" them, an indication that true meaning should be felt by the reader rather than dictated by the author. It is a singularly Salingeresque concept and a component that distinguishes his writings. Whether or not Hotchner perceived the nuance is uncertain, but Salinger's words express his writing philosophy with precision and were without doubt chosen deliberately.

The Greenwich Village phase of Salinger's life was telling. If we are to believe Buddy Glass in "Seymour," the author was uncomfortable playing the role of man-about-town and poker buddy, but certainly no less awkward than he had been at the beginning of the year playing husband to the intractable Sylvia. It appears that after she returned to Europe, Salinger was still trying to find a "normal" place to fit in and having difficulty finding it. During this phase, we recognize the Salinger of his youth, the awkward cadet awash in his uniform, striving to be liked by his peers but fleeing to sarcasm and bravado just in case he is not.

. . .

Salinger may have thrown himself into dating, nightclubs, and playing cards in a futile effort to forget Sylvia and the war, but the previous five years had changed him fundamentally. Whatever spiritual revelation he had experienced on the battlefield proved to be indelible and had already begun to mold his writing. As a result, two lasting elements of Salinger's work come into focus during the latter months of 1946, each with deep wartime roots: an inclination toward mysticism and the related conviction that his professional work was itself a spiritual exercise.

By late 1946 Salinger had begun to study both Zen Buddhism and mystical Catholicism.* Rather than being shaped by them, he embraced these religious philosophies because they reinforced positions he already held. Zen was especially attractive due to its emphasis on connection and balance, subjects that his writings often covered anyway. The study of these faiths created in Salinger a feeling of duty to offer spiritual enlightenment through his work.

As if making up for lost time, during the summer of 1946 Salinger began to write a number of stories simultaneously. Between the months of August and December, he completed "The Male Goodbye," "A Young Girl in 1941," and his most ambitious project yet, a 30,000-word novella entitled "The Inverted Forest."

"The Inverted Forest" should be viewed as a work that shows the author in transition. Back home in New York, he found himself attempting to live in two separate realities: the "inverted" world of spiritual creativity and the social world of Greenwich Village clubs and poker games. Mirroring this struggle, "The Inverted Forest" contains themes that will dominate Salinger's future writings. Through this story, the author asserts his conviction that art and spirituality are synonymous and his belief that inspiration is connected to spiritual revelation. It de-

---

*According to *Time* magazine, starting in late 1946, Salinger would distribute reading lists of Zen-related material to the women he was dating. This was apparently his way of gauging their spirituality.

picts life as a struggle between material and spiritual forces and raises questions regarding the ability of art to survive the hostility of modern society. However, considering Salinger's inner turmoil after the war and the difficulty he was having writing even the simplest of pieces during 1946, such ambitious themes were perhaps too complicated for a single story at the time and resulted in a novella that is disconnected and imprecise.

"The Inverted Forest" tells the story of Corrine von Nordhoffen, the rich daughter of a suicidal orthopedic-appliances heiress and a German baron, and of her outcast schoolmate Raymond Ford, who is abused by his alcoholic mother. The story is told in two parts. The characters are introduced as children, but the bulk of the story is told nineteen years later, when they reestablish their relationship. Corrine has since become a successful businesswoman, and Ford is now a professor at Columbia University and the author of two volumes of truly inspired poetry.* Ford found his poetry and his path in life by cloistering himself in the dusty library of an elderly patroness, where his seclusion created a poetry-filled world like an "inverted forest" deep within his soul.† Ford's connection to poetry has separated him from normal romantic inclinations, but Corrine determines to marry Ford regardless and after an extended courtship of sorts (consisting mainly of dates at a Chinese restaurant), the two are wed.

After a brief, lopsided marriage of twin beds, Corrine becomes the unwitting accomplice to Ford's artistic and spiritual downfall. The couple is visited by a young woman pretending to be a student and novice writer of poetry. She begs Corrine to have Ford, whom she claims to admire, read samples of her verse. When Ford reviews the girl's work, he speaks the most crucial lines of the story, a reference to Samuel Taylor Coleridge's "Kubla Khan," which reproaches the girl for not revealing art but constructing something that sounds artistic instead. "A poet doesn't invent his poetry—he finds it. . . . The place where Alph the sacred river ran—was found out not invented."[22] True

---

*There is a temptation to compare Raymond Ford to Charles Hanson Towne, Salinger's Columbia poetry professor, who, like Ford, authored a number of successful poetry collections. However, the character of Raymond Ford has little else in common with Towne.

†Salinger uses the occasion of this story to reject the pessimistic outlook of T. S. Eliot in his poem *The Waste Land*, as he did in "Last Day of the Last Furlough." Existence is "Not a wasteland," Ford declares, "but a great inverted forest. With all foliage underground."

art, according to Ford, is never created but always encountered. The line equates art with spirituality and true art with spiritual revelation.

In a way never completely explained, the girl somehow works her way into Ford's life with the intention of subduing him. After a short period of clandestine dating, Ford calls his wife and announces that he and the young woman, now known as Bunny, are running away together. Corrine tracks them down and finds them living in a run-down tenement. At this point, Salinger indicates that Bunny is a manifestation of Ford's mother and symbolic of a callous society determined to crush his divine inspiration and expel him from his inverted forest. The treachery is apparently accomplished, because Corrine discovers Ford completely destroyed, mired in alcoholism, and incapable of producing anything approaching true poetry.

In "The Inverted Forest," through the character of Raymond Ford, Salinger presents three stages of artistic and spiritual existence. Ford is first presented as a child, restrained by the influence of his mother, whose destructive powers threaten to suffocate him. Somehow, Ford's artistic spirituality overcomes this abuse by developing internally, as an inverted forest might grow underground. This leads to the second presentation of Ford, as an adult who has attained true artistry (with its many afflictions) despite his painful past. In this state, Ford is granted the ability to act as intermediary between the subterranean world of art and that of common callousness. In Ford's third manifestation, he enters the world aboveground, where the destructive influences of the first stage overwhelm his spiritual capabilities to counter them. In the end, Ford's inverted forest is torn up by its roots.

It is ironic that Salinger wrote the story at this stage of his life. "The Inverted Forest" condemns modern society for obstructing the revelation of spiritual and artistic truth. It also proposes that true artists cut themselves apart from the modern world in order to experience and serve that truth, much in the same way as monks cloister themselves to serve God. Meanwhile, in Salinger's own life, he was striving, perhaps more than at any other time, to live within the same society that his story condemns.

7. Recognition

When the German army surrendered on May 8, 1945, the world erupted in celebration, but, fearful of being engulfed by emotion, Salinger found himself unable to face the occasion. Instead, he spent the day alone, sitting on his bed, staring at a .45-caliber pistol clutched in his hands. What would it feel like, he wondered, were he to fire the gun through his left palm?[1]

The scene is a macabre one and speaks powerfully of Salinger's feelings of estrangement and imbalance after the war. These sentiments continued to percolate within him at the close of 1946, drawing him closer to that "trembling melody" that he recognized must be written—a melody of words that would give voice to all those who cowered in introspection while the world around them rejoiced. A year later Salinger would release the first chords of that melody.

In November 1946, Salinger was informed that *The New Yorker* was finally going to publish "Slight Rebellion off Madison" in its December issue. The news had come to his agent, Dorothy Olding, through William Maxwell, the same editor who, in January 1944, had declared the boastful Salinger "just not right" for *The New Yorker.*

Salinger was ecstatic. The anxious and compliant persona of his youth once again rose to the fore, just as it had in 1941, when the magazine had first accepted the story. After a year of inactivity and five months of furious writing, he was desperate to reignite his career. *The New Yorker* had held "Slight Rebellion" for five long years, and he had abandoned hope of ever seeing the story in print. And although he had never stopped submitting works to the magazine, he had nearly given up on *The New Yorker* itself. Now, when the opportunity to see his byline in the magazine he most coveted finally arose, he was willing and happy to do anything. This time he uttered no complaint when Maxwell requested revisions to the story before release, as he had in 1943.[2]

The timing of the news about "Slight Rebellion" was not without a happy irony. Salinger had recently completed "A Girl in 1941 with No Waist at All," which recalls the week most closely associated with "Slight Rebellion." This caused Salinger to relive his own anticipation of "Slight Rebellion"'s publication in 1941 and relive the circumstances that had put a halt to the story's release. It was as if he had put pen to paper and turned back time, resurrecting the very week that had determined the story's fate in order to bring it to a happier conclusion.

On November 19, Salinger wrote to thank William Maxwell for reconsidering "Slight Rebellion." In contrast to his 1944 note, in which he had stipulated terms for his story "Elaine," he told Maxwell that he would be happy to make any changes to the story that the magazine saw fit. He informed the editor that he was placing final touches on a seventy-five-page novella called "The Inverted Forest" that he had been working on since August and anticipated finishing in a day or two. As soon as he did, he would adjust "Slight Rebellion" for publication. Perhaps dazzled by his rising prospects, Salinger also notified Maxwell that Dorothy Olding was sending a new story for his approval, one entitled "A Girl in 1941 with No Waist at All." This new piece would arrive at Maxwell's office without demands, and it is doubtful that the editor ever perceived any irony in its submission.[3]

When "Slight Rebellion off Madison" appeared in *The New Yorker* on December 21, 1946, it was tucked away in the back pages among the ads. Salinger did not care. He had now been published by *The New Yorker*—his fondest dream since he had begun to write seriously. Salinger instinctively sensed that his belated *New Yorker* debut would alter his career. When he turned twenty-eight in January 1947, he finally left his parents' apartment on Park Avenue and struck out on his own, moving into a barren loft in Tarrytown, New York, a space he described to Elizabeth Murray as "a little, made-over garage which my landlady rather irritatingly calls the studio."[4]

The new surroundings were stark but affordable, and, despite his irritation, Salinger recognized it to be the perfect atmosphere for an aspiring artist. Its location in Westchester County was near enough to the city yet isolated enough to ward off its distractions. For someone who often sought a refuge in which to write, Salinger appreciated his cell-like space in Tarrytown as the first place where he could completely immerse himself in his craft, away from the scrutiny of his parents, the demands of war, and the diversions of Greenwich Village. Tarrytown was, in short, his own inverted forest.

At the same time that Salinger was moving house, *The New Yorker* rejected "A Young Girl in 1941 with No Waist at All." But Salinger remained undaunted. He was determined to enter the fold of what he had previously mocked as *The New Yorker*'s "little clique of Hemingways" and immediately, in January 1947, sent it another story, not "The Inverted Forest," as one might have assumed, but a far shorter manuscript entitled "The Bananafish." This effort sparked some interest in the magazine's editorial offices but contained major flaws. On January 22, Maxwell wrote to Salinger's agent about the new submission:

> We like parts of "The Bananafish" by J. D. Salinger very much but it seems to us to lack any discoverable story or point. If Mr. Salinger is around town, perhaps he'd like to come in and talk to me about *New Yorker* stories.[5]

Salinger had received such mixed messages from *The New Yorker* before, and they had always angered him. He saw himself writing unique stories of a new kind and had always hoped that the magazine would recognize his innovative approach. When it did not, he tended to ignore its decision and take his work elsewhere. This time was different. Instead of concentrating on the magazine's inability to perceive his accomplishments, he decided to swallow his pride and work with it. Within a short time, he was sitting in William Maxwell's office.

What *The New Yorker* recognized in Salinger's story was his stylistic precision, especially his gift for dialogue, which flowed naturally and was pleasing to the ear. Maxwell's dilemma lay in the fact that no one at *The New Yorker* could figure this new story out. It appeared to be excellently written but was at the same time unintelligible. The story began with a young man named Seymour Glass sitting on a Florida beach, entertaining a young girl named Sybil Carpenter. Maxwell and Salinger decided that it needed extensive revision in order to be understood. So Salinger took "The Bananafish" back to rework it and added an opening scene, introducing Seymour's wife, Muriel.

Salinger revised "The Bananafish" repeatedly. After adding the portion containing Muriel's character, he resubmitted it to *The New Yorker*, where the story was assigned to Gus Lobrano for editing. The magazine again returned it. One can only assume that Salinger was once more called down to the magazine's office for a conference. At least *The New Yorker*, unlike the slicks, was willing, in a process that lasted an entire year, to work in consultation with him and appeared to value not only his ability but also his opinion. Whatever bitterness accompanied these rejections and summonses to Maxwell's and Lobrano's offices, Salinger obliged. His career came first.

After numerous revisions, "Bananafish" was finally accepted in January 1948. By then he had renamed it "A Fine Day for Bananafish" and was once again contacted by the magazine, this time to discuss the story's title. There was some confusion at *The New Yorker* on exactly how Bananafish should be spelled. Was it one word or two? In a letter to Gus Lobrano on January 22, Salinger explained that it should appear as one word because two words would make too much sense. Lobrano apparently accepted this logic, and when the story was published on January 31, 1948, the title had been adjusted to "A Perfect Day for Bananafish."

The effort involved in completing "A Perfect Day for Bananafish" demonstrates not only the intense cooperation between Salinger and *The New Yorker*'s editors, who consulted him over every detail, but also the extent to which Salinger sharpened the story. Since he worked on the piece for a whole year, we can be sure that he scrutinized each word, producing a level of precision that also prompts a humorous speculation: considering the enigmatic nature of the story's final version, one can only sympathize with William Maxwell when imagining how incomprehensible the original version must have been.

From the opening lines of "A Perfect Day for Bananafish," readers know exactly who Muriel Glass is. She is staid and complacent. She is also frivolous and self-indulgent. In the most obvious symbol of superficiality, Muriel, like so many Salinger characters, has an extraordinary devotion to her fingernails. The simple fact that she is alone in her hotel room while her husband is on the beach, as well as her choice of reading material—"Sex Is Fun—or Hell"—establishes her as confident and independent. Muriel is, as Salinger states, "a girl who for a ringing phone dropped exactly nothing."[6]

When Muriel does answer the phone, her mother is on the line and the women engage in a conversation that centers on Muriel's husband, Seymour. Since returning home from the war, Seymour has not been the same. He has been acting increasingly irrationally. There is a strong suggestion that he has aimed his car at trees while driving, as well as references to seemingly small things—his aversion to the sun, his insistence upon playing the piano in the hotel lobby, and his fantasy of having gained a nonexistent tattoo while in the service. Although her mother is aghast at Seymour's actions and probably disgusted about the marriage itself, Muriel is surprisingly accepting of her husband's idiosyncrasies, disregarding any mention of Seymour's problems in favor of superficial banter over fashion.

Down on the beach sits Seymour Glass, his pale, thin body cocooned within his bathrobe. He is talking to a child whose mother has sent her off to play while she herself consumes martinis. The little girl's name is Sybil Carpenter, and her conversation with Seymour is as ordinary as it is intriguing. Sybil, though, is not a likable child. She is demanding, impatient, and given to jealousy. She is certainly not the insightful Mattie Gladwaller or the adorable Phoebe Caulfield. When Sybil brings up the subject of her rival, the young Sharon Lipschutz, Seymour quotes T. S. Eliot's poem *The Waste Land* in claiming the topic to be "mixing memory and desire." Salinger's use of this quote points to the source of Sybil's name. *The Waste Land* opens with a short introduction in Greek in which the young men of Cumae taunt the entrapped Sibyl with their freedom. In Greek mythology, Sibyl was granted a wish. In vanity, she chose eternal life. However, she forgot to request eternal youth at the same time, condemning her to grow old without end. Eliot presents Sibyl suspended within a jar, begging the gods for the very death that she has denied herself. It is a dark vision of humankind being perpetually mutilated by its own experience and frantically seeking release.

Climbing upon a rubber raft, Sybil coaxes Seymour into the water, where he tells the young girl the story of the Bananafish, which have a lethal desire for bananas that grow in great bunches within banana holes in the ocean. Entering the holes to consume their desire, the Bananafish fall victim to their own gluttony, an excess so great that they "become pigs" while in the hole and grow so swollen with their feast that they are cut off from escape. The correlation between Seymour's tale of the Bananafish doomed by greed and Eliot's Sibyl, cursed by relentless existence, is unmistakable.

In "Seymour—an Introduction," Salinger informs readers that the Seymour of "Bananafish" "was not Seymour at all but, oddly, someone with a striking resemblance to,—alley oop, I'm afraid—myself," adding that he was "using a very poorly rehabilitated, not to say unbalanced, German typewriter at the time."[7] From the terror of the Hürtgen Forest to the horrors of the concentration camps, the knowledge that strangles Seymour Glass may be the soul-wrenching realization of the cruelty of which humankind is capable. After experiencing such horrors, Seymour, much like his creator, perhaps found it impossible to fit into a society that ignored the truths that he now knew. The little girl on the raft may be called Sybil in reference to Eliot's poem, but her last name is Carpenter, and within her also resides the nature of William Blake's Lamb. Seymour may weigh the nature of humanity through the time he spends with Sybil, all the while grasping for some kind of hope or even deliverance from what he has endured.

When Sybil is delighted by the story and claims to see a Bananafish, Seymour pulls her toward shore against her will. He then presents her with a final act of blessing by kissing the arch of her foot, wishing her a path free of evil and pain, unlike the path that he himself has suffered. The action alarms the girl, and she runs from him "without regret." The interlude over, Seymour has drawn his own conclusions regarding the makeup of human beings and the world around him.

Back in the hotel room, Muriel is asleep on one of the twin beds, just as she has been asleep to Seymour's needs, pain, and perceptions and just as the world sleeps, disregarding the gentler possibilities of its nature. Gazing at her, Seymour no longer sees the woman he married, and she is referred to only as "the girl." Salinger then tells us that Seymour "took out an Ortgies caliber 7.65 automatic" from his luggage, sits upon the bed with it, and stares at his wife. Unwilling to further evolve in a world where the accumulation of pain and the knowledge of evil are as unavoidable as the accumulation of age is inevitable to the prisoner of Cumae, Seymour shoots himself in the head.

. . .

The bleakness of "Bananafish" is inescapable, and Salinger spent a fitful year reworking it. Throughout 1947, every aspect of his life was on the edge of change. As liberating a notion as his stark garage apartment in Westchester might have initially appeared, he soon found it too restricting and by winter had relocated to Stamford, Connecticut. This time the studio he rented was not in a garage but in a renovated barnlike structure that doubled as the summer home of Salinger's new landlord, Himan Brown. A well-known producer of radio programs, including *Inner Sanctum Mysteries,* with its tales of "mystery, terror, and suspense," Brown nearly refused to rent the house to Salinger upon learning he had a dog. When he reluctantly agreed to accept the schnauzer as a tenant, Salinger was relieved. The property had charmed him. Strategically nestled in a patch of woods, the small Connecticut studio was surprisingly comfortable and, according to Salinger, held a "nice fireplace, pretty grounds, and all the quiet in the world."[8]

It was also the last gasp for the slicks and the power they had held over him since 1941. With his budding relationship with *The New Yorker,* he sensed himself on the verge of a professional breakthrough. Consequently, his tolerance for the slicks and their tendency to alter his stories hit an all-time low. Yet this same confidence afforded him moments of magnanimity, such as when, on April 10, he gave his permission to Dorothy Olding for Burnett to republish his 1942 story "The Long Debut of Lois Taggett."[9]

In May, "A Young Girl with No Waist at All" came out in *Mademoiselle*. It contained a biographical attachment in which Salinger's aloofness or even outright derision as far as the slicks were concerned is all too evident. In fact, he declined to submit the profile, but the magazine worked around this and printed a short blurb that incorporated his refusal:

In 1947, Salinger rented this small house in Stamford, Connecticut. It was here that he wrote several of the *Nine Stories* and became one of the elite writers of *The New Yorker.* (Sherck)

J. D. Salinger does not believe in contributors' columns. He did say, however, that he started to write at eight and never stopped, that he was with the Fourth Division and that he almost always writes of very young people—as in his story [on] page 222.

In the meantime, Salinger was writing his last two stories ever to appear in the slicks. He named them "Wien, Wien" and "Needle on a Scratchy Phonograph Record," although they were later published as "A Girl I Knew" and "Blue Melody." At first glance the stories are very different, but when placed side by side, they reveal fundamental similarities. Both are pessimistic and convey a sense of despondency common to Salinger's writings after the war; both center on characters symbolic of youthful innocence, and each depicts murder through indifference.

"A Girl I Knew" closely recounts the events of Salinger's search for his Austrian family in 1945. It is narrated by a young man named John, whose father has sent him off to Vienna to study the family business after receiving failing grades at school. Once in Vienna, John establishes himself in a boardinghouse located in an inexpensive part of the city—a veiled reference to Vienna's Jewish quarter. During his five-month stay there, he becomes infatuated with Leah, the sixteen-year-old daughter of the family living in the apartment beneath him. When John observes her gazing from her balcony, he is transformed by her purity and fullness of beauty.

John returns home to New York. Years go by, and the war intervenes. After serving in Army Counter Intelligence, he returns to Vienna in the hope of finding Leah. After searching without success, he discovers from friends of her family that she and her parents have been killed by the Nazis at Buchenwald.

Attempting to gain a final sense of Leah, John travels to the old apartment house that the two of them shared years before. Once there, he finds that the building has been converted into living quarters for American officers. Entering the lobby, he encounters a staff sergeant sitting at a desk, cleaning his nails. John implores the sergeant to allow him to go upstairs and visit his former apartment. When the exasperated sergeant asks John why going up to the apartment is so important to him, John briefly explains about Leah and her fate. "She and her family were burned to death in an incinerator, I'm told," John tells him. The sergeant's response is cold and indifferent: "Yeah? What was she, a Jew or something?" In the end John is allowed up to the apartment—not because of the sergeant's sympathy but due to his lack of interest. As John gazes down upon the empty balcony below, he is aware that nothing of the past remains in this place except the four walls around him. Back downstairs, he thanks the sergeant, who wonders aloud about the proper way to store champagne.[10]

By the time they have finished the story, readers are filled with revulsion for the sergeant. Although not directly guilty of the death of Leah and her family, he is held responsible nonetheless because of his attitude and the realization that without such indifference the Holocaust would never have taken place. The character of Leah therefore represents more than a romantic interest. On the one hand, she symbolizes the fragile and beautiful things of life that have been crushed by the Second World War. On the other hand, her treatment even after her death touches on a broader moral issue: the very nature of humankind and our ability to commit or condone atrocities through indifference.

Although "Blue Melody" is set in the Deep South, it resonates with the same accusations as "A Girl I Knew." A story of jazz and segregation, "Blue Melody" follows the career of a gifted blues singer named Lida Louise as seen through the eyes of two children, Rudford and Peggy—this story's symbols of innocence. When Lida Louise suffers a burst appendix at an outdoor party, no hospital will treat her because of her race and she is left to die in the backseat of a car.

The story is Salinger's tribute to the blues singer Bessie Smith. When Smith bled to death in 1937 of injuries suffered in an automobile accident, it was reported that she had been denied admittance to the nearest hospital because she was black.

In "Blue Melody" Salinger makes a statement even more stinging than the story told about Smith. Lida Louise is turned away from several hospitals even though it is clear that she is dying. When refusing to admit her—in essence passing a death sentence—the hospitals' staffs hide behind the same excuse: "I'm sorry but the rules . . . do not permit Negro patients." They are just following orders. Salinger claims that the story is not "a slam" against the American South or "a slam against anybody or anything. It's just a simple little story of Mom's apple pie, ice-cold beer, the Brooklyn Dodgers, and the Lux Theater of the Air—the things we fought for, in short. You can't miss it, really."[11]

"Can't miss it," indeed. Salinger was plainly calling attention to the persistence of dehumanizing values within the society around him. He was asking whether these were the values for which Americans had fought and died. In doing so, he demanded an examination of those values before allowing his countrymen to condemn the cruelties of others and smugly turn their backs on their own brutality. In "Blue Melody" Salinger completed what he had begun in "A Girl I Knew": he brought the Holocaust home.

· · ·

As if expressing the professional transition that Salinger was experiencing, *The Inverted Forest* was published in a special issue of *Cosmopolitan* in December 1947, a month before the release of "A Perfect Day for Bananafish." Salinger appears to have already been embarrassed by the earlier story. He knew "Bananafish" to be a far superior work, and the novella's release, so close to its publication, elicited inevitable comparisons. After meeting with editors such as Maxwell and Lobrano at *The New Yorker* over the course of 1947, Salinger had learned a great deal about tightening up his stories, and "The Inverted Forest" now seemed foreign and immature to him. But *Cosmopolitan* proclaimed "The Inverted Forest" to be a novel and released it with great fanfare. The magazine prefaced the story by advising readers:

> To say that this short novel is unusual magazine fare is, we think, a wild understatement. We're not going to tell you what it's about. We merely predict you will find it the most original story you've read in a long time—and the most fascinating.[12]

"The Inverted Forest" was not a success. After struggling through it, readers of *Cosmopolitan* may indeed have found it unusual, but few thought it fascinating. Most were incensed at the magazine for having led them into a veritable maze. According to A. E. Hotchner, who was briefly employed by *Cosmopolitan,* the magazine's editor "was swamped with letters of protest, and from that point on . . . refused to publish anything in which the story-line was not clear-cut and definite."[13] This reaction did not dissuade the magazine from reprinting it in the Diamond Jubilee issue of March 1961. By then Salinger had hoped all memory of the novella had been long forgotten and, when he learned that the magazine planned to reissue it, begged it to reconsider. But by 1961, Salinger had become a world-renowned author, and *Cosmopolitan* reprinted the story regardless.

Salinger had better luck with *The New Yorker.* "Bananafish" was a success, and the magazine's readers were intrigued by its elusive meaning and powerful ending. Suddenly anxious to retain Salinger's talents after years of snubs, *The New Yorker* offered him the most coveted of contracts, one that kept him on retainer and paid him an annual salary for the privilege of being the first to review his works.* Called a "first reading agreement," it essentially freed him from being forced to write for the slicks in order to support himself. From this point on, all of

---

*It has been reported that *The New Yorker* paid Salinger $30,000 a year for the right to review his work first.

Salinger's stories would be written solely for *The New Yorker,* and he was obliged to find publishers elsewhere only if rejected by it. In exchange Salinger was bound to his new editor, Gus Lobrano, who had selected him to receive the rare honor.

It can be argued that no other editor—Salinger's future mentor William Shawn included—ever dealt with J. D. Salinger as deftly as Gus Lobrano. He had a gift for dealing with people, especially the sensitive, egoistic types employed by *The New Yorker,* who were largely a collection of touchy artists, all jealous of their positions at the magazine, which they viewed as a kind of literary Mount Olympus.

Lobrano had been a college roommate of E. B. White, whose wife, Katharine, was the magazine's powerful fiction editor. The Whites had decided to move to Maine in 1938, and they had brought Gus Lobrano on board the magazine before they left, throwing him a selection of contributors whom Katharine was not quite comfortable handling, for the most part Jewish authors. During his apprenticeship, it was William Maxwell, himself hired by Katharine White years before, who had innocently showed him the ropes. Maxwell did not consider Lobrano a threat, confident that he himself would succeed White as head of the fiction department. Just as the Whites were preparing to leave, Maxwell's uncle died suddenly, and when Maxwell returned from the funeral, he was shocked to discover Gus Lobrano installed in Katharine White's office. Maxwell promptly quit the magazine, but Lobrano lured him back and the two eventually became close friends.[14]

The resolution was an amazing feat that displayed the crux of Lobrano's brilliance. He had a gift for collecting around him a cadre of talent through an easy familiarity that was foreign to the sanctified halls of *The New Yorker.* From the day he took over from Katharine White, Gus Lobrano determined the direction of *The New Yorker'*s corporate culture—through the uniqueness of his personality, and always to his benefit. To advance this culture, as well as his personal following, Lobrano pioneered the idea of a "first reading agreement." The idea transformed major contributors into employees, bound authors to him personally, and created a kind of *New Yorker* "family." Just as the magazine's founder, Harold Ross, had wooed talent by stroking their egos at cocktail parties, Gus Lobrano molded his own array of artists during lunches, fishing trips, and games of tennis by making each feel part of a select group of insiders.

Salinger too felt chosen. Still bruised over his "betrayal" by Whit Burnett, he embraced the comfort Lobrano offered and basked in the satisfaction of being accepted among the elite of *The New Yorker.* Salinger and Gus would always be close, but they never established the kind of relationship that Salinger achieved with Maxwell, who was more bookish, sensitive, and kinder than Lobrano, all attributes that Salinger cherished. Salinger may have suffered fishing trips and games of tennis with Lobrano, but it was their mutual esteem for Maxwell that bound them together.

. . .

In February 1948, while still euphoric over his *New Yorker* success, Salinger received a familiar blow from the slicks. *Good Housekeeping* published his story about returning to Vienna in search of the shattered past, the story Salinger had submitted as "Wien, Wien" but now appeared as "A Girl I Knew." Recalling similar experiences in 1944 with *The Saturday Evening Post,* Salinger was incensed. Once again, a magazine had changed a title without consulting him. The editor, Herbert Mayes, though, did not understand why Salinger was offended: "I don't know what upset Salinger," Mayes wrote, "but he protested vehemently and ordered his agent, Dorothy Olding, never again to show me any of his manuscripts."[15] Alterations without author consultation were common practice among such magazines, but in *The New Yorker* Salinger had found a solution to his problems. His enforced tolerance for the slicks was at an end.

While these professional frustrations and triumphs took place, Salinger remained in his Stamford, Connecticut, barn-studio with his dog, Benny, and began to work on two stories that would swiftly find their way to the pages of *The New Yorker* and advance his reputation. The first of these stories, "Uncle Wiggily in Connecticut," is a portrait of unfulfilled lives, a glimpse into the disillusionment of Salinger's new suburban neighbors.

When Salinger moved to the suburbs, he encountered the newly emerging suburban middle class, a segment of society whose growth was explosive in 1948 and among whom he found endless fodder for his writing. When Salinger lived in Connecticut, unabashed Americanism and materialism were unquestioned values. His neighbors pursued these values religiously and weighed one another against a standard of conformity that often suffocated individuality. Salinger found such material irresistible. Having long exposed the phoniness of society, he now found himself living in a culture that not only esteemed this quality he so despised but also sought to infect all of its members with it.

"Uncle Wiggily in Connecticut" contains three major players: an upscale suburban housewife named Eloise, her former college roommate Mary Jane, and Eloise's daughter, Ramona. As the story opens, Mary Jane is visiting Eloise at her home in suburban Connecticut. As the day wears on, the two women become progressively drunk and begin reminiscing over the past. "Uncle Wiggily" is an orgy of cigarettes and cocktails representing affectation and escapism, two of Salinger's most frequent concerns.

In their stupor, Eloise recalls her lost true love, a soldier named Walt Glass, who was killed in a bizarre accident involving a small Japanese stove. The scene is broken by the entrance of Eloise's eleven-year-old daughter, Ramona, an awkward child in thick glasses. Eloise is almost disdainful of her daughter and especially derisive of Ramona's imaginary boyfriend, an invisible companion called Jimmy Jimmereeno. When Ramona announces that Jimmy Jimmereeno has been run over by a car and is now dead, readers realize that she has overheard her mother's confession about Walt Glass.

The climax of the story is driven by nuance. When Eloise, still drunk, stumbles into Ramona's bedroom at night to check on her, she finds her daughter compressed into a small portion of her bed as if to make room for an imaginary companion, as she had habitually done for Jimmy Jimmereeno. When confronted by her mother, Ramona admits she is making room for a new friend, the invisible Micky Mickeranno. Unable to replace her own true love, Walt Glass, Eloise becomes furious and physically forces her sobbing daughter to occupy all of the bed. There is then a moment of true tenderness between mother and daughter, followed by a pitiful recognition. Eloise picks up her daughter's glasses from the nightstand and holds the lenses to her cheek to catch her tears.

The final paragraph reveals that Eloise is now aware of her own phoniness. Returning downstairs, she wakes up her friend. Sobbing, she implores Mary Jane to recall a dress that Eloise had liked in college. In her parting line, she pleads with her friend to confirm that she had once been a "nice girl."[16] The lines are a powerful recollection of

Eloise's former sincerity, a genuineness that she has sacrificed for the approval of others. The power of these words lies not in the event itself but in Eloise's sudden recognition of what she has lost and what she has become. Salinger's message is clear. What readers witness through "Uncle Wiggily" is a tug-of-war between reality, with all its imperfections, and the false illusion of the suburban dream.

. . .

Salinger's next *New Yorker* story, "Just Before the War with the Eskimos," is an exploration of division; about barriers between people and between themselves and their dreams. It is existential in nature and revolves around the rescue of Ginnie Mannox from her drift toward alienation. An allegory rich in metaphor and symbolism, "Eskimos" is more parable than tale and reveals a spiritual exploration within the author as Salinger sought release from the pain of depression and answers to questions about life and the nature of mankind. Significantly, it is the first story in three years in which readers leave the protagonist better off than when they first encounter her.

At the beginning of the story, readers are introduced to the character of Ginnie Mannox, who, while playing tennis with her schoolmate Selena Graff, is secretly contemptuous of her. Ginnie is cynical, selfish, and uncaring. Clearly, something has happened that has hardened her. Seeking reimbursement for a taxi fare, Ginnie travels with Selena to the Graffs' upscale apartment. There she meets Selena's brother, Franklin, an unassuming but maladjusted twenty-four-year-old who is out of place in ordinary society. Franklin has cut his finger. He offers Ginnie half of his chicken sandwich. He also provides Ginnie with the awareness of her own separation and increasing alienation.

A transformation occurs within Ginnie through her conversation with Franklin, which plays out like a game of tennis. Franklin is bitter and antagonistic, yet somehow Ginnie comes to maturity through their discussion. Exactly how is a matter of interpretation. It may be that she is jolted into recognizing her own alienation by observing Franklin's pitiful state of estrangement or that she gains the insight to see beyond Franklin's hostile exterior and perceive the goodness within him. Either way, Ginnie becomes a better person through her connection with Franklin and finds a rebirth of faith within the obscurity of his misfit character.

That acquisition is represented by the chicken sandwich Franklin gave her, which Ginnie rediscovers in her pocket once on the street. Confronted with the choice of discarding or retaining it, she returns it to her pocket. Salinger then forces readers to reevaluate the story with the last line: "A few years before, it had taken her three days to dispose of the Easter chick she had found dead on the sawdust in the bottom of her waste-basket."[17]

In a story strewn with Christian symbolism, the Easter chick had lain for three days before Ginnie finally accepted that it would not rise from the dead. When discarded, it took with it her innocent trust and faith. Franklin has offered her that long-awaited resurrection as she once again begins to believe in the value of others as well as her own worth.

"Uncle Wiggily in Connecticut" was published on March 20, and "Just Before the War with the Eskimos" appeared on June 5. Readers scratched their heads over both stories but were delighted nonetheless. These were "*New Yorker* stories" written in the *New Yorker* style, described by the poet Dorothy Parker as being "urbane, clever, and absolutely well-written." With these successes, Jerry Salinger was embraced by the *New Yorker* family and would henceforth be expected to match expectations and to conform to the *New Yorker* doctrine.

8. Reaffirmation

When Salinger was a child and very much his parents' little Sonny, he had a habit of running away from home when confronted by conflict. One day when he was about three or four, his sister, Doris, was asked to watch him while their parents went out. An argument occurred between them, and Sonny rushed off to escape the quarrel. He packed a suitcase full of toy soldiers and stormed out of the apartment. When his mother arrived home, she found her son sitting in the lobby. "He was dressed from head to toe in his Indian costume, long feather headdress and all," Doris recalled. "He said, 'Mother, I'm running away, but I stayed to say good-bye to you.'"[1]

Salinger's stories grew to bask in the sheer delight of childhood. His writings evidence the opinion that children are closer to God than adults, allowing them to love more perfectly, oblivious to the divisions created and used by adults to separate themselves from one another. Since children enjoy such an elevated position in Salinger's writings, the spiritual purity of his adult characters can be measured by their closeness to the children around them. Perhaps the clearest example of this reflection appears in *The Catcher in the Rye* when Holden observes a woman and her son in a movie theater. Although the woman cries throughout the film's maudlin plot, she refuses to take the boy to the bathroom, causing Holden to judge her as being "Kindhearted as a goddam wolf."[2] Holden's pronouncement echoes Salinger's own philosophy, a belief that solidified in 1948.

That July, Salinger traveled on vacation to Wisconsin, where he spent the summer at a lodge on the shore of Lake Geneva. Sitting in his lakeside suite, a crowded but comfortable room decorated in a log cabin theme, he began to take notes on reading materials he had brought with him: a chilling endorsement of ethnic cleansing contained in the Nazi treatise *New Bases of Racial Research* and a May 1 article from *The New Yorker* entitled "The Children of Lidice."

It was the *New Yorker* article that captivated Salinger's attention, a shocking description of the savage slaughter of children during the war and the enslavement of those who had managed to survive because they looked German. "We know," Salinger recorded from the text, "that more than six thousand Jewish, Polish, Norwegian, French, and Czech children were killed by gas at Chelmno and burned in the crematorium."[3]

The quotation was a terrifying selection, chosen from an article that spoke not only to Salinger's own experiences but also to his persistent longing to deny the fate suffered by his Austrian family. It represented a burden of memory that seemed to grow more enormous with time and one that Salinger recognized must be subdued.

The conclusion of "Just Before the War with the Eskimos" had hinted at a new direction in his writing, away from the dark themes that had possessed his stories since 1946; but it had been a faint divergence, still hesitant, and part of his psyche remained ensnared by his experiences of war and the Holocaust.

The quotation that Salinger drew upon was not the article's final lines. The closing paragraph of the sad tale of the children of Lidice directly followed the words that Salinger had written down, and it was the power of those words—and not the despair of Salinger's selection—that would finally take hold and guide his pen: "I haven't given up hope," the article proclaimed. "None of us have given up hope."[4]

At Lake Geneva, something deep within Salinger shifted, persuading him to abandon the dark recess into which his writings had descended. Perhaps something in the *New Yorker* piece had encouraged him, or perhaps the shimmering view of the lake from his window. Salinger put away his notes on Nazi atrocities and began a new story, a short but significant piece entitled "Down at the Dinghy," a tale that would address the question of anti-Semitism but would complete the transformation of his work and deliver its players to salvation through love rather than damnation through hatred.

Originally entitled "The Killer in the Dinghy," it is easy to imagine Salinger writing this piece while gazing at the nearby docks of Lake Geneva.[5] Conveying insights provided by a child, it is reminiscent of the Caulfield series but its characters foreshadow future works through Boo Boo Tannenbaum and references to her brothers, Seymour and Buddy Glass.

"Down at the Dinghy" is divided into two acts and narrated in the third person. It is set at the lakeside summer home of Boo Boo Tannenbaum, her husband, and her four-year-old son, Lionel. Also in the house are their live-in maid, Sandra, and part-time cleaning woman, Mrs. Snell. Lionel is portrayed as an overly sensitive but perceptive child who habitually hides from the world when confused by conflict. Salinger connects Lionel's attitude to his own childhood by having him wear a shirt emblazoned JEROME THE OSTRICH. On this day, Lionel has hidden in the hold of his father's boat after overhearing something frightening. His mother has repeatedly gone down to the lake, attempting to retrieve her son and discover what has upset him.

In the Tannenbaums' kitchen, Sandra is pacing and nervous, repeatedly telling Mrs. Snell that she's "not gonna worry about it." Their conversation seems cryptic but when Sandra sneers that Lionel is "gonna have a nose just like the father," Salinger hints that she has blurted out an ethnic slur against the family.[6]

Upon the dock, Boo Boo makes another attempt to coax Lionel from the dinghy. But Lionel is defiant. From within the hold of the boat, he angrily throws a pair of goggles into the lake. When Boo Boo calmly explains that the goggles belonged to her brother Webb and had once belonged to her brother Seymour, Lionel selfishly answers, "I don't care." Rather than react to her son's rebellion, Boo Boo offers Lionel a gift of keys, a clear counterpart to the goggles he has thrown into the water—but not before ensuring that Lionel realizes that he has hurt her. She threatens to toss the keys into the lake as Li-

onel did the goggles. When he protests, Boo Boo mimics his retort of
"I don't care."

Salinger tells us that Lionel then looked at his mother with "perfect
perception." This moment is the climax of the story, the point at which
its pieces tumble into place. At that instant, Lionel realizes that he has
hurt his mother. He suddenly understands that he has stepped upon a
tangible connection that Boo Boo held with her brothers, Webb and
Seymour. Lionel wants the gift of keys but is aware that he no longer
deserves it. When his mother gives them to him regardless, he realizes
that her love is unconditional. It is a level of purity that transcends circumstances and allows Lionel to trust as completely as Boo Boo loves.
As an act of penitence, Lionel throws the keys into the lake. In doing
so, he creates an equilibrium through a seemingly small sacrifice that
actually allows him to connect once more with his mother. He then accepts Boo Boo into the dinghy. As their loves combine, both mother
and son derive strength from each other they did not possess before.
When Lionel reveals that he overheard Sandra call his father "a big-
sloppy-kike," Boo Boo's reaction is tempered by the power of that
love. Instead of viewing Sandra's insult as a personal affront, she considers the remark as it affects Lionel. She explains to her son that Sandra's comment "isn't the worst that could happen."

Lionel only instinctively perceives that Sandra has said something
bad. He does not understand the epithet she used and confuses "kike"
with "kite." But the issue of discrimination is one that Lionel will be
forced to confront during his lifetime, and Boo Boo does not protect
him from that confrontation. Instead, she offers a collective support.
In doing so, she herself learns some measure of acceptance, the ability
to rise above a challenging insult. Boo Boo and Lionel's combined love
creates strength greater than Sandra's attitude of blind contempt.

Through his mother, Lionel gains a crucial insight. He begins to
understand the value of interaction with others, his need for others,
and the need of others for him. He begins to realize that mutual dependence can be strength and that combined love is the purest form of
refuge. He is no longer alone in a frightening world.

Salinger displays the result of their mutual growth as mother and
son plan to take out the boat, which has lain stagnant for months. This
is a symbol of rebirth, but in order to accomplish it they will need
each other. "You'll have to help [your father] carry the sails down,"

Boo Boo tells her son. The story ends in a scene representing union, equality, and compromise, an affirmation of their need for each other and the power that their love contains. Together, Lionel and Boo Boo race home. And through the love of his mother, Lionel wins.

In writing this story Salinger relied heavily upon memories of his own childhood. His schooling and youth were generally populated by upper-class white Anglo-Saxon Protestants. Like Lionel, Jerry Salinger was likely to have been aware of the inevitable murmurings about him being half Jewish. Gloria Vanderbilt, the epitome of upper-crust society, thoughtlessly referred to the young Salinger simply as "a Jewish boy from New York."[7] The discomfort of being stereotyped in this way was still fresh in Salinger's mind when he wrote "Down at the Dinghy."

The story is not Salinger's personal complaint or gnashing of teeth; it is a reaffirmation of the faith in human connection he had found on the battlefields of France and had nearly lost in the agony of the death camps, a confirmation that began to reemerge in "Just Before the War with the Eskimos" and comes to fruition in "Down at the Dinghy." Upon returning home to Connecticut and after three long years of doubting the presence of God in man, Salinger proudly declared to Elizabeth Murray that, spiritually, "the old ship is steady again."[8]

. . .

When Salinger returned from Wisconsin, he was met by an unpleasant but all too familiar situation. *The New Yorker* had previously rejected his story "Needle on a Scratchy Phonograph Record" and Salinger had reluctantly submitted it to *Cosmopolitan,* where A. E. Hotchner was now an editor. Hotchner claimed to have influenced the magazine to accept the story since *Cosmopolitan* was still wary of Salinger after the problems surrounding "The Inverted Forest." But in doing so, it had taken the liberty of changing the story's title without consultation, releasing it as "Blue Melody." Not only was Salinger furious at *Cosmopolitan,* but he also blamed Hotchner, ending whatever still existed of their association. The incident signified the closing stage of Salinger's involvement with the slicks, but not before he was forced to endure one last embarrassment at their hands.

When "Down at the Dinghy" was submitted to *The New Yorker,* the magazine rejected it. Determined to see it in print regardless,

Salinger sold the story to *Harper's*. On January 14, 1949, he complained to Gus Lobrano that *Harper's* had asked him to shorten the piece. Salinger naturally hesitated but made the changes rather than abandon "Dinghy" altogether.[9] It was the last time he would make such concessions for the slicks and the last time a Salinger story would ever premiere in an American magazine other than *The New Yorker*.

A productive year, 1948 had proved to be a period of cleansing for Salinger in which he began to reevaluate his past while cementing his *New Yorker* relationship. And despite his scathing critique of his suburban neighbors in "Uncle Wiggily," that November, he happily renewed the lease on his studio apartment in Stamford.

As 1949 began, *The New Yorker* was holding Salinger's next story to appear in the magazine, a tale entitled "The Laughing Man." This piece shows the clear influence of Sherwood Anderson and is a fanciful adaptation of Anderson's 1921 story "I Want to Know Why."* It examines the fragile nature of childhood innocence and the power of the storyteller to construct and dismantle dreams. Salinger's most imaginative and playful story to date, readers found it captivating.

"The Laughing Man" and "Down at the Dinghy" were the only Salinger stories to be published in 1949. However, the records of *The New Yorker* reveal that he submitted three other stories in 1948 and another seven in 1949, all of which were rejected. Of the ten works returned, the identity of only five is known: "A Girl I Knew" and "Blue Melody" in 1948; "Down at the Dinghy" in 1949; and two pieces that remain unpublished, "The Boy in the People Shooting Hat" and a story that Salinger was especially fond of called "A Summer Accident."

Evidence indicates that the story Salinger submitted to *The New Yorker* as "A Summer Accident" was actually a version of "The Ocean Full of Bowling Balls." In his 1962 annotated bibliography of Salinger's work, Donald Fiene, Salinger's first bibliographer, reported that "The Ocean Full of Bowling Balls" was submitted to *Collier's* in 1950 or 1951.[10] Considering that Salinger was bound by contract to submit any story first to *The New Yorker*, he would have been obliged to submit "The Ocean Full of Bowling Balls" to it before it went to

---

*Salinger acknowledges Anderson's influence in "Seymour—an Introduction" when he confesses that he had written a story "that had a good deal to do with Sherwood Anderson." The reference may well allude to *The Catcher in the Rye*, but it is worded in such a way as to indicate a shorter work, leaving "The Laughing Man" as the best candidate.

Collier's and probably did so in 1949—the same year as "A Summer Accident" appears in its rejection files. Whether or not these two stories are indeed the same is interesting but largely academic. More important is what the situation says about Salinger's affection for "The Ocean Full of Bowling Balls" as a concept. He had abandoned the slicks by 1949, and if a story was rejected by *The New Yorker* he generally refused to submit it elsewhere. Yet he made a rare exception for "Ocean," confirming his attachment to it.

The circumstances surrounding *The New Yorker's* rejection of "The Boy in the People Shooting Hat" are especially ironic. When Gus Lobrano reviewed it, he was both impressed and appalled. He returned the story to Dorothy Olding along with a long letter conveying his regret over its rejection and his bewilderment over its plot. "Here, alas, is Jerry Salinger's latest story," Lobrano began. "I'm afraid it's impossible to express adequately our distress at having to send it back. It has passages that are brilliant and moving and effective, but we feel that on the whole it's pretty shocking for a magazine like ours."[11]

Readers of *The Catcher in the Rye* will recognize the title of this story as being descriptive of the red hunting hat defiantly worn by Holden Caulfield. Lobrano's letter confirms that the story contained a fight between the central character, a boy named Bobby, and a sexually experienced boy named Stradlater. The clash occurred over Bobby's feelings for an old girlfriend named June Gallagher. According to Lobrano, the magazine considered Bobby's character to be incomplete and suggested that "possibly the development of the theme of this story requires more space." Oddly, Lobrano interpreted the story as possessing a homosexual overtone. "We can't be quite sure whether his fight with Stradlater was caused by his feelings for June Gallagher," he explained, "or his own inadequacy about his age (which is brought into relief by Stradlater's handsomeness and prowess), or a suggestion of homosexuality in Bobby." Lobrano went on to advise that the story required "considerably more length," lamenting that Salinger had not delivered a "less-complicated theme." Bobby, of course, was actually an alias for Holden Caulfield, and this story covers much of chapters three to seven of *The Catcher in the Rye*.

In September, Salinger received a rejection notice from *The New Yorker* concerning an unnamed story, in all probability "The Ocean Full of Bowling Balls." Distressed by the decision, it was not until October 12 that he calmed down enough to approach Gus Lobrano over the verdict. He expressed his frustration to the editor but acknowledged how difficult Lobrano must find it to turn down his work.[12] He would resume work on his novel about the prep school boy, he said, rather than force the issue with Lobrano.

The timing of Salinger's return to *Catcher* may also explain the fate of the remaining rejected stories, five of which are unknown. Considering the quality of the work being produced by Salinger during these years, it would be sad if they were truly lost. However, since the rejected stories about which we do have information are both related to *The Catcher in the Rye,* it is probable that a number of these otherwise missing pieces were reworked into that novel.

. . .

Despite these rejections, by 1949, Salinger's *New Yorker* successes had earned him a level of recognition he had long desired, and his fame had spread far beyond the readership of the magazine itself. Especially drawn to his work were artistic circles nationwide: filmmakers, poets, and fellow authors. The talents of the emerging writers Kurt Vonnegut, Philip Roth, and Sylvia Plath crystallized in the freshness of Salinger's vision as they were inspired by his message and style. John Updike's avowal of having "learned a lot from Salinger's short stories" was not uncommon. "Like most innovative artists," Updike pointed out, Salinger "made new room for shapelessness, for life as it is lived."[13]

The readers of Salinger's shapeless reality multiplied in 1949 with a number of major reprints of his stories. Doubleday reprinted "Just Before the War with the Eskimos" in its collection *Prize Stories of 1949.* "A Girl I Knew" was reprinted in *Best American Short Stories of 1949,* edited by Martha Foley. In 1950, Foley went on to recognize "The Laughing Man" as "one of the most distinguished short stories published in American magazines in 1949."[14] Whit Burnett republished "The Long Debut of Lois Taggett" in *Story: The Fiction of the Forties.* And, sweetest of all to Salinger, *The New Yorker* recognized "A Perfect Day for Bananafish" as one of the decade's finest contributions and reprinted it in *The New Yorker's 55 Short Stories 1940–1950.*

These were heady days for Salinger, and he found it difficult to maintain his equilibrium. For someone who valued the notion of balance, the temptation to bask in the satisfaction of his accomplishments was a potential hazard that cut straight into a major vein of his personality.

J. D. Salinger was always concerned about how he was perceived. The opinions of others mattered a great deal to him. For this reason, his personal and professional correspondence was consistently guarded and geared to the ear of the intended reader. Above all else, he dreaded being considered smug, a frequent accusation throughout his youth and army years. As an adult, smugness became the most affronting of labels, and he went to great lengths to avoid being perceived as vain. Salinger possessed an inherent conceit that had been fostered by his adoring mother during childhood and fed by his persistent ambition later in life; and though pride and high self-esteem are feelings common to authors, for Salinger, to be considered arrogant struck an especially raw nerve.

When "Down at the Dinghy" appeared in *Harper's* in April 1949, it was accompanied by an autobiographical "contribution." Salinger's disdain for such self-indulgence had only deepened since *Mademoiselle* had requested, and not received, a similar sketch two years before. The fact that *Harper's* had forced his hand to shorten "Dinghy" certainly did not make Salinger any more compliant, but he was clever in his aversion. He constructed a curt response to appear in the magazine that revealed his impatience for such a frivolous request and contempt for those who enjoyed fulfilling it. "This time," Salinger promised, "I'm going to make it short and go straight home."

> In the first place, if I owned a magazine I would never publish a column full of contributors' biographical notes. I seldom care to know a writer's birthplace, his children's names, his working schedule, the date of his arrest for smuggling guns (the gallant rogue!) during the Irish Rebellion.[15]

The "gallant rogue" comment was an obvious swipe at Ernest Hemingway, whose conceit and bravado were well known.* In fact, Salinger occupied much of this piece criticizing the phoniness of writ-

---

*Elizabeth Murray's daughter, Gloria, later recalled Salinger speaking at length about Hemingway a few months before this piece was written. At that time, Salinger claimed to be grateful that Hemingway had not continued their relationship.

ers who enjoyed publicizing themselves, as Hemingway did. The tactic gave him the opportunity to criticize his competition while, in contrast, presenting himself as being humble. In case readers somehow missed the point, Salinger helpfully pointed out that he was indeed "modest almost to a fault."

Salinger's tirade against literary egos also averted the purpose of the sketch, which was to shed light on the details of his own life. The only personal facts he actually parted with were three short pieces of information that were important but not very enlightening. "I've been writing seriously for over 10 years," he told his readers. "I was with the Fourth Division during the war," and "I almost always write about very young people."

However, Salinger did allow a fragment of a revelation to slip onto the page. "I've written biographical notes for a few magazines," he confided, "and I doubt if I ever said anything honest in them." That much was certainly true. When it came to revealing the details of his life, the Salinger family attitude toward privacy emerged in full force. He considered such confessions to be an imposition and felt under no obligation to respect them. This, after all, was the same Jerry Salinger who, as a young man, had playfully falsified his own draft application.

A comparison of the few autobiographical profiles that Salinger granted reveals a number of deliberate contradictions. For *Story* magazine in 1944, he claimed that his father had dragged him off to Europe to slaughter pigs. For the 1951 dust jacket biography for *The Catcher in the Rye,* he recalled the same trip as being "a happy tourist year," while his interview with William Maxwell the same year confided that he had "hated it."

These aspects of Salinger's public persona reveal the way in which he dealt with emerging fame. He avoided disclosing personal facts regardless of how harmless they were and desperately attempted to appear humble. He protected himself with the defense that any attention drawn to him personally was a deflection from the work he was presenting. In truth, his displays of modesty were in deference to his work alone and in no way actually made him humble.

Amid the successes of 1949, the contributor's biography that accompanied "Down at the Dinghy" demonstrated that, in the heat of the public spotlight, Salinger was already beginning to squirm. As the year drew to a close, two events occurred that should have put his ego in check, alerting him to reconsider the consequences of the fame to which his ambition was driving him.

Salinger was friends with the poet Hortense Flexner King, who was currently teaching a creative writing class at Sarah Lawrence College, an all-girls' school in upscale Bronxville, New York.[16] When the autumn semester began, she invited Salinger to be a guest speaker. Salinger accepted, but, as he later recounted to William Maxwell, "I got very oracular and literary. I found myself labeling all the writers I respect . . . a writer, when he's asked to discuss his craft, ought to get up and call out in a loud voice just the names of the writers he loves." He then went on to name his favorite writers. "I love Kafka, Flaubert, Tolstoy, Chekhov, Dostoyevsky, Proust, O'Casey, Rilke, Lorca, Keats, Rimbaud, Burns, E. Brontë, Jane Austen, Henry James, Blake, Coleridge."

When the lecture was over, Salinger was embarrassed. Once on the speaker's stage, he had become a performer and displayed a persona that smacked of smugness. This was clearly not a comfortable position—or rather, he was too comfortable in the position, and it revealed aspects of his personality that he wanted kept from display. "I enjoyed the day," he commented to Maxwell, "but it isn't something I'd ever want to do again." In fact, it was Salinger's first and only public appearance in such a capacity. Authors routinely employ such appearances to sell their books, but for Salinger future speechmaking and book-signing appearances were out of the question.

Another prickly consequence of Salinger's fame occurred the following December. Shortly after the release of "Uncle Wiggily in Connecticut" the year before, he had sold the story's movie rights to Darryl Zanuck for the Hollywood producer Samuel Goldwyn. It had been Salinger's ambition to see his work adapted to the screen since "The Varioni Brothers" in 1942. The sale of "Uncle Wiggily" paid handsomely and assured Salinger increased exposure for his work. Potentially, it was a tremendous advance for his career. Though "Uncle Wiggily" might have fitted neatly onto the stage as a play, the story consisted almost entirely of dialogue and was simply too short for a film. Major enhancements would be necessary before it reached movie theaters. Salinger must have realized this, yet he sold the rights anyway. Moreover, on the advice of Dorothy Olding, who supported the sale, he abdicated any influence over the movie's production. This left

"Uncle Wiggily" completely in the hands of Goldwyn, who immediately employed the screenwriters Julius and Philip Epstein, of *Casablanca* fame, to write the script, reconstructing Salinger's story in the process.

Why Salinger allowed himself to be put into this position is a mystery. Here was an author who became furious over the mere suggestion that his work might be altered—when magazines had changed his story titles without consultation, he had been driven to frenzy. In 1945, he had warned Ernest Hemingway against the sale of movie rights to Hollywood. And though Salinger secretly adored films, his depiction of the movie industry in his stories was consistently scathing. There can be only one explanation why Salinger forfeited "Uncle Wiggily in Connecticut" to Hollywood: after struggling for so many years to attain literary success, his ambition had embedded itself so deeply as to become a reflex.

The film version of "Uncle Wiggily in Connecticut" was named *My Foolish Heart* and opened to the general public on January 21, 1950. The starring roles were played by Susan Hayward as Eloise Wengler and Dana Andrews as Walt Glass (Walt Dreiser in the movie). In order to become eligible for the 1950 Academy Awards, the film was given a limited release in New York and Los Angeles during December 1949. This is when Salinger would have first seen what Hollywood had done to his story.

The opening scenes of *My Foolish Heart* hold closely to Salinger's original version, and some of the initial dialogue is verbatim. Quoted repeatedly is the line "Poor Uncle Wiggily," which, in the film, is an expression of sympathy that falls flat and is overused. But the plot soon deviates into a tale that has little to do with the original. Early in the movie, the bitter and jaded Eloise discovers an old brown-and-white dress in the back of her closet that reminds her that she was once "a nice girl." The image then fades, accompanied by background harps, into Eloise's memories of Walt and her abandoned virtue.

To say that Hollywood took liberties with "Uncle Wiggily" when devising *My Foolish Heart* would be an understatement. Extra characters were thrown in to populate the film, among them Eloise's husband, Lew, and her parents. In contrast, the movie sidelines the crucial character of Ramona. A story crafted by Salinger as an exposé of suburban society and a call to personal examination was twisted by Hollywood into a love story that oozed sentimentality. *My Foolish Heart* portrays Ramona as being the love child of Eloise and Walt, a relationship that must have surprised the author. In the film, Walt dies nobly in an Air Corps training accident rather than the pointlessness of an exploding Japanese stove. Upon Walt's death, Eloise contrives to steal Lew from her friend Mary Jane to provide a father for the otherwise illegitimate Ramona. In the end, the memories provided by the dress convince Eloise to become "a nice girl" once again, and they all live happily ever after.

Salinger watched *My Foolish Heart* with horror. He detested the film but had resigned any control over his story's interpretation when he had sold the rights to Zanuck. As with his lecture at Sarah Lawrence College, his ambition had delivered an experience so shocking that he resolved never to repeat it, and it has long been believed that Salinger doggedly prevented the adaptation of any of his writings for stage or screen for the rest of his life. But that assumption is false. In years to come, Salinger would come dangerously close to repeating the mistake he made with "Uncle Wiggily," allowing his ambition to again prevail and lure him in the direction of Hollywood.

My Foolish Heart was attacked by critics for being overly sentimental, and Salinger doubtless held hopes that it would simply fade away. But no such thing happened. The film became widely popular, and Susan Hayward received an Academy Award nomination for her portrayal of Eloise. Also earning a nomination was the film's theme song, composed by Victor Young. It remains a well-known standard today.

In 1949, Salinger reached heights of literary success and fulfilled aspirations of which he had long dreamed. However, his autobiographical profile for *Harper's* and his lecture at Sarah Lawrence College revealed his reluctance for center stage, while the film adaptation of "Uncle Wiggily in Connecticut" taught him the artistic price often paid for popularity. Still, his ambition prevailed.

By October, Salinger and Benny had moved from their comfortable barn studio in Stamford into a house on Old Road in Westport, Connecticut, the same town in which Scott Fitzgerald had begun work in 1920 on his novel *The Beautiful and Damned*. Once settled in, Salinger described his new home as "snug and right to work in," the ideal place to resume his novel.[17] The unfinished *Catcher* had been his companion for the past decade, and he wanted very badly to see it finished. Before he could devote himself to that task, he needed to purge himself of another unfulfilled commitment.

In 1945, Salinger had decided that his fellow veterans "deserve some sort of trembling melody rendered without embarrassment or regret."[18] It can be argued that he began that melody with "The Stranger" or certainly "A Perfect Day for Bananafish" and added to it with succeeding stories; but before allowing himself to move on with his novel, he felt compelled to complete that melody. The result was "For Esmé—with Love and Squalor," widely considered one of the finest literary pieces to result from the Second World War.

In all likelihood Salinger had already completed the original draft of "For Esmé" when he moved to Westport. When it was returned by *The New Yorker,* Salinger was compelled to rework it. In February 1950, he reported to Gus Lobrano that the story had been shortened by six pages.[19] This edited version stands among Salinger's tightest works and shows an attention to detail reminiscent of "A Perfect Day for Bananafish." When released by *The New Yorker* two months later, there was little doubt in the minds of readers that Salinger had produced his finest work to date.

The goals of "For Esmé—with Love and Squalor" are "to edify, to instruct."[20] Through this story, Salinger sought to inform the civilian world of the lingering traumas borne by the soldiers in the Second World War. Yet its major purpose is to serve as a tribute to those soldiers themselves and as a lesson on the power of love to overcome what they had endured. This is Salinger's "trembling melody," his homage to his fellow soldiers. In crafting the story, Salinger reached deep into the events of his own life, producing an inspiration that only a veteran could deliver.

The story appeared in an age of unquestioned patriotism and increasing conformity. Five years after the war's end, the reality of the experience was receding into the background of public consciousness and being replaced by a more romantic notion. This ordered romance left no room for the inglorious messiness of post-traumatic stress disorder. For most ex-soldiers, shame and misunderstanding restrained any expression of the trauma they grappled with daily. They suffered in silence. Through "For Esmé—with Love and Squalor," Salinger spoke for those men as no one else had.

"For Esmé—with Love and Squalor" is narrated by someone who

sounds suspiciously like Salinger himself: a writer who served in Europe as an intelligence sergeant during the Second World War. After a short introduction, the story opens in Devon, England, on a rainy April day in 1944. The opening mood is heavy. The sergeant is intensely lonely, and there is an unspoken awareness that D-Day is only weeks away. Feeling restless, he takes a stroll into town, where he is drawn to a church where children are having choir practice. While listening to the choir, his attention becomes focused upon one member in particular, a girl of about thirteen. Upon leaving the church, he escapes the rain in a nearby tearoom, followed shortly by two drenched children, Esmé, the girl who had intrigued him in the church, and her seven-year-old brother, Charles. Sensing the narrator's loneliness, the girl joins him, and they engage in a conversation that is both polite and revealing.

Esmé and her brother are orphans. Their mother has recently died (we assume in the blitz) and their father has been killed serving with the British army. In his honor, Esmé proudly wears his enormous military watch. When she confides the loss of her father, she spells out the word s-l-a-i-n, attempting to spare Charles the hurtful reminder. Before leaving the tearoom, Esmé promises to correspond with the narrator. In return, she asks that he write her a short story about "squalor." Squalor has been her recent experience, but, challenging the devastation to her life, she has resolved to retain her compassion and to protect her brother from descending into bitterness.

The scene fast-forwards to Bavaria in May 1945. This is "the squalid, or moving part" of the story, we are told, and not only does the scene change, but "the people change, too." Now "cunningly" disguised as "Sergeant X," the narrator is billeted in an occupied German home along with other soldiers. X is seated at a table in his dark and chaotic room, attempting in vain to read. That very day, he was treated in a hospital for a nervous breakdown. His gums still bleed, his hands shake, his face twitches, and he sits in the dark after vomiting into a wastepaper basket. In front of X lie piles of unopened mail. He reaches into the heap and removes a letter written by his older brother back home requesting "a couple of bayonets or swastikas."

X tears up the letter in disgust and despair. The silence is broken by the entrance of Sergeant X's jeep partner, Corporal Clay (also referred to as "Corporal Z"). Adorned in ribbons and medals, Clay belches and makes casually insensitive comments on X's ravaged condition. He mentions that he has written to his girlfriend, telling her that X has had a nervous breakdown, amd suggesting that the sergeant must have been unbalanced before the war.

When the insufferable Clay finally leaves, Sergeant X is again alone with his depression and the heap of unopened mail. Delving absent-mindedly into the pile, he retrieves a small package. The box contains a letter from Esmé, who has also enclosed her father's watch. Her letter explains that the watch is "extremely water-proof and shock-proof" and that Sergeant X is welcome to wear it "for the duration of the conflict." At the letter's end, Esmé expresses her hope that Sergeant X will stay in touch, and Charles has added his own enormous greeting: "HELLO HELLO HELLO . . . LOVE AND KISSES CHARLES."

These simple words jolt Sergeant X to the memory of his former self. They prove that Esmé's love has preserved the innocent purity of Charles against all odds. They offer X the hope that love may have a similar triumph in his own life. After finishing the letter and examining the watch, Sergeant X becomes overcome by sleepiness, but not before assuring readers that he can now find the strength to conquer the squalor of his experiences and reconnect with the values he held before the war.

The story's primary symbol is Esmé's father's watch, its meaning shifting as the story progresses. In the first section, it is symbolic of the girl's connection with her dead father and calls attention to the tragedy suffered by Esmé because of the war. In the second section, when X discovers the watch enclosed with Esmé's letter, it becomes symbolic of the sergeant himself. Examining the watch, he notices that it has stopped keeping time and "its crystal had been broken in transit," a clear analogy to his own emotional state, with the watch's "transit" paralleling his own journey through the war. X then wonders if "the watch was otherwise undamaged," contemplating the ability of love to overcome the effects of trauma. Now recognizing that love can indeed survive squalor, Sergeant X is transformed.

The final words of the story are X's assurance that he can reclaim his f-a-c-u-l-t-i-e-s intact. They may also represent the rhythm of the watch, which readers are now convinced is only superficially damaged. This is Salinger's acknowledgment of hope. It is his comfort for and reassurance to his fellow veterans.

In writing "For Esmé—with Love and Squalor," it was necessary for Salinger to reach back into the events of his own past. That the story was written by a veteran who suffered the same traumatic stresses as those the narrative addresses gives "For Esmé" a certain moral authority. However, Salinger did not write the story as a personal recollection. Nor did he seek to draw attention to his own experiences. He instead grants authenticity through his own understanding. To those interested in Salinger's life, an examination of the parallels between author and character is enticing, but such an inspection defies the spirit in which the story was written. Though we may recognize Salinger in Sergeant X's character, veterans of the time recognized themselves.

The author's deepest self-expression was not contained in the story's dates, events, or settings at all but within a personal alignment with the emotional and spiritual postures of its characters. Esmé's words in the teahouse on retaining compassion were echoes of Salinger's own. In the spring of 1944, while based in Devon awaiting the D-Day invasion, he expressed the exact same determination to appear less cold and more compassionate to those around him.[21] Like Sergeant X, Salinger lost sight of that resolve after the war. Here Esmé's words call the author back to that resolution. In this way, Salinger himself partook of the healing that "For Esmé—with Love and Squalor" provides.

9. Holden

The New Yorker featured "For Esmé—with Love and Squalor" on April 8, 1950. After the crowded years of 1948 and 1949, Salinger published this single story between April 1949 and July 1951. "Esmé" was an immediate success. Readers recognized the tribute that it tendered and flooded Salinger with mail. On April 20, he marveled to Gus Lobrano that he had already received more mail for "Esmé" than for any other story he had written.[1]

Everyone waited in anticipation for his next release. Yet, at this recognized high point of his career, Salinger abandoned publishing anything until he had finished his beloved Holden Caulfield novel, The Catcher in the Rye.

The task was daunting. What Salinger had of his book was a tangle of disjointed short stories written as far back as 1941. As he had added to the manuscript over the years, his philosophy and outlook had shifted and changed, and the pieces of the novel that Salinger possessed in late 1949 held differing messages and themes. The challenge that lay before him was to weave all the strains together into a unified work of art.

In order to devote himself to the mission, Salinger cut himself off from distraction. He considered himself to be producing high art and consciously sought the refuge of his own inverted forest in order to reveal it. Reinforcing this self-image, his personal exploration of Zen Buddhism intensified while he was finishing *The Catcher in the Rye*. In 1950, he befriended Daisetz T. Suzuki, the renowned author and Zen master whose fascination with blending Christian mysticism into the expression of Zen ideas matched Salinger's own. For Salinger, the combination of Zen philosophy with his own conviction that art was connected to spirituality resulted in a faith that equated writing with meditation, a faith that had begun on the battlefields of France when he had turned to his work as a source of spiritual sustenance. In the years since, he had discovered that Zen Buddhism fitted seamlessly into his personal belief system. It had helped to buffer the despondency he experienced after the war and had added balance to his writings.

After Salinger's discomfort in the public eye during late 1949, his embrace of writing as a form of meditation was both fulfilling and natural, but it reinforced a situation in which he found it increasingly difficult to produce while under observation or scrutiny. Writing as meditation required isolation and total concentration. Once Salinger had embraced this method, he began to view the clamor of publicity and fame as keeping him from both his work and his prayer. Westport, therefore, became something of a personal monastery, a refuge in which he could connect the pieces of his Holden Caulfield book.

In 1961, *Time* magazine reported that Salinger had completed *The Catcher in the Rye* by isolating himself in "a sweatbox near the Third Avenue el" in some sort of self-imposed imprisonment.[2] "He locked himself in there," it claimed, "and ordered sandwiches and lima beans while he got the book out of himself."[3] *Time*'s depiction is fanciful and unlikely. Salinger was given to periods of loneliness, so although he had the opportunity to seclude himself at Westport when necessary, he considered it important to be within striking distance of New York City, where his friends and family lived, and it is probable that the "sweatbox" was actually an office at *The New Yorker*. The magazine frequently offered working space to its contributors, an arrangement that Salinger is known to have taken advantage of during the summer of

1950, when he used the offices of vacationing editors while completing *The Catcher in the Rye.*

Salinger was not completely alone when in Connecticut, either. There, he had Benny "for company and distraction."[4] Salinger was extraordinarily attached to the schnauzer. He enjoyed talking about the dog as much as a proud parent might speak of an only child. After everything they had been through together, from Germany to Connecticut, Benny alone, it seemed, understood his master. "You don't have to take time to explain to a dog," Salinger said, "even in words of one syllable, that there are times when a man needs to be at his typewriter."[5]

As much as Salinger may have viewed writing as a spiritual exercise, he did not undertake his labor on pure faith. By the time he settled in at Westport and focused on completing his novel, he had already secured a publisher. In the autumn of 1949, an editor at Harcourt, Brace & Company, Robert Giroux, wrote to Salinger in care of *The New Yorker* and offered to publish a collection of his short stories. Salinger never answered Giroux's letter but in November or December showed up unexpectedly at his office. According to Giroux, Salinger was not ready to publish a short-story collection. Instead, he offered the editor something rather more tantalizing:

> The receptionist rang my desk to say that Mr. Salinger would like to see me. A tall, sad-looking man with a long face and deep-set black eyes walked in, saying, "It's not my stories that should be published first, but the novel I'm working on."[6]

"Do you want to sit behind this desk?" Giroux asked. "You sound like a publisher." "No," Salinger answered, "you can do the stories later if you want, but I think my novel about this kid in New York during the Christmas holidays should come out first."

Giroux was surprised and delighted. In view of Salinger's recent successes, he had assumed that every publisher in America had already offered a book deal. He eagerly promised to publish Salinger's novel upon completion, and the two men shook hands to seal the deal. When Salinger left Giroux's office, he felt relieved of the burden of hunting for a publisher and could now devote himself to the book.

A similar event occurred in August 1950, when *Catcher* was close to completion. On the eighteenth, Salinger was contacted by the British publishing house Hamish Hamilton. The company's founder, Jamie Hamilton, had read "For Esmé—with Love and Squalor" in *World Review* and had been so impressed that he wrote to Salinger himself, telling him that he expected to be haunted by "Esmé" "for years to come," and inquiring about the British rights to his short stories.[7] Just as Giroux had, Hamilton envisioned publishing a Salinger collection. Salinger offered Hamilton the British publishing rights to *The Catcher in the Rye* instead.

Jamie Hamilton would play a significant role in Salinger's life for years to come. Together with *New Yorker* founder Harold Ross, Hamilton filled a void left in Salinger by the absence of Whit Burnett. In the case of Hamilton, this comparison would have a bitter irony. But as Salinger was finishing *The Catcher in the Rye,* Hamilton and Ross were the two individuals whom he most genuinely liked and professionally respected.

At first glance, Harold Ross and Jamie Hamilton appear remarkably similar. Both men were self-starters and had forged the most respectable of literary establishments. Ross had fathered *The New Yorker* in 1925 from his apartment on Manhattan's East Side, forcibly nurturing it into the most reputable literary magazine in America. Jamie Hamilton had launched the publishing house of Hamish Hamilton (proud of his Scottish heritage, Hamilton used his Celtic name "Hamish" rather than the English "James" when naming the company) in 1931. His editorial prowess and strength of character soon established Hamish Hamilton as one of the most innovative publishers in Britain. Both men attracted the finest talents through their intense interest in their authors. Yet Ross and Hamilton were actually very different people, and Salinger was attracted to them for very different reasons.

Harold Ross was unusually indulgent of his authors, many of whom became close personal friends. Overlooking Ross's somewhat bellicose style, Salinger described him as "a good, quick, intuitive, child-like man."[8] What especially drew Salinger to Ross were his childlike qualities, which managed to survive despite the weight of responsibility.

That Salinger should connect with Jamie Hamilton was inevitable. They were intense personalities cut from the same cloth. A former

Olympic athlete, Hamilton was both competitive and tenacious. He was an emotional man who disliked critics and viewed the world in terms of "us" and "them." When he thought that someone had wronged him, he had the ability to cut him or her off completely, refusing even to enter the same room. Above all, both men were driven by ambition. Such individuals often connect through their similarities, but Hamilton and Salinger were perhaps too similar, and the ambition of one man would eventually clash with the ambition of the other.

. . .

After working on the novel for a year, in the autumn of 1950, Salinger completed *The Catcher in the Rye*. The achievement was a catharsis. It was confession, purging, prayer, and enlightenment all encased in a voice so distinct that it would alter American culture. More than a collection of reminiscences or a tale of teenage angst, the novel was a cleansing event in Salinger's life. Holden Caulfield, and the pages that contained him, had been the author's constant companion for most of his adult years. Those pages were so precious to Salinger that he had carried them on his person throughout the war. In 1944, he had confessed to Whit Burnett that he needed them with him for support and inspiration. Pages of *The Catcher in the Rye* had stormed the beach at Normandy; they had paraded down the streets of Paris, been present at the deaths of countless soldiers in countless places, and been carried through the death camps of Nazi Germany. Now, in his refuge in Westport, Connecticut, Salinger placed the final line on the final chapter of the book. Immensely relieved at having finished it, he sent the manuscript to Robert Giroux at the office of Harcourt, Brace for publication. Another copy was sent by Dorothy Olding to Jamie Hamilton at Hamish Hamilton.

When Giroux received the manuscript, he "thought it a remarkable book and considered [himself] lucky to be its editor." He was convinced that the novel would do well but later confessed that "the thought of a best-seller never crossed [his] mind." Assured of the novel's distinction and having already sealed a verbal contract with a handshake, Giroux sent *The Catcher in the Rye* to Harcourt, Brace vice president Eugene Reynal.

After Reynal reviewed the manuscript, it became clear to Giroux that the publishing house would not recognize the verbal contract. Worse still, it was apparent that Reynal did not understand the novel at all:

> I didn't realize what big trouble I was in until, after he'd [Reynal] read it. He said, "Is Holden Caulfield supposed to be crazy?" He also told me he'd given the typescript to one of our textbook editors to read. I said "Textbook, what has that to do with it?" "It's about a preppie, isn't it?" The textbook editor's report was negative, and that settled that.[9]

Giroux broke the news to Salinger in the worst way possible: he took the author to lunch. Humiliated, he confessed that Harcourt, Brace wanted Salinger to rewrite the book. To Salinger, the scenario was doubtless a nightmarish replay of Whit Burnett and the *Young Folks* anthology. He did his best to restrain his fury throughout lunch (Giroux had brought along another Harcourt, Brace employee for support) but, immediately upon returning home, called Harcourt, Brace and demanded his book back. "Those bastards," Salinger wailed.[10]

There was trouble too in London, where Jamie Hamilton was having his own reservations about publishing *Catcher*. Personally, Hamilton thought the manuscript brilliant, but he worried that it might be a professional risk. He himself was half American and more tolerant of the slang in which the novel was written, but he was doubtful that other Britons would accept Holden Caulfield's language. Expressing his concerns to a colleague, Hamilton said:

> I think that Salinger, whose first novel this is, has remarkable talent and that the book is extraordinarily funny, though whether the idiom of adolescent American will appeal to English readers I cannot say.[11]

Hamilton's instincts prevailed, and he published *The Catcher in the Rye* in Britain. Back in America, Dorothy Olding had sent the retrieved *Catcher* manuscript to the fiction editor John Woodburn at Little, Brown and Company in Boston. Woodburn was enchanted, and Little, Brown snatched it up immediately.

After overcoming the apprehension of Hamish Hamilton and the shock of Harcourt, Brace's abandonment, Salinger at last felt secure. But he would endure one final blow to the novel, and it would come from the institution closest to his own heart. At the end of 1950, Dorothy Olding delivered *The Catcher in the Rye* to the offices of *The New Yorker,* a gift from Salinger to the magazine that had stood by him for so long. He intended for *The New Yorker* to print excerpts from the book in proud affirmation of his talents and fully expected its reception to be warm and enthusiastic.

On January 25, 1951, Salinger received *The New Yorker*'s reaction from Gus Lobrano. According to Lobrano, the *Catcher* manuscript had been reviewed by himself and at least one other editor, possibly William Maxwell.* Neither of them liked it. Its characters were considered to be unbelievable and the Caulfield children, in particular, too precocious. In their opinion, "the notion that in one family (the Caulfield family) there are four such extraordinary children . . . is not quite tenable." As a result, *The New Yorker* refused to print a single word of *The Catcher in the Rye.*[12]

In addition to the verdict on *Catcher,* Lobrano's letter included a lecture on Salinger's writing style. Immediately after finishing the novel, Salinger had written a short story entitled "Requiem for the Phantom of the Opera." Lobrano's letter containing the *Catcher* rebuff was ostensibly a rejection letter for that story. Lobrano felt that Salinger had attempted "Requiem" too soon after completing *Catcher.* "I can't help but wonder," he commented, "if you were still imprisoned in the mood and even the scenes of the novel." Lobrano went on to criticize the story as being "too ingenious and ingrown." He reminded Salinger that *The New Yorker* took a dim view of any story that displayed "writer-consciousness."

Despite Salinger's hurt over the novel's rejection by *The New Yorker,* it seems that he took much of Lobrano's criticism to heart. Perhaps in reaction to the editor's homily on "writer-consciousness," Salinger adopted an attitude to publicity and publishing that mirrored

---

*Lobrano did not reveal the identity of the other editor who reviewed *Catcher.* However, upon the novel's completion, Salinger personally read its contents to his friend William Maxwell, who was unlikely to have expressed a negative reaction in Salinger's presence.

The New Yorker's concept of the "proper" relationship between an author and his work. The magazine promoted a literary philosophy that elevated the story and subjugated the writer. If the author's presence was too strident in a story, it was viewed as flouting the magazine's creed on "writer-consciousness." It felt that any literary acclamation was the reserve of the magazine. All *New Yorker* stories were to be written in the *New Yorker* style.

The Catcher in the Rye was not such a work. It had been conceived a decade before, and those who knew Salinger clearly saw the author's individual imprint. To Lobrano, this approach was authorial conceit, and he probably coupled the rejection of "Requiem" with the rebuke of *Catcher* in order to make the point. What was not perceived at *The New Yorker* was *Catcher*'s uncanny ability to speak to individuals on a level so personal as to remove the author completely. Salinger was not about to rewrite *Catcher* to please Gus Lobrano, but his letter may have cast doubt into his mind, causing him to redouble his efforts to emulate the literary philosophy of a magazine he still profoundly respected.

More important, that philosophy also fit in with Salinger's Zen beliefs. In 1950 and early 1951, he was following a line of Zen thought that demanded ego detachment as an element of meditation. If Salinger indeed equated writing with meditation at this time, he would have shied away from publicizing himself in connection with his book. Self-promotion—more than just appearing smug or un–*New Yorker*—would have been sacrilegious to him. Publicity would have seemed like taking credit for the authorship of prayer, defeating the very purpose of meditation itself. After incorporating himself into every page of the novel, from this point forward Salinger sought a level of anonymity that would prove impossible to obtain.

Detachment did not mean that Salinger would remove himself from how his book was to be presented. He was not about to let unknown editors have their way with it. Neither was he prepared to have them challenge his personal beliefs for the sake of profit. While avoiding attention, he still wanted control over every aspect of the novel's production. Though *The New Yorker* may have understood the philosophies of consultation and writer-consciousness, Little, Brown and Company certainly did not. Between its acceptance of *Catcher* at the end of 1950 and its release in July 1951, what transpired between Salinger and his publishers was a series of episodes in which Salinger appeared to fight every effort to make his book a success.

An example of what it was like to negotiate with Salinger was experienced by the New American Library, which had been appointed by Little, Brown to produce the novel's paperback edition. The company had contracted a well-known artist, James Avati, to design the book's cover. His design included an illustration of Holden Caulfield wearing his red hunting hat. Salinger detested the image. It reminded him of the "gay *Post* illustrations" that had competed with his stories years before. He himself envisioned a sublime drawing of Phoebe Caulfield gazing wistfully at the Central Park carousel. "It was a nice idea," said Avati, "but it didn't get to the guts of the story." In reality, both artist and publisher had become exasperated with Salinger, who had rejected every idea they had offered. Finally, Avati put his foot down:

> I asked him, "Can I talk to you?" and we went into a little side office. Then I just told him, "These guys know how to sell books. Why don't you let them do it?" In the end, he said okay.[13]

Salinger may have acquiesced to the Holden cover, but it was certainly not "okay."

Little, Brown had wisely avoided an inevitable skirmish with Salinger over his book's hardcover design by accepting an illustration by Michael Mitchell, a personal friend of Salinger's from his days living in Stamford and now a fellow Westporter. Salinger was naturally delighted by the choice of artist, an opinion justified by Mitchell's design. Depicting a stylized red horse rampant in fury, the image eloquently conveyed the depth of the novel within and remains emblematic of *The Catcher in the Rye* to this day.

When Little, Brown sent the novel to galleys, Salinger called John Woodburn and requested that no promotional copies be sent to book reviewers or the press. It was normal practice in the publishing world to distribute advance copies of a book before publication. Woodburn was dumbstruck at Salinger's request. When he pointed out that the advance transcripts were necessary for publicity, Salinger told him that he did not want any publicity. In addition, he was having problems with Little, Brown's design and wanted his photograph removed from the back cover. It was, Salinger said, simply too big.*

Alarmed and frustrated by these demands, Woodburn appealed to the vice president of Little, Brown, D. Angus Cameron. He explained the situation and asked for help. Cameron immediately left Boston for New York City and met with Salinger. "Do you want this book published or just printed?" he asked. Salinger held his resentment in check and agreed to allow Little, Brown to distribute copies, but Woodburn would soon pay for having involved Cameron.

In March 1951, amid his struggles with Little, Brown, Salinger had his first meeting with Jamie Hamilton. The publisher traveled to New York with his wife, Yvonne, to meet his American authors and bonded with Salinger immediately. Salinger was equally impressed and especially relieved by Hamilton's apparent concern to accommodate his wishes. After his ongoing confrontation with John Woodburn, Salinger felt he had found in Jamie Hamilton an editor who would do justice to his book. His feelings seemed confirmed when Hamilton returned to Britain and sent him a gift of books along with a very flattering letter. Salinger was delighted by the gesture. He sensed that he had found not only a worthy editor but a kindred spirit.

Preparations for the release of *The Catcher in the Rye* had occupied Salinger since late 1950. Each step of the process—publicity, correcting proofs, examining galleys, and presentation—had been an ordeal. By April, Salinger found himself embroiled in a whirlwind of prepublication commotion that he despised. Disillusioned and increasingly uncomfortable, he could not wait for the process to end.

One day in early April, Salinger was washing his car at Westport when the telephone rang. Annoyed at the timing, he rushed into the house and ran up the stairs to answer the call. On the line was the excited John Woodburn. "Are you sitting down?" he asked. Salinger was wet and out of breath. Woodburn broke the news that after receiving a galley copy of *The Catcher in the Rye,* the Book-of-the-Month Club had chosen it to be its summer release. The selection would guarantee the novel instant popularity and was a publicity coup bar none.

---

*The photograph of Salinger that appeared on the back of *Catcher* was one of two taken by the famous photographer Lotte Jacobi. For some unknown reason, the photograph was reversed when transferred to the dust jacket. When asked her opinion of Salinger as a sitter, Jacobi responded that she found him "interesting."

Salinger, who had never expected to make a great deal of money from the book, was afraid the deal would only postpone the book's release and prolong his stress. "I suppose that will delay publication, won't it?" he asked.[14] It was not the reaction that Woodburn had expected. He did not know how to deal with Salinger or how to interpret his reactions. Making light of Salinger's response to the Book-of-the-Month Club deal, he repeated the story to columnists. When Salinger read Woodburn's rendition of their telephone conversation in the press, he was incensed. He told Jamie Hamilton that the story "made me look smug." As far as Salinger was concerned, Woodburn had committed an unpardonable sin.*

For a short time it appeared that Little, Brown would indeed postpone the release of *Catcher* for several months in deference to the Book-of-the-Month Club. In the end, it held to its release for mid-July. In the meantime, editors at the Book-of-the-Month Club were having problems with the novel's title. When they asked Salinger to change it, he became indignant. Refusing, he maintained that Holden Caulfield would not agree to the idea, and that was that.[15]

By now Salinger had endured all he could stand of the process and decided that it was best to remove himself from the situation. He abruptly made plans to leave the country and avoid being present when the book came out. In escaping, it was only natural that he should seek out the company of Jamie Hamilton, so he bought himself a ticket aboard the ocean liner *Queen Elizabeth*, bound for Southampton, England.

In the background, Salinger's former mentor Whit Burnett monitored events with morbid envy. With the acceptance of Salinger's novel by the Book-of-the-Month Club assuring its success, Burnett appears to have become acutely resentful of Little, Brown and Company. When he read a publicity release for *The Catcher in the Rye*—the book that should have been his—that resentment overtook him. With clear indignation, he wrote to the publicity department of Little, Brown on April 6, scolding the publisher for ignoring his contribution to Salinger's career:

*The episode so irritated Salinger that by December 11, eight months after the phone call, he had yet to reestablish direct contact with Woodburn.

I should like to call your attention, with a protest, to the inaccurate method of publicizing a friend of mine, a discovery of Story Magazine, and a young man whose first stories I have edited, published, and sponsored. . . . Your publicity Department says, "his previous work consists of only four short stories which have appeared in the New Yorker." This is nonsense. I have printed several stories by Mr. Salinger in Story Magazine where his first one appeared after he was a student in my class at Columbia University.[16]

Burnett went on to recite every Salinger story he had ever published and a list of other authors who had appeared in the magazine. "Perhaps in your future publicity," Burnett concluded, "this error might not occur again." To Little, Brown's credit, Burnett soon received a respectful and sincere apology from D. Angus Cameron himself.[17] But the damage had been done: Burnett had been denied not only the novel he had so long coveted but also any benefit of being connected to it.

. . .

On Tuesday, May 8, Salinger left for Britain, anxious to avoid the tumult of publication. He knew that with *The Catcher in the Rye* he had crafted his finest work to date. Yet the same ego that assured him of the novel's quality made it unbearable for him to watch as publicists cheapened it and critics dissected it. His original plan was to sit out the American release of *Catcher* through a long, unscripted tour of the British Isles. He would end his trip prior to the novel's release in Britain, hoping that by the time he returned to New York, the commotion over the book would have begun to fade. When he boarded the *Queen Elizabeth* for England, he could not have realized that he was taking the first step in a flight from scrutiny that would never end.

When he docked at Southampton, he made straight for his publisher's offices. Hamilton treated Salinger's arrival in London as a triumphal entry. He presented the author with a special copy of Isak Dinesen's *Out of Africa,* the same book that Holden Caulfield had so enjoyed in *Catcher,* as well as a copy of the British version of his own novel. To Salinger's satisfaction, it bore a subdued cover that he actually liked, tastefully declaring its title and author against a field of red and white, without any photographs or biographical details.

Hamilton began a nightly ritual of taking Salinger out on the town, where they eventually took in every decent play in London's West End.[18] On one such occasion, Salinger first experienced some of the discomfort that *Catcher*'s publication would generate. Treating Salinger to the theater, Hamilton had chosen two Cleopatra plays starring the legendary actor Sir Laurence Olivier and Olivier's wife, Vivien Leigh. "The Oliviers," as Hamilton referred to them, were personal friends of his, and he had chosen the plays to impress his new colleague. After the theater, Olivier and Leigh invited Hamilton's group to their Chelsea home for dinner. While Salinger thought it a "very posh evening," he was also uneasy. In *The Catcher in the Rye*, Holden Caulfield describes seeing Olivier in the 1948 film *Hamlet*. "I just don't see what's so marvelous about Sir Laurence Olivier," Holden complains. "He was too much like a goddam general, instead of a sad, screwed-up type guy."[19] In other words, Holden considered Olivier a "phony," and there was Salinger, forced to sit through dinner and exchange niceties with the very brunt of his condemnation. As the night wore on, he felt more and more like a phony himself. The incident still resonated with Salinger after he had returned home, and he sent Hamilton (who, having read the book, should have known better in the first place) a long letter explaining that he did not share the same viewpoint as Holden Caulfield on the sincerity of Olivier's acting. He asked Hamilton to pass the sentiments and his apology on to Olivier.* Hamilton did so, and Salinger received a gracious letter from the actor in reply.[20]

While in London, Salinger purchased a Hillman car that he used to explore Britain. With no set itinerary, he drove through England and Scotland and visited Ireland and the Scottish Hebrides. He was enthralled by everything he saw, and his letters and postcards sparkle with enthusiasm and childlike delight. At Stratford-upon-Avon, he paused before the theater and debated with himself between paying homage

---

*Salinger's distress over the encounter with Olivier, though certainly sincere, appears somewhat belated. In letters written home from England, he mentioned having met Olivier and Leigh with self-satisfaction. Only after returning home and learning that the Oliviers were planning a visit to New York and wanted to see him did Salinger pen his letter of apology.

J. D. Salinger in 1950. This photo embellished the original back cover of *The Catcher in the Rye*. The photograph so irritated Salinger that he insisted it be removed. (Lotte Jacobi, University of New Hampshire)

to Shakespeare and rowboating with a young lady. The lady won out. In Oxford, he attended Evensong at Christ Church. In Yorkshire, he swore that he saw the Brontë sisters running across the moors. He was delighted by Dublin but fell in love with Scotland most of all and actually wrote of settling down there.[21]

After seven weeks in Britain, Salinger succumbed to a sense of anticipation and decided to return home in time for the American debut of *The Catcher in the Rye*. Making his way back to London, he met again with Jamie Hamilton and purchased a first-class ticket to New York. On July 5, he boarded the *Mauretania* at Southampton and arrived home on the evening of July 11, five days before his novel's publication.[22] He did not return alone; he brought the Hillman with him.

. . .

The Catcher in the Rye was published on July 16, 1951, in both the United States and Canada. After the success of "For Esmé—with Love and Squalor," expectations were high. When critical reviews of the novel began to appear, they exceeded those expectations. The depth of reaction also indicated that *The Catcher in the Rye* would have a greater public impact than Salinger could have hoped for, or perhaps could deal with.

Playing on the "Esmé" theme, *Time* magazine ran a review of *Catcher* entitled "With Love & 20-20 Vision." It praised the novel's depth and (to Salinger's certain delight) compared the author to Ring Lardner. "The prize catch in *The Catcher in the Rye*," commented *Time*, "may well be Novelist Salinger himself."[23] *The New York Times* called *Catcher* "unusually brilliant." *The Saturday Review* praised it for being "remarkable and absorbing." On the West Coast, the *San Francisco Chronicle* confirmed it to be "literature of a very high order." Most satisfying of all to Salinger, despite their initial reservations over the book, critics at *The New Yorker* found it "brilliant, funny," and "meaningful."*

Naturally, there were also less favorable reviews, but these were relatively few in number and they generally found fault with the novel's language and idiom. A number of critics were offended by Holden's repeated use of "goddam" and especially the phrase "fuck you." In 1951, these were shocking expletives for any novel. Not surprisingly, *The Catholic World* and *The Christian Science Monitor* found such language "repellent" and "vulgar." *The New York Herald Tribune* reacted by saying that the novel "repeats and repeats, like an incantation . . . casually obscene."

Mimicking Holden Caulfield, James Stern of *The New York Times* published a clever article on July 15 titled "Aw, the World's a Crumby Place." Using Holden's voice, the article follows a girl named Helga, who, after reading "For Esmé—with Love and Squalor," excitedly consumes Salinger's novel. Though the article appears to taunt Salinger and mock his writing style, it ends with Helga "reading this

---

* *The New Yorker* took advantage of the publicity surrounding *Catcher* and, two days before the novel's release, published "Pretty Mouth and Green My Eyes," a story Salinger had written in 1948.

crazy 'Catcher' book all over again" and noting, "That's always a good sign."[24]

Catcher soon emerged onto the *New York Times* best-seller list and would remain there for the next seven months, reaching the number four spot in August. Its popularity was due largely to the delivery of the Book-of-the-Month Club edition on the doorsteps of thousands of homes, which multiplied the novel's readership exponentially and ensured Salinger's fame in households throughout the nation.

Apart from the gigantic photograph that he so abhorred, the Book-of-the-Month Club version also came with a lengthy profile of the author. Salinger had agreed to grant the interview only because it was to be conducted by *New Yorker* editor William Maxwell, a friend whom Salinger trusted to present him in the kindest of lights. Still, as with previous interviews, he gave away as little personal information as possible.

The profile cited Salinger's childhood, his army service, and the highlights of his career—which, not surprisingly, consisted of his *New Yorker* stories. It also dwelled upon Salinger's professionalism. According to Maxwell, Salinger wrote "with infinite labor, infinite patience and infinite thought for the technical aspects of what he is writing, none of which must show in the final draft." He added that "Such writers go straight to heaven when they die, and their books are not forgotten." The summary then quotes Salinger commenting with deliberate humility that the "compensations" of writing "are few, but when they come, if they come, they're very beautiful."[25]

Above all, Maxwell's interview stressed the author's connection with New York City, especially places associated with the movements of Holden Caulfield in the book. By placing Salinger in Central Park and its lagoon, and taking a cab to Grand Central Station while home from boarding school, Maxwell drew attention to the similarities between J. D. Salinger and Holden Caulfield. From a publicity point of view, the move was brilliant. But if the author sought to dissuade readers from perceiving him as the novel's protagonist, the Maxwell interview crushed that possibility. By aligning himself so closely with Holden's character in the biographical description, Salinger sparked an immediate interest among his readers to learn more about the author. How Salinger, so concerned with protecting his privacy, did not suspect this outcome remains a mystery.

Maxwell's piece stated that Salinger "is now living in a rented house in Westport, Connecticut, with, for company and distraction, a Schnauzer named Benny, who, he says, is terribly anxious to please and always has been." This disclosure must have made Salinger nervous. Westport was not a large community, and Salinger doubtless envisioned himself pursued by readers seeking out a lanky young man (whose features they would recognize from the book's jacket cover) walking a schnauzer. When Salinger came back from Britain, he did not return to Westport. Although back home, he was still in flight.

. . .

What readers encountered within the covers of *The Catcher in the Rye* was often life-changing. It would also alter the path of American culture and help define its psyche for generations. From the novel's opening line, Salinger draws the reader into the peculiar unrestrained reality of Holden Caulfield, whose meandering thoughts, emotions, and memories populate the most completely stream-of-consciousness experience offered by American literature. The disordered nature of Holden's narration is evident from the first page. Its opening sentence of sixty-three words and first paragraph running to more than a page defied literary convention and alerted readers that they had embarked upon a unique experience.

For all of its unconventionality, *The Catcher in the Rye* carries on a literary tradition begun by Charles Dickens and welded to American culture by Mark Twain.* As a successor to *David Copperfield* and *The Adventures of Huckleberry Finn, The Catcher in the Rye* continues an observation of mankind as seen through the lens of an adolescent and rendered in a language true to the narrator's location and age. The repetitive slang of the New York street was attacked by some critics who failed to recognize the subtle innuendos veiled within the phrases.

The influences of other writers can also be sensed in the novel and

---

*Holden's reference to Dickens's *David Copperfield* in chapter 1 perhaps delivers a secondary message. The first chapter of the Dickens novel cites Copperfield as having been born in a caul, a membrane that surrounds newborns. Holden Caulfield's name has been analyzed repeatedly, often with this reference in mind. The conjunction of "caul" with "field" and the similarity between "Holden" and "Hold on" easily satisfies. However, Salinger first named Holden Caulfield in 1941, years before he ever conceived of a field of rye. This date also precludes another theory that Salinger joined the names of the actors William Holden and Joan Caulfield. Joan Caulfield's film career did not begin until 1945.

evoke Salinger's notion that he had accepted a literary inheritance from Ernest Hemingway in Paris in 1944. The voice of Holden Caulfield is descended from the narration of Hemingway's 1923 story "My Old Man," which was itself influenced by Hemingway's mentor, Sherwood Anderson, and in particular by Anderson's 1920 story "I Want to Know Why," in essence binding together three generations of great American authors.

Holden's story is told from a hospital in California. His tale covers the events that have resulted in his hospitalization and occurred during a three-day period the previous December. His account begins on a Saturday afternoon at his boarding school, Pencey Prep, in Agerstown, Pennsylvania. Having failed every class but English, Holden has been asked by the school's administration not to return after the Christmas holiday. The setting of the opening scene establishes Holden as an outcast. He is alone on top of Thomson Hill, separated from his peers, watching them from afar while presenting a monologue that expresses his alienation and disgust with the phony world around him. From this first scene, readers realize that Holden Caulfield is a disturbed young man.

Holden then introduces a variety of classmates and teachers, among them the pathetic Robert Ackley and Holden's self-absorbed roommate, Ward Stradlater. Stradlater has a date with Jane Gallagher, a childhood friend of Holden whose innocence Holden has come to idealize.

Holden Caulfield is a character of contradictions. Even his physical description displays the opposites that make up his personality. At sixteen, he is clearly caught between adolescence and adulthood, with a tumult of conflicting emotions. The most prominent of Holden's contradictions involves his condemnation of "phoniness," which he rails against while indulging in fabrication and pretense, going as far as to call himself "the biggest liar." Such attitudes sometimes annoy readers, who, looking for a character with qualities that are easily identifiable, find fault in Holden's apparent hypocrisy. His contradictions serve a number of purposes. They portray his inconsistencies and lend reality to his character, which is lifelike in its complexity. They also define him as a typical adolescent. On another level, Holden's contradictions serve to mirror the balance in which *The Catcher in the Rye* is constructed.

Before Stradlater leaves for his date with Jane Gallagher, he pressures Holden into writing an essay for him. Holden chooses to write a description of a poem-strewn baseball glove once owned by his younger brother Allie. As he writes, Holden relays the story of ten-year-old Allie and his death from leukemia three years before. Although he tells the story in an almost nonchalant way, it is among the most sobering portions of the book. Only at this point do readers begin to understand the scale of Holden's anguish. All of his traits and reactions are dominated by his brother's death. In his memory, Allie possesses something that Holden cherishes above all else and has lost: his innocence. Holden lost it on the night he lost Allie, and the two losses are inseparably entwined. In his mind, to enter adulthood would be to abandon Allie and, in doing so, sever his tie to the memory of his own innocence.

Holden goes beyond preserving Allie through memory. He idealizes his dead brother, elevating him to a near-holy status. In the absence of adult supervision, he reinvents Allie as a reproachful parent-god. When he becomes depressed, he searches out his brother for comfort, and if he feels besieged, he actually prays to Allie. As Holden moves into adulthood, he drifts away from Allie, farther from his own ability to live up to the standards of purity and genuineness that Allie represents to him.

Depressed over his memory of Allie and frustrated over the possible spoiling of Jane Gallagher's innocence, Holden has a fistfight with Stradlater. Bloodied and dejected, Holden packs his suitcase and decides to leave Pencey that night, although he is not expected home until Wednesday.

Holden's rebellion against the world around him contains a judgment on mankind. Salinger's postwar preoccupation with the opposing forces of human nature developed into a vision of the world as being divided between the genuine and the phony, the enlightened and the insensitive, the Tyger and the Lamb. Holden Caulfield also divides the world between camps of "us and them," but his camp is a small one indeed, consisting only of his sister, Phoebe, his dead brother, Allie, and, perhaps, the reader.

Once in New York, Holden decides to check into a hotel and avoid being home when his parents receive word that he has been expelled from school. After arriving at Grand Central Station, he catches a cab and gets a room at the seedy Edmont Hotel. He finds the hotel "full of perverts." Supplied with Christmas money sent by his grandmother, he goes out on the town. He visits two bars, where he meets three girls who stick him with the bill and a former girlfriend of D.B., his older brother. Returning to the hotel, Holden is approached by an elevator operator named Maurice, who offers him a prostitute for five dollars. Holden accepts.

While valuing innocence, Holden is still attracted to adult situations. Bars, prostitutes, the backseats of cars, all lure him. Upon entering these situations, he cannot deal with them. By cutting himself off from the world around him, Holden has left himself no other figure to turn to for advice than Allie. Without guidance, which Allie's now-eternal youth cannot provide in these adult situations, Holden recoils from them and from any transition that takes him where Allie has never been.

He defends his alienation with scorn for adult society and a refusal to compromise with it. Holden's contempt is not reserved for adults alone. He identifies many of his own age and younger as being equally phony. Holden's problem is actually with the living—those who continue to live the life that his pure brother has been denied. He measures the quality of the lives around him not by his own standards but by Allie's. The challenge that Holden encounters is to reevaluate his perceptions in order to find a place in the world of the living.

Holden's acute perception is also a source of his own self-derision. Already corrupted by the things he disdains, he seeks refuge in flights of fancy. These are only momentary flights, and he finds himself increasingly having to deal with reality. Although he would like the world to accept him on his own terms, he knows that he will eventually have to compromise. In a way, his weekend in New York is his last great flight of fancy. But it is an adult flight and belies the truth that Holden must face: that he is already grown and the time has come to compromise.

As readers accompany Holden through his three-day journey, they encounter a series of settings and characters that contrast to one another and are symbolic of larger issues. Pretense and illusion are conveyed through upscale boarding schools and Upper East Side apartments, while the grimy Edmont Hotel and Holden's makeshift bed in the waiting room of Grand Central Station speaks to a very different reality. The stark sobriety of Mr. Spencer's bedroom, permeated by Vicks nose drops, contrasts with the affluence of Mr. Antolini's apartment, which is cluttered with the remnants of a cocktail party. Mr. Spencer may have greeted Holden bare-chested in his bathrobe, but it was Mr. Antolini's well-guarded facade of normalcy that proved threatening in the end. *Catcher*'s shifting scenes amplify Holden's contradictions and inner conflict. One page finds him drunk in a bar while the next finds him in a school playground. The question presented to readers is whether Holden actually belongs in either of these settings.

When Sunny, the prostitute, arrives, Holden finds her younger than he had expected. The situation depresses him, and he attempts only to have a conversation with her. Sunny is not interested; she collects her money and leaves. During the night, Holden is awakened by Sunny and Maurice at the door. They demand five more dollars. Refusing to pay, Holden fights with Maurice, who bloodies him and takes the money from his wallet. Maurice and Sunny are the most decadent and immoral characters Salinger introduces. They have fallen victim to the darker forces of their nature, to the Tyger of William Blake's poem. While Maurice is loathsome, Sunny is pathetic and has been degraded, corrupted not only by the treacherous Maurice but also by her compliance with the world around her. If Holden had avoided the fight by surrendering the five dollars demanded, it would be an admission that this is what the world he is about to enter is about: cheating, lying, and tawdriness. From this point, Holden begins to put away his childhood, but perceiving no redeeming qualities in the world he is about to enter, he also begins to despair.

Two nuns appear at the center of the story and signal the point of transition. Their position contrasts to that of the two characters that directly precede them, Maurice and Sunny. Again using the analogy of Blake's poetry, the nuns are *Catcher*'s equivalent of the Lamb. Holden is inspired by these women. His donation of $10 to them elevates his fight with Maurice to something approaching nobility. Most important, the nuns are the first adult characters Holden encounters whom he actually respects without qualification. The simplicity, thoughtfulness, and self-sacrifice of their lives show Holden that it is possible to become an adult and not be phony. From the point when he meets the nuns, Holden's emotional and physical state deteriorates rapidly, but he begins to accept responsibility and change.

. . .

After leaving the nuns, Holden becomes engrossed by a couple and their little boy walking down Broadway. Holden's depiction of this image is perhaps the most surreal that he offers. Behind his parents, the little boy is walking close to the curb, but in the street. In essence, he is taunting a metaphorical cliff. While walking, the boy sings the Robert Burns song so vital to Holden's story, "If a body catch a body coming through the rye." The boy is in extreme peril. The traffic on Broadway is heading straight for him, and drivers honk their horns and slam on their brakes to avoid hitting him. Amid this commotion, his parents saunter down the avenue, oblivious to the danger. Oddly, rather than being alarmed and angry with the couple for ignoring their son, Holden relates how happy the scene made him. It is possible that, for the first time, the appreciation of innocence outweighs Holden's feeling of obligation to be the Catcher in the Rye. It is also possible that this child does not exist at all and is a figment of Holden's imagination or a hallucination of himself.

After purchasing a jazz record, *Little Shirley Beans,* for his sister, Phoebe, he meets his old girlfriend, Sally Hayes, for a date. This portion of the novel closely resembles "Slight Rebellion off Madison," with Sally and Holden going to the theater and having an argument at the Rockefeller Center ice-skating rink. Alone and miserable after the quarrel, Holden attends the Christmas Pageant at Radio City Music Hall and meets his former classmate Carl Luce for drinks at the Wicker Bar. After an argument with Luce, who is portrayed as a pretentious braggart, Holden becomes drunk and again calls Sally, offering to help trim her Christmas tree, as he did in the earlier story.

In the dawning hours of Monday morning, Holden is in a drunken stupor and wanders around Central Park. He goes to the lagoon and numbly drops the *Little Shirley Beans* record, shattering it. Exhausted and despondent, he collects the broken fragments from the ground and decides to sneak home to see Phoebe, who is perhaps the last glimmer of hope left in his life. Creeping into his family's apartment, he goes directly into D.B.'s room, where Phoebe is sleeping. With him is the shattered record, a common Salinger symbol of the irretrievability of the past. As he did in "I'm Crazy," Holden briefly watches Phoebe sleep. When he awakens her, she accepts the pieces of the record and they engage in the most genuine conversation of the novel, the only one that Holden has completely without judgment.

Phoebe is only ten (the same age as Allie when he died), but she soon realizes that Holden has been thrown out of school. She challenges him to "name one thing" that he truly likes. All Holden can think of is Allie. Holden then tells Phoebe his fantasy of being the Catcher in the Rye. It is a dreamlike image in which Holden is the only adult in an overgrown field of rye teeming with little children at play. But the rye, grown well above the children's heads, hides a treacherous cliff. Holden sees himself as responsible for protecting the children from falling off the cliff.

The Catcher in the Rye is a central image and a necessary one for understanding Holden's frame of mind, but it is not the major point of the scene. That point occurs when Phoebe reminds Holden that Allie is dead and he has misquoted Burns. Only then does something within Holden begin to tumble into place.

In 1974, *The Catcher in the Rye* was first published in Israel. When the time came for Salinger to approve the contract with the publishing house, Bar David, he was startled to learn that it planned to change the title to *I, New York and All the Rest*. In defense of its decision, Bar David maintained that the present title made no sense when translated into Hebrew. Naturally, Salinger refused the change. He explained that, by itself, the term "catcher in the rye" had no more meaning in English than it did in any other language. The words, he reminded them, were a misquotation from Robert Burns, the meaning of which was explained in the book.[26] While the significance of Holden's misquotation was emphasized by Salinger, it is often virtually ignored by readers and academics. By replacing "Gin a body meet a body" with "When a body catch a body," Holden changes the connotation of the poem. To "catch" children from falling into the perils of adulthood is to intervene by rescuing, preventing, or forbidding. But to "meet" is to support and share, which is a connection. In a sweeping sense, Holden's entire journey is discovering the mistake that he has made when misquoting Burns. His struggle comes to an end only when he recognizes the difference between catching and meeting. When that recognition occurs, it is an epiphany.

In his final attempt to avoid responsibility, Holden decides to run away to Colorado. His plan evolves into a fantasy of living a life pretending to be a deaf-mute. He reveals this to Phoebe and borrows her savings in order to finance his flight. But Holden has neglected to consider what effect this will have upon his sister. He is about to recognize that unlike the dead, who can suffice on remembrance, the living require consideration in the present.

When she learns of Holden's intentions, Phoebe is rightly angry and hurt. She devises her own plan. She will call Holden back to reality by packing her bags and feigning to go with him. This will force Holden to choose between her and Allie, between responsibility and memory. She meets Holden the next day, carrying her suitcase. When Phoebe tells Holden she is going with him, he does not take well to the idea and tries to convince her that she cannot go. Refusing now to speak to her brother or allow him to touch her, Phoebe switches roles—playing the part of Holden and forcing him to deal with her as an adult would.

The moment of connection, of Holden's passage into adulthood, does not occur at the carousel. It happens beforehand, while he and Phoebe are arguing. In this scene, Holden promises to collect his bags and go straight home but only if Phoebe will return to school. This is catching, not meeting, and Phoebe is not convinced that Holden is sincere. She tells her brother to do whatever he wants to do, but she is not going back to school regardless. Then she tells her brother to shut up. The words are a slap across the face, and Holden is changed. He asks Phoebe to walk with him to the Central Park Zoo. "If I let you not go back to school this afternoon and go for a little walk, will you cut out this crazy stuff?" he asks. "Will you go back to school like a good girl?" Despite the maturity of Holden's words, Phoebe is still switching roles. She runs away from Holden, just as he had planned to run away. But Holden is unmoved. He then utters perhaps the most significant lines of the novel: "I didn't follow her, though. I knew she'd follow me."

The derivation of this scene and the course of Holden's transformation can be found in previous stories. The power of Charles's words to rejuvenate Sergeant X in "For Esmé—with Love and Squalor" is similar to the power of Phoebe's words to awaken her brother Holden. Lionel Tannenbaum's realization of the pain he has caused his mother in "Down at the Dinghy" is like the awareness Phoebe's words deliver to Holden. The strength found through mutual dependence and compromise by Babe and Mattie Gladwaller as they sled down Spring Street is also found here. This is not simply the moment when Holden Caulfield enters adulthood. It is the moment of connection, when he stops catching and begins to meet others. There are other stories too where portions of this scene can be found, but its message is most clearly expressed by Holden's younger brother in "The Ocean Full of Bowling Balls." In that story, Kenneth—now Allie—warned Vincent against being too reticent to relinquish self and embrace the connection with others that comes from selfless love. In the same story, he lamented Holden's inability to compromise and wondered if Holden would ever surmount that inflexibility.

By relinquishing his own needs, Holden does compromise. He compromises out of love for his sister. Holden's compromise is not surrender. It is balance. It is the same balance that Seymour Glass teaches his brother Buddy when playing marbles. It is balance attained by releasing oneself in order to find the place of perfect connection. And from that point on, Holden Caulfield speaks as an adult. He does not enter adulthood because he has been beaten into submission by the world around him or by seeing the virtue of maturity. He becomes an adult because that is what his sister needs.

There is a delicate but pervasive element of Zen belief in *Catcher*'s carousel scene that elevates it to a spiritual event. Its magnitude is transmitted through the reader's instinct rather than narrative text. The message of Holden's transformation is intangible and is experienced by the reader rather than dictated. Salinger did not need to deliver a sermon on Zen or innocence or even love. The combination of subtle props and small events that surrounds this scene converges within the reader to deliver the weight of its value.

Holden watches Phoebe as she rides the carousel. As he does, his connections are sublime and occur on many levels. He connects with Phoebe and, in doing so, mystically with his brother Allie, finding in his sister an embodiment of the same innocence that had kept him tied to Allie. In finding Phoebe, Holden releases Allie, whose values and purity he now recognizes have been born again within his sister. By releasing the dead, he embraces the living. In a very real way, just as the memory of Allie held Holden to stagnancy, his union with Phoebe releases him to life.

Perhaps most important, Holden connects with himself. As he watches Phoebe, he does so as an adult. Yet he is overwhelmed by her beauty and touches a remnant of his own innocence. Realizing that he has retained these capabilities, Holden cries from joy and relief. He accepts that he can enter the adult world and not be phony. As an adult, he can still be "swell."

For J. D. Salinger, writing *The Catcher in the Rye* was an act of cleansing. Through it, he relieved himself of a weight he had carried since the end of the war. The crush of Salinger's faith, threatened by the terrible events of war, so full of blackness and death, is reflected in Holden's loss of faith, caused by the death of his brother. The memory of fallen friends haunted Salinger for years, just as Holden was haunted by the ghost of Allie. On this point, Salinger made a slip of the pen. In renaming the character of Kenneth Caulfield, he chose a term used to represent fellow soldiers of the Second World War.

The struggle of Holden Caulfield echoes the spiritual journey of the author. In both author and character, the tragedy is the same: a shattered innocence. Holden's reaction is shown through his scorn of adult phoniness and compromise. Salinger's reaction was personal despondency, through which his eyes were opened to the darker forces of human nature.

Both, however, eventually came to terms with the burdens they carried, and their epiphanies were the same. Just as Holden comes to realize he can enter adulthood without becoming false and sacrificing his values, Salinger came to accept that the knowledge of evil did not ensure damnation.

10. Crossroads

J. D. Salinger wrote a masterpiece, *The Catcher in the Rye*, recommending that readers who enjoy a book call up the author;
then he spent his next 20 years avoiding the telephone.
—John Updike, 1974[1]

In creating the intimacy between Holden Caulfield and readers of *The
Catcher in the Rye*, Salinger employed the lesson taught to him by Whit
Burnett in 1939 when Burnett read William Faulkner without coming
"between the author and his beloved silent reader."[2] Like countless
other Americans, Faulkner himself was experiencing that same intimacy during the summer of 1951, glimpsing within the pages of
Catcher a reflection of himself. "Salinger's *Catcher in the Rye*," he remarked, "expresses so completely what I have tried to say." Yet, by experiencing Holden's character through the echo of his own reflection,
Faulkner saw the journey of Holden Caulfield as an unredeemed misery. "His tragedy," Faulkner felt, "was that when he attempted to enter
the human race, there was no human race there."[3]

William Faulkner's appreciation of Salinger's novel brought full circle an inspiration that he himself had unwittingly catapulted. But his interpretation also foreshadowed the predicament that Salinger now faced: different people were drawn to *Catcher* for different reasons. By virtue of Holden's character being so absorbing and because the novel allowed so many interpretations, readers were anxious for its meaning to be clarified or to have their personal sensation of it confirmed. In the attempt, it was only natural that they would seek out the author himself. After all, Holden seemed to be talking about Salinger when he declared that after finishing a good book "you wish the author that wrote it was a terrific friend of yours and you could call him up on the phone whenever you felt like it."[4] Many readers took this line to be an open invitation. Nothing could have been farther from the truth.

In reality, Salinger hated every moment of the celebrity that now enclosed him. "It's a goddamn embarrassment, publishing," he moaned. "The poor boob who lets himself in for it might as well walk down Madison Avenue with his pants down."[5] Impatiently, he waited for book sales to subside and his notoriety to fade, but the furor over *Catcher* showed no sign of abating. By the end of the summer the novel was already in its fifth printing and climbing the *New York Times* best-seller list.

Still Salinger held out hope that he could resume a normal life. As late as February 1952, although *Catcher* stubbornly remained on the book charts, he insisted that he could put the novel's publication behind him and retrieve the past.* In an interview granted that month to the *Daily Mirror* in England, he was optimistic. "The fact is," he stated prematurely, "I feel tremendously relieved that the season for the success of *The Catcher in the Rye* is over. I enjoyed a small part of it but most of it I found hectic and professionally and personally demoralizing. Let's say I'm getting good and sick of bumping into that blown-up photograph of my face on the back of the dust-jacket. I look forward to the day when I see it flapping against a lamp post, in a cold, wet Lexington Avenue wind."[6] The allusion Salinger used in describing the dust jacket was a reference to the final scene of "The Laughing Man," whose narrator is terrified by a piece of red tissue paper flailing against a lamppost. For Salinger, the enormous photograph of himself

---

* *The Catcher in the Rye* last appeared on the *New York Times* best-seller list on March 2, 1952, when it held the number twelve position.

on the book's back cover irritated him to the point of obsession. In the short lull between the novel's second and third printings, he finally managed to have the photograph removed and would never repeat the mistake of allowing his image on a book. In fact, he developed such an acute aversion to being photographed at all that to this day he is recognized almost exclusively by that single photograph.*

Against his new fame, Salinger attempted to construct something of a normal life. After returning from Britain, he moved back to New York City, where he hoped to blend into the population, settling into an apartment at 300 East 57th Street in the Sutton Place district of Manhattan. The area was pleasant and middle class, and Salinger had been familiar with it for years. Dorothy Olding, who had secured the apartment for him while he was in England, lived just a few buildings away. His friend Herb Kauffman also lived nearby, and the Sutton Cinema was his favorite movie house. Once moved in, Salinger found that something of the area's comfort now embarrassed him. Like success itself, the location seemed to violate the values of humility and simplicity that he strove to embrace. So he took an apartment that was small and obscure and decorated it in a style that was shockingly ascetic.

All accounts agree as to the grim severity of Salinger's new living quarters. According to the author Leila Hadley, whom Salinger briefly dated in 1952, the apartment contained few furnishings aside from a lamp, a drawing table, and a photograph of himself in uniform. Everything but the walls was black: the furniture, the bookshelves, even the bedsheets. To Hadley, these surroundings, and the self-portrait especially, reinforced her opinion that Salinger took himself far too seriously.[7] Others held an even darker view of Salinger's tastes, believing the blackness of the new apartment matched his own despair.[8]

The apparent contradiction involved in creating a cell-like atmosphere in a Sutton Place apartment was typical of Salinger throughout 1951. The year was among the most pivotal of his life, and his actions revealed the paradox of his personality in ways strikingly similar to Holden Caulfield. After asking John Woodburn not to send him re-

---

*Salinger's decision to remove his photograph from the back cover of *The Catcher in the Rye* raised the value of the copies that contained the photograph exponentially. A first edition of *Catcher* with the dust jacket has been known to sell at auction for as much as $30,000. Second editions sell for less but still far more than later editions without Salinger's photograph.

views of *Catcher* and bragging about having cut himself off from any source of news while in Britain, once he settled in at East 57th Street, he seemed to digest every critical article he could acquire. Already disdainful of literary critics, his opinion quickly turned to disgust. Yet he continued to absorb every word.

Rather than embracing positive reviews and remaining contemptuous of those more negative, Salinger lashed out at them all. He thought them pedantic and smug. None, he claimed, expressed how the novel actually made the reader feel, and he condemned even the most glowing reviews for analyzing *Catcher* on an intellectual rather than spiritual level, therefore stripping the novel of its intrinsic beauty. So, though critical opinion certainly mattered a great deal to Salinger, he did not condemn the critics for attacking him personally. Rather, he blamed them for their inability to feel the experience of *The Catcher in the Rye,* and for that sin he pledged his undying scorn.[9]

When *Catcher* was published in Britain at the end of August, it was confronted with a far chillier reception. If a number of American critics had been unperceptive, the British appraisals were outright condescending. In a typical review, *The Times Literary Supplement* skewered the novel for what it called its "endless stream of blasphemy and obscenity." Worse yet was a generally snobbish contempt for the novel's literary construction. It wasn't so much the American vernacular that had put off British reviewers, as Jamie Hamilton had feared, as the seemingly random nature of the novel's structure. Consequently, British sales of *The Catcher in the Rye* were not good and Salinger was embarrassed when Hamilton began to suffer the penalty. His ire quickly turned on the unworthy Little, Brown and Company, which was enjoying far greater profits than his friend in London. After weighing the British reviews and sensing Hamilton's distress, Salinger swore never to have anything more to do with Woodburn or his detestable colleagues at Little, Brown again. "Damn them all," he said with a scowl.[10]

Salinger's social life also suffered contradictions after *Catcher*'s release. As might have been expected, he now found himself more popular than before. Party and dinner invitations poured in. Women were anxious to date him. Strangers sought his autograph. There was an explosion of fan mail. Salinger admitted to having initially enjoyed the attention. After all, it was what he had worked for all his life. Nevertheless, once placed in these situations, he squirmed under their demands. His newfound inclination to cloister himself came into conflict with his social instincts. He dated women he could not trust. He accepted invitations to events at which he found himself uncomfortable, drinking too much and regretting having attended them in the first place. Then, the following week, he would accept another invitation. Like Holden Caulfield, Salinger appeared uncertain of which direction to move in.

Aside from *Catcher*'s publication, a number of events occurred in 1951 that would affect Salinger for years to come. During the previous autumn, he had attended a party given by Francis Steegmuller of *The New Yorker* and his wife, the artist Bee Stein. It was there that he met Claire Douglas, the daughter of the renowned British art dealer Robert Langton Douglas and half sister of Baron William Sholto Douglas, marshal of the Royal Air Force. Claire was only sixteen but was instantly drawn to the thirty-two-year-old Salinger. In turn, he was enchanted by the demure young girl with the large, expressive eyes and childlike nature. The following day, he called the Steegmullers to express his interest in Claire, and they gave him her address at Shipley, ironically the same private school that Jane Gallagher attends in *The Catcher in the Rye*. Salinger contacted Claire that week, and the couple dated intermittently for the next year.

At times their relationship was intense, although chaste by all accounts. During the summer of 1951, it was interrupted by Salinger's visit to Britain and the death of Claire's father, which took her to Italy for the funeral. When each returned to America, the romance was revived. However, in a December letter to Jamie Hamilton, Salinger revealed a serious romance with a girl he called "Mary," confiding to Hamilton that he and Mary had actually considered marrying before coming to their senses. Salinger's tone made it plain that he was still captivated by this girl despite attempts to be "rational."[11] The chances are that there was no "Mary" and Salinger was actually referencing Claire Douglas. Jamie Hamilton would have immediately recognized Claire—and her young age—had Salinger identified her by name. The Douglases held power in Britain, and the family was well known.

The rationality that Salinger referred to in putting away his romance was, in fact, religion. After returning home from Europe he began to frequent the Ramakrishna-Vivekananda Center on East 94th Street, around the corner from his parents' apartment on Park Avenue, which taught a form of Eastern philosophy centered on the Hindu Vedas, called Vedanta. There, Salinger was introduced to *The Gospels of Sri Ramakrishna,* a huge volume of complicated religious doctrine that explicitly advocated sexual restraint. As a result, although he dated often during 1951, there has never been a whisper that he engaged his companions sexually. In fact, Salinger's dates were more likely to share religious discussions than physical contact.

. . .

The close of 1951 delivered a shock when *New Yorker* founder Harold Ross, who had turned fifty-nine that November, fell ill with a mysterious ailment.

Just how serious Ross's illness was became apparent late that summer, when he could no longer make it to the magazine's offices. Ross had edited every issue of *The New Yorker* since 1925, and his absence was ominous. Alarmed, Salinger wrote to him expressing his concern and his hope that Ross would soon return to work. The editor did return in mid-September and life at the magazine appeared to go back to normal. Salinger made plans to visit Ross for a weekend that October but suddenly came down with shingles and was forced to postpone the trip. On October 23, Ross sent Salinger his own sympathies, comforting him with rearranged plans for their visit. "I'll put you down for spring," he promised.

On December 3, recovered to health and feeling the need to escape the clamor of the city, Salinger reported to Gus Lobrano that he was going away for a few weeks in an attempt to finish a story. It was a trip he would never take.

Despite his returning to work and making plans for the following year, Harold Ross's health worsened. Traveling to Boston, Ross consigned himself to the New England Baptist Hospital, where he underwent exploratory surgery on December 6. Surgeons found that a large tumor had enveloped his right lung, and, while they deliberated what to do, Ross died on the operating table.

Salinger was staggered by the news. His affection for Ross had been absolute. On December 10, he attended the funeral with the entire *New Yorker* "family." Besides their shock and grief over the loss of their leader, there was a feeling of apprehension. Ross's death had been unexpected, and he had not named a successor. Among the mourners, two names were whispered as likely candidates to head the magazine. Foremost was Salinger's own editor, Gus Lobrano. The other was William Shawn, who had been on the *New Yorker* staff since 1933.

. . .

Salinger would never again attain the level of productivity he had achieved in 1948. He spent most of 1951 wrestling with "De Daumier–Smith's Blue Period," the only story he is known to have written that year. Salinger claimed to have worked on the piece for five months, but it actually took far longer.

It appears that Salinger began writing the story soon after the rejection of "Requiem for the Phantom of the Opera" in January 1951. The first available reference to the story is contained in an undated letter to Gus Lobrano.* Just before Salinger left for Britain on May 8, Lobrano had taken him to lunch at the Algonquin Hotel, where they had discussed the story. Salinger had then rushed home to complete the piece, which he had promised to deliver to Lobrano the previous Saturday and was now late.

Upon submitting the story, Salinger told Lobrano that he was uncertain of it. He considered it long and meandering and was afraid readers might find it "offensive."[12] Lobrano not only agreed, he also thought the story "bizarre." His final rejection letter did not appear until November 14, but it is probable that Salinger had already ineffectively reworked and resubmitted it before its rejection.

According to Lobrano, "the piece wasn't successful as a short story, perhaps because the idea and characterization were too complex for so much compression."[13] *The New Yorker* commonly used the term "compression" to indicate that a story needed to be shortened. Salinger spent innumerable months during his career "compressing" his stories to acceptable *New Yorker* length. Lobrano's use of the word in this letter helps to explain why Salinger had worked on the story for so long. Salinger responded to Lobrano the next day. He told the editor that he wouldn't protest the rejection but would go on to another

---

*Though the letter was undated, Salinger mailed it from Westport, which places it before May 8. The letter's tenor and content also indicate that it was written very close to Salinger's departure for overseas. In addition to its hectic tone, it reports Salinger having purchased a coat with a fur collar—an item he certainly wouldn't have needed in New York during the spring.

story instead.[14] Yet his resentment was palpable in his reply, and despite his claiming otherwise, it was clear that he was unwilling to give up on it regardless of *The New Yorker*'s verdict. Still chafing at the rebuff on December 11, Salinger shared his disappointment with Jamie Hamilton. Rather than shelve the story, Salinger told him he was debating adding it to a collection or even expanding it into a novel.

It was likely Hamilton who came to Salinger's aid. "De Daumier–Smith's Blue Period" was published the following May, not in *The New Yorker* or any other American magazine but in the British *World Review*, the same publication in which Hamilton had first read "For Esmé—with Love and Squalor." Not only was "De Daumier–Smith" the last Salinger story ever to appear outside the pages of *The New Yorker*, it is the only story initially published outside the United States.

. . .

After *The Catcher in the Rye*, the aim of Salinger's ambition shifted and he devoted himself to crafting fiction embedded with religion, stories that exposed the spiritual emptiness inherent in American society. In doing so, he was forced to deal with the question of how to deliver that message through fiction. The aim of fiction is the re-creation of realism, but Salinger was seeking to transmit spiritual epiphanies that were in essence intangible. His first attempts were not successful, and it took years for him to develop the appropriate vehicle for his message.

Salinger's first attempt at religious fiction, "De Daumier–Smith's Blue Period," is the story of a disturbed young man who is saved by a transcendent epiphany. The story is narrated in the first person by John Smith and offered in memory of his late stepfather. A reflective tale, the story is told by Smith as an adult, looking back upon events that took place in 1939, when he was nineteen.

Believing himself to be a great artist, John Smith is presented as pretentious and self-pleased, using his intellect to feed his ego and his contempt for those he considers untalented. Knowing what we do of Salinger's connecting of art with spirituality, Smith's elevation of the intellect over the spiritual not only signals his disconnection with the world around him but also the alienation between himself and his art. His ego is enormous. He notes his resemblance to El Greco and admits without self-consciousness to having painted seventeen self-portraits. Most of all, Smith is lonely, a condition amplified by his description of a vision of New Yorkers playing a game of musical chairs from which he is excluded. After issuing a prayer to be left alone by his fellow man in reaction to the scene, Smith reports that the prayer was answered. "Everything I touched," he admits, "turned to solid loneliness."[15]

In May 1939, Smith finds what he believes to be a way out of his impasse. In a French-language newspaper, he discovers a classified ad in search of an instructor for a Montreal correspondence "art academy" named Les Amis des Vieux Maîtres, an institution headed by Monsieur I. Yoshoto. Smith answers the ad, embellishing his credentials and claiming to be the great-nephew of the artist Honoré Daumier as well as a close friend of Pablo Picasso, the two relationships that provide the story with its title. As a pseudonym, he chooses the pretentious and phony Jean de Daumier–Smith to mask the banality of his true identity.

Smith is accepted as an instructor and heads for Montreal. It never occurs to him that he may have been the sole applicant. In fact, his haughty attitude is undisturbed by what he finds there. As it turns out, the high-sounding Les Amis des Vieux Maîtres is nothing more than the Yoshotos' tiny apartment, sharing a tenement with an orthopedic-appliance store in the worst section of the city.

During his time in Montreal, Smith indulges his fantasies so completely that he actually begins to believe them. "I lied," he admits, "in 1939, with far greater conviction than I told the truth." He becomes so immersed in his fictional persona that when asked to translate for M. Yoshoto, he becomes indignant. "Here I was—a man who had won three first-prizes, a very close friend of Picasso's (which I actually was beginning to think I was)—being used as a translator." His lies and embellishments are important only to him, and the story masterfully contrasts his own rich imaginings with the negligible reactions of those around him. In other words, Smith is lost in his own inverted forest but rather than being seeded with inspiration, his forest is overgrown by illusion and ego.

If the realities of the art "academy" and Smith's position as "instructor" fail to discourage him, the comic ineptitude of his correspondence students stuns him into dismay. Smith is initially given charge of three students. Reviewing the work and profiles of his first two proves to be an ordeal. First, there's Bambi Kramer, a housewife whose favorite artists are Rembrandt and Walt Disney. Bambi submits a painting of three misshapen boys fishing in an equally distorted body of water. The boys ignore, or cannot read, a nearby NO FISHING! sign. Bambi solemnly titles the creation "Forgive Them Their Trespasses." Smith's next student is a "society photographer" named R. Howard Ridgefield. Ridgefield, whose wife has urged him to "branch over into the painting racket," names his favorite artist as the painter Titian. Ridgefield's submission is as charming as Bambi's. It depicts a young girl being sexually molested in church by a minister "in the very shadow of the altar." The descriptions are among the most humorous that Salinger ever penned; but Jean (John) is not amused. Instead, he's driven deep into frustrated despair by the hopelessness of his situation.

Jean's third student offers salvation. A nun of the order of the Sisters of St. Joseph, Sister Irma teaches at a convent elementary school. Unlike the first two students, she neglects to provide her age and encloses a photograph of her convent in place of one of herself. She states that her favorite artist is Douglas Bunting, a painter completely unknown to Smith, and that her hobbies include "loving her Lord and the Word of her Lord." Sister Irma submits an untitled and unsigned painting of the burial of Christ. The small painting displays such talent that Jean falls instantly in love with its beauty. Enraptured and elated by this student's prospects, Smith immediately writes Sister Irma a long, excited letter.

Like Holden's encounter with the nuns in *The Catcher in the Rye,* Smith discovers Sister Irma exactly midway through his tale. Also like the scene in *Catcher,* the event in "De Daumier–Smith" signals the point of transition. The letter that Jean pens to Sister Irma in response to her submission graphically explains the roots and depth of his spiritual void. This portion of the story addresses the connection between art and spirituality and touches upon the notion of balance by pointing out the clash between the spiritual and the intellectual.

By this point in the story it becomes plain to readers that the subject of spiritual faith cannot be ignored. There are simply too many references. Smith professes agnosticism in his letter to the nun while insincerely aligning himself with the name of Saint Francis of Assisi. Somehow, Smith determines that he has found a kindred spirit through art in Sister Irma. This is another of Smith's delusions. The nun is clearly set in contrast to him, and his letter reveals just how wide the rift between them is.

Smith experiences two near-mystical incidents that together form the climax of the story. The first is muted and is a chilling insight into his own alienation that brings him to the point of collapse. After taking a walk one night, he is drawn to the lighted display window of the orthopedic-appliance shop on the ground floor of the school building. As he gazes at the contents on exhibit—enamel bedpans and urinals overseen by a wooden dummy wearing a rupture truss—he experiences an abrupt stripping of his ego that reveals his alienation. He suddenly comes to realize that no matter how technically perfect his art might become, it is tied to intellectual logic and he will always remain uninspired, adrift in a world he considers mundane and ugly. He now recognizes that he is spiritually unconscious, with no connection to the divine inspiration that true art requires or true living demands. His art is polluted by ego.

Smith attempts to deal with his experience and the resulting feelings of insignificance by retreating into his own fantasy world and dreaming of Sister Irma. Here is the "ribald" portion of the story that readers were warned of in its opening paragraph. In Smith's fantasy, he rescues Sister Irma from her convent. In his imagination, she is young and beautiful and Smith chivalrously whisks her away in a romantic whirlwind.

The illusion is short-lived. The next day, Smith receives a letter from Sister Irma's convent, informing the school that she can no longer continue her art studies. Smith is stunned and embittered, and his reaction is cruel: he cuts loose his remaining students, spitefully telling them to abandon any hope of ever being artists. He then pens another letter to Sister Irma. Smith's ego having entrenched his spiritual obstinacy, he cautions the nun that she will never perfect her art without further technical instruction.

Smith describes his second experience as being "transcending." It is the most blatant epiphany that any Salinger character experiences. Like Saul on the road to Damascus, he is transformed by divine revelation delivered through a blinding light. While straining away from labeling his experience as mystical, Smith stresses that the event actually occurred.

In the evening's twilight Smith is once again drawn to the lighted display window of the orthopedic-appliance shop. Peering through the window, he becomes fascinated by the figure of a woman changing the truss on the wooden dummy. Suddenly realizing that she is being watched, the woman becomes disoriented, falling to the ground in confusion. Embarrassed but mustering nobility, she lifts herself up and resumes her task.

The girl in the window corresponds to Sister Irma. Both are devoted to a lowly calling. Yet it is actually a beautiful thing that they do because they do it with humility. Salinger made a similar point in *The Catcher in the Rye*. Holden and Allie were mesmerized with appreciation for the kettledrum player of Radio City Music Hall orchestra. Although the drummer struck his instrument only once or twice during the performance, he did it with such genuine dedication that Holden and Allie thought him the best drummer they had ever seen. Salinger likens this selfless dedication to spirituality when Holden comments that Jesus Himself would have liked the kettledrum player for the purity of his art.

However, the central figure in this scene is not the girl in the window or even Smith. The prop of the storefront dummy, which Smith likens to God, holds greater meaning. In the first encounter, he saw the dummy as the powerless god of a world filled with enameled urinals who ruled over his banal life of alienation as a blind, muted spectator. But the dummy changes meaning when Smith encounters it during his epiphany, and it takes on the most important message of the story—the meaning around which all other themes revolve.

> Suddenly . . . the sun came up and sped toward the bridge of my nose at the rate of ninety-three million miles a second. Blinded and very frightened, I had to put my hand on the glass to keep my balance. When I got my sight back, the girl had gone from the window, leaving behind her a shimmering field of exquisite, twice-blessed, enamel flowers.

In a burst of light Smith experiences the revelation that beauty and value are inherent in all things, even the most lowly and untalented. Moreover, this value proclaims the presence of God. The lowly bedpans and orthopedic supplies are not just transformed into beautiful enamel flowers. They are transformed and "twice blessed." Smith, too, is changed. He quickly reinstates his students, telling them that their previous dismissals had been an administrative mistake. He then releases Sister Irma to pursue her own destiny. "Tout le monde est une nonne," he concludes. "Everybody is a nun."

The end of "De Daumier–Smith's Blue Period" contains a brief segment that returns Jean de Daumier–Smith back to ordinary but fulfilled John Smith, living in the present moment. It shows what he has learned from his experience and how his life has been stripped of phoniness and ego. In the process, Smith does not forsake his art but rather becomes his art—a more faithful rendering of the value held within self than he could have ever reproduced through his seventeen self-portraits.

Like its main character, "De Daumier–Smith" shows Salinger on the road to enlightenment, in search of spiritual direction. Consequently, despite its numerous Roman Catholic metaphors, the story is not an endorsement of Christian dogma. The experience of John Smith is basically Zen Buddhist in nature. In Zen, Smith's epiphany is called "Satori." A key goal of Zen Buddhism, Satori is a sudden flash of enlightenment. It is individual and intuitive and the opposite of intellectual knowledge. Often obtained through meditation, Satori can be experienced by anyone of any faith. A sudden burst of light, it is abrupt and momentary, coming out of the "blue," usually after a blow to one's ego.

"De Daumier–Smith's Blue Period" is a humorous story containing deep meaning. All the same, Gus Lobrano was correct in his criticism. In constructing it, Salinger attempted to make too many points on too many levels within too little space. As a result, no single message is completely clear and the varied themes that make up this story tend to run together and obscure one another.

. . .

In light of the success of *The Catcher in the Rye,* Salinger had hoped that living in Manhattan might afford him a measure of anonymity. He was disappointed. He developed a fear of being recognized that, coupled with the lures of the city, with its social gatherings and romantic distractions, made it impossible for him to live a normal life in New York and still write with the devotion he sought. He had a new novel planned, and it would require greater solitude than the city would allow.

Salinger made arrangements to leave soon after January 1 for

Florida and Mexico, where he hoped to begin his book in earnest.[16] Events, however, predominantly the changing of the guard at *The New Yorker,* conspired to keep him in the city until March.

Most of the *New Yorker* "family" believed that fiction editor Gus Lobrano would succeed Harold Ross. Doubtless, Salinger also hoped that his friend would assume the lead role. If Lobrano was often dissatisfied with Salinger's writings, he was, at least, respectful in his disapproval. Among the magazine's editors, Salinger had gained a reputation for being difficult to deal with. Oversensitive to criticism and unusually protective of his work, he was known to become sullen and even angry when a story was contested.* Lobrano had learned how to deal with Salinger and treated him with deference. His criticisms were deliberately soft and apologetic, accompanied with expressions of upset, pain, and regret over being forced to rebuff any story. Lobrano was also not above acknowledging Salinger's occasional anger over his verdicts and—perhaps most important of all—knew how to leave the author alone when it was wise to do so. Having established this rapport, Salinger probably felt it in his interest that Lobrano rise to the helm of *The New Yorker.*

Out of the shadows emerged the hazy figure of William Shawn. When it was announced at the end of January that Shawn had been selected to succeed Ross, Salinger was disappointed, and Lobrano was embittered. What Salinger could not have realized at the time was that William Shawn would become the greatest champion of his career and was uncannily similar to what Salinger himself would someday become.

Despite having occupied a series of positions at the magazine since 1933, Shawn was barely known by the staff. He was an intensely private person, close to no one, and his reputation consisted of whispers and innuendos. The differences between Ross and Shawn were obvious from the start. Harold Ross had been lively and social and had run the magazine with a loud audacity, while Shawn was temperate and withdrawn, his management style oppressively polite. Shawn's first act

---

*In a rare television interview, given in 1995, William Maxwell recalled Salinger's indignation over the editorial insertion of a comma into one of his manuscripts. "There was hell to pay," Maxwell remembered. The comma was removed. When asked what the incident said about Salinger as a writer, Maxwell became solemn. "Salinger's idea of perfection is really perfection," he said, "and it shouldn't be tampered with."

as editor was to demolish Ross's office and move to the opposite end of the building. The gesture seemed threatening to the preening *New Yorker* "family," and rumors began to fly. One story was that in 1924, Shawn had been an intended victim of the infamous murderers Leopold and Loeb. Keen to verify or refute the rumor, amateur sleuths from *The New Yorker* secretly traveled to Chicago in 1965 to view the transcripts of the Leopold and Loeb trial. Finding no reference to a William in the transcripts, they returned to New York convinced that the tale was untrue. Yet none of the curious staffers dared ask Shawn himself.[17] That would have been unthinkable.

Born William Chon in Chicago in 1907, Shawn had never graduated from college. After changing his name, which he felt sounded confusingly Asian, he developed a personality that valued courtesy and loyalty but was highly eccentric. Aside from an obsession with privacy, Shawn was riddled with fears. He was claustrophobic and terrified of fire, machines, animals, and heights. It was said that he carried a hatchet in his briefcase in case he became trapped in an elevator.[18] The weight of these phobias should have constricted his prospects, but Shawn possessed raw talent and insight, a sharp editorial instinct that balanced his phobias and cast him onto center stage despite his shyness. By all accounts, he was a consummate professional who valued his authors' opinions and respected their privacy as much as his own. "Here at *The New Yorker*," Shawn declared, "if we tell someone we want to do a profile and that person doesn't want to cooperate, we don't do the profile."[19] Artistic and sensitive (Shawn had moved to New York aspiring to be a composer), no editor could have complemented Salinger as well or understood him better.

Oddly, within weeks of Shawn's ascendancy, Salinger was contacted by his former mentor Whit Burnett. *Story* magazine was planning a special issue, and Burnett wondered if Salinger, in light of his *Catcher* success, would contribute a story. "It is a long time since we have seen a story by you," Burnett commented.[20] Salinger declined. He had not forgiven Burnett for the *Young Folks* anthology episode. And he never would.

At the same time, Salinger found himself forced to deal with John Woodburn and "those bastards" at Little, Brown and Company. It had been seven months since the publication of his novel, and both Little, Brown and Dorothy Olding were pressuring Salinger to consider putting together a collection of short stories, a project that had been under discussion since April 1951 and a desire Salinger had held since 1944. He first met with Roger Machell, who represented Jamie Hamilton in New York, to discuss the project. When Machell reported Salinger's intention back to London, Hamilton was thrilled over the prospect and Salinger seemed reconciled; but when it came to dealing with John Woodburn, Salinger hesitated.

Still stinging from the Book-of-the-Month Club incident, he decided to deal with the editor only through his agent. By March, though, he decided to postpone the short-story collection, at least temporarily. Imagining himself reliving the misery he had endured the year before, Salinger explained that he did not feel ready for the commotion of publication just yet.[21]

In fact, Salinger was having a difficult time on a number of levels. He acknowledged not staying "rational" concerning his relationship with the mysterious "Mary," and moreover, he was having trouble dealing with his notoriety. He found himself in fear of being recognized and confessed that venturing outside his apartment gave him the uncomfortable sensation of being watched. He began to avoid people, and most of his time was spent cowering in his gloomy quarters, unsuccessfully attempting to write, while telephone calls went unanswered and party invitations sat unopened. Within a short time he began to complain of feeling trapped and cut off from others. In an effort to crawl out from what was clearly a looming depression, Salinger left on the trip to Florida and Mexico that he had planned for the previous January.

His itinerary on this trip was deliberately vague. He wanted to get away from the city and relax on a beach in obscurity. And though his original plans had been to begin a new novel while away, later correspondence indicates that he did little actual writing while on holiday. He seems to have been in no hurry to return home, however, and remained in Mexico until June. In the meantime, "De Daumier–Smith's Blue Period" was published in London's *World Review* in May. That same month, Salinger was honored with the 1952 Outstanding Alumnus Award by Valley Forge Military Academy. The awards dinner was planned for May 24, and it was expected that Salinger would attend, give a speech, and receive his honor. Salinger's sister, Doris, who was taking care of his apartment while he was away, retrieved the announcement and invitation.* After consulting her brother, she mailed the school a curt reply that was startling in its firmness: "My brother, J. D. Salinger is inaccessible somewhere in Mexico." The note allowed Salinger the opportunity to avoid the dinner and still appear gracious. Upon his return to New York in June, he sent a letter to the Alumni Association thanking it for the honor and expressing his humility over receiving it.[22]

The award from Valley Forge highlighted a number of contradictions evident in Salinger's character. There is no reason to believe that he was not flattered by the presentation, and his thank-you letter appears sincere. Yet he was also relieved to have been out of the country when the award was given. Ironically, the academy was rewarding him for his success with *The Catcher in the Rye*, a book that mocked the school. It's doubtful that the academy realized it at the time, but Salinger certainly did, and he would not have risked repeating the Olivier dinner experience on such a grand scale.

While Salinger was away, Dorothy Olding resumed negotiations with Little, Brown and Company over publishing a short-story collection. By the first week of July, they had reached an agreement, and Salinger wrote to Jamie Hamilton to offer him the British rights. He also offered Hamilton the source of his own epiphany, what Salinger called "the religious book of the century," *The Gospels of Sri Ramakrishna*. Confident that Hamilton would be as inspired by the text as he had, Salinger promised to send a copy of *The Gospels* to London and urged the publisher to read it and consider releasing an unabridged version in Britain.

The Gospels of Sri Ramakrishna record the conversations of the Bengali saint Sri Ramakrishna with his devotees. Written by an ardent disciple known only by the pseudonym "M," *The Gospels* were published in 1897 and brought to the United States by Swami Vivekananda. The collection is long and intense and the philosophy both sublime and complicated. Salinger doubtless studied the text for many months, perhaps years, before assimilating its tenets.

---

*It is possible that Doris accompanied her brother on part of the trip. Photographs taken about this time show her and Salinger enjoying themselves at a Florida beach resort.

According to the Ramakrishna-Vivekananda Center in New York, where Salinger first encountered his teachings, the life of Sri Ramakrishna was "literally an uninterrupted contemplation of God." The beliefs espoused by Sri Ramakrishna are known as Vedanta, and through *The Gospels,* the teachings of Sri Ramakrishna introduced Vedantic thought to the West. According to the center, "the four cardinal principles of Vedanta may be summed up as follows: the non-duality of the Godhead, the divinity of the soul, the unity of existence and the harmony of religions."

First and foremost, Vedanta is monotheistic. It teaches that there is only one God and that God is present in all things. In Vedanta, God is the ultimate Reality, and the names and distinctions that human beings apply to the things around them are illusion. These distinctions do not exist because all is God. In Vedanta, therefore, each soul is holy because it is part of God, and the body is merely a shell. The aim of Vedanta is to see God, to become one with God, by looking beyond the shell and perceiving the holiness within. Sri Ramakrishna called this form of enlightenment "God-consciousness" and taught that it could be obtained only through personal experience. Vedanta is a tolerant philosophy, accepting all faiths as being valid as long as they lead to the recognition of God. Without God-consciousness religion becomes sterile and loses the power to transform individual lives.[23]

Sri Ramakrishna espoused many beliefs that Westerners rarely associate with Hindu philosophy. Vedanta asserts that truth is universal and all humankind and existence are one. Rather than defy beliefs that Salinger already held, Vedanta supported and enhanced those beliefs and was especially in concert with Zen Buddhism. From 1952 until the end of Salinger's publishing career, Vedantic thought became entrenched in his work. The challenge that lay before him in 1952 was how best to introduce such an Eastern philosophy to American sensibilities without preaching and without appearing so odd as to turn readers away.

If Salinger had experienced a spiritual epiphany through *The Gospels of Sri Ramakrishna,* it was difficult to discern from his bearing. He remained depressed and withdrawn. He had suffered from depression for years, perhaps throughout his entire life, and was at times afflicted by episodes so intense that he could not relate to others. The irony of Salinger's frequent depressions was that they were usually caused by loneliness. Once having taken hold, his melancholy estranged him from others, deepening the very loneliness that had spawned it.

Salinger expressed his depression through his characters, pain that can be felt through the despair of Seymour Glass, the frustration of Holden Caulfield, and the misery of Sergeant X. Yet most of those characters were granted salvation, a road to wellness, often found through human connection. And though the author often shared the sorrow of his characters, he rarely possessed their cures, and there came a time in Salinger's life when living vicariously through the fictional epiphanies of his characters no longer sufficed.

Salinger's attraction to Vedanta was simple. Unlike Zen, Vedanta offered a path to a personal relationship with God, something that Salinger found enormously attractive. This allowed him hope, a promise that he could obtain a cure for his depression, live the resurrection he had gifted his characters, reconnect with himself and those around him, and find God and, through God, peace.

In July, Salinger decided that he was finally ready to resume work, the fourth time in seven months that he had made such a claim. This time, he attributed his renewed initiative to the hot July weather rather than any religious inspiration. In fact, he would not finish his next story until November. Once completed, it would be saturated with his new faith.

. . .

By the autumn of 1952, it became clear to Salinger that he could no longer live in New York City and still work. Manhattan was too neurotic. It held too many distractions, too many people, and not enough solitude. He had spent seven of the past fourteen months out of the country, and he simply couldn't afford to keep a Manhattan apartment while constantly seeking refuge from the city. He had accumulated a modest bankroll from the sales of *Catcher,* but in 1952, no one anticipated the novel's continued success. So, with frugality in mind, Salinger began to consider purchasing his own home. It would have to be away from the city but not an impossible distance from the offices of *The New Yorker.* Not surprisingly, he seems to have ruled out a suburban environment. Instead, he was drawn to the more rustic areas that had inspired him in his youth and where he had spent his childhood summers. He contacted his sister, Doris, who was recently divorced, and asked if she would accompany him in his search for a home. Doris readily agreed, and she, her brother, and Benny the schnauzer set off for New England.

They first traveled to Massachusetts, where Salinger fell in love with the old fishing towns along the coast of Cape Ann. After looking at a number of properties, he decided they were too expensive, and the trio moved on. They then traveled along the Connecticut River north into Vermont. In the town of Windsor they stopped at a diner for lunch. There, they struck up a conversation with a local real estate agent named Hilda Russell. She offered to show them a piece of property in nearby Cornish, New Hampshire, that she felt might be perfect for Salinger.

The village of Cornish is 240 miles north of New York City, but to Salinger it seemed a world away. Set among rolling, wooded hills, the rural hamlet exudes tranquillity. On a drive along its lonely roads, as the landscape dips and climbs, the wholesome scenery of Cornish woods, fields, and farmhouses is occasionally broken only by an exalting view of the Connecticut River Valley. Cornish was indeed ideal for Salinger. Seeking anonymity, he could have found no better place. The village itself is nearly anonymous. It has no town center or hub of activity, no business district or industry. Its beauty and solitude had attracted artistic minds for generations. It was home to the revered artist Maxfield Parrish, who had immortalized its pastoral scenery in his paintings.* At the turn of the twentieth century, Cornish had become famous as the home of Augustus Saint-Gaudens, the renowned sculptor whose studio had been a beacon for artists for decades. In fact, as part of the Dodge estate, the property that Russell showed Salinger was owned by Saint-Gaudens's granddaughter.

The land was located deep in the woods, at the end of a long road that climbed a hill. At the summit, the woods had been cleared to reveal a small, red, barnlike structure that Russell identified as "the house." The clearing containing the property melted into a meadow that fell downward so abruptly that it resembled a cliff. At the bottom of the meadow, a brook laced into the lushness of the surrounding

---

*Parrish lived in Cornish until his death in 1966, at the age of ninety-six. It is not known whether the artist ever met his equally famous neighbor.

woods. From the top of the meadow, the view was magnificent: before them lay the Connecticut River Valley with breathtaking vistas of rolling fields and woodlands and misty mountains beyond.

In contrast to the beautiful setting, the house was in a very poor state. It was actually a barn, dilapidated beyond livability. Renovated untold years before to include a two-story living room with exposed beams, a tiny loft, and a small kitchen off to the side, it offered all the deprivations of the frontier. It had no running water, no bathroom, and no heat to buffer the harsh New England winters. Despite these short-comings, Russell quoted a price that would have exhausted Salinger's savings. He could afford to buy the property but would have no funds left to renovate it.

When Salinger expressed an interest in the property regardless, his sister was appalled. She thought it inconceivable that her brother would entertain the notion after being raised on Park Avenue. A buyer for Bloomingdale's who had married a successful garment merchant, Doris's entire life had been lived in style. But Salinger knew depriva-tion firsthand. He had slept countless nights in frozen foxholes and had struggled for comfort in renovated garages and barns before. Moreover, this was his chance to fulfill the dream of Holden Caulfield, to escape to a cabin in the woods, far away from the phoniness of soci-ety, deep within his own inverted forest. Here was the ideal place to write and meditate, a place where he could release the characters of his imagination. Before year's end, he had placed a binder on the 90-acre property. Realizing Holden's dream, he would remain in Cornish for the rest of his life.[24]

. . .

When "De Daumier–Smith's Blue Period" was rejected by *The New Yorker* on November 14, 1951, Salinger began to revamp an old story that took place on a cruise ship.[25] How much work Salinger put into the story before he left for vacation in March is unclear, but his letters indicate that he wrote little during those months. Not until the au-tumn of 1952 did he regain his writing stride, enabling him to com-plete the manuscript by November 22. The gap in time can be sensed while reading "Teddy." The story's beginning has a distinctly looser feel than the remainder of the story. It also seems apparent that, while negotiating his next book with Little, Brown and Company, Salinger intended to include "Teddy" in the collection before it was actually finished. This influenced the story, causing Salinger to deliberately contrast and complement the collection's intended opening story, "A Perfect Day for Bananafish."

Excited by *The Gospels of Sri Ramakrishna,* Salinger rushed to present its values through his work. With the story "Teddy," messages that he had previously embedded into his stories as personal meditation, therapy, or acts of cleansing were made completely public for the first time, shared with readers as duty to his faith.

In 1952, most Americans thought their way of life superior to that of Eastern cultures. Salinger was well aware of this chauvinism. It was clear to him that his reading audience was not going to accept the notions of mysticism or reincarnation easily. So, in order to present them and still maintain reader interest, he created a ten-year-old American child, middle class and intriguingly intelligent—someone whom he was comfortable writing about and whom he hoped Americans would be interested in reading about.

Through the story, readers are introduced to the remarkable character of Teddy McArdle, the ultimate enlightened child. Young Teddy is a mystic-savant, a seer so far advanced in his spiritual quest for oneness with God that his attachment to the physical world around him, including his parents, has reached the point of evaporation. The story takes place aboard an ocean liner. Teddy, his parents, and his sister, Booper, are returning to the United States from a European trip, where Teddy, the subject of academic curiosity for most of his life, has been grilled, recorded, poked, and prodded by academics and casual partygoers like a show dog.

The story's opening scene is set in the stateroom of Teddy's parents, who, sunburned and apparently hungover, are trying to sleep late despite the activities of the precocious genius. Teddy's brilliant mind ticks away at light speed on impossible levels. His father, a bellicose actor and not in the best of moods, struggles to assert his authority over his child. Teddy's mother lies under the covers in bed, taunting her husband and listlessly issuing commands to Teddy in an attempt to irritate his father. Teddy's interactions with his parents are detached. He hears them only on the surface, and it's plain that he places little weight on their words or attitudes.

Standing on his parents' Gladstone suitcase, Teddy leans out of the porthole as if it were the interface between two worlds, the spiritual and the material, the world of reality and the world of illusion. He becomes fascinated when he spots a mass of orange peel that has been thrown into the ocean. As the pieces begin to sink, he ponders how they will soon exist only in his mind and how their existence actually depended upon his noticing them in the first place. While he peers out of the porthole in solipsistic contemplation, his parents insult and snap at each other. Salinger's descriptions of his characters accentuate the differences between them. Teddy's priorities are spiritual ones, and he is only dimly concerned with the physical world around him.

Teddy's parents are described as being materialistic and self-centered. They squabble over the quality of their luggage, which Teddy uses as a stool. Teddy's father is obsessed with retrieving his expensive Leica camera, which Teddy has given to his sister, Booper, as a toy, unconcerned about its material worth.

Teddy's interest in the orange peel speaks of the Zen notion of impermanence and the Vedantic belief that separate existence is an illusion. It also foreshadows the story's ending. Leaving his parents' stateroom in search of his sister, Teddy cautions his parents that they may never see him again outside their minds. "After I go out this door," he reports, "I may only exist in the minds of all my acquaintances. . . . I may be an orange peel." Despite this morose prediction, he still refuses to give his mother "a nice, big" kiss before leaving.

Teddy has acquired what Sri Ramakrishna called "God-consciousness." He perceives the inner spirit rather than the outward appearance. He also has little regard for the labels that he feels Western minds wrongly attach to people and objects. In contrast, his parents perceive only the shell. They appear indifferent to his enlightenment and insist upon treating him like a child. Their spiritual delinquency is the source of their discourse and the reason Teddy appears cold to them. While still respecting their position as his parents, he perceives the immaturity of their inner spirits and reacts accordingly.

After experiencing Teddy's relationship with his parents, it may seem odd that Teddy is amazingly tolerant of his sister, Booper, who is perhaps the most vicious child ever discharged by Salinger's imagination. But the rationale behind Teddy's tolerance of this cruel little girl, who claims to hate everyone, is simple.* He recognizes that she has only just begun her spiritual journey and has many incarnations ahead of her.

After finding Booper and making plans to meet at the swimming pool, Teddy settles into a lounge chair on the sundeck and begins to add to his diary. As he writes, Bob Nicholson, an academic from an unnamed university who has heard one of Teddy's taped interviews during a party, approaches him. He imposes himself on Teddy and begins to pepper him with philosophical questions. Nicholson's character serves two purposes. Salinger uses him as a sounding board against which Teddy can express Vedantic and Zen viewpoints that Nicholson reacts to skeptically. He treats Teddy not as a child or even as a human being but as a thing of intellectual curiosity. In short, Nicholson embodies the logic that poisons God-consciousness, and he represents the power of the intellect to blind individuals from spiritual truths.

Through Teddy, Salinger clarifies major tenets of Vedanta. He points out the difference between love and sentimentality, which he claims to be an "unreliable" emotion. Expounding on the philosophy of nonattachment, Teddy explains that the body is merely a shell and outward things are not reality. Only unity with God is real. Teddy is detached from those outward appearances because he is enlightened and sees only the godliness within.

To make these points clear to Western minds, Salinger uses a common Judeo-Christian image: the fall of Adam and Eve from grace. Teddy tells Bob that what Adam and Eve ate in the Garden of Eden was an apple containing logic and intellectuality and that one should vomit it from the system. The trouble, he explains, is that people don't want to see the way things actually are and that they are attached to their physical existence far more than they are connected to God.

From the subjects of logic and reincarnation, the topic turns to death. Teddy explains death as being a progression of life, giving himself as an example. He reveals that he has a swimming lesson in five minutes and points out that he could arrive for his lesson unaware that

---

*Booper's claim that she "hates everybody in this ocean" adds a dimension to the story's setting, which casts its characters adrift in an environment with no definable borders, no beginning, and no end. This setting mirrors the Zen and Vedantic concept of existence. The characters of "Teddy" are delivered to the reader in real time and are not connected to future events.

the pool is empty of water. He could walk to the edge of the pool, be pushed in by his sister, and fracture his skull. Yet he feels that were he to die in this way, it would not be tragedy. "I'd just be doing what I was supposed to do," he reasons, "wouldn't I?"

The story's most mystical event is a quiet one and nearly invisible. Soon after Nicholson settles into the lounge chair next to Teddy, Teddy becomes unfocused, his attention mysteriously diverted to the area of the sports deck where the swimming pool is—as if hearing some inner voice coming from that direction. Lost in whatever thoughts have mesmerized him, Teddy absentmindedly interrupts Nicholson with a haiku written by Bashō: "Nothing in the voice of the cicada intimates how soon it will die."

After Teddy leaves for his swimming lesson, Nicholson sits in contemplation of their discussion. Suddenly he springs from the deck chair and races through the ship to the area of the pool. Salinger then presents the most widely criticized ending of any story that he ever published. Having not quite reached the pool, Nicholson hears

> an all-piercing, sustained scream—clearly coming from a small, female child. It was highly acoustical, as though it were reverberating within four tiled walls.[26]

Most readers have interpreted the closing lines of "Teddy" as indicating Teddy's death at the hands of Booper. This conclusion is derived from Teddy's own prediction rather than the text itself. Salinger's words intimate that it is Booper, and not Teddy, who screams from within the empty pool. The reader, therefore, is left with three options. Booper may well have pushed her brother into the pool in an act of cold-blooded murder—as Teddy had predicted. Yet, according to the text, it is just as likely that Teddy, recognizing the threat that his sister poses, pushes her over the edge before she has the chance to take his life.* The third possibility is that Teddy accepts his death and allows Booper to push him into the empty pool but, anticipating her action, holds Booper and takes her down with him. By doing so, Teddy may

---

*A number of scholars have offered this explanation without recourse. If this line of thought is followed through, it points directly to the possibility that Teddy planned Booper's murder and predicted his own death in an effort to shift blame. This line of thought would transform the entire story and present Teddy as Salinger's most insidious character.

usher his sister into her next incarnation. Scornful of the Western fear of death, the genius-child may well feel it his obligation to speed along his sister's spiritual journey, considering himself to be "doing what [he] was supposed to do" in the process.

None of these explanations is completely satisfying. Consequently, the story's critics—many of whom found fault in its Eastern tenets—conveniently delivered the brunt of disapproval to the story's ambiguous ending rather than condemn cultural philosophies they did not understand. Salinger himself recognized the story's failure, conceding that though "Teddy" might have been "exceptionally Haunting," and "Memorable," it was also "unpleasantly controversial, and thoroughly unsuccessful."[27]

As 1952 drew to a close, Salinger remained at a crossroad: if he were to continue presenting religious doctrine through his work, he would have to find another vehicle, stories that *The New Yorker* would actually print and characters whom the public would accept.

11. Positioning

I'd build me a little cabin somewhere with the dough I made.
I'd build it right near the woods, but not right in them, because
I'd want it to be sunny as hell all the time.

—Holden Caulfield in *The Catcher in the Rye*

On February 16, 1953, J. D. Salinger became the official owner of 90
acres of hillside property in Cornish, New Hampshire.[1] The temptation to interpret Salinger's move as life imitating art is compelling. In
The Catcher in the Rye Holden Caulfield dreams of running away to
neighboring Vermont and finding a cabin in the woods where he can
live a life of seclusion. To ensure his separation from the world, Holden
plans to pretend he is a deaf-mute. "Then I'd be through with having
conversations for the rest of my life," he rationalizes, "and they'd leave
me alone."

That winter found Salinger blissful, cutting firewood and drawing
water from streams. In this, the first home that he actually owned, he
attempted to forge a life, not as an unresponsive malcontent but as a
fully engaged member of the community. He envisioned Cornish as a

place where he could write in peace, join with the world around him, and actually be happy. If Salinger did share Holden Caulfield's dream, it was not a longing for seclusion but a dream of a place to call his own.

Cornish indeed had an amazing effect on him. After the depressed months of 1952, Salinger found there the most genuine happiness that he had experienced since before the war. He eagerly set himself to renovating his new property and making his hovel an actual home. Scraping together the last of his savings, he ordered repairs on the house, mended gaps in the structure, installed storm windows, and had work done on the grounds. He then set out to establish himself among his new neighbors.

The village of Cornish hugs the Connecticut River, which separates New Hampshire from Vermont. The hamlet itself has no real place where its citizens can gather, and the area's social life is largely centered in the neighboring Vermont town of Windsor. Windsor too is a tiny community but contains a cluster of shops that, in this rural setting, passes for a business district. Among its establishments in 1953 were the coffee shops Harrington's Spa and Nap's Lunch, where the area's high school students congregated. Salinger often crossed an ancient covered bridge into Windsor to pick up his mail and buy supplies, hoping to mingle with the townspeople as he did. With Harrington's Spa and Nap's Lunch among the shops he frequented, he inevitably encountered the Windsor High School students.

On November 20, 1952, Salinger had sat for the acclaimed portrait photographer Antony di Gesu. Salinger wanted a portrait of himself to give to his mother and, di Gesu claimed, his "fiancée."*

> Since I didn't [know] as much then as I do now, I set up the camera and light and sat him right down. His expression was so rigid and self-conscious [that] I was at my wits end. Nothing happened. I decided on something I had never done before with an adult. I excused myself, went up to my apartment and came down with "Catcher in the Rye" . . . and suggested he

---

*Di Gesu's claim that Salinger wanted a portrait for his fiancée is possible, although his recollection occurred thirty years after the incident and may have been flawed. Salinger was indeed romantically involved in late 1952 with either the mysterious "Mary" or Claire Douglas.

do anything he pleased. Read to himself. Read aloud or just smoke . . . I took 48 5×7 negatives. Serious, thoughtful, smiling, laughing, howling with laughter.*

Di Gesu's account reveals the child that still lived within Salinger at the time he moved to Cornish. Salinger's ability to connect with the remnants of his own childhood was what had given him the insight to create the voice of Holden Caulfield.†

With such a background, Salinger naturally bonded with the local teenagers. In a short time he began to frequent the coffee shops, joining clusters of students, whom he often treated to food and drinks and engaged in conversations that sometimes lasted hours. On some days he allowed groups of adolescents to crowd into the jeep that he had bought for his house-hunting trip and would drive them to his home. There they discussed their lives. They talked of school, sports, and relationships, often while playing records and eating snacks. "He was just like one of the gang," recalled a student, "except that he never did anything silly the way the rest of us did. He always knew who was going with whom and if anybody was having trouble at school and we all looked up to him, especially the renegades."[2]

Despite being thirty-four and a famous author, Salinger was surprisingly comfortable among these young people, as if he were reliving his own adolescence through them—this time as the most popular member of the group. Yet, while spending time with his young friends, Salinger never lost sight that he was the adult. He chaperoned them to sporting events, took them on camping trips, and was trusted enough by the children's parents to head the local church youth group. By every account, he conducted himself honorably as a contented overseer, an adult who understood the teenage mind with uncanny perception.

. . .

*From the unpublished memoirs of Antony di Gesu, San Diego Historical Society. The fact that Salinger allowed di Gesu to take forty-eight photographs of him is a testimony to the photographer's method. In contrast, the famed photographer Lotte Jacobi managed to obtain far fewer images before Salinger bolted from her studio.

†Salinger requested that di Gesu not show any of the photographs he had taken, a promise the photographer honored for thirty years. When he asked Salinger why he was so reluctant to be recognized, Salinger told him that people reacted oddly around him in fear that he would write about them.

But Salinger did not limit himself to the company of teenagers. Many of Cornish's adult residents recalled him being friendly and talkative, frequently visiting his neighbors and staging cocktail parties. Entertaining his guests, Salinger was anxious to discuss religion and local events, demonstrate methods of meditation and yoga, and show off the transformation of his new home. He also mimicked the locals and set out to build a life as a simple country gentleman. He cleared some of the woods around his cottage, allowing it to be "sunny as hell." He planted a vegetable garden and began to grow corn. With these rural pastimes in common with his neighbors, he began to foster a feeling of community with them.

In order to build this new life, Salinger allowed his professional ambition to recede briefly. Occupied with domestic renovations, he canceled a number of business trips to New York City. The most conspicuous cancellation was one with Jamie Hamilton in February. The two men were scheduled to discuss the upcoming British release of Salinger's short-story collection. At the last minute Salinger claimed he was needed in Cornish instead. The excuse was convenient; he and Hamilton had suffered something of a rift over the collection, and it's likely that Salinger was happy to avoid the meeting.

The first strain in Salinger's relationship with Hamilton had occurred in November 1952. Hamilton's reaction to *The Gospels of Sri Ramakrishna* was not what Salinger had expected or hoped for. When Hamilton received the massive text, he was aghast. Clearly, there was no revenue possibility in his releasing it in Britain. In fact, he was unable to get through the text.

He seems to have avoided the subject, and Salinger was forced to prod him into addressing the issue. Finally, Hamilton awkwardly admitted his inability to absorb the volume. "I feel terribly guilty about the Ramakrishna book," he acknowledged. "I received it safely and read much of it with enjoyment and profit, though some I confess defeated me."[3] Conveniently claiming that another publisher was considering an abridged version of *The Gospels,* Hamilton begged off Salinger's suggestion that he publish the complete book. Salinger reported to Hamilton that he understood the editor's reluctance and appeared to overlook the disagreement, but deep inside he was hurt and disappointed that Hamilton had not shared his enthusiasm for such a vital subject.

A greater departure arose over the upcoming release of Salinger's short-story collection. Ober Associates had negotiated with Little, Brown and Company to have the book published in the early spring. The timing was designed to coincide with the release of *The Catcher in the Rye* in paperback. After the conflicts over the publication of *Catcher,* both Little, Brown and Hamish Hamilton were reluctant to approach Salinger with any differences of opinion over the forthcoming collection. For his part, Salinger had become even more stubborn.

An example of Salinger's entrenchment can be seen with his story "Teddy." Apparently, Salinger was unwilling to consider the possibility that it might not equal the quality of his finest selections. He presented the inclusion of "Teddy" to Little, Brown and Hamish Hamilton as a fait accompli. The story sailed through the offices of *The New Yorker* in a similar manner, quickly accepted by both William Maxwell and Gus Lobrano despite its heavy religiosity and shocking ending. At the time Lobrano was still stinging from the appointment of William Shawn, and it is unlikely that either he or Maxwell felt strong enough in their uncertain positions to challenge Salinger, who was now clearly the magazine's premier contributor. *The New Yorker* published "Teddy" on January 31, 1953. Salinger was instantly flooded by mail from readers, receiving even more letters for "Teddy" than he had for "Esmé." Most of the reaction was outrage, but Salinger remained undaunted and never considered rethinking the story's inclusion in his book.

Salinger applied the same controlling attitude to the collection's title. In November 1952, he chose nine of his best pieces—including the just-finished "Teddy"—for the anthology. Determined that no single story should label the entire collection, he then expressed to Jamie Hamilton his refusal to consider any title such as *A Perfect Day for Bananafish—and Other Stories*. Salinger went on to speculate, "I may end up just calling it *Nine Stories*."[4] Hamilton was appalled at the idea. The kind of title that Salinger so adamantly opposed was exactly what Hamilton had envisioned. Remarkably, he planned to call the British version *For Esmé—with Love and Squalor and Other Stories* and was incredulous over Salinger's suggestion. The title *Nine Stories,* he claimed, "would be about as big a handicap as could be provided for any book at birth, and we sincerely hope that you weren't serious."[5] Salinger was indeed serious and was now sullen over Hamilton's reaction.

In March, *The Catcher in the Rye* was released in paperback by

Signet Books (a division of New American Library), selling for 50 cents. Salinger cringed over its presentation, but he had been forced to agree to it back in 1951 and was helpless to alter it now. The design, which Salinger had fought over two years earlier, depicted Holden Caulfield decked in his red hunting hat and carrying a suitcase, peering naively into a seedy nightclub. Standing next to Holden was an obvious "fallen woman" lighting a forbidden cigarette. The tawdry cover promised the most provocative of contents. "This unusual book may shock you," it proclaimed, "will make you laugh, and may break your heart—but you will never forget it." The back cover heralded *Catcher* as "a literary sensation" and contained a six-line biography of the author that offered no new information.

Happily, Salinger could ignore the paperback release of his novel. For him, the event was primarily a precursor to the publication of his short-story collection, which he had indeed decided to title *Nine Stories*. But the Signet release of *Catcher* reinforced Salinger's belief that he needed to keep a close eye on Little, Brown and Company, which controlled the paperback rights to his books and was to blame for Signet's offense. In Salinger's mind, Little, Brown was in the business of selling ink on paper and cared nothing for the presentation of art. Salinger actually refused to refer to the publisher by name, derisively calling it "the House of Hits" instead. This time Salinger had his way: The cover of *Nine Stories* contained no illustration. Gone was any biography of the author, save a mention that he had written *The Catcher in the Rye*. Also absent was any photograph of Salinger. On that, he had been particularly adamant.

Nine Stories was published on April 6, 1953. Opening with "A Perfect Day for Bananafish" and ending with "Teddy," the collection included everything Salinger had published in *The New Yorker* between 1948 and 1953 in addition to "Down at the Dinghy" and "De Daumier–Smith's Blue Period," which had been published in other magazines. Salinger rightfully dedicated the anthology to his editor, Gus Lobrano, and his agent, Dorothy Olding, without whom few of the book's contents would have reached the reading public. When Salinger finally held the collection of which he had dreamed for so many years, he was disappointed. He said that it seemed meager and toothless.[6] But there was no question that *Nine Stories* would be popular. With the paperback release of *The Catcher in the Rye* reigniting interest in the au-

26360-9 ✳ IN U.S. $3.95 (IN CANADA $4.95) ✳ A BANTAM BOOK

Nine Stories by J. D. Salinger

A PERFECT DAY FOR BANANAFISH

UNCLE WIGGILY IN CONNECTICUT

JUST BEFORE THE WAR WITH THE ESKIMOS

THE LAUGHING MAN

DOWN AT THE DINGHY

FOR ESME— WITH LOVE AND SQUALOR

PRETTY MOUTH AND GREEN MY EYES

DE DAUMIER-SMITH'S BLUE PERIOD

TEDDY

thor and, most conspicuously, allowing younger readers to experience the novel, public appetite for the collection was enormous. Yet it was precisely the success of *Catcher* that now handicapped *Nine Stories.*

The critical reception of *Nine Stories* ranged from approving to enthusiastic. Most of the criticism was directed not at Salinger's craftsmanship, which was undeniable, but at his perceived inability to sustain the level of quality established by *The Catcher in the Rye.* Although unfair, the comparison was inevitable. On April 9, Charles Poore of *The New York Times* reported that *Nine Stories* was "somehow disappointing, coming from the man who wrote the outstanding first novel of

1951." Poore went on to explain the dilemma that now plagued Salinger. "That's the penalty Salinger has to pay for being such a good author," he observed. "The result is that when he comes along with a book that would make the reputation of any one of a dozen gifted young fogies we complain because it's not better than 'The Catcher in the Rye.' "[7] After grieving that "the business of playing tunes on the nerves of [Salinger's] characters can become fairly monotonous," Poore went on to condemn both "A Perfect Day for Bananafish" and "Teddy" for what he called their "bang! bang!" endings and to praise "For Esmé—with Love and Squalor" as the greatest story to result from the Second World War. Poore's critique was typical of many reviews of *Nine Stories,* affirming Salinger's talent while conveying disappointment at his not producing exactly what was expected of him.

Poore's review was less forgiving than that of the novelist Eudora Welty, which appeared in *The New York Times Book Review* on April 5. Welty showered Salinger with praise, calling him an artist whose writings are "original, first rate, serious and beautiful." A personal friend of Salinger, Welty understood him extraordinarily well, and although their friendship derailed her neutrality, her review of *Nine Stories* was indisputably inspired. "Mr. Salinger's stories," she observed, "honor what is unique and precious in each person on earth. Their author has the courage—it is more like the earned right and privilege—to experiment at the risk of not being understood."[8]

The reading public snatched up *Nine Stories* faster than it could be placed on shelves. The book soon rose to ninth place on the *New York Times* best-seller list and remained in the top twenty for the next three months. This was a rare accomplishment. For a collection of short stories, which normally sold far fewer copies than a novel, the achievement was extraordinary. Successful despite the fact that it was underpublicized and contained no distracting personal information, *Nine Stories* appeared to validate Salinger's contempt for publicity and affirmed his resolve for greater control over his product.

Salinger himself determined to ignore the book's reception. He tried his best to stay away from newspapers and magazines for weeks after the collection's release and asked Dorothy Olding and Gus Lobrano to see that no one sent him any reviews or clippings. He said he feared being unbalanced by the attention and explained that scrutiny distracted him from his work.[9]

In the meantime, agreement was reached with Hamish Hamilton on the collection's release in Great Britain. Evidently to preserve their relationship, Salinger uncharacteristically acquiesced to Hamilton's choice on the book's title. In June, Hamilton released *Nine Stories* as *For Esmé—with Love and Squalor and Other Stories*. As with the British reception of *The Catcher in the Rye,* sales were lukewarm. This was the second time Hamilton had taken a hit for Salinger. He believed fully in the author's talents, but his friendship was beginning to clash with his business sense, which by all accounts was the driving force of his life. As the weeks wore on and sales stubbornly dwindled, he began to consider how he could turn a profit from his risky investment.

. . .

Today, *Nine Stories* is understood on two levels: as being a collection of loosely connected but self-contained works and also as a chronicle of the steps along the path of J. D. Salinger's spiritual exploration. Gilbert Highet, who reviewed the book for *Harper's,* the magazine in which "Down at the Dinghy" had been published, came admirably close to this perception in 1953. Highet intuitively sensed Salinger's presence in each story and expressed his feeling that through *Nine Stories* readers experienced stages of the author's journey of self-examination. He also relayed his fear that the enormity of Salinger's talent was in danger of being ensnared by the compactness of his focus. Highet saw in each of the *Nine Stories* a character who was unmistakably Salinger, "a thin, nervous, intelligent being who is on the verge of a breakdown: we see him at various stages of his life, as a child, as an adolescent, as an aimless young man in his twenties."

When the pieces that make up *Nine Stories* are placed together, it becomes clear that they are indeed steps along the path of a spiritual journey. With "A Perfect Day for Bananafish," the collection opens with a tale of irredeemable despair. The next three stories, "Uncle Wiggily in Connecticut," "Just Before the War with the Eskimos," and "The Laughing Man," deliver that despair into the average moments of everyday lives. This first section of *Nine Stories* conveys bleak accounts of the spiritual agonies inherent in modern-day America. They are populated by characters who ineffectively grapple to elevate themselves above the darker forces of human nature. But *Nine Stories* also offers hope. The book's philosophies are divided by "Down at the

Dinghy," a work that liberates readers from the prevailing hopelessness of the first four stories by offering an alternative to despair through genuine love. The power of hope is continued through the rest of the book, with the possible exception of the morality play "Pretty Mouth and Green My Eyes," which appears in the collection out of time. In "For Esmé—with Love and Squalor," the simple answer of strength through human connection begins to take on miraculous overtones, until in "De Daumier–Smith's Blue Period" the revelation previously provided by human connection becomes a completely spiritual event. "Teddy," the book's final installment, was crafted especially to finalize the destination of *Nine Stories'* journey. Through "Teddy," readers reach a place where the power of love through human connection has been transformed into the power of faith through union with God.

Many critics and scholars have viewed "Teddy" as being a retelling of "A Perfect Day for Bananafish." Salinger himself reinforced this thought when, in "Seymour—an Introduction," he compared Teddy's eyes to those of Seymour Glass. "A Perfect Day for Bananafish" and "Teddy" were deliberately situated in *Nine Stories* as symbolic bookends and were published exactly five years apart to the day. Both stories contain "bang! bang!" endings that result in the deaths of their main characters. Both tragic finales involve water and little girls. Seymour Glass and Teddy McArdle are both estranged from the world upon which they are impaled. It seems apparent that Salinger used the death of Teddy to reexplain the suicide of Seymour from a later perspective in an attempt to embed a spiritual acceptance into Seymour's character that "Bananafish" alone does not supply. In other words, Salinger used "Teddy" to rewrite "Bananafish," or at least to reroute the direction of readers' interpretation.

. . .

Mid-1953 found Salinger happy and content. He was at ease in his new home in Cornish, which he was transforming into a comfortable country cottage. He was friendly with his new neighbors, who all seemed to like him, and he had developed a mutually satisfying rapport with the local youths. Cornish also stimulated his creativity, and he claimed to be writing some of his finest works to date.[10] His career was soaring through the paperback version of *The Catcher in the Rye* and the positive reception of *Nine Stories*. Salinger finally seemed to have found his niche, the dream of Holden Caulfield—somewhere he actually belonged.

During these months, references to the mysterious "Mary" disappeared from Salinger's correspondence and Claire Douglas reemerged to share his happiness. Claire was now nineteen, Salinger's junior by fifteen years, and attending Radcliffe. For Claire, whose own father had been thirty-five years her mother's senior, the age difference was particuarly not an issue, but Salinger was acutely aware of the gossip it might generate and strove to keep the relationship as private as possible. Gleefully, the couple devised ways in which they could see each other without the knowledge of others, going as far as to fabricate imaginary friends to explain Claire's long weekends away from school. Within a short time, Salinger had fallen in love with Claire, just as Claire's world began to revolve around him, embracing his religion, his opinions, and his tastes.

The harmony was short-lived. According to Claire, Salinger asked her to quit school and move into the Cornish cottage with him, much as Holden Caulfield had asked Sally Hayes. But Claire refused, and Salinger recoiled. "When I stood up to him on that one thing, college," she later recalled, "he vanished."[11]

Salinger was not the only romantic interest in Claire's life at the time. There was also a twenty-three-year-old Harvard Business School MBA student named Colman M. Mockler, Jr., whom she had met at school. Mockler was artistically sensitive, unassuming, highly principled, and a formidable competitor for Claire's attention. Salinger was distressed over Claire's additional admirer. He also knew that when she was at school, she was likely with Mockler. So, when he asked Claire to leave Radcliffe and move to Cornish, he was plainly attempting to secure her affections and separate her from his competition. Claire responded with a clear choice, one that began to disintegrate Salinger's contentment. She not only refused his request but, during the summer of 1953, traveled with Mockler, to Europe, where the couple stayed in Italy and where Mockler was likely introduced to Claire's mother.[12] Her decision to spend the summer overseas with Salinger's rival had an understandably chilling effect on their relationship. When she returned from Europe in mid-September, Salinger refused to see her.

Salinger's falling-out with Claire Douglas was exacerbated by an event that occurred in November. Among his Windsor High School friends was a senior named Shirlie Blaney. Blaney asked Salinger if she could interview him as part of a school project, and Salinger agreed. On November 9, they met at Harrington's Spa. Salinger ordered lunch, and Blaney (who had arrived with a friend for support) began her interview. The girl's questions were straightforward and not particularly intrusive: Where did Salinger go to school? When did he begin writing? What did he do during the war? Was *The Catcher in the Rye* autobiographical? Salinger had answered each of Blaney's questions before, most notably for William Maxwell in his Book-of-the-Month Club interview, and he thought nothing of answering them now with a candid innocence common among friends.

On November 13, 1953, Shirlie Blaney's interview appeared, not in a school project but in the local newspaper, the *Daily Eagle–Twin State Telescope*. The article was short, juvenile, and riddled with errors—it enrolled the author at New York University for an extra year, sent Sol Salinger to Austria and Poland with his son, and relieved Salinger of two years of army service. Blaney also reported things that she had obviously misinterpreted, erroneously claiming that Salinger was traveling to London to make a movie and that he had purchased his Cornish home two years before. The article is best remembered for Salinger's reported quotation on *The Catcher in the Rye*. When asked if the novel was autobiographical, Salinger appeared to hesitate. "Sort of," he hedged. "I was much relieved when I finished it. My boyhood was very much the same as that of the boy in the book, and it was a great relief telling people about it." The line is still frequently quoted but, again, was nothing more than he had revealed previously to Maxwell.

A bittersweet portion of the Blaney article was contained in its preface, which included a short description of the author:

> A very good friend of all the high school students, Mr. Salinger
> has many older friends as well, although he has been coming
> here only a few years. He keeps very much to himself, wanting
> only to be left alone to write. He is a tall and foreign looking
> man of 34, with a pleasing personality.*

---

*In descriptions of Salinger the terms "foreign looking" and "exotic" arise repeatedly. With little doubt, the expressions were used to convey Salinger's Jewish heritage.

Salinger's reaction to the article was deep hurt. In his view, Blaney had deceived him by asking for the interview for a school project. It seems apparent that the *Daily Eagle* had used the young girl, but that was not the point. To Salinger, the incident implied that the infringement and subterfuge he so hoped to have escaped when he left New York was alive here too, in this seemingly idyllic community.

As the episode came so soon after Claire Douglas's defection, Salinger's reaction was extreme. He stopped going into Windsor and ended his relationship with the students. He began to avoid his neighbors. There would be no more cocktail parties or trips to basketball games, no more lunches at Harrington's Spa or conversations over records and potato chips. Salinger withdrew from the people of Cornish as he had the crowds of New York. When the students went to his cottage to find out what had happened, Salinger sat inside motionless and pretended not to be home. Within weeks, he began to build a fence around his property.

From that point on, J. D. Salinger would turn his ambition away from being accepted by those around him and concentrate instead upon his own methods of finding comfort in life. In this concluding act of 1953, Salinger's life once again resembled his art, but tragically. The *Daily Eagle* article had the same effect upon the author as the final "Fuck you" had upon Holden Caulfield. And, like Holden, Salinger resigned himself to the pitiful reality that Holden had acknowledged:

> You can't ever find a place that's nice and peaceful, because there isn't any. You may think there is, but once you get there, when you're not looking, somebody'll sneak up and write "Fuck you" right under your nose.[13]

12. Franny

Whereas Salinger's break with Claire Douglas in the winter of 1953 may have put him into isolation, for Claire it proved to be devastating. When Salinger disappeared from sight, to the extent that Claire thought he had actually left the country, she physically collapsed.

During the opening days of 1954, Claire was diagnosed with glandular fever and hospitalized. Doctors decided to remove her appendix at the same time, leaving her physically depleted and emotionally exhausted. Throughout the ordeal, she heard nothing from Salinger. Keeping watch over her bedside was Colman Mockler, who provided the attention and affection she needed, while at the same time tapping Claire's vulnerability with incessant pleas to marry him. Claire finally agreed, and they were soon wed.

Little has been reported about Claire's first husband. In a 1961 interview with *Time* magazine, her half brother Gavin offered the ambiguous opinion that he "wasn't a bad guy . . . but he was a jerk." In fact, Mockler's later life was exceptional. The namesake of numerous foundations and scholarships, many of them faith-based, Mockler went on to achieve remarkable success as the CEO of the Gillette Company while maintaining an admirable balance among his career, his family life, and an intense religious conviction.

It was precisely Mockler's religious devotion that shaped his marriage with Claire and affected the story "Franny." According to his second wife, Mockler experienced a profound religious conversion about the time he was married to Claire.[1] Having embraced Salinger's spiritual views, Claire was likely thrown into a crisis, forcing her to choose between her growing Zen and Vedantic convictions and the fundamentalist Christian commitment of her new husband. Claire's decision appears to have been swift and complete. After only a few months with Mockler, she returned to Salinger and her marriage was annulled.

At the time Claire could not have suited Salinger better had he crafted her himself. Her life bore a remarkable resemblance to that of the fictional character of Esmé. Claire Douglas was born on November 26, 1933, in London. Salinger loved all things British, and Claire's nationality certainly added to his attraction. Like Esmé, Claire was raised by a governess and her childhood was overwhelmed by the Second World War. In 1939, she and her older half brother, Gavin, were sent from London into the countryside to avoid the blitz, Claire to a convent, while their parents stayed behind in the capital. In 1940, the family's London home was destroyed by a bomb. To ensure their safety, Claire and Gavin, at ages six and eight, were whisked out of England by their mother, who accompanied them to the United States.

Jean Douglas and the children arrived in New York on July 7, 1940, aboard the SS *Scythia*.[2] Once in America, Claire's mother remained in New York City awaiting the arrival of her husband, while the children were sent to a series of foster homes for the duration of the war. By 1941, Claire's parents settled in Manhattan, remaining separated from their children, who continued to be shuttled between foster homes.[3] So, though Claire and Gavin's parents remained alive and well during the war, they were just as separated from their children as the parents of Esmé and Charles had been by death.

Though Salinger could grant spiritual and emotional sustenance to Esmé and Charles in his story, the real-life impact of war left Claire and Gavin bereft of direction. Gavin was especially hard hit by events and not as miraculously preserved as Charles was in "For Esmé." Anchorless, the Douglas children were bounced from one foster home

Claire Douglas as she appeared in 1951. Claire had met Salinger the year before and in 1955 would become his second wife. (Shipley School/Claire Douglas)

to another until they had seen seven by war's end.* Claire was then sent again to stay with nuns, this time to Marydell Convent in Suffern, New York, before moving on to Shipley, where she was enrolled when she met Salinger in 1950.

Considering her chaotic history, it is easy to understand how Salinger became Claire's father, teacher, protector, and lover all rolled into one, while to Salinger, Claire's background, youthful beauty, and delicate charm may well have made her appear as Esmé incarnate. The couple also shared many interests. Both were fascinated by religion, and at Shipley, Claire had excelled at many of the same subjects as

---

*One of the foster homes in which Claire and Gavin were placed was located in Sea Girt, New Jersey, a short distance from the home of Oona O'Neill and the town mentioned by Mattie Gladwaller in her letter to Babe in "A Boy in France."

Salinger had at Valley Forge: dramatics, languages, and sports. Claire was an intelligent woman, an honors student at some of the most prestigious schools in the nation, and despite her delicate disposition in 1954, she was not an empty vessel to be filled by Salinger's whims. She was, however, deeply in love with Salinger and possessed an uncanny ability to draw him out of his defenses. When he was around her, he was playful and unguarded, able to reconnect with his own youthful innocence. Claire saved him from loneliness and depression, and she probably knew it. Both were exactly what the other needed at that time in their lives. It was time to settle down, burn their histories, and build a new life.

Salinger's relationship with Claire Douglas proved to be his focus throughout 1954, and he published nothing new that year. His career did not suffer from neglect. Both *The Catcher in the Rye* and *Nine Stories* continued to sell at amazing rates. In addition, the year witnessed a number of stories reprinted in various collections. "Uncle Wiggily in Connecticut" appeared in *American Short Story Masterpieces,* published by Dell; "Just Before the War with the Eskimos" was reprinted for Bantam in *Manhattan: Stories from the Heart of a Great City;* and *Nine Stories* was released in paperback by the New American Library. It had no cover illustration.

At the same time that Salinger's work was enjoying added exposure, Sir Laurence Olivier approached him via Jamie Hamilton, requesting permission to adapt "For Esmé" into a radio drama for the BBC. "He's most anxious to include 'For Esmé,' " Hamilton reported, "and hopes you will feel like agreeing." Salinger would have been the only contemporary author that Olivier had thus far included in his radio series, and he should have been flattered; he refused nonetheless. *My Foolish Heart* was still fresh in Salinger's psyche, and even Olivier could not be allowed to do an interpretation of "Esmé" that might betray its spirit. If Olivier was surprised at Salinger's refusal, especially after the 1951 dinner faux pas, Jamie Hamilton felt absolutely rebuffed.

. . .

The drama of Salinger's relationship with Claire Douglas is the backdrop for "Franny," the only story he completed in 1954. Since its publication, scholars have consistently pointed to Claire as being the inspiration for Franny's character. Salinger often embedded such personal items into his stories, and there can be little doubt that Franny's character reflects Claire Douglas. Her half brother Gavin also believed this to be true. In 1961 he told *Time* magazine that "the navy blue bag with the white leather binding," carried by Franny in the story, was the very bag that Claire owned when she visited Colman Mockler. Gavin scornfully went on to accuse Salinger of inflicting the same Jesus Prayer that drives the story "Franny" on his sister while he was writing the story. "She was hung on the Jesus Prayer," Gavin recalled. "Jerry is very good at hanging people on things." Despite Gavin's derision for Salinger, his claim has never been disputed. If true, it grants Salinger a sympathy for the prayer that is seldom accorded by readers.

Another parallel between the fiction of "Franny" and actual events is created by the character of Franny's boyfriend, Lane Coutell. It has long been speculated that Lane's character was based upon Claire's first husband. However, Salinger presents Lane as pompous and condescending, too intellectual to respond to Franny's spiritual needs. In truth, it was Mockler who experienced the religious breakthrough shared by Franny's character and not Claire, although that event may indeed have sparked a spiritual crisis within her.

It also seems that Salinger devised the basic plot of "Franny" long before Claire's fleeting marriage. In fact, the story's concept may be nearly as old as *The Catcher in the Rye*. When "De Daumier–Smith's Blue Period" was rejected by *The New Yorker* in 1951, Salinger told Gus Lobrano that he was considering doing "that college story" instead.[4] So, though Salinger may have imbued "Franny" with numerous personal references, the story itself is not a retelling of his own relationship. The inspiration of many of Salinger's characters often sprang from actual people, but in short time the author's imagination took control and obscured these sources. Consequently, Lane Coutell may not resemble Colman Mockler any more than Robert Ackley resembled Salinger's own classmate or Raymond Ford resembled Charles Hanson Towne.

. . .

"Franny" is the tale of a young woman who questions the values of people around her. Believing there must be more to life than ego-filled pretension and competition, she determines to seek a spiritual path to happiness. Desperate for insight, when Franny encounters a little green book entitled *Way of a Pilgrim,* she is drawn to it immediately.* Readers soon realize that Franny is engrossed by the book's contents—the story of a wandering Russian peasant who seeks to fulfill the biblical exhortation to "pray without ceasing"—and has become addicted to the book's Jesus Prayer, "Lord Jesus Christ, have mercy on me," a mantra she repeats until it synchronizes with her heartbeat and becomes self-activating.

At first glance "Franny" appears to be a stationary piece of literature. It consists almost entirely of dialogue and contains only two speaking characters and little change of venue. However, Salinger's manipulation of shifting narrative perspective is especially well done in "Franny." When the story begins, readers are eased into its situation through the guidance of its third-person narration, which reveals the motives and inner thoughts of the characters. But once the reader becomes comfortable, the narration pulls away. When Franny begins to conflict with her boyfriend, Lane, the narration stops revealing her inner thoughts, forcing the reader to concentrate on the dialogue in order to understand her motives. By the story's end, the narration is cold and merely relays events, delivering the full responsibility of interpretation solely to the reader.

Salinger drenched each line of "Franny" in a symbolism that displays Franny as being in the world but no longer part of it. She becomes a pilgrim wandering through the American wilderness of ego-filled phoniness in search of an uncertain truth. Salinger recalled past images in order to foreshadow Franny's spiritual dilemma. He reached back to "Just Before the War with the Eskimos" and resurrected the image of the chicken sandwich as symbolic of Holy Communion—this time completing it with a lowly glass of milk. He also reused the comparison in "Teddy" between ego-filled intellect and the spiritual fall from grace to explain Franny's condition. From the moment Franny and Lane are seated in an upscale French restaurant, Salinger begins to parallel Franny's character with the seeker of *Way of a Pilgrim.*

*When Franny's character is later included as one of the Glass children, Salinger will change her first encounter with *Way of a Pilgrim.* In "Franny," we are told that she discovered the book while taking a class on religion, but in "Zooey," he tells us that she found the book on her late brother Seymour's desk.

The most symbolic image of "Franny" occurs at the center of the story and marks a shift in narrative perspective. It is perhaps the portion that most resembles the later "Zooey" in its construction from pieces of figurative setting, description, and gesture.

Lane begins to brag ad nauseam about a term paper he has written on Gustave Flaubert. He delivers a monologue on literature and academia that is condescending and self-satisfied. Franny interrupts his opinionated harangue and compares his ego to that of a "section man," an assistant who fills in for a literature professor and whose near-sighted ego tears down each author he presents. Lane is stunned, and Franny begins to feel overwhelmed. She retreats to the ladies' room, where she tearfully confines herself in the most remote stall. Cringing in embryo position, deep inside herself, Franny screams. Here readers are given the image of Franny as a spiritual seeker whose quest for enlightenment is restrained by the human tendencies that confine her, the four walls of the stall: ego, intellectualism, phoniness, and conformity, all of which conspire to keep her from her spiritual pursuit. She attempts to block out these pressures by isolating herself and obscuring her vision but is overwhelmed nonetheless. She then sobs in despair—not because she is in spiritual uncertainty but because she knows the true direction but feels cowed by the world around her. Only the little green book, pressed to her heart, gives Franny the strength to collect herself and continue on. It is a scene similar to the first ego-shattering epiphany of Jean de Daumier–Smith and paves the way for the final experience of Satori.

Franny believes she is going insane. But in fact she is not losing her mind. Her sense of reality is shifting. She is shedding the conventions that have previously blinded her, fading from the material world and shifting into a different perception. Conventions and outward appearances are becoming less real. The effect is not only emotional and spiritual but physical as well. Franny appears pale, begins to sweat, and becomes ill.

Collapsing under the encroaching weight of her physical deterioration, Franny is carried to the restaurant office, unconscious. When she begins to revive, readers are left with the story's final scene, presented as a fading image and rendered without narrative comment:

> Alone, Franny lay quite still, looking at the ceiling. Her lips began
> to move, forming soundless words, and they continued to move.[5]

As Franny gradually vanishes into the power of the Jesus Prayer, she inches toward a spiritual state. Yet she is not presented as completely heroic or selfless, or as having attained holiness. Her use of the Jesus Prayer is accompanied by a lack of conscious input that riddles it with flaws.* Her newfound perception is loveless. It produces its own snobbery. It is no less derisive of others than Lane's ridiculing of those he considers intellectually inferior. Franny's condemnation of Lane's attitudes is truth, but her spirituality contains a contempt that threatens to overwhelm its benefits.

Attempting to pray without ceasing by synchronizing the Jesus Prayer with her heartbeat, Franny is overtaken by the mantra and dislodged from the conventional world, the only world she has ever known. Franny's crisis, therefore, is that she cannot live in two worlds at the same time. It is a dilemma markedly similar to the struggle that confounded Salinger himself, torn between the social world around him and the spiritual hermitage of pure art.†

. . .

When "Franny" appeared in *The New Yorker* on January 29, 1955, it caused a sensation, becoming an instant favorite of critics and a fashionable topic of conversation among readers. Not only did Salinger once again receive more mail than he had for any previous short story, but "Franny" garnered *The New Yorker* more mail than it had received for any other story in its history. It appeared that in the eyes of the public, J. D. Salinger could do no wrong. Unfortunately, although Salinger went out of his way to avoid the mistakes he had made in "Teddy" and constructed Franny's character to be so compelling and natural that it lacks any hint of sermonizing, the story was even less well understood.

The 1950s produced a scholarly backlash against spirituality that caused readers and academics to embrace any interpretation other than the one Salinger had intended. Many readers construed the story

---

*Delivering a subtle verdict, Salinger, although overwhelmingly sympathetic to Franny's character, hints at her misapplication of the Jesus Prayer when he causes her to miss the ashtray while explaining the theory behind the prayer.

†This is also the dilemma of the seeker in *Way of the Pilgrim*. As the book begins, he states, "The first Epistle of St. Paul to the Thessalonians was being read, and among other words I heard these—'Pray without ceasing.' It was this text, more than any other, which forced itself upon my mind, and I began to think how it was possible to pray without ceasing, since a man has to concern himself with other things also in order to make a living."

as a condemnation of contemporary academia. Others viewed it as Franny's transition into adulthood. Some even believed Lane Coutell to be the true protagonist. Nearly universal was the misconception that Franny was pregnant.

The New Yorker's editors themselves believed Franny was pregnant. When Salinger found out, he made several changes in the hope of removing the assumption. But he was torn. Delivering a clear-cut message defied his philosophy of writing. He had too much respect for readers to remove their personal analysis. On December 20, 1954, he wrote to Gus Lobrano of his impasse, telling the editor that he himself did not believe that Franny was pregnant but it was not for him to know or decide. The reader alone was worthy of that conclusion. And though Salinger cringed at the thought that readers might view the story through the lens of Franny's pregnancy, he refused to defile the confidence he held with them. After making several substantial changes to the text of "Franny," he reconsidered and finally decided to insert but two lines and to take his chances. He added "Too goddam long between drinks. To put it crassly," and hoped that readers would understand it as a reference to the time between sexual encounters rather than menstrual periods.[6] It was a gamble that Salinger lost and that he regretted.*

Franny's attraction to the mantra of the Jesus Prayer was a reflection of Salinger's own interest in Eastern philosophies and of his complaint that American culture frustrates spirituality. Salinger cast Franny as a wanderer in the jungle of American intellectualism very much as the Siberian peasant is forced to wander in *Way of the Pilgrim*. Unfortunately, the author was perhaps too delicate in his objectivity. Though the point is clear that "Franny" bemoans Western society for its spiritual insensitivity, the lack of narrative verdict allowed the frequent misinterpretation of this story as being a condemnation of the method of Franny's spiritual quest. Whereas, in reality, Salinger likely had an enormous respect for the Jesus Prayer and the mystical powers that it represents, many readers viewed the prayer's culminating effect upon Franny as something of which she should be cured.

---

*In his 1963 book *J. D. Salinger* (p. 139), Warren French justly observed that the inserted line actually reinforced the notion among the reading public that Franny was pregnant.

13. Two Families

On February 17, 1955, Jerome David Salinger was married to Claire Alison Douglas in a private ceremony performed by a justice of the peace. The wedding took place twenty miles west of Cornish, in Barnard, Vermont, and was attended by only the closest of family and friends. The couple had taken their prenuptial blood test on February 11 and taken out their marriage license the following day. Perhaps symbolic of their new beginning together, Claire and Salinger refused to acknowledge their previous marriages on the license, and the document claims to be the first union for both.[1]*

Upon returning to Cornish after the ceremony, the newlyweds hosted a small wedding reception. In attendance were Miriam Salinger, J.D.'s sister, Doris, and oddly enough, Claire's first husband, Colman. As gifts to his guests, Salinger presented each with an inscribed copy of

---

*The misinformation is characteristic of Salinger. It was his lifelong habit to alter facts that he did not consider to be anyone's business. He especially enjoyed manipulating the indirect details of official documents, as he had done with his draft registration in 1942. Salinger's marriage license, however, affirms his knowledge of his mother's Iowa birthplace, a small fact that he would later allow to be denied.

The Catcher in the Rye. To Claire, he presented his latest story, the tribute "Franny." Cornish residents added to the occasion with their own tradition, electing the new groom to the honorary post of town hargreave. The appointment was a local custom that Salinger doubtless viewed with suspicion, as it jokingly required him to round up stray pigs, an activity the author had renounced years before while dragging swine by their hindquarters in Poland.

Once married, Salinger and Claire set about building a life for themselves in step with the purity of their religious beliefs and independent of the 1950s obsession with status and appearance. It was a life void of the phoniness and materialism that Salinger had repudiated in his writings and that both had renounced through their convictions, one of simplicity with an emphasis upon spirituality and nature. It was an austere existence—a Zen Buddhist version of Salinger's apartment on East 57th Street. The couple drew their water from an old well. They grew their own food, and Salinger in particular developed a life-long passion for organic gardening. Both vowed to respect all living things and, according to Gavin Douglas, refused to kill even the tiniest of insects. Afternoons were filled with meditation and yoga. At night, they snuggled and read together, often *The Gospels of Sri Ramakrishna* and Paramahansa Yogananda's *The Autobiography of a Yogi.*

Exactly how Salinger felt about his new life can be gauged through a story that Claire's half brother relayed to *Time* magazine reporters in 1961. "He wanted to be self-sufficient," Douglas commented. "He had this vegetable garden, and Maxwell and all the others would send him things to grow. It was a primitive sort of life—you could call it Zen or whatever you like." When Salinger took Gavin on a tour of the property shortly after the wedding, he pointed out an abandoned barn. "They're gone," Salinger said of the previous owners. "They couldn't make it. But I'm here now. And I'm going to make the land profitable." In an exceptional moment of perception, Claire's brother interpreted Salinger's declaration as "an affirmation . . . a statement of belief in humanity."[2] Indeed, Salinger seemed to thrive in his new life. When his friend the author S. J. Perelman visited the newlyweds that June, he remarked on the positive effect the marriage and lifestyle had had upon Salinger.* "Jerry, in all justice, looked better than I've ever

---

*Perelman has long been credited with having introduced Salinger to Claire in 1954. The misconception was fostered by Salinger himself, who believed his early relationship with

seen him," he told Leila Hadley, "so evidently he's flourishing under matrimony or over it."[3]

Yet the cottage at Cornish bore two faces, each reflecting a mood of the couple's life there. The face that overlooked the sloping meadow with its spectacular view of the Connecticut River Valley was bright and indeed "sunny as hell." But the cottage was also enveloped by dense New Hampshire woodlands, a face of Salinger's reality that was veiled in shadows.

From the start Salinger worried that Claire would be unable to adapt to the solitude and simplicity of life at Cornish. Her life had thus far been a turmoil of constant movement, and she had always been surrounded by people. She had grown up in a family of intellectuals with homes throughout the world, a rarefied aristocracy that exuded wealth and position. Like Oona O'Neill before her, she might have been comfortable in the company of wealthy socialites, but the life of a New England farmer was something foreign to her.

During their engagement the couple had spent much of their time traveling, as if Salinger were staving off Claire's reaction to the austerity that awaited her. They had frequently visited New York, where they had stayed with Salinger's parents and Claire had been introduced to his professional family at *The New Yorker*. Salinger had also taken her to the Ramakrishna-Vivekananda Center around the corner from his parents' apartment. Claire fell in love with the center, as Salinger had hoped she would, but whether or not she could sustain a life of pious simplicity in rural New England was a question that time alone would answer.

The relationship began to falter almost immediately. Within a month of their marriage, Claire apparently began to reexamine her idealistic view of Salinger's Vedantic faith—just as Salinger himself was becoming increasingly immersed in it. Inspired by their readings of *The Autobiography of a Yogi* during their engagement, the couple had written to the book's publisher, the Self-Realization Fellowship, inquiring where they could find a teacher who might guide them in further studies. In response the fellowship suggested that they visit the guru Swami Premananda, who maintained a temple at College Park, Maryland. In

---

Claire Douglas to be a private affair and was perhaps wary of the innuendo of being romantically tied to Claire while she was underage.

March 1955, they boarded a train bound for Washington, D.C., to meet with Premananda.

Aside from her studies alone with Salinger, Claire's previous experience with Vedantic philosophy had been limited to her visits to the Ramakrishna-Vivekananda Center in New York City. Well funded and located in a brownstone in an upscale neighborhood, the center had entranced with its luxurious atmosphere and exotic decor. The temple in Maryland was a different story: an insignificant redbrick storefront situated in a low-class neighborhood that must have made Claire uncomfortable. Once inside, one noted the cheapness of its furnishings. After services and meditation, Claire and Salinger met privately with Swami Premananda, who, to Claire, seemed as unremarkable as the temple itself. After receiving instructions on breathing exercises and bestowing a donation on the guru, the couple was given a mantra to repeat, just as Franny had recited the Jesus Prayer, and were initiated into the Self-Realization Fellowship. Claire was disillusioned by the experience, but Salinger was rapturous. On the train back to Cornish that night, the couple made love, an event that Claire later recounted to her daughter, Margaret, as the occasion of her being conceived. Claire Salinger had become pregnant just two months after marriage.

As the pregnancy progressed, Claire became increasingly unhappy. Her sex life, she told friends, with Salinger had been sporadic at best, but she now accused him of treating her with physical revulsion. Claire believed that once her pregnancy became noticeable, Salinger reverted back to the disapproval of Sri Ramakrishna regarding women and sex. Ramakrishna had taught that sex was a worldly indulgence that should be reserved for procreation alone. Once Claire was pregnant, sex became a sin. *The Gospels* left little room for interpretation and was far less forgiving of romantic relationships than *The Autobiography of a Yogi* or the Self-Realization Fellowship:

> By meditating on God in solitude the mind acquires knowledge, dispassion, and devotion. But the very same mind goes downward if it dwells in the world. In the world there is only one thought: woman and gold.[4]

Even within marriage, the *Gospels* equated pleasurable sexual relations with damnation. So Claire was distraught during the last half of

1955, and to make matters worse, Salinger was absorbed by his work, which included frequent trips to New York City, where he holed up in the offices of *The New Yorker.* As Claire's pregnancy progressed, her ability to travel with her husband decreased, until by winter she found herself alone in the Cornish cottage. Working furiously, Salinger was happy in his new life, but Claire, isolated, began to see herself as a virtual prisoner.

The life that Salinger had built for himself and Claire in 1955 has often been regarded with scorn, used by detractors as a demonstration of his eccentricity and an accusation that he abandoned or even abused his wife. An understanding of Salinger's nature and devotion to his craft reveal a grayer truth. Living in Cornish itself inevitably created solitude. The town was remote and sparsely populated. Life there had changed little in decades, perhaps centuries. Isolation is often the exchange made for living in a place of unspoiled beauty, and S. J. Perelman described their property as a "private mountaintop overlooking five states"—testimony that the beauty of Salinger and Claire's Cornish home was, even by Perelman's high standards, beyond compare.

Cornish remains a rural village today, but in 1955 it was especially at the mercy of nature. Winters were long and severe, and any sizable snowfall spelled instant isolation. Few roads were paved, and the spring thaw turned them into impassable streams of mud. For the village locals, many of whom had held their plots for generations, isolation and self-sufficiency were the assumed way of life, and no one thought Salinger's lifestyle strange, especially as he had a new wife to consume his attentions.

It was also natural that Salinger chose the existence he did: a life of privacy, of regulation and absolute devotion to his craft. In his youth he had been considered something of a loner and had long struggled to find peaceful solitude in which to write. Over the years he had constantly fled New York in search of privacy and inspiration. While in the army he'd spent many weekends and furloughs in cramped hotel rooms, pecking away at his portable typewriter while his friends chased girls. Now, with a place of his own, one with extensive property, Salinger could finally create the refuge that his creative passions so desperately needed.

Professionally, 1955 was a very productive year. Salinger spent its opening days putting the final polish on "Franny" before its release and immediately afterward began to pen a ninety-page novella that would prove seminal in his body of work, a story through which many of his past efforts would converge to blaze a new path for his writings: "Raise High the Roof Beam, Carpenters," the first true saga of the Glass family.

Salinger worked tirelessly on the story for most of the year. He paid the novella a devotion that he had not employed since *The Catcher in the Rye*. It was continually reworked, refined, and "compressed" until it reached a quality and size that *The New Yorker* would accommodate.* This process seldom involved Gus Lobrano, whose health was beginning to fail. Instead, Salinger collaborated with the magazine's editor (and Lobrano's nemesis), William Shawn. For all of Shawn's eccentricities, he was universally praised as being a brilliant editor whose contribution could make the most lackluster of works shine. For months, he and Salinger secluded themselves in Shawn's *New Yorker* office and worked on the story. When it was finally completed in November, "Carpenters" bypassed the normal process of evaluation by the magazine's editorial staff (the same assessors who had so misinterpreted "Franny") and went directly to publication.

. . .

The opening pages of "Carpenters" are exquisite. In them, the narrator recalls a night that occurred twenty years earlier, when his ten-month-old sister was moved into the room that he and his brother shared as teenagers. When the child began to cry during the night, his brother calmed her by reading an ancient Taoist tale of a Chinese duke who sends a seemingly ordinary vegetable hawker on an impossible quest for the perfect steed. When the hawker proves himself incapable of distinguishing even the horse's sex or color, the duke becomes dismayed. How can such a man be a judge of quality? Yet, when the horse arrives, it proves to be the most superior of animals. Chiu-fang Kao,

---

*Despite the attention paid to refining "Raise High the Roof Beam, Carpenters," its original *New Yorker* publication contained two typographical errors that have survived succeeding reprints. Page 68 (Little, Brown and Company 1963 hardcover edition) uses the term "God damn," while page 69 hyphenates the term into "God-damn." The most noticeable error occurs on page 18, where a printing omission resulted in the line "In doing it, I hit my head a very audible crack on the roof."

the lowly vegetable hawker, had chosen it by perceiving its spiritual essence and ignoring its outer details.

With a masterful tenderness, this opening passage gently shepherds the reader into the fold of Salinger's imaginary world. His ability to draw the reader into his work, a maneuver whose gentleness seemed to have been refined with each previous story, reached its summit in "Carpenters." Through the story's first lines, the yet-unknown narrator reintroduces the reader to two characters who are already familiar: Franny, the distressed protagonist of Salinger's most recent work, and Seymour, the tragic hero of the celebrated "A Perfect Day for Bananafish." The reader's feelings of intimacy and comfort with these characters are immediate, and the short story that the narrator tells of his brother Seymour reading a Taoist tale to the infant Franny is sublime.

A collision with reality soon follows. Readers are quickly reminded that Seymour, now understood to be exceptional in wisdom, perception, and kindness, is actually dead. But it is too late for them to retreat; they have already entered the matrix of Salinger's craft. Fixed there, their sympathies are instinctively delivered to the storyteller, who lays bare his grief over Seymour's death. This grief attaches a bittersweet quality to the Taoist tale. "Such a man [as the insightful vegetable hawker], gifted with the eye for the core of reality, was Seymour," he mourns. And since Seymour's suicide in a Florida resort seven years before, the narrator has been unable "to think of anybody whom I'd care to send out to look for horses in his stead." The storyteller of "Raise High the Roof Beam, Carpenters" is Seymour's younger brother, Buddy Glass, and when Seymour's tale of the duke and Kao ends, it is Buddy's tale that begins.

Buddy's story takes place on the day of Seymour's wedding during the Second World War, in June 1942, and is the first story he narrates. After reintroducing readers to Seymour's character, Buddy continues to set the stage by describing the rest of the Glass family. The description not only serves to familiarize the reader with Buddy and his siblings but also explains why he is alone in representing Seymour's family at the wedding.

At the request of his sister Boo Boo who has been forced to "fly to parts unknown for the war effort," Buddy has traveled from Fort Benning, Georgia, to New York City to attend his brother Seymour's wedding.* Crowded into "an enormous old brownstone" with other guests, Buddy awaits Seymour's arrival. After waiting in vain for an hour and twenty minutes, the bride-to-be, Muriel Fedder, finally accepts that she has been stood up at the altar and is guided out of the brownstone by her family and whisked away in the waiting bridal car, without her intended groom.

The Fedders, humiliated by events and furious with Seymour, announce to the guests that despite their being forced to call off the wedding, the reception will take place. The crowd then clumsily files into a series of waiting cars to make their way to the Fedders' home.

The awkwardness of Buddy's position, which is unique among the guests, is painful. To make matters worse, Buddy finds himself in a limousine with Muriel's greatest champion, the matron of honor, along with the bride's aunt and great-uncle and the matron of honor's husband, "the Lieutenant." The matron of honor is exploding with fury. Her attacks on the absent bridegroom are so rabid that Buddy is placed in a difficult position. No one knows that he is Seymour's brother. Does he admit his relation to the errant groom and defend his brother, whose absence Buddy himself doesn't understand, or does he continue to remain silent and attempt to conceal his relation to Seymour?

After a series of amusing and sometimes bizarre incidents, the limousine is barred from reaching the Fedders' apartment by a parade and the wedding guests wind up not at the reception but at the apartment that Buddy shares with Seymour. When the matron of honor continues to attack Seymour, even within the haven of his home, Buddy finally rises to his brother's defense. In doing so, he is forced to admit that he is Seymour's brother, and he receives the brunt of the matron of honor's rage.

During this conflict, Buddy finds Seymour's diary stashed away in the bathroom. Reading it enlightens him to his brother's motivation for having stood up his bride at the altar. It also enlightens readers as to Seymour's character and personality.

The story's two major conflicts, the one between Buddy and the

---

*In June 1942, Salinger was stationed at Fort Monmouth, New Jersey, where Seymour was encamped when he wrote his "Carpenters" diary entries. However, Salinger still aligns himself with Buddy Glass through this reference. Fort Benning is easily a euphemism for Bainbridge Army Base, both situated in Georgia. Furthermore, Fort Benning had been the home base of Salinger's 12th Infantry Regiment.

matron of honor and the one between Buddy and himself (as he attempts to rationalize Seymour's seemingly callous selfishness), come to an end when the matron of honor calls the bride's family and returns to the group with the announcement that Seymour and Muriel have eloped.

Besides parallels with previous stories, "Carpenters" contains similarities with Salinger's own life that are unmistakable. Both he and Seymour were corporals and served in the Army Air Corps during the war. Like Seymour, Salinger underwent basic training at Fort Monmouth, New Jersey, before being transferred to Georgia, where Buddy is stationed. On a private level, by placing the events in 1942, Salinger draws a personal comparison between Muriel Fedder and Oona O'Neill. In the story Buddy has never met Seymour's intended bride. However, in her letter, his sister Boo Boo describes Muriel as being physically beautiful but intellectually vacant, a description remarkably similar to those given to Jerry's own 1942 belle. In addition, Seymour's diary entries describing his trips from Fort Monmouth to New York to meet Muriel correspond to Salinger's own routine in 1942 while he was dating O'Neill.

The connections between the plot of "Carpenters" and Salinger's life in 1955 are especially obvious. "Carpenters" is a story about a wedding written the same year that Salinger himself was married. In addition, it was written while his wife was pregnant, giving a special depth to this first true Glass family story as heralding the nativity of two families: the Glass family and Salinger's own. In naming this story, Salinger (through Boo Boo Glass) called upon a wedding poem by the Greek poet Sappho. It is easy to envision Salinger watching workmen as they expanded his Cornish cottage in 1955, thinking of Sappho's poem and adding his own personal twist: "Raise High the Roof Beam, Carpenters!"

Also wrapped within "Carpenters" are a number of Zen and Vedantic themes, presented more subtly than in previous stories. Foremost among them is the topic of indiscrimination, which is actually the application of God-consciousness to individual lives and its clash with the world of accepted convention. Buddy presents this theme from the story's opening tale, when the vegetable hawker selects a superior steed by sensing the horse's inner spirit rather than by evaluating its external appearance. Throughout the story, the theme is extended by

Buddy's dilemma. He reveres and loves Seymour but cannot quite understand his actions. Some appear to be selfishly cruel: Seymour's abandoning Muriel on their wedding day and his striking Charlotte Mayhew with a rock as a child. Buddy faces the challenge of seeing beyond the surface of these acts and perceiving the true motivation behind them. This is an exercise of faith for Buddy, who begins to doubt his brother's virtue as he is pressured by the judgment of those around him.

Seymour's diary entries recount his dates with Muriel and his visits to the Fedders' home. They explain the relevance of the opening Taoist tale to this story. Seymour describes Muriel as materialistic and egotistical but says that the virtue of her simplicity outweighs those traits. When she presents Seymour with a dessert made by her own hands, he cries with grateful joy. It is the goodness contained in Muriel's simplicity that Seymour most perceives, not Muriel's conventionality. Speaking in the terms of the Taoist tale, Seymour has chosen a superior horse despite all outward appearances to the contrary. Yet Buddy is reluctant to accept this logic, and his actions show his disapproval of Seymour's choice. When he reads Seymour's words, he throws down the diary in anger and begins to drink heavily.

Buddy's actions blend into another important theme presented by "Carpenters": acceptance through faith. The incident with Charlotte Mayhew speaks to Salinger's ongoing fascination with the competing forces of human nature. Seymour aspired to saintliness but was still capable of cruelty. This cruelty was not premeditated. It was instinctive. Although the character of Seymour Glass represented Salinger's aspirations to the qualities of the Lamb, Seymour was also home to the Tyger, just as the darker forces of human nature live side by side with spirituality.

When Salinger penned "Carpenters," he was still struggling to rationalize the coexistence of these forces. He did not understand why God imposed conflict through human nature but had come to accept it as part of God's inscrutable plan. In "Carpenters," Seymour employs the example of a kitten to condemn the human tendency to mask the crueler realities of creation with false sentimentality. "We are being sentimental when we give to a thing more tenderness than God gives to it," he reasons. God's plan is perfect and must be accepted, even if it conflicts with social concepts. The inclination of human beings to deny the existence of both sides of human nature and to mold their concept of God to fit their sentimental illusions is condemned by Seymour as sacrilege. "The human voice conspires to desecrate everything on earth," he warns.[5]

In "Carpenters," true acceptance is based upon faith and not logic. Seymour accepts Muriel despite her materialism. Buddy accepts Seymour despite his perceived cruelties. As the story ends, Buddy still does not understand why his brother threw a rock at Charlotte Mayhew as a child. Neither do readers. But the point being made is this: if we are to accept Seymour Glass, we must accept him in all of his complexity and flaws, as well as his virtues, because each is holy.

The value of acceptance through faith is symbolized by the character of Muriel's tiny great-uncle. He is by far the most attractive character of the story and the only one who does not pass judgment. Salinger amplifies his connection with the themes of acceptance through faith and God-consciousness by depicting him as a deaf-mute. The next-to-final scene of "Carpenters" leaves Buddy Glass alone with this symbol, signifying that Buddy has obtained these capabilities through his experience. In the story's closing line, Buddy considers sending this character's cigar butt (suddenly used up after remaining unlit throughout the story) along with a blank sheet of paper (symbols of acceptance and indiscrimination) to Seymour as a wedding present—proof of the lessons he has learned.

"Carpenters" has been acclaimed as Salinger's most masterful character study. Its players are completely natural human beings and its dialogue moves along at a pace. Atop its underlying questions on the nature of humanity and examples of God-consciousness, the story exudes a playfulness that Salinger's shorter *New Yorker* stories never accommodated. "Carpenters" was crafted to deliver the sheer joy of reading, and there is every indication that Salinger wrote it with an exhilarating joy of authorship. There is a feeling of wholesomeness as readers are drawn into the lives of the members of the Glass family, as Salinger's new vehicle of exploration. Much of this feeling is due to familiarity with the story's characters, but more is due to the attitude with which Salinger wrote "Carpenters" and readers absorb it. Every word of this story, every silence, every sideward glance, bears meaning. But it is often meaning that needs little analysis. Much of "Carpenters" is enjoyable simply because it reflects the average moments of average lives. Salinger crafted the Glass family, and Seymour Glass in particular, to call attention to the divine beauty alive within us all.

In Salinger's own life, the story held a meaning that was intensely personal and supremely positive. The character of Seymour Glass represented Salinger's affirmation of humanity—the presence of divinity within each human being that triumphs over despair. As a creation, Seymour represented the victory of Salinger's faith in humanity, which after years of doubt slowly resurrected until it came ablaze through the Glass family. The Caulfields had questioned the meaning of life. They often fell short of their goals and regularly complained. The Glass family instead confirms the meaning of life; yet they are no less ordinary than the Caulfields. The powers that Seymour developed through his concentration upon God were powers that Salinger believed to be within everyone. Personally, Salinger would hold the image of Seymour Glass, in Seymour's ever-increasing saintliness, up to his own life as an example not of how he envisioned himself but as a goal to attain.

On the dust jacket of the 1961 hardcover edition of *Franny and Zooey,* Salinger wrote an author's note that applies to "Raise High the Roof Beam, Carpenters" with exactness. It clarifies his personal vision of the Glass family sagas as a body of work and reveals the tenderness that he felt for them:

> Both stories are early, critical entries in a narrative series I'm doing about a family of settlers in twentieth-century New York, the Glasses. . . . I love working on these Glass stories, I've been waiting for them most of my life, and I think I have fairly decent, monomaniacal plans to finish them with due care and all-available skill.[6]

Salinger's introduction of that family of settlers to the world was a gamble. His name was already synonymous with another fictional family, that of Holden Caulfield, a family the world had embraced and come to love. The public craved tales of the Caulfields, and Salinger was aware that many readers would be reluctant to embrace a competing group of characters.

But after two attempts at religious fiction that he considered unsuccessful, Salinger felt he had finally found the ideal vehicle to convey his message. By collecting characters from past stories and binding them together into a single family, he would employ the seven children of Bessie and Les Glass to portray the agonies of searching for nobility and eternal truths while striving to survive in modern society. He would also use these characters to begin the search that eventually enters the lives of all spiritual and religious people: the quest for perfection.

14. Zooey

On December 10, 1955, Claire gave birth to a seven-pound, three-quarter-ounce baby girl at Mary Hitchcock Memorial Hospital in Hanover, New Hampshire, and J. D. Salinger became a father.[1] The new parents named the baby Margaret Ann.* Salinger had wanted to name her Phoebe, after Holden Caulfield's sister, but Claire protested and won out at the last minute. So it was perhaps a compromise that, once legally named, Margaret Ann's parents would actually call her Peggy, after the child heroine of "Blue Melody."†

Salinger's joy over Peggy's birth was absolute. Here was a man from whose imagination had come Mattie Gladwaller, Phoebe Caulfield, and the remarkable Esmé. Even before Peggy was born, Salinger's writings had expressed his anticipation and his resolve to be a good father. Seymour's diary in "Raise High the Roof Beam, Carpenters,"

*The name Margaret was probably Claire's suggestion. It was a traditional name in the Douglas family, who proudly traced their lineage to Henry VIII through his daughter Margaret Tudor and, through her, to the Scottish House of Stuart.

†Margaret Ann's birth certificate contains an error: the document mistakenly reverses Claire's middle and first names, renaming her Alison Claire Salinger.

presented to the world exactly three weeks before Peggy's birth, gave voice to Salinger's own hopes and aspirations:*

> I've been reading a miscellany of Vedanta all day. Marriage part-ners are to serve each other. Elevate, help, teach, strengthen each other, but above all, serve. Raise their children honorably, lovingly, and with detachment. A child is a guest in the house, to be loved and respected—never possessed, since he belongs to God. How wonderful, how sane, how beautifully difficult, and therefore true. The joy of responsibility for the first time in my life.[2]

Actually, Salinger and Claire were unprepared for parenthood. Their pasts, temperaments, and circumstances had left them ill equipped for the everyday demands of raising a child. Claire was twenty-two. Her own parents had been nearly absent during her childhood, and she had little experience to draw upon aside from memories of nannies and foster parents. She was also increasingly vulnerable, exasperated by the isolation of Cornish and insecure in her marriage. Though almost thirty-seven, Salinger was also unready for the realities of fatherhood. Although the ideals of parenthood elated him, his own experiences with children, outside the realm of fiction, were limited at best. The rudimentary details of caring for an infant, changing diapers, and re-sponding to demands for attention were concerns his fiction had never considered. In a story told by the Salinger family, he was holding his infant daughter when she urinated. Salinger threw up his arms, tossing the baby into the air. Peggy landed safely on a cushion but almost paid dearly for her bad timing and her father's inexperience.

Other challenges, less common to new parents, foreshadowed problems of greater concern. For Claire and Salinger, Cornish sud-denly seemed like a wilderness where the custody of an infant was a fearful thing. And Peggy was born in early December, a precursor to four months of the winter whose isolation and loneliness had hounded Claire the year before. As the days grew colder, the cottage must have seemed to shrink around her, making Claire into a prisoner once

---

*Here the timing did not cooperate. Salinger's daughter was due to be born on Novem-ber 19, the same day as the scheduled publication of "Raise High the Roof Beam, Carpen-ters" by *The New Yorker.* However, she had her own plans and was overdue by three weeks.

again. Intensifying her situation, the baby had naturally become the center of Salinger's attention, and Claire likely found herself competing for her husband's affections. Suddenly burdened with the inescapable duties of motherhood, Claire could be forgiven for beginning to resent her own child.[3] In 1956, little was known of postnatal mood shifts; women suffered in silence, with feelings of guilt and confusion that often nearly overwhelmed them. Salinger's letters of the period reveal that he was aware of his wife's discomfort but only dimly.

As an infant, Peggy suffered a series of common childhood ailments that apparently baffled her parents. With the nearest hospital twenty miles away in Hanover, the Salingers admitted living in a constant state of terror.[4] Although Salinger attempted to treat the child through prayer, Peggy was seldom in good health and cried constantly. Crowded in the cottage with a sullen wife and wailing child, Salinger found that he could not work. So, not long after Peggy's birth, he made a decision that was professionally advantageous but personally disastrous.

Across the stream and about a hundred yards from the cottage, he built a small concrete structure as a private hermitage in which to write. His detached studio has often been referred to as his "bunker," but the unit was surprisingly comfortable—if stark—and was not a refuge from others as much a place where his imagination could run free.

Salinger carved a subtle path through the meadow adjacent to the cottage. At the point where the meadow gave way to woods, the ground suddenly dropped, and the path transformed into a series of stepping-stones installed as a staircase. At this point, the ground leveled off and the path resumed, leading into an open field. Here, the sound of rushing water could be heard. Separating the field from the dark forest beyond was a flowing stream that contained a spring and small waterfall.* Over the stream Salinger constructed a simple wooden bridge, across which lay his retreat, built of green concrete cinder blocks to blend into the surroundings.

Within the bunker, a wood-burning stove warmed the cold New Hampshire winters. On sunny days, a generous skylight lighted the space. The building was furnished with a bed, shelves, a filing cabinet,

---

*The spring gushed cool water, even during the summer, and Salinger used it as a kind of makeshift refrigerator, often storing bottles of Coca-Cola in the water, at arm's reach from the path.

and a long table that the author used as a desk and upon which his precious typewriter was enthroned.* Salinger did not use a chair. Instead, he had a tremendous leather car seat upon which he often sat in the lotus position. But the most magnificent aspect of Salinger's sanctuary was the complication of its walls: they were strewn with an ever-increasing menagerie of notes. As the saga of the Glass family spilled from Salinger's mind, one drop at a time, he would pen his ideas and post them around him. The personal histories of his characters, the genealogy of the Glass family, past and future story ideas, all found their position in the chaotic organization of Salinger's chamber walls.

After completing the bunker Salinger developed a routine that he would maintain until very old age. He awoke at six thirty in the morning and meditated or did yoga. After a light breakfast, he would pack his lunch and disappear into the seclusion of his workplace. There, he was not to be disturbed. Twelve-hour days were normal. Sixteen-hour days were not unusual. At times, he would come home for dinner, only to return again to the bunker. Many nights, he did not come home at all.

The decision to construct a hermitage in the woods has long been derided as the greatest symbol of Salinger's seclusion from the world. In hindsight, the choice wreaked havoc on his personal life. But he remained convinced that his work was worth the sacrifice. His insistence upon maintaining a daily routine that cloistered him away from his family speaks to the stubbornness of his ambition. In the comfort of his own design, freed from the distractions that had always plagued him, the richness of his art came vividly to life. Within his cloister, reality and imagination were allowed to blur, and the bunker became the realm of the Glasses. Here the characters of his imagination reigned supreme, dictating their stories to him as spirits might channel messages to a medium from other worlds. With no outside disruption to

---

*Salinger was superstitious about his typewriter. He changed it as infrequently as possible and used the same machine to write "Hapworth 16, 1924" as he had *The Catcher in the Rye*. In fact, he may have changed his typewriter only three times throughout his career, due more to obligation than to choice. His wartime stories were written using an army-issue typewriter different from the one he had used at Park Avenue. This typewriter delighted the author. After returning home from the war, he appears to have purchased one like it, and it was that one he took with him to Cornish. Despite his love of the machine, Salinger never learned how to touch-type and wrote all of his stories using no more than two fingers at a time.

obstruct them, they became as real to the author as flesh-and-blood people.

. . .

Come spring, Peggy's ailments began to subside and Salinger boasted that she was blossoming into a happy child full of smiles and laughter and that he and Claire were falling more deeply in love with her each passing day.[5] Additions were made to the still-primitive cottage. A running-water system was finally set up, complete with a washing machine, and Salinger reluctantly installed a telephone in his private bunker, warning Claire that he was to be disturbed for emergencies only. The season's thaw also brought visits to the Maxwells, always with Peggy in tow. Salinger joyfully tended to his garden and devoted himself to a diet of organic foods. He could be spotted driving into town in his jeep or in nearby Windsor, picking up supplies. In Windsor, Salinger developed a lifelong friendship with Olin and Marguerite Tewksbury, local farmers from whom he often bought produce. Salinger spent hours sitting on the Tewksburys' porch with Olin, surveying the fields and discussing local events while Claire introduced Marguerite to the then-radical concept of organic farming, a method the Tewksburys slowly came to embrace. Though corn and fertilizer were accepted topics of conversation with the Tewksburys, Salinger's work was not. That subject, Marguerite later recalled, was strictly taboo.[6]

Most anticipated by the Salingers was the springtime arrival of their nearest neighbors, Judge Billings Learned Hand and his wife, Frances. An elderly couple,* the Hands spent only six months a year in Cornish, arriving with the thaw and retreating to New York before the onslaught of winter. When they were in residence, dinner at the Hands' was a weekly ritual for Salinger and Claire; there they enjoyed reading aloud together and discussing current events and spiritual and social topics, as well as daily life in Cornish. During the winter months, Salinger wrote to Hand frequently, keeping the judge updated on what was going on during his absence. The enthusiasm with which Salinger and Claire (and, when she grew older, Peggy) looked forward to the arrival of their neighbors cannot be overstated. On the Hands' return

*Born in 1872, Judge Hand was age 84 in 1956.

after the long winter, Salinger wrote with grateful relief, "They bring only peace and joy, those two."[7]

Serendipity had always been a remarkable aspect of Salinger's life. He often encountered the right person at exactly the right time. Had he not studied under Whit Burnett, he might well have gone into acting. He had met Hemingway at the very moment his soul needed an anchor. He had been approached by Jamie Hamilton when he most craved a kindred spirit and was exasperated with his editors at Little, Brown. William Shawn had entered his life when he most needed professional affirmation. And Claire's return in 1955 had saved him from a pit of despair that might well have consumed him. Salinger's friendship with Judge Learned Hand was a prime example of that same fortune.

Billings Learned Hand is widely regarded as having been the most important judge in American history never to sit upon the highest court. He was often called "the tenth justice of the Supreme Court" in recognition of his impact upon American law. A 1944 speech on the nature of liberty delivered by Hand was so thoughtful and eloquent that it catapulted him to instant fame and is still required study in law schools throughout the nation. During his fifty-two years on the federal bench, Judge Hand forged a reputation as a champion of individual liberties and a fierce protector of the freedom of speech.

Aside from similarities of conviction, Judge Hand and Salinger shared personal traits that bonded them together. Hand was himself an author, whose works remain as important to constitutional law as Salinger's works are to fiction. Both men valued their right to privacy and were wary of those who might twist their words to serve purposes not intended. Both were intensely fascinated by religion and enjoyed conversations on spiritual topics that often consumed hours. Sadly, both men were enmeshed in troubled marriages, a fact that both painstakingly concealed from others. Perhaps most important, both Salinger and Learned Hand suffered from periods of deep depression, a penchant toward melancholy that fused them together in a way unique to such sufferers. During the final years of Learned Hand's life, his relationship with Salinger was perhaps the fullest he enjoyed, while Salinger's gratitude for their friendship was unmistakable. His letters to Hand were frequent. In them, he confided his inability to deal with Claire's loneliness and feelings of isolation. It was to Hand that Salinger first announced the birth of his daughter. It was Hand whom Salinger chose to be Peggy's godfather.

. . .

On March 1, 1956, Salinger's longtime editor, Gus Lobrano, died of cancer at age fifty-three. Lobrano's death came as a shock to the *New Yorker* family. "He was such a nice man," Salinger mourned, "I can't begin to tell you . . . I miss him tremendously."[8] For all their professional disagreements, Salinger and Lobrano had worked well together. Their relationship had spanned a decade. Gus Lobrano had also been a physical link to the memory of Harold Ross who had taught Lobrano a rare respect for writers, which was vital when dealing with Salinger.

As head fiction editor, Lobrano had held a powerful position at *The New Yorker,* and his death created a void that invited chaos and was potentially lethal to Salinger's relationship with the magazine. In Lobrano's sudden absence, hopeful candidates scurried to fill the vacancy. Foremost among them was Katharine White, whom Lobrano had himself succeeded back in 1938. Having since returned to *The New Yorker,* the Whites were now anxious to reassert their influence. That J. D. Salinger would find a viable replacement for Gus Lobrano among this clash of egos was improbable.

The struggle within the editorial offices of *The New Yorker* indeed claimed victims. Salinger's friend S. J. Perelman suspended his association with the magazine in disgust over the ensuing frenzy. Perelman had been close to Lobrano and bewildered at the succession of Shawn to replace Ross. Watching the jockeying of positions in the shadow of Lobrano's death, he was amazed and appalled. Even the magazine's contributors seemed drawn into the bedlam, "acting," as he put it, "as though they invented the paper." On one occasion Perelman actually came to blows with the cartoonist James Thurber. "Thurber was going on ad nauseam about his influence and how he'd set the style for the whole enterprise, etc. I finally got a snootful and said mildly, 'Come, come, it's just another 15-cent magazine.' Though nearly blind, he leapt at me and tried to throttle me. It took two burly copy editors to drag him off me."[9]

When the Byzantine intrigue at *The New Yorker* finally subsided, it was Katharine White who slipped into Lobrano's position. She and her husband were now viewed as something of a cabal at the magazine, and many of those who had been close to Lobrano were distraught. "Following Gus Lobrano's death," Perelman reported, "White has consolidated her editorial power to such an extent that she sits astride the magazine and is slowly throttling the life out of it."[10]

Conceding the new reality, Salinger tried his best to work with White, an effort that would prove futile. White first approached Salinger shortly after Lobrano's death with a letter of condolence plainly aimed at solidifying her position with the magazine's premier contributors. Salinger responded on March 29 with an expansive reply. He admitted having a difficult time accepting Lobrano's passing but told White that her support had made things easier for him and he was grateful. "To leave much unsaid," he abruptly injected, "I do have a story going, and I expect to submit it very soon."[11]

Just as Salinger was settling into his routine at Cornish and trying to keep abreast of events at *The New Yorker*, he received word that *Cosmopolitan* had chosen to republish his story "The Inverted Forest" in its Diamond Jubilee issue. Although he was without legal recourse, Salinger objected to the reprint and pleaded with the magazine to reconsider, but to no avail. The possession of Salinger's first novella was simply too much of a temptation for *Cosmopolitan*'s editors, who were anxious to capitalize on the author's recent fame.* Accompanying the story, they inserted a short profile of the author (Salinger naturally refused to supply even the most evasive autobiographical note) and reminded readers that they possessed two Salinger works, "The Inverted Forest" and "Blue Melody," both written before the publication of *The Catcher in the Rye*. Salinger was incensed that, aside from this minor disclaimer concealed at the bottom of the story's opening page, *Cosmopolitan* allowed the illusion that "The Inverted Forest" was a new work.

This was the first instance in which Salinger sought to prohibit the republication of his earlier, pre–*New Yorker* stories. Previously, he had allowed them to be rereleased without complaint. He had even put aside personal animosity and agreed to Whit Burnett's use of "The Long Debut of Lois Taggett" six years before. However, Salinger had been embarrassed by "The Inverted Forest" when it had first appeared

---

*Salinger shared billing in *Cosmopolitan*'s Diamond Jubilee issue with several names greater than his: Winston Churchill, Pearl S. Buck, and Ernest Hemingway were also featured.

in 1947 and had not warmed to it since. Now engrossed in crafting the Glass family series, the last thing he wanted was the reappearance of older works that might confuse readers by colliding with the structure and messages of his new project.

As justified as Salinger may have been in protesting the republication of "The Inverted Forest," the incident foreshadowed a tendency that would soon become a fixation. It signified his growing reluctance to allow his less polished stories to be scrutinized by the reading public. As early as 1940, he had expressed his discomfort with rewitnessing the imperfections of past attempts. "When I'm finished with a piece," he had said, "I'm embarrassed to look at it again, as though I were afraid I hadn't wiped its nose clean."[12] In truth, Salinger often missed the simplicity of his earlier stories.[13] Yet, with each installment of the Glass family series, he felt compelled to strive for a greater measure of perfection. Beginning in 1956, with the popularity of *Nine Stories* and the advent of the Glass family promising a body of future works, Salinger increasingly began to call his uncollected stories, with all their glaring imperfections, back from the gaze of readers and into obscurity.

. . .

No story reveals Salinger's quest for perfection better than the novella "Zooey." Salinger worked on the piece for a year and a half, agonizing over each word and punctuation mark. The construction of "Zooey" is in itself a saga that involved the politics of *The New Yorker* and influenced Salinger's personal life immeasurably. Its reception at the magazine's editorial offices, under the new regime of Katharine White, nearly ended his association with it. And the single-minded devotion with which he wrote "Zooey" became so paramount in his life that it nearly ended his marriage.

On February 8, 1956, Salinger received his yearly (first-rejection contract) salary from *The New Yorker*. The check was delivered to Salinger's agent along with a note from William Maxwell that expressed the magazine's desire to publish Salinger's next work. "It would give this magazine delight to get its editorial hands on a new story by him," Maxwell stated.[14]

Within his bunker, Salinger was indeed working on his next project that February. But it was not intended to be a short story. He had actually begun to write a novel about the Glass family. It had been his intention to write a second novel as soon as he had completed *The Catcher in the Rye,* but that had never come to pass. Now, after creating an atmosphere of privacy in which to work and having envisioned a cast of characters who infatuated him, he felt the time was finally right. His correspondence during 1956 and 1957 was strewn with excited references to his new book. They also make it plain that the novella that we now know as "Zooey" was originally a large portion of that intended novel.

In attempting such an ambitious work, Salinger tried to employ the same method that had worked for him so well when he had penned *The Catcher in the Rye:* he sought to construct the new book by sewing together pieces that could also stand on their own as self-contained stories. "Zooey" is a prime example of this method. While his letters leave no doubt that "Zooey" was intended to rest within the new novel upon the book's completion, the story's most immediate purpose was to stand alone as a sequel to the story "Franny."[15]

Salinger had nearly completed "Zooey" by mid-April 1956.[16] He was, however, unsure of it at the time and, considering the chaos at the offices of *The New Yorker,* was fearful that it would be rejected by the magazine. He had good reason to be apprehensive: reaction to "Raise High the Roof Beam, Carpenters" had been muted.

"Carpenters" came close to structural perfection—a fact that had saved it from critics anxious to attack its religious content. As author Ben Yagoda observed years later, the saving grace of "Carpenters" was that Salinger's "obsession with the holy Seymour and the rest of the Glasses is restrained by an allegiance to literary and narrative values."[17] According to Salinger, "Zooey" held no such religious moderation, and unless he could duplicate the precision he had achieved with "Carpenters," critics and editors would surely dismiss it.

Salinger tried his best to subdue the religious content of "Zooey," but he found it impossible. Had he sat at his typewriter determined to write "a love story about a stolen pair of sneakers," he said, the result would still be a religious sermon. It was something that he claimed to have no control over, and he seems to have given up trying. "The choice of material has never seemed to be really mine," he said resignedly.[18] Clearly, Salinger's faith had become so intertwined with his work that they were now indistinguishable. The question that presented itself was how the public would receive such a union of prayer and authorship.

When Salinger submitted "Zooey" to "the editorial hands" of *The New Yorker*, it was scrutinized with vigor. The submission presented the new editors an opportunity to assert themselves by bringing the magazine's most prestigious contributor into line. They deemed the story too long and meandering. Its characters were seen as too precious, presented by an author overly enamored of them. But most damning of all, they charged that the story was saturated with religion. "Zooey" was not only rejected by *The New Yorker* editorial staff—it was rejected unanimously.

With Gus Lobrano gone, the task of informing Salinger fell to William Maxwell, who sought to spare Salinger's feelings by citing a *New Yorker* policy against publishing sequels as the reason for "Zooey" 's rejection.* But the truth was plain, and Salinger was distraught over the snub. He had worked long and hard on "Zooey," and by 1956 there could be no consideration of submitting it elsewhere.

Salinger found himself in a difficult position. He had grandiose plans for his Glass family series that he was unwilling to abandon. The rebuff of "Zooey" seemed to block his aspirations. There were also financial considerations. *Nine Stories* and *The Catcher in the Rye* sold consistently at a brisk rate. The royalties were handsome but not guaranteed. Salinger now owned his own home on 90 acres of property and had recently done extensive work on the grounds and cottage. He also had a wife and newborn baby. If cut off from *The New Yorker*, he may have worried, how would he support his family?

In this uncertain atmosphere Salinger did a desperate thing: he turned his eyes to Hollywood. He swallowed his disgust over the mistreatment of "Uncle Wiggily in Connecticut" by filmmakers in 1949 and considered selling the movie rights to yet another of his *Nine Stories,* this time "The Laughing Man." To represent him to filmmakers, Salinger employed H. N. Swanson, who was a business partner of Ober Associates. Swanson, known to his friends as "Swanie," was the most renowned and successful writers' agent in Holly-

---

*The insincerity of Maxwell's excuse for the rejection of "Zooey" was awkward for him and Salinger alike. The editor should have remembered that *The New Yorker* had accepted Salinger's first contribution, "Slight Rebellion off Madison," with an appeal for a sequel including Holden Caulfield.

wood.* He had represented William Faulkner, Ernest Hemingway, and, most notably, F. Scott Fitzgerald. If Salinger were forced into the distasteful position of relinquishing the rights to "The Laughing Man" to an industry he loathed, he would, at least, be in prestigious company.

When Swanson approached Hollywood producers with Salinger's offer, their reaction was predictable. They were excited, but it was the prospect of transforming *The Catcher in the Rye* to the screen that thrilled them. This Salinger refused. In fact, his offer came with a further caveat: he would in no way participate in the adaptation of his work. He was willing to sell the movie rights to "The Laughing Man," and that was the end of it.

Broadway too had its eyes on *Catcher*. The famous director Elia Kazan implored Salinger to allow the adaptation. When the breathless Kazan had persuaded his last, Salinger simply shook his head and murmured, "I cannot give my permission. I fear Holden wouldn't like it." The matter was over but the story quickly became legend.[19]

There was perhaps another explanation for Salinger's sudden reticence toward Hollywood and Broadway, aside from the wishes of Holden Caulfield. On November 8, 1956, Salinger received a check from *The New Yorker* for "Zooey." William Shawn had overridden the decision of his editors and determined to publish the story despite them. Moreover, Shawn had resolved to edit "Zooey" himself. For Maxwell and White, the event must have been chilling. In overruling them, Shawn had not only chastised the editorial staff for its arrogant shortsightedness but also aligned himself with Salinger completely. For the next six months, Shawn and Salinger alone would work on revising "Zooey," away from the scrutiny and influence of anyone else at the magazine. They barricaded themselves into Shawn's office for days, relentlessly refining the story one word at a time. As they did, the two men became the closest and most devoted of friends. William Shawn saved not only Salinger's novella but also his association with *The New Yorker* itself, and Salinger would never forget it.

In revising "Zooey," the greatest obstacle seems to have been the story's length. As it had with "Raise High the Roof Beam, Carpenters,"

---

*Swanson's resemblance to Les Glass, who is described in "Raise High the Roof Beam, Carpenters" as "hustling talent for a motion picture studio" in Los Angeles, may—or may not—be coincidental.

The New Yorker demanded that Salinger "compress" the story to fit the magazine before it would publish it.* In its final form, "Zooey" runs to 41,130 words and is Salinger's longest work apart from *The Catcher in the Rye*. That he labored to condense the story for an additional six months after Shawn purchased it is some indication of its original size.

Naturally, Katharine White grew enviously fascinated by the clandestine goings-on within Shawn's office. Attempting to expand her involvement in the project, she sent a number of letters to Salinger expressing her keen interest. By late November 1956, Salinger appeared to be making substantial progress in reworking the story, and White congratulated him on his accomplishment with calculated affectation:

> I just wanted to let you know how happy I am—for you and for the magazine—that you were able to bring it down to publishable length. Sorry it can't be used at once . . . we simply have to wait for that special issue that can absorb a story of that length.[20]

Six weeks later she again wrote to Salinger but sounded far less certain about his progress than before. In a tone that must have made Salinger wary, the letter is reminiscent of Whit Burnett and his cajoling for *The Catcher in the Rye:*

> I have been thinking about you a great deal, and sympathizing with you in your labors to cut the long section of the novel to feasible *New Yorker* length. I realize what an agonizing process it must be for you and I do very much hope that it is going alright and is not taking too much out of you or slowing up too much the process of the novel that we all wait for so eagerly.[21]

White had also addressed the eagerly awaited novel in her earlier letter. "I can't help but hope that new and shorter stories from the novel will come along soon," she wrote, "so that we can publish them right away."[22]

---

*In 1943, a younger, less pliable Salinger had referred to *The New Yorker*'s demands for the "compression" of "Slight Rebellion off Madison" as its "smug wordage requirements."

There is another intriguing aspect to White's letters apart from Salinger's incomplete novel. The story that he and Shawn struggled to "compress" and that scholars assume to have been "Zooey" is in fact referred to by both White and *The New Yorker* only as "Ivanoff the Terrible."* Academics have since ignored the "Ivanoff" title, confident that it refers to "Zooey," but their reasoning may be more emotional than logical. The misfortune of having lost such a major work and a large section of an unpublished novel about the Glass family is simply inconceivable.

. . .

Home in Cornish, the singular devotion that Salinger paid to reworking "Zooey" forced his disappearance into his bunker for days on end. For Claire, the advent of her third winter in New Hampshire was further embittered by his absence. As she had during previous winters, she sank into hopelessness, becoming brooding and forlorn. Salinger barely noticed. But the consequences of his ambition to perfect "Zooey" would soon collect its debt in Claire's deepening despondency.

During the third week of January 1957, Jamie Hamilton and his wife, Yvonne, visited New York from London. Seeing the perfect opportunity to introduce the baby (and to meet with Shawn over "Zooey"), Salinger and Claire happily bundled up Peggy and set out for the city.

With his mother and sister away on a Bermuda cruise, Salinger opted to take a Manhattan hotel room rather than stay on Park Avenue. Reintroduced to the once-familiar comforts of New York, Claire found the prospect of returning to another lonely Cornish winter unbearable. She waited for Salinger to leave the hotel, and when he did she fled with the baby. When Salinger returned, he found the hotel room empty.[23] Whatever remorse gripped him as he returned to Cornish alone—and later events prove that his remorse was considerable—he bore in silence. None of his personal letters or professional correspondence ever addressed the issue of Claire's absence or the loss of Peggy. Instead, he continued to labor on "Zooey."

At the same time, the already humbled Salinger received word from

---

*When chronicling editor-author correspondence, it was common practice at *The New Yorker* to cite the story that was the subject of any given letter at the bottom of the document.

his Hollywood agent, H. N. Swanson. The negotiations to sell the movie rights to "The Laughing Man" had collapsed. The story had last been in the hands of the producer Jerry Wald, who had envisioned creating a comedy from the tale. Wald, however, considered the story too short to be made into a film and complained of Salinger's unwillingness to revise it.

> I feel that the particular elements captured in the writing which give the story its special charm and pathos would be difficult to convey when blown up to screen-size reality. . . . Naturally, this would require a writer in perfect tune with the idea, and . . . Mr. Salinger will not consider working on it himself. My main complaint is that "The Laughing Man" gives me too little to work on.[24]

Wald's decision to reject "The Laughing Man" ended Salinger's appetite for Hollywood conclusively. He never again considered relinquishing any of his stories to film producers or stage directors. From that point on, he would guard each of his works as jealously as he protected *The Catcher in the Rye,* in whose defense he had never wavered. In the same letter that declines "The Laughing Man," Wald continued to appeal for the rights to *Catcher.* "Will you please convey to Mr. Salinger," he implored Swanson, "that I am still interested in his brilliant *Catcher in the Rye.* I wish there was something I could do to convince him that it should be brought to the screen." Considering other products of Wald's résumé (the producer was working on an adaptation of *Peyton Place* at the time) and his intention to interpret "The Laughing Man" as a comedy, the rejection fortuitously saved both the story and its author from almost certain humiliation.

Once he had completed "Zooey," Salinger determined to reunite with his wife and child. During the first days of May 1957, he traveled again to New York, where Claire and Peggy were living in an apartment paid for by Claire's stepfather. After delivering the now-finished "Zooey" to William Shawn, Salinger sought out Claire to try to convince her to return with him to Cornish. Claire was apprehensive, but three times a week she had been seeing a psychiatrist, who encouraged her to enter into a dialogue with her husband.

Meeting with Salinger, Claire delivered a series of demands before she would consider reconciliation. Salinger was to spend more time with her and Peggy. When he was away at work, she and the baby were to be allowed frequent visitors. The cottage was to be renovated and expanded. A nursery was to be added. The grounds were to be manicured and redesigned to provide a playground. Above all, she insisted upon the freedom to travel, not just to New York when Salinger needed to meet with his editors but to warmer climates when the winter became oppressive and overseas on long vacations when she became restless.

Salinger agreed to it all and set to work. He hired contractors to build a nursery and gardeners to landscape the grounds.* He promised Claire that they would entertain more often and that he would spend more time with the family. Together, they planned a long vacation to the British Isles, a reproduction of the trip that had so delighted him in 1951 to the country where Claire had spent her childhood. He excitedly wrote to Learned Hand and Jamie Hamilton of their plans to visit Europe. Perhaps, he mused, they would not return to Cornish at all but would settle down in Scotland, a fantasy he had long entertained.

. . .

"Zooey" finally appeared in *The New Yorker* on May 17, 1957.† From its outset, readers are advised that "Zooey" is not actually a story at all "but a sort of prose home movie."[25] Here is the author's intention to write "about a stolen pair of sneakers," a glimpse into the life of the Glass family centering on the two youngest children, Franny and Zooey, just as "Carpenters" had centered on Seymour and Buddy. Expanding the reader's intimacy with the Glass family consumes much of the novella, but it is soon overwhelmed by Salinger's compulsion to focus on spiritual issues. The resulting layers of meaning within "Zooey" are also revealed in the opening pages, which warn that "In Zooey, be assured early, we are dealing with the complex, the overlapping, the cloven."

---

*According to Peggy, her father insisted upon designing the nursery himself with disastrous results. Forgetting the consequences of nature, he instructed the builders to construct the nursery with a flat roof. Winter snows had to be shoveled from the roof, and rain collected on it, often seeping through into the nursery.

†In fact, there was room for little else in the mid-May issue of *The New Yorker*.

In October 1945, Salinger told *Esquire* magazine that he had trouble writing simply and naturally. "My mind is stocked with some black neckties," he observed, "and though I'm throwing them out as fast as I find them, there will always be a few left over."[26] In 1957, some black neckties remained in Salinger's writing, but they had transformed themselves from the remnants of literary pretensions to an inclination toward spiritual snobbery that divided the world between the enlightened and the unaware. In "Zooey," Salinger sought to discard the last of his neckties on both the literary and spiritual levels. Written simply and naturally, "Zooey" attempts to purge Salinger's work of the spiritual conceit from which it suffered and that drove Franny Glass to the point of collapse. Here is where "Zooey" overlaps with his previous works. The story opens three days after the events of "Franny," with Franny curled up on the Glass family couch, suffering from the spiritual and physical crisis brought on by her absorption in the Jesus Prayer. The story is also prefaced by the narrator coyly admitting that he is actually Franny's brother, Buddy Glass, although he is determined to relate events in the third person.

At first glance, the brilliance of the Glass children seems to construct an enclave against a boorish world, or, as Buddy Glass puts it, "a sort of semantic geometry in which the shortest distance between any two points is a fullish circle." This chauvinism may seem to be the haughtiest of Salinger's "neckties"—a love of a closed society of overly precious characters that derails objectivity. However, a close examination of "Zooey" reveals that the story actually concentrates on its characters' flaws and not their virtues.

As foreshadowed in her own story, Franny's faith in the Jesus Prayer and *Way of the Pilgrim* has fostered a spiritual snobbery that has cut her off from the rest of the world and now threatens to alienate her from her own family. Encountered largely on its own in "Franny," this elitism is portrayed as an inheritance from her brothers Seymour and Buddy in "Zooey."* In order to arrange this point, Salinger was forced to retract the portion of "Franny" that explains her encountering *Way of the Pilgrim* in her school library. In "Zooey," the book is discovered instead on Seymour's desk, where it has lain since his death seven years

---

*Although Buddy largely blames himself and Seymour for much of Franny's spiritual predicament, his narration also hints at Franny's personal tendency toward elitism by revealing that she sees herself as being languid and sophisticated.

before. Through this correction, Salinger not only condemns Seymour for imposing dogma on the youngest of his family members but also connects the crisis of Franny's spiritual conceit with the aloofness of the Glass clan itself.

Readers are first introduced to Franny's older brother, Zooey, who is cornered in the bathtub by their mother, Bessie Glass. Bessie persuades Zooey to attempt to lift Franny up from her malaise, but Zooey is also suffering from a subtler but no less damaging spiritual crisis. He is consumed by a personal struggle with his own ego, and his growth has been stunted by a religious upbringing so advanced that it has turned him bigoted against others.

Salinger causes Zooey to refer to the bathroom as his "little chapel" and Bessie to recite more than forty items in the bathroom medicine chest. Each object is clearly tied to ego. Creams, nail files, powders, and toothpastes are mixed with ignored mementos of individual family lives: seashells, ancient tickets to a play, and a broken ring. Lest readers somehow miss the connection with these items and the affliction of ego, Zooey then engages in the most common Salinger demonstration of self-centeredness: he pays extraordinary homage to his nails.

The story's second section takes place in the family living room and consists of a conversation between Zooey and Franny. The setting of this scene is perhaps the most highly symbolic of the story. When first presented, the room is being used by Franny as a kind of spiritual tomb and is infested with the ghosts of the past. Crammed with articles and furniture, it is dark, heavy, and dust-laden. Each eclectic piece of furniture, every nick and stain, book and family keepsake, is described in both physical and historical detail. Each object and imperfection carries flashbacks that haunt the scene and seem to hover over the sleeping Franny like the ghosts of children long grown or long dead.*

Ostensibly, the room is awaiting the arrival of painters to cover the myriad historical blemishes and renew it with a fresh coat of paint. In preparation for the workers, Bessie removes the heavy damask curtains from the windows as Franny sleeps on the couch nearby. Suddenly,

---

*In describing the Glass family apartment, Salinger inserted one of the tiny misleading details that he enjoyed injecting into his stories. The Glasses' apartment is plainly based upon Salinger's parents' apartment on Park Avenue. However, Buddy Glass refers to the apartment's southern exposure. Salinger's Park Avenue apartment had no southern exposure, and his parents' much-coveted corner apartment faced north and west, toward Central Park.

perhaps for the first time in countless years, the room is awash in sunlight, illuminating the clutter that will clearly make the painters' job impossible.

The description of the Glass family apartment is unique in Salinger's work. The setting of no other story is so intricately described. Rooms, surroundings, and furniture are consistently ignored by Salinger, while articles of clothing often hold a prominent position in his text. But the clothing of Franny and Zooey is ignored. As characters, they are represented instead by the rooms in which they are encountered. Readers first meet Zooey in the chapel of ego. Franny is encountered in the living room, where the Glass family memories are entombed. More than any other memory, the ghost of Seymour saturates this place. It is a ghost that has driven Franny to silent desperation and Zooey to rage. "This whole goddam house stinks of ghosts," he wails.

The room also symbolizes Franny's spiritual and emotional state. Recognizing the setting as being symbolic of Franny allows it to explode with meaning and to foreshadow the story's eventual epiphany. For aside from Franny and Zooey, the novella's second scene contains a third character: the sun. When Bessie takes down the old, heavy curtains and the sun washes into the room where Franny cringes on the ancient couch, it allows the outside world—where children are playing on the school steps across the street—into the Glass enclave like light into a tomb.

Zooey attempts to awaken Franny from her malaise by reasoning with her over her obsession with the Jesus Prayer, telling her that she is misusing it. He accuses her of attempting to lay up spiritual treasure by reciting the prayer as a mantra. He then equates the desire for spiritual treasure with the lust for material wealth. Worse still, he accuses Franny of spiritual snobbery, telling her that she is "beginning to give off a little stink of piousness." He charges his sister with conducting a "little snotty crusade" in which she sees herself as a martyr in a world populated by personal enemies. In other words, she is using the Jesus Prayer to bolster her own self-righteous image and to separate herself from the rest of the world, which she now considers spiritually inferior. Zooey's speech drives Franny to near hysteria, but he is relentless. He continues by arguing that if she insists upon having a breakdown, she should go back to school rather than have it at home, where she is the baby of the family and keeps her tap shoes in the closet.

Zooey, now caught up in his own tirade, questions the sincerity of Franny's faith. He asks how she can continue with the Jesus Prayer if she will not accept Christ for who He is. He reminds Franny that when she was a child she was incensed to discover that Jesus had elevated human beings above the sweet, cuddly fowl of the air. That simply didn't fit in with Franny's concept of who Jesus should be. To Franny, Jesus should be lovable, more like Saint Francis of Assisi than an angry prophet rudely overturning tables in the temple. Zooey advises Franny that in order to use the Jesus Prayer properly and live a life of constant prayer, she must first see the face of Christ Himself, an ability that he calls "Christ-Consciousness," a living communion with God. "God almighty, Franny," he shouts. "If you're going to say the Jesus Prayer, at least say it to Jesus, and not to St. Francis and Seymour and Heidi's grandfather all wrapped up in one."[27]

"Zooey" contains a number of religious symbols that are unmistakable. However, the beginning of true spiritual revelation for Zooey's character is sublime in its delicacy. To craft it, Salinger departed from the explanatory nature of his more recent works and reached back into the indistinct softness of his Caulfield era.

In the middle of his argument, Zooey glances out of the window and becomes distracted by a simple scene playing out on the street below. The sight captivates him, but initially he is not sure why. A small girl, about seven years old and wearing a navy blue pea jacket, is playing hide-and-seek with her dog. The girl conceals herself behind a tree, and the unsuspecting dachshund loses sight of her. Distraught and confused, the dog scurries back and forth, desperately searching. Just as the dachshund's agony becomes nearly unbearable, he catches the girl's scent and springs to her side. The girl screams in delight, and the dog yelps with joy. Their reunion is sealed with an embrace before the pair stroll off toward Central Park and disappear from Zooey's view.

The delicacy of this scene is perhaps marred by Zooey's explanation of it. "There are nice things in the world," he reasons. "We're all such morons to get so sidetracked. Always, always, always referring every goddam thing that happens right back to our lousy little egos." The lines can be interpreted as a marriage of Salinger's former and contemporary themes. A chance glimpse of a common event allows Zooey to be awakened to the presence of beauty in the world. It occurs through the innocent purity of a little girl, very much in the same way as it had to the previous Salinger characters Babe Gladwaller and Holden Caulfield. But "Zooey" goes beyond the revelation of Babe and Holden by pointing out the tendency of ego to obscure the divine beauty so abundant in everyday life.

Salinger derived the inspiration for "Zooey" from two primary sources: a book published by the Self-Realization Foundation and his own personal struggle with ego. While writing "Zooey," Salinger continued his involvement with the Self-Realization Foundation that he had begun in 1955. The foundation had been organized in 1920 by the Indian sage Paramahansa Yogananda. When, in 1954, Salinger read Yogananda's book, *Autobiography of a Yogi*, it reaffirmed his own religious convictions and influenced his marriage to Claire. After studying *Autobiography* in depth and incorporating many of its teachings into his own work, just as he had done with *The Gospels of Sri Ramakrishna,* he immersed himself in Yogananda's other writings. Foremost among them was Yogananda's immense two-volume work *The Second Coming of Christ: The Resurrection of the Christ Within You.* The religious tenets presented in this book are the foundation of the spiritual message delivered by Salinger in "Zooey."

Yogananda claimed to have received the only true interpretation of the Christian Gospels and the life of Christ through divine revelation.* His weighty text is an explanation of the words and deeds of Christ as he interpreted them. *The Second Coming of Christ* examines the four Gospels verse by verse. According to Yogananda, Jesus was so filled with God-consciousness that he actually became one with the Almighty, or, in Yogananda's view, a Son of God. This was a position that implied holiness but not divinity. The yogi felt that everyone was a child of God and could awaken the holiness within themselves through prayer and meditation. It was his contention that the awakening of that holiness was the true meaning of resurrection. The second coming of Christ, therefore, was not an actual physical event to occur in the future. Instead, Yogananda believed that Christ's promise to return could be fulfilled at any time by any person through the attainment of

---

*Among Yogananda's revelations was the disclosure that Christ had spent many years in India before beginning his ministry. Equally expedient was Yogananda's use of Gnostic and apocryphal texts to shore up assertions not supported by the four Gospels proper.

spiritual oneness with God. Yogananda's text terms this spiritual awakening "Christ Consciousness" and describes it as the ability of mankind to become holy by recognizing the presence of God within all things.

Critics have asserted that Zooey is Salinger's most perfectly crafted character, apart from Holden Caulfield. While Salinger and Buddy Glass narrate "Zooey" with a single voice, it is within the character of Zooey Glass that Salinger is most deeply embedded. From the time he completed *The Catcher in the Rye,* Salinger maintained the philosophy that his work was the equivalent of spiritual meditation. That philosophy only deepened when the solitude of Cornish buffered him against the distractions of publicity and fame. The public's interest in Salinger, with its fan mail and flattery and the constant barrage of reviews and articles praising his work, only served to fracture his meditation, and he protested that attention and scrutiny hampered his writing and he was unable to produce if he felt himself "in the news." Yet a part of J. D. Salinger still privately thrived on the same attention and affirmation that he publicly eschewed. The great irony of Salinger's life lay in the paradox of this situation. Since he viewed writing as a form of meditation, the perfecting of his writing resulted in the very product that fed his ego.

As an actor, Zooey finds himself in a similar position. His chosen work feeds the ego that he realizes is his spiritual downfall. And Zooey approaches his work with the same prayerful attitude as did Salinger. In his letter, Buddy exhorts Zooey to pursue his acting career with the same fullness with which Seymour will later exhort Buddy to write—with all of his stars out, as an act of faith. Salinger reiterates the philosophy that total dedication to one's work is a spiritual endeavor by fastening quotes from the Bhagavad Gita on the door of Buddy and Seymour's room: "You have the right to work, but for the work's sake only. You have no right to the fruits of work. Desire for the fruits of work must never be your motive in working." The second quotation also foreshadows the story's ending: "Perform every action with your heart fixed on the Supreme Lord. Renounce attachment to the fruits." The challenge that faced both Salinger and his characters was how to pursue their work with all of their strength and not be seduced by the fruits of their labor.

Zooey recites a procession of spiritual truths, to no effect. Franny instead begins to cry, and Buddy tells us that Zooey smelled the defeat of his argument in the air, causing him to leave the room in frustration. Zooey's contentions to Franny were logical. Yet something vital was missing from Zooey's logic that caused his presentation to fail. At this point in the story, Zooey himself still doesn't understand the reason why, a fact that's again proved by his rude and impatient attitude toward his mother on his way out of the living room.

The story's final act takes place in Buddy and Seymour's childhood room, where Zooey makes a phone call to Franny, pretending to be Buddy. The room has been kept as a shrine. It remains exactly as it was seven years before, upon Seymour's suicide. Buddy has insisted upon keeping a phone on the desk in Seymour's name as a connection to his brother and in denial of their separation. Within the room, which is childlike in its trappings and overflowing with books, Zooey is drawn to the phone "as though marionette strings were attached to him." He picks up the receiver, covers the mouthpiece with a handkerchief that he has been wearing on his head, and dials a number.

The richest of Salinger scenes are those that offer a simple act that ignites a spark of meaning, which in turn ignites its own series of flames. "Zooey" contains one of the most surreal images ever to appear in a Salinger work. When Franny is called to the phone by her mother, she is told that her older brother Buddy is on the line. On her way to take the call, Franny walks down the hall to her parents' bedroom. Around her, the apartment is in varying states of disarray and renewal. The hallway is drenched with the smell of fresh paint and Franny must walk on old newspapers spread on the floor as protection. As she makes her way to the phone, she grows physically younger with each step she takes. By the time she reaches the end of the hall, she has become a little child. Even her silk nightgown has been mysteriously transformed "into a small child's woolen bathrobe." The image is a fleeting one and the narration at the end of "Zooey" is aloof, yet, mixed into the scent of fresh paint and the echoes of Zooey's calls to Christ-Consciousness, Franny may mystically embody the words of Jesus Himself, who said, "Except you be changed, and become as little children, you shall not enter into the Kingdom of Heaven."

It is during the final conversation between Franny and Zooey that the story's parts converge. For an extraordinary period of time, Franny is convinced that she is speaking to her brother Buddy, calling from his

cloister in the woods of New York State.* The misconception gives
Franny the opportunity to vent her anger at Zooey and to express her
opinion that Zooey is in no spiritual position to pass judgment on the
Jesus Prayer. Most convicting of all, she accuses Zooey of bitterness.

Inevitably, it dawns on Franny that she is actually speaking to
Zooey. What then transpires between brother and sister is remarkably
similar to the confrontation between Holden and Phoebe at the end of
The Catcher in the Rye. Although he is found out, Zooey is determined
to continue the conversation despite Franny's irritation. Franny reluctantly agrees to listen to him make one last point, but she demands that
he do it quickly and then leave her alone. Franny's words "leave me
alone" cut into Zooey just as Phoebe's demand that her brother "shut
up" struck Holden. There is a heavy silence on the line, and Franny realizes that she has overstepped her bounds.

Zooey's reaction to Franny's words is to release his own ego and
submit to the needs of his sister. His attitude is transformed. In a tone
brimming with compromise, Zooey tells Franny to continue with the
Jesus Prayer, but he implores her to say it properly, asking that she first
recognize the holiness in a simple bowl of chicken soup that is offered
with unconditional love. Painfully, he encourages Franny to continue
her acting career. His pain comes from his confession that acting is a
direct result of desire, the desire for acclamation and the fruits of one's
labor. The religious life, he laments, is dependent upon detachment—
the very opposite of desire. He cannot see that Franny has a choice.
She must act because that is the gift that God has given her. And she
must act with all her might, striving to attain balance in the process.
"The only religious thing you can do, is act," he tells Franny. "Act for
God, if you want to—be God's actress."

Zooey, of course, is speaking as much to himself and his own struggle as he is to Franny. Zooey does not instruct Franny or lead her to
the place of revelation. They reach that place together. What had been
missing in Zooey's logic and in the Jesus Prayer itself was not spiritual
truth but the divine enlightenment offered through human connection. The holiness inherent in a mother's bowl of chicken soup and the
joy shared between a little girl and her dog are not mundane banalities
of everyday life. They are miracles that display the face of God. Zooey

*To carry out his ruse, Zooey calls Franny by the nickname "Flopsy" when pretending
to be Buddy.

then relays the story of the Fat Lady, a tale that has become one of Salinger's most inspiring and famous images. When very young, Zooey appeared on the radio quiz show *It's a Wise Child*. One evening, as he was about to go onstage, his brother Seymour approached him and told him to shine his shoes first. Zooey was incensed. He thought the studio audience imbeciles. He thought the producers imbeciles. And he was not going to shine his shoes for them, especially since his feet would be hidden onstage anyway. But Seymour sternly rejected this argument. He told his brother to shine his shoes "for the Fat Lady." Seymour never explained who the Fat Lady was, and Zooey developed an imaginary image of a cancer-ridden woman sitting on her porch and playing the radio. With this image and Seymour's insistence in mind, Zooey shined his shoes each night before going out on stage. Franny too had developed a similar concept of her own Fat Lady, for whom Seymour had encouraged her to be funny.

This was Seymour's encouragement to both Franny and Zooey to be their best with all of their might. But exactly who this "Fat Lady" was, or what she represented, had been unclear to them for all of these years—until the moment of epiphany, the moment when the connection between brother and sister allowed them Christ-Consciousness and the ability to glimpse the face of God. "Don't you know who that Fat Lady really is?" Zooey asks. ". . . Ah, buddy. Ah, buddy. It's Christ Himself. Christ Himself, buddy."[28]

The tale of the Fat Lady is a parable. It is an acknowledgment of the presence of God within us all. For Zooey it is a path away from the clutches of his ego as he is forced to recognize the holiness within all people. For Franny it is an explanation of how to "pray without ceasing," always to have God in her heart, not by mumbling lines written by others but by doing everything in life, even shining one's shoes, as a sort of prayer, a holy act.

Zooey no more understood why he shined his shoes than Franny understood the Jesus Prayer she recited. In essence they were performing the same prescribed ritual in the hope it would deliver comfort. The beauty of Seymour's exhortation is that it does not overthrow the Jesus Prayer. It is the Jesus Prayer, the modern-day American version of the pilgrim's ancient Russian plea to see God more clearly through grace.

Overcome by the joy of understanding, Franny reacts in the same way that Babe Gladwaller and Sergeant X reacted when they received their own revelations: she falls blissfully asleep.

Salinger bared his soul in "Zooey," exposing the war that raged between his spirit and his ego. The pain of the Glass children, who feel cut off from those around them, was a pain that the author knew well. The struggle to accept others and to recognize the goodness in the world was shared not only by Franny and Zooey but also by the author who gave them life. In "Zooey," Salinger also shared perhaps his greatest frustration. When despair and loneliness compelled him to seek God through his writings, he found that his work was itself the greatest potential barrier to that communion. Somehow, he would have to discover a way to continue honoring God through his work, while avoiding the material rewards of his labor.

15. Seymour

"Zooey" proved popular among readers of *The New Yorker.* The novella's acceptance silenced, or at least subdued, pundits who had convinced themselves that it would be Salinger's public downfall. These critics (who included Katharine White's cadre at the magazine itself) attributed the novella's success to the sophistication of the average *New Yorker* reader, who had become accustomed to the unpredictability of Salinger's style. Still, the story's detractors continued to believe that if "Zooey" were presented to a general audience it would not survive. Few believed Salinger to be brazen enough to release it in book form. "Zooey" had been born within the pages of *The New Yorker,* and it was within those pages that it was expected to grow old and die.

The silence of critics did not completely save "Zooey" from degradation, at least in Salinger's eyes. On May 21, 1957, a mere week after "Zooey" 's release, Signet Books took out an ad in *The New York Times* that compared the novella to its paperback editions of *Nine Stories* and *The Catcher in the Rye.** Salinger detested those presentations

*Signet had released the paperback edition of *Nine Stories* in 1954. The book's presen-

of his work and was infuriated with their being connected to his new effort. He naturally blamed Little, Brown and Company for the affront and impulsively dashed off a furious telegram to Boston, deploring the analogy and Signet's tactics. Little, Brown's apologies were immediate and profuse. It claimed to be unconnected to the ad and unaware of its appearance. Salinger collected himself and after a few days responded to Ned Bradford, editor in chief at Little, Brown, with a calmer but no less indignant approach. He reiterated his aversion to paperback releases in general and explained that Signet's ad was so close to the debut of "Zooey" as to make it "unattractively timely."[1]

The episode is seemingly minor, but it displays Salinger's simmering contempt for publishers. The dispute with Signet and Little, Brown over the *New York Times* ad spotlights his opinion that he was embroiled in a constant struggle to protect his work from the very publishers that held charge over it. Striving as he was for perfection, the thought of allowing his work to be mangled by editors in the pursuit of profits incensed him. And money was very much the point. In Salinger's view his publishers raked in far too much profit, and his letters brimmed with complaints of their greed.

The incident spoke directly to the dilemma that Salinger had presented in "Zooey," the conflict between the production of art and the gleaning of profits. Salinger went to great lengths in "Zooey" to rationalize his continuing publication despite the spiritual pitfalls of success. Zooey had told Franny that she had no choice but to act because God had given her the gift. Salinger felt the same about his own vocation and believed it his duty to continue publishing in the effort to share his point of view. But when his writings were successful, profits were inevitable, as applause was inevitable if Franny acted well on stage. These were the fruits of labor against which Seymour and Buddy had so sternly warned. They were tied to ego and spiritual death. The religious consequence of the profits produced by Salinger's work made him extremely uncomfortable, but it was Little, Brown and Company that took the lion's share of those profits, and that fact made Salinger furious.

---

tation was tasteful if not aesthetically pleasing. It had no garish cover illustration, as did the Signet version of *Catcher,* and was void of a provocative marquee. By then, however, Salinger had become disgusted with the idea of paperback (or "throwaway") books in general and was as scornful of Signet's *Nine Stories* as he was of its *Catcher.*

Salinger's disgust with his publishers was soothed by the return of Claire and Peggy to Cornish. By summer 1957, the renovations on the cottage had been completed. Peggy moved into the nursery and played on the newly landscaped lawn. The family room held a television and a piano, almost in mimicry of the Glass family apartment. Barely three years old, Peggy was a special delight to her father, and Salinger's letters overflowed with recounts of her antics and the joy she provided daily. According to her father, Peggy was a happy, active child, whom Salinger had nicknamed "the Dynamo." He reveled in playing jazz records for his daughter and teaching her to dance. She had begun to talk, and in January Salinger bragged to Judge Hand that she even recognized her last name. Of course, she believed that everyone was named Salinger, even characters on television.

The same letters that celebrated Peggy's childhood also cursed the long winter and conveyed Salinger's anxiety over its possible effect upon Claire. Even as "Zooey" was hitting the newsstands, he was already engulfed in his next project, yet another Glass story that would consume him. When the time came to fulfill his promise to Claire and embark on the long vacation to Europe, he found that he could not leave Cornish or the work he had begun. "The fact is, I suppose," he explained with some embarrassment, "I love this place for working."[2] According to Salinger, Claire remained patient and good-natured despite the postponement, for which he was grateful. He lamented that he realized how much his rigorous writing schedule took a toll on his wife and sarcastically moaned that it must be "Heavenly to be married to a man who'll give you a weekend in Asbury Park in five years."[3] Despite his contriteness, Salinger's obsession with his work only deepened. When Jamie Hamilton had his American representative, Roger Machell, attempt to arrange a meeting with Salinger in New York in February 1958, Salinger declined. It might be a number of years until he could tear himself away from his work, he said in excuse.[4]

The message that Salinger delivered through these apologies is unmistakable: his family meant a great deal to him and he was happy to have them back, but his work came first. In a very real sense, he was becoming prisoner to it. His Glass family series had become a compulsion that demanded satisfaction at all costs, even at the price of losing Claire and Peggy yet again. Consequently, throughout 1958 and well into 1959, the life of J. D. Salinger and the construction of the next Glass family installment melted into a single story. By the time he completed his next work, a novella titled "Seymour—an Introduction," he had become completely entrapped by his own creation.

. . .

When Salinger turned thirty-nine on January 1, 1958, he was writing steadily, satisfied with both the pace and the results of his work.[5] Eight months later, however, he had still not completed the story. By then *The New Yorker* had arranged to set aside an entire issue to feature the new work, which by autumn had already surpassed "Carpenters" in length. After working tirelessly for an entire year without a break, Salinger began to fall ill. In late summer, he suffered a series of colds and influenzas, leading to a chest infection serious enough to lay him up and pause his writing. Meanwhile, *The New Yorker* was growing increasingly impatient to see his new story or at least obtain a firm date for its completion, charging that the delay was wreaking havoc at the magazine. Come October, after bolstering his health with an intensive regimen of vitamins, Salinger had convinced himself that he was well enough to resume work.[6] But he had lost months and found it difficult to resume where he had left off. Early 1959 saw the novella still incomplete, and *The New Yorker*'s tone became increasingly exasperated.

When encountering spells of writer's block, Salinger had often traveled, believing that changes of scenery awakened his creativity. The success of many of these excursions is debatable, but Salinger was desperate to finish "Seymour." In March 1959, he left Cornish alone and took a room in an Atlantic City hotel. Claire's reaction to Seymour Glass being granted a trip to the Jersey shore while her own vacation had been denied can only be imagined, but such a declaration of Salinger's priorities almost certainly fed into her increasingly bitter resentment.

Salinger found himself no more capable of completing "Seymour" in Atlantic City than he had been in Cornish. Now frenzied, he again relocated, this time to New York City, and took a room a block away from the offices of *The New Yorker*. As he had in 1950 when completing *The Catcher in the Rye*, Salinger used an office at the magazine in an effort to work. This too failed. Within days of arriving in New York, Salinger again fell ill with influenza. Despairing, frustrated, and now infirm, he returned home to Cornish with the novella still in pieces.[7]

When Salinger finally finished "Seymour" in the spring of 1959, the manuscript went directly to William Shawn, who accepted it immediately and refused any input from the *New Yorker* fiction department. Katharine White was incensed by being shut out of the process yet again. It was up to William Maxwell, who understood Shawn's motivation and was perhaps closest to White, to soothe her feelings. "I do feel that Salinger has to be handled specially and fast," he told her, "and think that the only practical way of doing this is as I supposed Shawn did do it—by himself. Given the length of the stories, I mean, and the Zen Buddhist nature of them, and what happened with 'Zooey.' "[8]

Aside from being a diplomatic consolation, Maxwell's note to White helps to explain how "Seymour—an Introduction" avoided *The New Yorker*'s usual editorial gauntlet. While excusing Shawn by painting Salinger as being difficult to work with, Maxwell's final reference to "Zooey" reveals his and White's overriding reluctance to challenge Salinger's new work and risk being embarrassed as they had been over "Zooey."

. . .

Between the publication of "Zooey" in May 1957 and the appearance of "Seymour—an Introduction" on June 5, 1959, the most important occurrence in Salinger's life was conducted on a stage far larger than the settings of Cornish, New Hampshire, or the office of *The New Yorker*. During this time, the public perception of J. D. Salinger suddenly lurched from that of short-story writer into the realm of legend. The myth of Salinger as an ascetic hermit reluctantly dispensing jewels of enlightenment became indelibly ingrained in the American consciousness. Just as Salinger had elevated the character of Seymour Glass to a position of sainthood, he himself found that he had been equally elevated by a segment of the population too large to ignore. His search for humility through privacy had endowed him with an aura of pious inapproachability that readers found alluring. It also added an ambiguity to his image that easily lent itself to a vast variety of interpretations. In a very real way, the author had become indistinguishable from his work. And just as the name of Holden Caulfield was invoked in the defense of a rising call to social dissatisfaction, the name of J. D. Salinger began to be called upon to defend myriad social issues.

The mid-1950s witnessed the spontaneous emergence of a youth movement that felt alienated from the materialistic society of its parents. Rebelling against the rigid conformity that had infused American society since the war, many young people of the 1950s sought a collective voice through which they could express their disillusionment and frustration with the world around them. They looked for validation of their emerging discontent, which would grow steadily until it changed society beyond recognition. Many found this validation in *The Catcher in the Rye*. Years after *Catcher*'s initial publication, the youths of America suddenly seized upon the character of Holden Caulfield as the spokesperson for their generation. Feeling that Holden spoke directly to them and that Salinger, with his battle against phoniness and consumerism, expressed their own dissatisfactions with society, they began to rally around Salinger's work with devotion. The result has often been referred to as "the Cult of *Catcher*," an almost religious frenzy that began to surround the novel and the author who had created it. Among students it became fashionable to be seen carrying *The Catcher in the Rye* or *Nine Stories*. Young men mimicked Holden Caulfield in their attitudes and their dress. Ironically, in a subculture where non-conformity was the measure of worth, association with the character of Holden Caulfield became a requirement.

Looking upon their students in bewilderment, the reaction of academics was surprising. The years 1956 and 1957 witnessed the first serious intellectual analysis of Salinger's work. The writer who himself had never graduated from college and had derided the academic community at every opportunity suddenly found himself the topic of furious academic discussion. At university campuses across America, Salinger became a scholarly preoccupation of both professors and students.

An example of Salinger's new position occurred as early as the close of 1956, when he received an offer from the University of Michigan at Ann Arbor, asking him to take a position on the school faculty. Shortly after his thirty-eighth birthday, Salinger responded with a gentle scolding, declining the offer and explaining that he found it difficult to work around people and felt it best that he remain in Cornish. There were other reasons too, Salinger confessed, why he felt an academic position in Michigan was out of the question. These had to do "with personal convictions about how and where a practicing fiction writer should live," which he characterized as being "firm" but "not interesting."9

The University of Michigan offer naturally recalled Salinger's discomfort at Sarah Lawrence College in 1949 and the conflict that subsequently raged between his convictions and ego. That Salinger's ego was immense is indisputable. Yet, in deference to his religious beliefs, he struggled to contain it all of his life, perhaps explaining why the relative seclusion of Cornish—away from the constant buzzing of admirers—was so attractive to him and vital to his work.

As Salinger continued to write and to publish, his influence grew. By 1959, the call to rebellion that the public had come to associate with Salinger's work began to bleed into mainstream society. The theater became infused with the ideas of playwrights such as Bertolt Brecht, Jean-Paul Sartre, and Arthur Miller, who depicted the alienation of individuals in conventional society in ways remarkably concurrent with the complaints of Holden Caulfield. American bookshelves began to collect the works of writers such as John Updike and Kurt Vonnegut, authors who had been profoundly influenced by Salinger at a young age. The controversial novel *Lolita,* which Vladimir Nabokov admitted had been inspired by "A Perfect Day for Bananafish," wedged its way into American awareness despite having been banned in 1955. During these years, Sylvia Plath, admittedly dazzled by Salinger's intensity, completed her first draft of *The Bell Jar,* a novel clearly fashioned after *The Catcher in the Rye.* Not even Hollywood was immune to Salinger's influence. The actor James Dean was in many ways Holden Caulfield personified, and movies like *Rebel Without a Cause,* a film still compared to *Catcher,* were instant sensations.

When Salinger began to pen "Seymour—an Introduction," the Beat Generation had taken center stage. Writers such as Jack Kerouac and William Burroughs continued the dialogue Salinger had begun, taking the discussion of alienation and displacement to new levels.*

---

*The correlations between Salinger and Kerouac are fascinating. Kerouac is said to have coined the phrase "Beat Generation," to describe his contemporaries as being wearied by the conformity of society, in ways similar to Holden Caulfield. Salinger certainly addresses Kerouac directly in "Seymour—an Introduction" by condemning "the Dharma Bums," the title of Kerouac's 1958 novel. Interestingly, only a single semester separated Salinger's and Kerouac's time at Columbia University, and had Columbia not mandated that Kerouac briefly attend prep school in New England, the two would have been classmates. Professionally, Salinger and Kerouac were similarly ambitious but eventually repulsed by their own fame. Icons of a generation, both authors were equally distressed to be invoked in defense of issues and positions they did not support. Salinger's reaction was to cloister himself in religion and seclusion, while Kerouac descended into the alcoholism that led to his early death.

For these "beatniks," poetry had become a major vehicle of expression, and great poets such as Allen Ginsberg continued Salinger's questioning of mankind's place in the world in a way particularly close to Salinger's heart.

For all the poetic complaint of the Beat poets and writers, their message was void of salvation. Salinger had become an icon to these creative rebels, but the author called them out with derision. To him, they were truly "the Dharma Bums," and he scolded them as being "the Beat and the Sloppy and the Petulant," and, most damning of all, "the Zen-killers." Yet it was clear that many of the shifts in society had been set into motion by Salinger himself, and he found that he was in the awkward position of deploring the aimlessness of fans who invoked his name while his works enjoyed a new understanding and a new reverence through their benefit.

Buffered deep within the woods of Cornish, Salinger tried to ignore the commotion that swirled around him. It was impossible. Strangers began to show up at the cottage. His mail overflowed with essays and term papers for evaluation.[10] Stories and rumors about him began to appear in the press. This was only the beginning, a small slice of the insistent attention that would harass him for decades to come and that he would be forced to address through his writings.

In the autumn of 1962, Salinger received an interesting piece of fan mail. Or rather, his response to it was interesting. A certain "Mr. Stevens," probably a college student, confided to the author his disgust with the materialistic values of adult society. He held an academic knowledge of Eastern philosophies and was frustrated with the importance that others placed upon "things" rather than the spirit. Doubtless, Mr. Stevens mailed his letter off to Cornish with satisfaction. If there was anyone in the world who would understand his anxiety, it was J. D. Salinger.

On October 21, Salinger penned a response to Mr. Stevens that was characteristically polite and unusually candid. After thanking Stevens for his letter and giving a cursory nod to his views, Salinger cut to the chase. What had struck him most about the letter was the quality of the ink: Mr. Stevens's typewriter ribbon was running dry. "For me," Salinger disclosed, "before anything else, you're a young man who needs a new typewriter ribbon. See that fact, and don't attach more significance to it than it deserves, and then get on with the rest of the day."[11]

To some, Salinger's response may seem dismissive, as it most certainly did to Mr. Stevens. But it faultlessly records Salinger's emerging attitude to the reverence his fans had imposed upon him. He was neither guru nor the Great Oz. His stories had never delivered their players to the place of absolute accomplishment. Neither was he a rebel or a prophet. Though he condemned the shallowness of society, he always placed responsibility upon individuals. It was with the same attitude and dry sense of ironic humor conveyed in his response to Mr. Stevens that Salinger wrote "Seymour—an Introduction." If his fans were seeking an icon to affirm their own stances, they had best look elsewhere—to the details of their own lives—and continue on their way.

. . .

"Seymour—an Introduction" is again narrated by Salinger's admitted alter ego, Buddy Glass, who, like Salinger himself, is forty while writing the story. The novella attempts to describe the nature of Buddy's older brother Seymour, an enlightened God seeker who remains a mentor for the Glass family despite his suicide in Florida in March 1948. As Buddy writes the novella, he encounters a series of emotional and physical difficulties that result from his reexamination of Seymour's life and character. These episodes repeatedly threaten to derail Buddy's project, and he shares them freely with the reader.

From the beginning, Buddy warns of a narration that will be long and unwieldy, often digressing to visit subjects he finds interesting. A foretaste of the unrestrained nature of his text is offered when he presents readers with a bouquet of parentheses. By speaking through Buddy, Salinger sought to blaze a trail of innovation into new literary territory. Through the story's narration, style, and subject matter, he discarded many rules of construction and embarked in a direction as yet unexplored. No other work that Salinger penned stands in such direct contrast to the dogma of *The New Yorker* against "writer-consciousness" as does "Seymour," which expressly violates every tenet of authorship that Salinger had been taught. Yet it is within this seemingly chaotic construction that Salinger's philosophy comes to a final clarity.

As a work "Seymour" has an enigmatic liquid quality. Its parts flow and counterflow simultaneously, like diverse currents in a stream. While the novella can be loosely divided into a number of sections, each with its own narrative thrust, there are always countercurrents flowing beneath the surface, enhancing the meaning of each topic that Buddy addresses. This makes any review of "Seymour—an Introduction" precarious, as it's often the unseen undertow that carries readers through.

The novella begins with two preambles, quotations by Franz Kafka and Søren Kierkegaard, as well as a personal foreword by Buddy himself. The opening quotations address the relationship between an author and his works. They express the love between a fiction writer and his characters and explain the power of that love to determine the direction of an author's writing. Buddy then addresses readers directly, calling them "bird-watchers" and accusing them of imbuing his authorship and private life with fantastic qualities they do not contain. This line of thought melts into the story's second section, through which Buddy denounces critics and their methods of analysis and the Beat Generation for their spiritual blindness. The flow between sections is seamless, deftly sewn together by Buddy's abhorrence of intellectual rather than spiritual analysis of his works as he condemns those who attempt to dissect his stories intellectually as "a peerage of tin ears."

In the third section of "Seymour," Buddy offers his thoughts about presenting the story as a biographical sketch. This is perhaps the coyest section of the novella. It introduces the story as not only a biographical glimpse of Seymour Glass but also of Buddy and, through Buddy, of J. D. Salinger. Its placement in the story is tinged with sarcasm as it inevitably perks up the ear of even the most lethargic of bird-watchers when Buddy references his past works, each of which is familiar to Salinger readers.

Section four is a lengthy analysis of Seymour's poetry, highly influenced by Japanese and Chinese verse. In this portion Salinger reiterates his conviction that poetry represents spirituality—a belief he has held since "The Inverted Forest." He repeats the dogma that true poetry is the result of divine inspiration, stating, "the true poet has no choice of material. The material plainly chooses him, not he it." Through Buddy Glass, then, Salinger again equates the quality of poetry to spiritual perfection, calling Seymour not only a true poet but also perhaps the greatest of poets. This alerts readers to Seymour's saintliness and aligns him with the most suffering of God seekers.

Seymour Glass was not perfect. Buddy quickly establishes his brother's humanity in the story's fifth section, which recounts Seymour and Buddy's vaudevillian heritage. Within this section are a number of symbolic memories, including of Zozo the clown, Gallagher and Glass, and Buddy's recollection of Seymour riding the handlebars of Joe Jackson's nickel-plated bicycle, one of the most hauntingly beautiful portions of the novella; but it's a story that Salinger does not completely explain.

Jackson, also known as the "Tramp Cyclist," was a famous vaudeville clown who traveled the world, enchanting audiences with his trick bicycle act. Dressed as a tramp and gesturing in mime, he would mount his bike and struggle to ride it as it slowly fell to pieces. In 1942, Jackson had just finished a performance at New York's Roxy Theatre when he suffered a fatal heart attack. As he lay dying, the sound of his grateful audience was still within earshot and his last words were "They're still applauding." His son, Joe Jackson, Jr., took over the bicycle act upon his death, keeping it exactly as his father had performed it. Through their combined careers, Joe Jackson's nickel-plated trick bicycle delighted audiences for a hundred years.

The vision of Seymour Glass at age five, joyously riding the handlebars of Joe Jackson's disintegrating bicycle "all over the stage" and "around and around," speaks volumes on the subject of trust and faith. And that is how, we are told, Seymour lived his life: so enraptured by the sheer exhilaration of living as to be unaware, or at least uncaring, of the decomposing forces around him. That is also how Salinger wrote his story, by ignoring the perils that his style and innovation would surely attract. Seymour and Salinger share the handlebars of Joe Jackson's nickel-plated bicycle, and they also share the question that this scene inevitably raises. If Seymour Glass loved the fullness of living and rode it with such unsuspecting trust, why did he end his own life— and why did Salinger, enjoying the liberation of writing freely and without regard to opinion, similarly end the life of his authorship?

The sixth section of "Seymour" provides a glimpse over the shoulder of the writer at work and explores some of the reasons that Buddy has been absent from publishing: his difficulty in writing, health problems, and Seymour's shifting image. In this, the most interactive portion of the novella, Buddy addresses the reader with increasing intimacy. As the narration loosens, letting go of self-awareness, Buddy becomes progressively liberated and happy. Within this passage, Buddy shares a letter written by Seymour in 1940. Addressed to "Dear Old Tyger That Sleeps," a reference to the poem by William Blake, Seymour's words directly reflect Salinger's own philosophy on writing. "When was writing ever your profession?" Seymour asks. "It's never been anything but your religion. Never. . . . Since it is your religion, do you know what you will be asked when you die? . . . Were most of your stars out? Were you busy writing your heart out?"[12] Buddy next offers a curious physical description of Seymour and a long narrative "home movie" inlaid with childhood memories that read like a series of Zen parables. Each reminiscence, every story and example that Buddy conjures, causes Seymour's spirit to strengthen its hold over him until, by "Seymour" 's eighth and final segment, the relaying of Buddy's "home movie" has clearly exhausted him. But it has also delivered enlightenment. Intensely satisfied, Buddy explains that he has come to peace with his life, the world around him, and perhaps even his brother's death.

. . .

Buddy's account is so tinged with personal sadness that it actually forces multiple emotions. And well it should, for "Seymour—an Introduction" is actually written on a number of levels. If Salinger had indeed purged his literary wardrobe of pretentious black neckties by delivering "Zooey," he soon fashioned another, far more garish accessory to dress up this story: a necktie that glowed in the dark and spun around.* Much of "Seymour" is vaudeville, and Salinger knew it. Through the work, he astounds readers with a three-ring circus, with all the acts occurring simultaneously.

Presumably, the novella is an installment of the Glass family series, a narration by Buddy Glass to expand the chronicle of his family. Here biography and religious instruction merge together as the events of Seymour's life double as episodes of spiritual instruction and Buddy uses a series of koanlike† reminiscences to familiarize readers with his

---

*In fact, Salinger's necktie in "Seymour" is described as being "crocus yellow." But the 1946 metaphor remains. Buddy admits that it is inevitable that his necktie will show up in his prose.

†A koan is a story, dialogue, question, or statement in the history and lore of Zen Buddhism, generally containing aspects that are inaccessible to rational understanding yet may be accessible to intuition.

brother's character while instructing them on spiritual issues. These koanlike parables are the life-giving force of the novella. Encapsulated throughout like a series of Fabergé surprises, they endow Buddy's story with the enlightened beauty of soft-spoken meaning.

The novella can also be viewed as the story of an author writing a story. Buddy expresses himself intimately to the reader, relaying his personal circumstances and inner emotions as he writes. He not only relays text but also shares his personal feelings about the text he is writing.

As a family history and spiritual instruction, "Seymour—an Introduction" is fascinating. But it is the novella's third aspect that readers have found most compelling: "Seymour—an Introduction" is often interpreted as an autobiographical sketch of J. D. Salinger himself.

In this view, Salinger transforms his Glass family series when presenting the novella. He does not tell an ongoing story in the traditional sense, apart from Buddy Glass's trials and tribulations of authorship, but instead uses the text to address a number of issues affecting his own life: the "Dharma Bums," his own celebrity, and his longing for privacy. In doing so, Salinger addresses readers directly, exposing their fascination with his private life and their misconceptions about his image. He then appears to set the record straight through the character of Buddy Glass. After scolding readers for being bird-watchers and leaving tire tracks on his rosebushes, he seems to offer numerous insights into his own life. Yet, the sensation of knowing Salinger better after reading "Seymour" is a finely crafted illusion. Similarly to Seymour's poetry, Salinger goes through the entire novella "without spilling a single really autobiographical bean."

In actuality, none of these interpretations is completely true, while, at the same time, they all are. Three parallel narrations occur in "Seymour—an Introduction," two biographical and one autobiographical. None is stationary or linear. Instead, the three stories that Salinger delivers in this single text continuously meld together, separate, shift, and reblend. The result has alternately dazzled and confused readers for decades.

To identify the autobiographical kernels within "Seymour—an Introduction" or to distinguish the traits that Buddy Glass held in common with the author are fascinating but parenthetical readings of the novella. The greatest mystery of "Seymour—an Introduction" is in its title character; and its greatest power is the sacrifice of creation.

The ghost of Seymour Glass floods this story. Buddy's pain over Seymour's physical absence is etched into every thought he conveys. (When Seymour stands on the curb watching his brother play marbles in the encroaching twilight, the scene is not only envisioned by readers but also felt, heard, and tasted by them.) It was Salinger who instructed A. E. Hotchner that fiction was "experience magnified." The great mystery of "Seymour—an Introduction" is this: What reservoir of experience did Salinger draw upon to portray the subtleties of Seymour's character, with their lifelike exactness? Where within the soul of the author did the deep pain of Buddy Glass find its terrible origin? Salinger had no brother. No one in Salinger's life, either relative or friend, ever came close to resembling the character of Seymour Glass. Neither, at forty, had Salinger ever known anyone who had died by his own hand. In fact, aside from the deaths of Ross and Lobrano, Salinger had been happily removed from death since the war. Yet the character of Seymour is so real as to indicate that he must have had some basis in fact. And the grief of Buddy Glass is far too fresh and poignant not to have been a recital of living emotions.

In "Seymour," Buddy relays an interesting story. While in the army, he was stricken with a case of pleurisy which plagued him for more than three months. His illness was finally relieved in an almost mystical way: by placing a poem by William Blake in his shirt pocket, where it exuded a healing power like a poultice, or as Buddy puts it, like an "unusually fast-working form of heat therapy." Buddy offers his story as an example of the power of spirituality to heal. He uses the memory to explain his motivation for collecting and publishing Seymour's poems. But the story may also touch upon motives behind Salinger's work more personal than spiritual edification.

If we assume that Buddy's story represents actual events in Salinger's life, it may shed light on the inspiration for Seymour's character as well as the source that Salinger tapped to invoke Buddy's grief. The most logical assumption is that Buddy's story recounts the pain that Salinger experienced between October 1944, when he crossed the Siegfried Line toward the Hürtgen Forest, and December of that year, when he finally staggered out of the bloodbath. It was in those months that

Salinger turned to writing poetry as a comfort. And it was in Hürtgen that Salinger completed "A Boy in France," a story that takes the William Blake poem "The Lamb" as its source of spiritual sustenance.

Buddy's reaffirmation of the values that Salinger clung to for survival during combat reminds the reader that the author became painfully accustomed to the grief of fallen brothers during the war. The absence of subsequent events in Salinger's life that might inspire the depth of mourning displayed by Buddy Glass for his brother indicates that Salinger may well have reached back into the anguish of those years in order to replay their emotions on the written page. The forerunner of Seymour Glass, Kenneth Caulfield, had been born during the war as a symbol of hope and triumph over death, as a reaction to despair. Salinger likely used this same wartime motivation when developing Seymour's character, and it can be said with reasonable certainty that Seymour Glass was actually born in the misery of active combat.

What inspires admiration about these connections is Salinger's apparent ability, fourteen years after the war's end, to relive its anguish so vividly as to give it fresh life. Yet the heartbreak of Seymour's death and the subsequent sadness felt by Buddy are not the major thrust of these characters. Instead, they represent Salinger's affirmation of life—his enduring enchantment with the beauty of the world and his belief in its power of redemption. Through Buddy's account, Seymour Glass is portrayed as a fleeting poem, a holy transient haiku. His value was not in his longevity but in the simple fact that he existed and touched the lives of those around him. Buddy sees it his duty to continue the enlightenment that came from knowing his brother, and he feels obligated to share that enlightenment with the rest of the world by collecting and publishing Seymour's poems. Salinger, therefore, portrays the poems of Seymour Glass not as mere works of art but as an "unusually fast-working form of heat therapy," a poultice offered as remedy to a spiritually aching world.

The enlightenment and inner beauty that Seymour represents and Buddy's appreciation of Seymour's gifts, despite the weight of his personal grief, stood in stark contrast to the negative cynicism of Salinger's generation. Seymour's and Buddy's characters challenged the Beat generation for its aversion to beauty and its emphasis upon the ills of the world around it. As Salinger offered faith and hope, the beatniks tendered only complaint and spiritual blindness. Employing the long-suffering, God-loving characters of Buddy and Seymour, Salinger condemned these "Zen-killers" for looking "down their thoroughly unenlightened noses at this splendid planet where—Kilroy, Christ, and Shakespeare all stopped." To Salinger then, the Beat poets and writers were not creative or spiritual equals to be embraced. Like professional readers, they were a "peerage of tin ears" to be rebuked.[13]

In the final analysis, Salinger's truest motivation for penning "Seymour—an Introduction" is found not in literary intent or biographical messages but within the spirit of a letter that he wrote to Learned Hand in 1958. "Remain in peace in the unity of God and walk blindly in the clear straight path of your obligations," he counseled. "If God wishes more from you his inspiration will make you know it."[14]

In the past, Salinger had sought to make his work exacting by using the tenets of *The New Yorker* as a guideline to perfection. By 1959, he was beginning to perceive the difference between perfection and the clinical flawlessness that *The New Yorker* demanded. He believed the difference to be a spiritual one. Salinger's words to Judge Hand reiterate his 1956 conviction that the subjects of his writings were not his to choose; they were the inspiration of God. Like Franny in the novella "Zooey," who was said by her brother to be "God's actress," Salinger now viewed himself as being God's author. And just as Buddy Glass was obliged to share the inspiration of Seymour's poetry with the world, Salinger felt obliged to share the beauty of his own personal revelation—delivered with steadfast love through the characters that now absorbed him completely. He may well have considered "Seymour—an Introduction" not as a story to be systematically crafted but as divine inspiration flowing in accordance with a freedom that only faith can provide, the same faith with which Seymour Glass rode the handlebars of Joe Jackson's nickel-plated bicycle. And here is the true source of Buddy's happiness: the delivery of inspiration freed him from the rules of conventional literature. The final arbiter of "Seymour" was not *The New Yorker*, the critics, or even readers. It was God Himself.

That is the revelation of Buddy Glass in "Seymour—an Introduction." The obligation of an author is to his inspiration alone, to his stars, and the truest measure of his work is the faith with which it is delivered. Once having fulfilled his sacred obligation, Buddy's eyes are opened to the truth around him. He now recognizes that every place on earth is Holy Ground. He finds peace through his connection with others, even the terrible and misinformed girls in room 307, whom he acknowledges as being his sisters as much as Boo Boo or Franny. And, like Franny before him, Buddy greets his own revelation with a conclusion by now common to Salinger characters who have attained similar enlightenment: a satisfied, peaceful sleep.

16. Dark Summit

> It is my rather subversive opinion that a writer's feelings of
> anonymity-obscurity are the second-most valuable property on
> loan to him during his working years.
>
> —J. D. Salinger, *Franny and Zooey* dust jacket, 1961

The *New Yorker* issue containing "Seymour—an Introduction" was published on June 6, 1959.* The magazine's cover featured an illustration of three children playing in a field, eyes fixed skyward in delight. For ardent Salinger fans the eclectic story within the magazine's pages was delightful indeed, but the general reaction to "Seymour" was mixed at best. Most readers simply did not know what to make of the novella. Was it a rebuke or an affirmation? A story of fiction or an autobiographical confession? A work of art or an exercise in self-absorption?

While readers were perplexed by its meaning and critics were nearly dumbfounded by its seemingly unrestrained style, the discussion over the nature of Salinger's new work was immediate and furious. As a re-

*Almost the entire issue of *The New Yorker* was devoted to "Seymour—an Introduction."

sult, "Seymour" became a literary must-read for 1959 and the magazine quickly sold out—exactly the reaction that *The New Yorker* had
anticipated. Regardless of the story's merits—which were largely unknown to William Shawn when he had accepted "Seymour"—the
story was expected to sell through the sheer force of Salinger's fame.

The same assurance that guaranteed sales for *The New Yorker* also
put Salinger into an awkward position. Even as newspaper and magazine articles began to review his new story with both disdain and admiration, the issue itself quickly became unobtainable, rapidly seized by
Salinger fans lucky enough to find copies. For the rest of his admirers,
who had now reached global proportions as *Catcher* and *Nine Stories*
had been translated into various languages and published overseas, it
seemed unfair of the author to publish exclusively for a tiny section of
the population who had access to *The New Yorker*. It had been nearly a
decade since the appearance of *The Catcher in the Rye* and six years
since Salinger had published *Nine Stories*. That he would release a new
novel about the Glass family was not only anticipated, it was now expected. In fact, Salinger had been promising a Glass novel to *The New
Yorker* since 1955.

When "Seymour" was released, the reading public easily perceived
the author coyly wrapped within the character of Buddy Glass. Buddy's
very protest, that readers "have somewhere picked up the bogus information that I spend six months of the year in a Buddhist monastery
and the other six in a mental institution," only served to validate the
popular notion that Salinger was an enlightened, if eccentric, hermit.
For his part, Salinger played his role well. Almost in mimicry of Buddy
Glass's character, he began appearing in the academic halls of Dartmouth College soon after the release of "Seymour," where he spent
hours working in the school's library, very much resembling the literary aesthetic one might imagine Buddy Glass to be. He briefly grew a
beard and sported a rugged backwoods dress of denim and plaid cot-
ton shirts, an appearance suited equally to chopping wood as to
scholastic endeavor. To complete the aura of the pensive genius, he
took up smoking a pipe from which wafted billows of sweet-smelling
Sobranie tobacco.

While playing this role, Salinger kept himself visible in the eye of
public curiosity but always at arm's length from intense inspection.
Plainly put, he made sure that he presented the right image to the pub-

lic, but he kept that image at a distance, close enough to inspire admiration but far enough to discourage close scrutiny. It was a game he played at his own peril and one he was destined to lose.

By the end of 1959, Salinger had played many roles: struggling artist, war hero, spurned lover, spiritual ascetic, the voice of a generation. But a piece of his image was still missing. On the eve of the 1960s, American society was awakening to an awareness of social and political issues in a way unprecedented since the Civil War. Topics such as the atom bomb, racial segregation, and the disparity of wealth found voices in the arts and champions among poets, authors, and playwrights. Salinger, however, had never shown much interest in politics, and, aside from his damnation of racism in "Blue Melody," his stories were largely void of contemporary social issues.

Privately, Salinger derided politics of all stripes. His letters to Learned Hand reveal that he believed strongly in the ideals upon which American society had been founded and had faith that the shortcomings of government, politics, and culture were worth overcoming in defense of those ideals.[1] He also had close relationships that gave him unique insights into current events and the principles that bound society together. In addition to Hand, who remained deeply engaged in current events, Salinger kept in close touch with John Keenan, his counterintelligence partner throughout the war, who had reacted to his experiences by joining the New York Police Department, where he was now a chief.* With the insights of such knowledgeable friends at hand, Salinger made his first and only foray into the arena of public social comment.

In the autumn of 1959, the *New York Post* ran an article by Peter J. McElroy entitled "Who Speaks for the Damned?" The editorial drew attention to the finality of a New York State law that denied the possibility of parole to prisoners given life sentences. For Salinger, who was

*The contrast between Salinger and Keenan is fascinating. As Keenan was Salinger's CIC partner, his wartime experience resembled Salinger's more than anyone alive. Yet the two men's reactions to the same events were vastly different. Salinger was torn apart by what he witnessed and spent the rest of his life weighing the deeper meanings that informed his experience. Keenan appears to have taken a noble but more detached approach. Upon returning home from the war, he joined the homicide division of the New York Police Department, in essence continuing the career he had begun with the Counter Intelligence Corps. Keenan's attitude may have perplexed Salinger in 1950, when he wrote "For Esmé—with Love and Squalor," but his friend served New York City well. He became chief detective of homicide for the City of New York and headed the infamous "Son of Sam" investigation in the 1970s.

most likely familiar with the law through his friendships with Hand and Keenan, the article's title was a challenge. On December 9, the *Post* printed his response on page 49 of the newspaper. "Justice," Salinger wrote, "is at best one of those words that make us look away or turn up our coat collars, and justice-without-mercy must easily be the bleakest, coldest combinations of words in the language."[2] Salinger's position was clear and his letter to the editor was scathing. What flawed the New York State law prohibiting parole was not only its lack of "mercy" but also its denial of the existence of redemption. Even if a prisoner experienced a complete change of character, the law was so ironclad that it removed any reconsideration of the sentence. Rather than allow for the possibility of penitence, the state insisted upon incarcerating these convicts for the rest of their lives without recourse, "to rust to death," as Salinger noted with derision, "in a sanitary, airy cell superior in every way to anything offered in the 16th century." For Salinger, to whom salvation was the goal of life, its denial by the state of New York was sacrilege. And the victims of that sacrilege, those imprisoned without hope of change, seemed to him to be "the most crossed-off, man-forsaken men on earth."

. . .

An uncomfortable episode began on November 7, 1959, when Salinger received a letter from his former editor and mentor Whit Burnett. A decade before, *Story* magazine had fallen upon hard times, a situation that Burnett blamed on an unscrupulous business manager. As a result, the magazine had been forced to suspend regular publication and existed only through sporadic hardcover collections of former contributions. In 1949, Salinger had permitted the rerelease of "The Long Debut of Lois Taggett" for one of those editions. Burnett now planned to resurrect the magazine and wrote to Salinger asking for a similar donation. Not only was the request ill timed, but it also had a tone that bordered on reproach. "This will probably come as a surprise—to hear a voice from the past," Burnett began, "but not a past as long as the Columbia days when you sat looking out the window."[3] Burnett went on to ask for permission to publish two Salinger stories still in his possession that had never been released.* Both had been re-

---

*Burnett had held "A Young Man in a Stuffed Shirt" and "Daughter of the Late, Great Man" since 1945, when Salinger had submitted them for inclusion in the *Young Folks* anthol-

jected by him years before. Now, in light of Salinger's success and fame, they had taken on a new appeal. "One is a wartime story and might seem dated," Burnett reasoned. "It is 'A Young Man in a Stuffed Shirt' and it is, I think, one of the best of its kind we have read. The other, more like 'Elaine' and 'The Long Debut of Lois Taggett'— is 'The Daughter of the Late, Great Man.' "

Salinger may well have forgotten about both stories until Burnett's appeal. By mentioning "Elaine" and "Lois Taggett," two of the few pieces that *Story* had actually published, Burnett hoped to remind Salinger of past favors he had performed. Salinger was in no way inclined to allow *Story* to publish the other pieces. The most superficial reading of "Seymour—an Introduction" should have warned Burnett of Salinger's aversion to the release of old stories, especially a pair that directly pointed to his wartime experiences and his failed romance with Oona O'Neill, stories his critics and fans would sift through relentlessly.

As if to intensify the futility of the request, Burnett ended his letter by rehashing the 1946 *Young Folks* anthology debacle that had ended their friendship and insisting that he had not been responsible for the outcome. "It has always been one of our deepest regrets," he lamented.

Salinger was unmoved. He not only instructed Dorothy Olding to deny Burnett's request to publish the stories but also demanded that Burnett give them back. Three days later, Olding broke the news to Burnett. It was an awkward chore for Salinger's agent, who had known Burnett almost as long as she had known Salinger. Furthermore, and unknown to Salinger, Olding had already accepted payment for the stories and was forced to return the checks that Burnett had sent.[4]

On December 15, Burnett again wrote to his former pupil, asking Salinger to reconsider, especially when it came to "A Young Man in a Stuffed Shirt." But the tone of this letter is one of bitterness, and it appears that he had resigned himself to the conclusiveness of Salinger's position:

---

ogy. This reminder of the events surrounding the anthology most certainly steeled Salinger's determination to refuse Burnett's request.

At what I understand is your request, I'm returning the two
stories—"A Young Man in a Stuffed Shirt" and "The Daughter
of the Late Great Man"—which you sent us in 1945 or 1946.
I'm sorry not to have had a little note from you personally but
I understand that you do not write notes any more.

Salinger was not only closing the doors on past friendships; he was
locking them behind him.

. . .

At 3:13 on the morning of February 13, 1960, J. D. Salinger again became a father. At the age of twenty-six, Claire gave birth to a son,
Matthew Robert Salinger, at nearby Windsor Hospital, a tiny wooden
structure built as a private home in 1836.[5] From the beginning of
Matthew's life, Salinger saw his own strengths and shortcomings reflected in his son. He commented that the newborn possessed an intelligence and cheer that radiated through his eyes but worried that
Matthew also appeared more delicate and sensitive than his sister,
Peggy. Advancing the years to Matthew's adolescence, Salinger envisioned him becoming a scholar, "thin, shy, very shaggy, and loaded
down with books," a near mirror image of himself as a youth.[6]

Salinger's joy over Matthew's birth was tempered in April 1960,
when he received a professional and personal shock. Aside from
William Shawn, who had become his greatest champion, Salinger's
most trusted professional friend was his British editor, Jamie Hamilton. Salinger felt forced to scrutinize every action of Little, Brown and
Company and its surrogate, Signet Books, in order to protect the integrity of his work. In contrast, Hamilton had always proved himself
respectful of Salinger's wishes and had earned the author's confidence
with renditions of Salinger's work that were faithful to their spirit.
Consequently, Salinger allowed Hamilton almost carte blanche when
making decisions.

Back in February 1958, Salinger had mentioned to Roger Machell
that he had received a contract from an English paperback publisher
for the British version of *Nine Stories*, called *For Esmé—with Love and
Squalor*. Although derisive of paperbacks in general, Salinger had reluctantly signed the document because Hamish Hamilton had made all
the arrangements. He appears to have given the incident no further

thought, but when Machell reported Salinger's comments back to London, Jamie Hamilton was horrified. Hamilton had not planned for Salinger to receive a copy of the contract and had purposely withheld the circumstances surrounding the British paperback release of *For Esmé—with Love and Squalor.* In fact, had Salinger realized the implications of the contract, he never would have signed it, and Hamilton knew it.

For Esmé—with Love and Squalor was released in paperback at the end of 1959, but Hamilton did not send a copy to Salinger. By April 1960, the author had not yet seen the new rendition of his book and was beginning to hear curious rumors about its presentation. He and Claire were making plans to spend Easter at Park Avenue, where Salinger's mother was anxious to fawn over her new grandson. Salinger happily made arrangements with his friend Roger Machell, Hamilton's American representative, to meet together in New York during his trip. He had only one request: that he finally see the British paperback version of *For Esmé—with Love and Squalor.* Although the work was his own, Salinger made the request almost apologetically and promised that he would not "save" the copy.[7] Such was his faith in his British business partners.

Salinger never met with Machell that Easter. By then he had obtained a copy of the paperback himself. When he saw it, he was stunned. The collection had been packaged to imitate the cheapest of dime novels. Gazing out from the book's cover, which was printed in garish tones of yellow, was an alluring woman many years older than the character of Esmé. In case her come-hither stare was not enticement enough, the publishers heralded the tawdry nature of the book's contents in bold letters strung over her head, calling the book "a painful and pitiable gallery of men, women, adolescents and children." Salinger was crushed. He had argued with Hamilton over the dignity of the collection's title in 1953 and had allowed the title only to preserve their personal friendship. Now combined with the sleazy illustration and the provocative marquee, it appeared to Salinger that Hamilton had planned on cheapening *Nine Stories* from the very beginning, in order to make a profit.

In his defense, Hamilton pleaded innocence. He claimed that he had submitted the collection to Penguin Books, which had tastefully handled the British paperback edition of *The Catcher in the Rye,* but it had refused it. Hamilton had instead sold the rights to Harborough Publishing and its paperback imprint, Ace Books. When Ace released Salinger's collection with what Hamilton later called "a jacket of singular vulgarity," Hamilton claimed to have been appalled but powerless to alter events.[8] In truth, though Salinger was ignorant of the nature of Ace's product when he hastily signed the contract, Hamilton certainly was not. Further incriminating the editor was the naked reality that his transaction with Ace Books was by far the most profitable he had ever reaped from a Salinger work to date.

Once again Salinger felt betrayed by an editor whom he held in the highest regard as both a colleague and a friend. His hurt and fury with Jamie Hamilton were unrestrained. Hamilton begged him for understanding and then forgiveness. He had his wife, Yvonne, and Roger Machell both appeal to Salinger on his behalf and even offered to come to America to discuss the issue if Salinger would meet with him. Salinger refused them all. And although Hamish Hamilton held first rejection rights to Salinger's next hardcover in England, Salinger told Hamilton that he would prefer to go unpublished in Britain rather than allow Hamilton to abuse another of his works. That was the last exchange between the two men, who had been close friends for nearly a decade. Salinger never spoke a word to Jamie Hamilton again.

For all of his difficulties with publishers and his complaints about their methods, Salinger compulsively clung to a series of editors for support throughout his career, often to the point of blurring personal and professional relationships. This meant that a business decision that he considered disadvantageous was also translated into a personal betrayal. It was a situation that had scorched him time and again and a lesson that he never learned completely. In 1961, he would dedicate *Franny and Zooey* to William Shawn, designating him as "my editor, mentor, and (heaven help him) closest friend."[9] Shawn would prove to be the last such exception. After the incident with Jamie Hamilton, the suspicion of editors that was already second nature to Salinger became engraved in stone. From the Hamilton debacle on, Salinger would make certain that every contract, including foreign translations of his works, held clauses granting him final say over their presentations, down to the narrowest of details. For this reason, nearly all subsequent Salinger publications are devoid of illustrations, marquees, descriptions, biographies of the author not written by Salinger himself, and, least surprisingly, his photograph. Few authors have ever exercised as much control over their finished product. Though many have viewed his preoccupation with such details as an eccentric compulsion, Salinger always considered that he was merely protecting the integrity of his work, a lesson taught to him well by Whit Burnett, John Woodburn, and Jamie Hamilton.

. . .

By the spring of 1960, Salinger had decided that the time was right to release a new book but not the Glass novel that he had been promising. He instead determined to defy his critics and combine "Franny" and "Zooey" for national release. In doing so, his ambition again outweighed his reluctance to deal with publishers—this time Ned Bradford, who had replaced John Woodburn at Little, Brown and Company after Woodburn's death, much in the same way that William Shawn had taken over managing Salinger after the death of Gus Lobrano at *The New Yorker*. While striving to stay as far removed as possible from the publishing process, Salinger insisted upon control over publicity and presentation. He delivered a series of demands to Little, Brown via Dorothy Olding and instructed Ober Associates to deal directly with the publishers. Still, within a few months, rumors of Salinger's upcoming book slipped out and caused a media uproar, spurring a level of attention from newspapers and magazines that should have caused Salinger to reexamine the direction in which he was heading.

The first major encroachment into Salinger's private life came from *Newsweek,* which, along with *Time,* was one of America's most popular and respected newsmagazines. Despite its respectability, the tactics used by *Newsweek* to collect information on Salinger evoked those used by modern-day paparazzi. This, naturally, was due to Salinger's reputation as a recluse who avoided encounters with the press at all cost. Regardless of Salinger's well-known wishes to keep his personal life private, *Newsweek* was determined to get its story. It sent the reporter Mel Elfin to Cornish to investigate the secretive author. Elfin staked out his subject for a week but was unable to catch even a glimpse of Salinger. Forced to interview Salinger's friends, neighbors, and acquaintances instead, Elfin found few who were willing to talk, and those who did shed little new light on Salinger. Elfin learned that Salinger could converse for hours about music, detective novels (which he read in abundance), Zen Buddhism, Japanese poetry, and yoga. One neighbor added the odd detail that he had practiced standing on his head before he was married. But most descriptions kept Salinger's public persona neatly intact. "Jerry works like a dog," the artist Bertrand Yeaton told Elfin. "He's a meticulous craftsman who constantly revises, polishes, and rewrites."[10]

With Elfin, *Newsweek* had sent a photographer to record Salinger's image. One day, the photographer was staked out in his car, parked on the roadside leading to Salinger's cottage. Salinger appeared on the path with Peggy in tow, probably on their ritual trek into Windsor to collect the family mail. Catching the stranger off guard, Salinger approached him. Perhaps it was the author's inherent politeness or the presence of four-year-old Peggy, but the photographer felt a tinge of shame over the subterfuge of his task. As the story was later recounted, "when he saw Salinger walking along, unaware, with his young daughter, the cameraman's resolve melted. He stepped from his car, introduced himself and explained his mission." He confessed that he had been sent by *Newsweek* to take the author's photograph. Salinger did not turn and run. He thanked the cameraman for his honesty and went on to explain why he avoided having his picture taken in the first place. "My method of work is such that any interruption throws me off," he explained. "I can't have my picture taken or have an interview until I've completed what I've set out to do."[11]

This story, now famous, was not part of the May 30, 1960, *Newsweek* article. Its origin is a later *New York Post Magazine* article by Edward Kosner, who quoted Nelson Bryant of the *Claremont Eagle,* who in turn quoted the photographer quoting Salinger. In a letter to Donald Fiene dated May 9, 1961, Bryant claimed that the actual story differed from Kosner's published rendition. In Bryant's later version, the photographer was on foot and Salinger was driving in his car with Peggy. Noticing the man on the road leading to his house, Salinger pulled over and asked if his car was broken down and he needed help. The photographer said no, and Salinger drove on. After realizing that he had just spoken to his subject, the photographer continued on to Salinger's cottage, where he shamefacedly explained his assignment.[12] Regardless of the version, the story of Salinger and the *Newsweek* photographer is poignant and gentle, but it is a tale very much like that of Hemingway and the chicken. The chance that it survived three retellings unadulterated is slim.

The *New York Post* story did not appear until April 30, 1961, almost a year after the *Newsweek* feature. By then Salinger had made certain that even the meager disclosures obtained by *Newsweek* had vanished. *Post* reporter Edward Kosner found that fewer people would talk to him than Elfin. His final article complained at great length of the refusal of Salinger's friends to be interviewed. William Shawn had told him that "Salinger simply does not want to be written about." At Harold Ober Associates, Kosner was informed that Salinger deserved privacy and should be left alone. Undaunted, Kosner traveled to Cornish, where absolutely no one would talk with him. Nevertheless, he published his article even though it was devoid of any information not already commonly known.

Such events could not help but disrupt Salinger's world, putting what little normalcy his life contained into jeopardy. He had taken joy in strolling with Peggy and taking her into Windsor to visit the post office and eat at the local diner. Now strangers lurked about his property, attempted to scale his fence, and waited on the road to ambush him and his family. He had regularly attended town meetings and church socials. But reporters hid in darkened doorways and photographers stalked the village center. In this threatening atmosphere, Salinger was attempting to raise a four-year-old daughter and a newborn son, seeking to protect the magic of their innocence from encroaching fears. Claire must also have been uneasy. If she had felt trapped in the past, the constant presence of prowling strangers completed her imprisonment. Even more menacing, some of Salinger's followers were mentally unstable. As his fame and reputation for aloofness grew, he began to receive threats in the mail—and, worse yet, threats against the children. Any shadow in the woods, any lurking figure on the road or loitering stranger in town, might well have been a crazed fanatic, determined to harm him and his family.

At the same time that Salinger's friends and family were dodging reporters, the State Department began its own investigation of the author. The Bureau of Educational and Cultural Affairs sent a questionnaire to the most respected of Salinger's associates inquiring about his character. In light of what was commonly known of the author, the purpose of the survey was shockingly obtuse. "We wish to add the name of Jerome David Salinger to our file of possible American Specialists for use in our Cultural Exchange Program overseas," the letter began. "We should appreciate a brief and frank opinion of his professional and personal qualifications."[13]

One such letter was sent to Judge Hand, who endorsed Salinger with enthusiasm. "He is a close friend of mine and I have the utmost regard, not only for his intelligence, but for his personal character." Hand went on to explain Salinger's intense interest in Eastern philosophies and highlighted his tenacious dedication to his craft. "He works with most untiring industry, writing and rewriting, until he thinks he has expressed his thought as well as it is possible for him to do so."[14]

Judge Hand remained uncertain as to the exact duties of a "cultural ambassador" and ended his letter requesting an explanation of precisely what the State Department had in mind for his friend. A week later, he received a reply informing him that Salinger "would no doubt be asked to speak informally before interested professional and lay groups in the various countries he would visit, hold informal round table discussions and spend some time just talking shop with his counterparts."[15] Hand was incredulous. With regard to Salinger's character, the government's lack of understanding was colossal. Clearly irritated by its lack of research, Hand attempted to set the State Department straight on who J. D. Salinger actually was and what it was up against. "He likes to be alone and to live alone," Hand scolded. "I can think of hardly anyone who would be less likely to 'hold informal round table discussions,' and spend time 'talking shop' with his counterparts."[16]

The notion of J. D. Salinger traveling the globe and giving lectures is amusing, but the episode annoyed Judge Hand and made Salinger wary. Considering the certainty of Hand's final response, it might be assumed that the government quickly abandoned all hope of recruiting Salinger for an official position. But this was not the case. In future years, various branches of government, including the president of the United States himself, would stubbornly attempt to press Salinger into service.

. . .

The rumor that Salinger was planning a book was confirmed in January 1961, when Little, Brown released a series of advertisements in selected newspapers. The ads showed multiple copies of *Franny and Zooey,* stacked upon one another in pyramid form or aligned like a row of dominoes. Salinger allowed the advance publicity but ensured that it was as muted and austere as the book cover itself, which had no illustration. Despite Salinger's puritan control over this new publication, Dorothy Olding and Little, Brown and Company gently attempted to persuade him to accept a number of book club offers, as he had with *The Catcher in the Rye.* As early as May 1961, Salinger had already turned down offers by the Book-of-the-Month Club, the Reader's Subscription Book Club, and one by the Book Find Club that he described to Ned Bradford as being so horrible it was almost beautiful.* Ironic, in hindsight, was Salinger's opinion that *Franny and Zooey* might struggle without a book club deal but would eventually "move along" despite it.[17]

But the editors at Little, Brown were masters of the sale and found clever ways to promote the book beyond Salinger's tight restrictions. The earliest ads, printed six months before the actual release, teasingly declared *Franny and Zooey* to be "what America is reading." The premature boast threw Salinger fans into a frenzy, sending them rushing to bookstores only to be met by disappointment.

Advertising *Franny and Zooey* so long before its actual release had consequences beyond titillating readers. It gave critics ample time to load their guns and take aim. Their moment had finally come, as Salinger had always known it would. When the time for publication finally arrived, during the second week of September, *Franny and Zooey* suffered an onslaught of critical scorn.

A few initial reviews of *Franny and Zooey* were deceptively positive. Even Charles Poore, the critic for *The New York Times* who had been so dissatisfied by *Nine Stories* eight years earlier, delivered a near-glowing review on September 14. "*Franny and Zooey* is better than anything Mr. Salinger has done before," he announced, and was "perhaps the best book by the foremost stylist of his generation." After having scorned the endings of "Teddy" and "Bananafish" in his previ-

---

*Salinger's reply to Bradford declining the book club deals was accompanied by an intriguing document. For some unstated reason, Salinger had compiled a list of his stories published between July 1941 ("The Hang of It") and April 1950 ("For Esmé—with Love and Squalor"). This document lends itself to a suspicion that Salinger and Little, Brown were contemplating a future collection of Salinger stories, perhaps those related to the Second World War.

ous review, Poore had since become enthralled with the Glass characters. "Long may the Glasses jabber," he proclaimed. "A miraculous vitality rides with their ritual-riddled despair."

Poore's review was the exception. Most critics derided the book.
They attacked it in sections, segmenting it between its two parts,
usually praising "Franny" for its characterization, tone, and structure
while belittling "Zooey" for its religiosity, formlessness, extreme length,
and (most damning of all) Salinger's obvious indulgence of his characters, charging that it denied Zooey any hint of reality. In short, "Zooey"
especially was loudly subjected to the same litany of criticism on a
national scale that it had suffered in the editorial offices of *The New
Yorker* in whispers.

What most critics dispensed was not a review of the merits of the new
book but a public rebuke of the author. The sullen resentment of critics,
held at bay for years while Salinger grew increasingly famous, suddenly
exploded. Some reviews were blatantly vicious, others timid in their condemnation. But none matched the insight of Norman Mailer in 1959
when he voiced the suspicion that such criticism of Salinger's work (and
success) "may come from nothing more graceful than envy."[18]

Aside from Salinger and his characters, a favorite target of critical
attack was Salinger's readers, who were perceived to be young, upper
middle class, and educated to the point of boredom. In his review for
The Atlantic Monthly, Alfred Kazin appeared to blame Salinger for
catering to the self-consciousness of such readers, while deftly inti-
mating that profit was the goal of his manipulations. "Salinger's vast
public," he opined, ". . . think of themselves as endlessly sensitive, spiritually alone, gifted, and whose suffering lies in the narrowing of their
consciousness to themselves, . . . in the drying up of their hope, their
trust, and their wonder in the great world itself."[19] Other critics
agreed. In *National Review*, Joan Didion charged Salinger with the
"tendency to flatter the essential triviality within each of his readers,"
and condemned "his predilection for giving instructions for living."[20]

Perhaps the most important and subsequently famous critique of
Franny and Zooey was written by the novelist John Updike and appeared in the Sunday *New York Times Book Review* on September 17.*

---

*In fact, Updike's article, entitled "Anxious Days for the Glass Family," was featured on
the cover of *The New York Times Book Review* that Sunday, making it the most widely read of
all Salinger reviews.

Updike had always revered Salinger and cherished his works. Yet he too fell into line with the storm of critical fury. Updike's criticism was muted and somewhat apologetic. It still reads with the embarrassed tone of a young man asking to be repaid a few dollars by an old teacher who had once lent him a fortune without expecting to be repaid.

Regardless of its self-conscious nature, Updike's review remains a superb example of the faults that most critics found with *Franny and Zooey*. Though he excused the stories separately, he felt that together they "distinctly jangle as components of one book."* Comparing the Franny character of the first story with the Franny of "Zooey," it became clear that Updike, like most critics, favored the shorter story over the longer. To Updike, "Franny" took place in a world that he easily recognized, while "Zooey" appeared to occur in a dreamworld: a haunted apartment where Franny somehow finds consolation through a dialogue that Updike found meandering and "condescending."

Updike criticized the Glass characters as a concept—in essence questioning the direction of Salinger's authorship. The Glass children were too beautiful, too intelligent, and too enlightened, he said, and Salinger loved them too deeply. "Salinger loves the Glasses more than God loves them," he grieved (mimicking Seymour's comment in "Raise High the Roof Beam, Carpenters"). "He loves them too exclusively. Their invention has become a hermitage for him. He loves them to the detriment of artistic moderation. 'Zooey' is just too long; there are too many cigarettes, too many goddams, too much verbal ado about not quite enough."

For all its bite, there is not a mean-spirited word in Updike's review, and it was written with a measure of honor that has endeared it to even the most defensive of Salinger fans.† After delivering his criticism, Up-

---

*Updike did recognize in his review that the presence of "Zooey" put to rest the misconception that Franny had been pregnant in the first story, concluding that "the very idea seems a violation of the awesome Glass ethereality."

†*The New York Times* received considerable mail in reaction to Updike's review of *Franny and Zooey*. On October 8, the newspaper printed a letter to the editor claiming to "correct some of the misstatements of fact and misleading implications" that Updike had presented. Updike himself answered the reproach in a long reply to the editor that proved his meticulous knowledge of Salinger's works and his admiration for the author. He nonetheless defended his stance. "I should be sorry to believe that even the most ardent Salingerite could honestly regard my review as hostile. I did not mean it to be so and, on re-reading it, do not find it so."

dike exited his article with grace, reminding readers that its subject, regardless of how flawed, was still the work of a great artist:

> The Glass saga, as he has sketched it out, potentially contains great fiction. When all reservations have been entered, in the correctly unctuous and apprehensive tone, about the direction he has taken, it remains to acknowledge that it is a direction, and that the refusal to rest content, the willingness to risk excess on behalf of one's obsessions, is what distinguishes artists from entertainers, and what makes some artists adventurers on behalf of us all.[21]

The novelist Mary McCarthy, in what was by far the most searing assault, delivered no such grace. McCarthy had built her reputation through a series of blistering essays that aimed to demolish literary sacred cows. Her personal views were as far removed from Salinger's as was humanly possible. Her autobiography, *Memories of a Catholic Girlhood,* had recounted her disgust with religion, her descent into atheism, and the transfer of her faith into her own intellect—the very antithesis of Franny in Salinger's book. That McCarthy should attack *Franny and Zooey* and Salinger especially came as little surprise to those who knew her. But it was the vehemence of her attack that caught everyone off guard.

Writing for the English Sunday newspaper *The Observer* in early 1962, in an article later reprinted in *Harper's,* McCarthy accused Salinger of having stolen his characterizations from Hemingway. She then went on to condemn not only *Franny and Zooey* but *The Catcher in the Rye.* "Salinger sees the world in terms of allies and enemies. [Even] *The Catcher in the Rye,* like Hemingway's books, is based on a scheme of exclusiveness. The characters are divided into those who belong to the club and those who don't." The "club" obviously now referred to the Glass family, and McCarthy rightly perceived that the most effective way to strike at the author was through his imaginary children. "And who are these wonder kids but Salinger himself?" she asked. ". . . to be confronted with the seven faces of Salinger, all wise and lovable and simple, is to gaze into a terrifying narcissus pool. Salinger's world contains nothing but Salinger."[22]

In one fell swoop McCarthy had struck three targets simultaneously: the thrust of *Franny and Zooey,* the originality of *Catcher,* and the motivation of the author.* Perhaps worst of all to Salinger, who was incensed by McCarthy's review, was that she had accused him of being two things he most detested in the world: an egotist and a phony. Such strikes could not go without response. However belatedly, William Maxwell rose in Salinger's defense. His argument was in reaction to McCarthy's review in particular but may well have applied to all the attacks that Salinger had suffered at the hands of critics. "Oh, God, there's too much blood in the water," Maxwell mourned. "His virtues were not of a kind she would have appreciated—the charm of his dialogue and economy and total absence of intellectual pretense at that point. The Glass stories are not intellectual. They're mystical."[23]

Today, *Franny and Zooey* is widely regarded as a masterpiece. It has been revered by generations of readers who have embraced it as a story suffused with empathy, humanity, and spirituality. To modern ears, the mockery and scorn of its contemporary critics have the tinny echo of concepts long since passed away, while *Franny and Zooey* remains timeless. We cannot imagine "Franny" without "Zooey," and in no way consider "Zooey" unrestrained or too long. And though most of the pronouncements of doom against Salinger's book have faded into oblivion, *Franny and Zooey* has remained in print every year since 1961, with the demand for copies increasing as time goes on.

Salinger did not have to wait for the passage of years for vindication. Nor did he need to depend upon friends such as William Maxwell for defense. Satisfaction for Salinger and the supreme answer to his critics came on Wednesday, September 14, 1961, the day Little, Brown and Company published *Franny and Zooey.* Lines of enthusiastic readers formed in front of bookstores, anxious to purchase Salinger's new release. Within the first two weeks of publication, the book sold more than 125,000 copies and was catapulted to number one on the *New York Times* best-seller list, a position never attained by *The Catcher in the Rye.* The presses of Little, Brown could barely keep up with the demand. In its first year *Franny and Zooey* underwent no fewer than

---

*Contemporary suspicion held that McCarthy's tirade against Salinger also served as a personal attack against *The New Yorker.* The magazine had supported McCarthy with a first-rejection contract until that year, when it had allowed it to lapse. It was common knowledge that McCarthy was furious over the snub. When her article appeared, deriding the magazine's star contributor, it was interpreted as revenge upon *The New Yorker* as much as a critique of Salinger. McCarthy admitted as much in a June 16, 1962, letter to William Maxwell.

eleven hardcover printings and remained on the best-seller list for six months. Even after falling off the list, it stubbornly slipped back on, placing it among the best-selling novels of both 1961 and 1962.

Within the sober cover, the stories "Franny" and "Zooey" remained unaltered from their original appearances in *The New Yorker*. For new material, Salinger had chosen to write a short commentary that he added to the book's jacket flap, detailing the position of both stories as sections of an ongoing saga about the Glass family. Aside from the Glass stories already published, Salinger promised his public that more sections of the series were awaiting release by *The New Yorker*. This, of course, was not true, but Salinger led readers to believe that *Franny and Zooey* was but the first of many such installments. "I have a great deal of thoroughly unscheduled material on paper, too," he claimed, "but I expect to be fussing with it, to use a popular trade term, for some time to come."[24]

There can be little doubt that Salinger fully expected to fulfill his promise to his readers when he released the jacket flap commentary, but less forgivable is the self-serving untruth with which he closed the segment. "My wife has asked me to add, however, in a single explosion of candor, that I live in Westport with my dog." This unnecessary aside was, of course, false and the inclusion of the word "candor" especially unfortunate. It was common knowledge that Salinger lived in Cornish, and to claim otherwise not only showed his desperation for privacy but proved that he was out of touch with the extent of his own fame.

The reality of Salinger's position became inescapable on September 15, the day after the release of *Franny and Zooey*. As lines once again formed in front of bookstores and newspapers continued to scream of Salinger's unseemly love for his characters, *Time*, the most widely circulated and respected newsmagazine in the nation, hit the newsstands with Salinger on its cover. American culture held few greater acknowledgments of celebrity; to make the cover of *Time* was to be cherished and envied. But for Salinger, it was an assault. Reflecting on the experiences of previous attempts to uncover the details of Salinger's life, *Time* determined to leave no stone unturned. It had sent reporters to Cornish, where they badgered his neighbors, his grocer, and even his mailman. The magazine's investigators were dispatched to Valley Forge and Washington to track down old classmates and members of the 12th Regiment. Others were sent to stalk the offices of *The New Yorker*, to lurk about Park Avenue, and to ambush Salinger's sister, Doris, at her job at Bloomingdale's.

The resulting feature article, entitled "Sonny—an Introduction," began in a way that must have made Salinger's heart sink. It relayed the supposed findings of an unnamed group of Cornish locals who, driven to madness by curiosity, sneak over Salinger's fence to spy on the goings-on of his compound. After lurking about apparently unseen, the prowlers describe what they have observed: Salinger's daily routine, the articles of his clandestine bunker, even the shade of his complexion. The article then continued by citing the major events of Salinger's life and rendering a fair critique of *Franny and Zooey*. In all, the *Time* feature had far more bark than bite and was more tribute than exposé. Although it attempted to cater to the rising obsession of readers with Salinger's private life, it offered few actual revelations. The greatest secret that *Time* claimed to expose came not from researchers or fence-scaling neighbors but from Salinger himself. "The dark facts are," *Time* breathlessly reported, "that he has not lived in Westport or had a dog for years."25*

Salinger hated the *Time* article, a fact that he was anxious to share with anyone who would listen. In the first place, he saw it as an invasion of his privacy. Not only did it dash any hopes he held of detouring gawkers away from Cornish to Westport, but the article's sarcastic disclosure of the subterfuge made him look foolish in the attempt. Most of all, Salinger detested the magazine cover. That was not surprising. *Time* covers were archived and commonly collected. Salinger had taken great pains to ensure that his books held no such likeness. *Time* knew this; in fact, it had made a point of relaying his distaste for such images in the article. So it was with apparent relish that it emblazoned Salinger's face across its cover. A portrait by Robert Vickrey, the image depicted Salinger clearly aging, his hair graying, his face drawn. His eyes at once focused upon everything and upon nothing, he seemed to be mentally inverted, sadly pensive. The background was, naturally, an overgrown field of rye with a small, childlike figure, arms outstretched, teetering on the precipice of a cliff.

When Russell Hoban, the artist who had designed the spread, learned of Salinger's derision for the layout, he felt dejected. Hoban was among Salinger's most ardent fans. His own daughters, Phoebe and Esmé, were both named in honor of Salinger characters. Yet a result of his admiration had been to estrange the author. Nineteen sixty-one was perhaps Salinger's most publicly successful year, the summit of his career. But it reaped dark consequences. If admirers of J. D. Salinger ever held the hope of someday befriending the author, maybe even calling him on the phone, as Holden suggests in *The Catcher in the Rye*, that hope was extinguished in the autumn of 1961.

*Actually, in 1961, Salinger did have a dog, which was photographed by a cameraman from *Life* magazine about the same time as the *Time* article appeared. Salinger's reference to living in Westport with his dog was taken from his 1951 *Catcher in the Rye* interview with William Maxwell and refers to his beloved schnauzer, Benny. After Benny's death, it may have been difficult for Salinger to find a suitable replacement, and the dog photographed by *Life* was still a puppy and ostensibly belonged to Peggy.

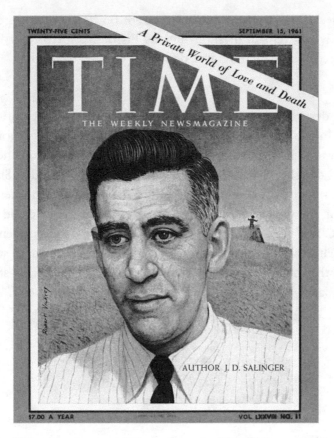

A portrait of Salinger on the cover of *Time* in September 1961. The recognition heralded the publication of *Franny and Zooey* and signaled the height of Salinger's professional success. (*Time*, a division of Time Inc.)

The enormous success of *Franny and Zooey* and the countless articles that accompanied it advanced a public fascination with Salinger's private life that he could not have imagined just a year before. Media articles with titles such as "The Mysterious J. D. Salinger" made for good copy. They were intriguing to readers and sold magazines. But they fabricated a myth that Salinger was an ascetic recluse who had spurned the real world for the refuge of his imagination. Reporters then set out to unravel the mystery that they themselves had created. The consequence of this manipulation was to produce in reality what had been fabricated on paper—and to curse the author in the process. With their relentless scrutiny and invasion of privacy, the media drove Salinger into a seclusion he might not have sought on his own, strengthening his resolve to remain in anonymity as his desire for privacy became more precious to him the more difficult it became to secure.

. . .

Winter descends quickly in Cornish, and late September offers few gifts of Indian summer. On such a rare day in 1961, the barefoot Claire Salinger took her nine-month-old son into her arms and took her four-year-old daughter by the hand, and set out to enjoy the day. Stepping outside the cottage, she heard shouting from just beyond her fence. Alarmed, she walked to the gate as quickly as little Peggy could follow. When Claire peeked through the door, the day's contentment must have melted away. On the other side was Ernest Havemann, who explained that he had been sent by *Life* magazine to research a story on her husband. "Oh Lord," Claire lamented, "not another one."[26]

17. Detachment

On July 8, 1944, little more than a week after the fall of Cherbourg, a staff sergeant of the 12th Infantry Regiment, a man whom Salinger had served with since D-Day, was abruptly killed when his jeep hit a land mine. The staff sergeant was posthumously awarded the Purple Heart, and his grief-stricken parents were consoled with the assurance that their son had died for a noble cause. Yet the accident had occurred between engagements, at a time when he should have felt safe. After surviving Utah Beach, Émondeville, and Montebourg, death had chosen the moment of least suspicion in which to strike him down.

The arbitrary nature of death made a lasting impression upon Salinger and wended its way into his work. The fate of Vincent Caulfield, killed by mortar fire while warming his hands in the Hürtgen Forest, and of Walt Glass, slain by an innocent-looking Japanese stove, are Salinger's cries against the random structure of the hair-thin line that separates life and death. Salinger was encircled by such misfortunes throughout the war, and he came to recognize that death held no nobility and chose its victims without purpose. He himself had survived; but it was an outcome without reason. He could just as well have been driving that jeep in July 1944 or fallen victim to unseeing mortar fire in the forest. Consequently, when Salinger left the service, he took with him an entrenched fatalism that would echo throughout his life.

By 1960, it became clear that Salinger's tendency toward fatalism had gained the power of religious conviction. In 1957, he told Jamie Hamilton that he held no control over the subjects of his own writings, that a higher force mandated them. He counseled Judge Hand in 1959 that if God wanted more from him, He would make it known. Even Salinger's characters echoed this conviction. In "Seymour—an Introduction," Buddy Glass advised readers that "the true poet has no choice of material. The material plainly chooses him, not he it."[1]

In April 1960, Salinger had a dark vision. He saw himself seated in a ballroom, looking on as dancers waltzed to the music of a band. Strangely, the music was becoming dimmer and dimmer to his ears as the dancers appeared farther and farther away. It's a lonesome image of Salinger withdrawing from the world around him—not so much out of choice as out of fate. "I've been expecting this kind of seating arrangement for years and years," he mourned. Yet in the end, he refused to complain. It was, he maintained, the only way he knew how to work, and he recognized that separation from the world was the price that his work demanded.[2]

Each winter at Cornish seemed to grow longer, and Salinger's feelings of remoteness deepened. He was frequently depressed but refused to allow anything to tear him from his work.[3] To worsen his situation, in September 1961, Peggy began school. Salinger had always lavished attention upon his daughter, and their daily walks together had become the highlight of his days. Her absence left a void in his schedule, and the hours previously spent with Peggy now found him entrenched in his bunker. Before long, work began to take precedence over everything else, and he frequently neglected opportunities to be with his family. During the winter holidays in 1961, Salinger and Claire flew with the children to New York City, where they stayed with Salinger's parents on Park Avenue. But that trip was an exception. The following winter, Peggy and Matthew both developed bronchitis and Claire took them to Saint Petersburg, Florida, while Salinger remained home at his typewriter.[4] In the winter of 1962, Claire and the children traveled to

Barbados to spend time with Claire's mother.* Again Salinger stayed behind, this time giving work on his new book as an excuse.[5]

At the same time, Salinger found he had few friends to whom he could turn. He had abandoned many. Along with Jamie Hamilton, he had discarded Roger Machell, who under different circumstances might have been his truest friend. After December 1959, there was little hope of renewing any bond with Whit Burnett. And those who had dared speak with reporters in 1961 had been swiftly cut away.

Perhaps unknown to Salinger at the time, the amazing serendipity of relationships that had blessed him throughout his life was at an end. No figure would arise to fill the gap left by departing friends or provide comfort when he needed affirmation. Those who had fallen away would now leave only empty spaces, reminders of just how far removed Salinger's ballroom chair had become.

On July 2, 1961, Ernest Hemingway, Salinger's friend and strength during the war, committed suicide at his home in Idaho. Six weeks later, on August 18, Judge Learned Hand, Salinger's closest friend and confidant, passed away in New York. For Salinger, the music had begun to fade into silence. The seclusion begun by his work habits and hardened by the media had evolved into a loneliness that was locked into place by the fatalism he embraced.

Salinger did not deliberately choose to withdraw from the world. His isolation was an insidious progression that slowly enveloped him. Sadly, he recognized the shadows descending but felt powerless to change course. His work had become a holy obligation, and he accepted that loneliness and seclusion might well be the price it demanded for fulfillment. In the jacket flap autobiography he wrote for *Franny and Zooey,* Salinger shared those feelings with the public. He confessed that he felt himself vanishing into his work and confided, "there is a real enough danger, I suppose, that sooner or later I'll bog down, perhaps disappear entirely, in my own methods, locutions, and mannerisms." He still held out hope that he would survive the demands of his calling. "On the whole, though," he stated, "I am very

---

*Salinger harbored some bitterness toward his mother-in-law and her second husband after they took in Claire and Peggy in 1957. Because her father was wary of allowing too much contact between Jean Douglas and Salinger's family, Peggy Salinger reports the 1962 trip to Barbados as being the first time she ever met her grandmother. Although Claire and the children visited Jean with increasing frequency in subsequent years, a certain remoteness always permeated the relationship between mother and daughter.

hopeful."⁶ Yet nowhere in his public confession was there any indication that he was willing to alter the path he was now traveling. To the outside world, this was proof that he had left his life to the whims of fate. But to Salinger himself, he was simply obeying the will of God. It would never have occurred to him to do otherwise.

. . .

As successful as *Franny and Zooey* had been, Salinger's reputation still rested upon *The Catcher in the Rye,* which, in 1960, had slipped back onto the *New York Times* best-seller list (at number five) and by 1962 had sold more than two million copies. It is therefore perplexing that Salinger remained silent when the novel was severely opposed by libraries, school boards, and faculties, potentially eliminating a vast segment of youthful readers who had kept its sales thriving.

The Catcher in the Rye was first challenged in 1954 by a school board in California. Since then, many dozens of attempts have been made to censor the book, demanding that schools ban it from the classroom and forbid their instructors from recommending the novel. Libraries, school boards, and parents' groups have cited Holden's use of profanity and his attitudes toward authority, sexuality, and education as reasons to suppress his voice. *Catcher*'s success propelled this controversy. The more popular the novel became, the more often it was opposed. *Catcher* may have been suitable for certain college curriculums, but as its popularity grew among academics, high school teachers began to suggest the book to their students. Some even tested the system by teaching the novel openly in the classroom. When they did, *Catcher*'s effect upon students was immediate. Many embraced Holden Caulfield as articulating their own deepest feelings. But parents were often appalled to find their children enraptured by a character they considered to be indecent and profane, one who drinks, smokes, and curses while visiting cocktail lounges and paying prostitutes. The resulting furor put *The Catcher in the Rye* into a curious position. In a 1962 survey, California college professors placed the novel at the top of their list of titles to recommend to their students. At the same time, *Catcher* was quickly becoming the most banned book in the United States.

Salinger is known to have made only one public statement on the issue and even that statement is diluted by the fact that it was in anticipation of events rather than a reaction to them. Shortly before the book's publication, Little, Brown and Company issued a limited publicity release in which Salinger was quoted as lamenting the possibility that *Catcher* might be censured for its language and content. "Some of my best friends are children," he began. "In fact, all my best friends are children. It's almost unbearable for me to realize that my book will be kept on a shelf out of their reach." This short comment, sent mainly to distributors, remains the only public statement on censorship made by the author.

By 1960, even this lukewarm opposition to the prospect of *Catcher*'s suppression had melted away into fatalistic acceptance. Once again, Salinger gave his work as an excuse for that fatalism. For some years he had received a number of letters from a relentless graduate student named Donald Fiene. He was a former high school English teacher who had been dismissed from his position for recommending *The Catcher in the Rye* to his students. Now a lecturer at the University of Louisville in pursuit of his master's degree, he had set himself the daunting task of compiling a complete bibliography of all Salinger works and translations for his master's dissertation. After several letters asking for Salinger's help went unanswered, Fiene was stunned to receive a response from the author in September 1960. In it, Salinger apologized for being unable to help Fiene in his project but went on to address his personal feelings concerning the debate that raged over *Catcher*'s suppression. "It distresses me very much," Salinger wrote, "and I often wonder if there isn't something I can do about it." He said he had decided to ignore the controversy completely. He explained to Fiene that in order to devote himself to the new work he was currently "buried under," he had chosen to let go of his feelings of responsibility toward old works.[7]

. . .

During the first week of June 1962, *Franny and Zooey* was published in Great Britain. After the falling-out with Hamish Hamilton, Salinger attempted to withdraw from personal contact with publishers, while demanding yet greater control over his products' presentation. He placed Ober Associates in charge of locating a suitable agent for him in England. Olding chose Hughes Massie & Co., which also managed Harper Lee, and assigned it the task of finding a publisher for *Franny and Zooey.* Among the first publishing houses to place a bid was Hamish Hamilton, which offered £10,000 for rights that, legally, it already possessed. Salinger ignored the offer by Hamilton and accepted a £4,000 bid by William Heinemann instead. Jamie Hamilton could well have sued Salinger for breach of contract but chose not to in an attempt to put an end to what he would later describe as the most painful experience of his career.

For William Heinemann and Hughes Massie, however, the pain was only just beginning. They soon experienced the exasperation that for Little, Brown and Company had become routine. Salinger immediately sought to apply the same level of perfection he demanded of himself to his new agent and publisher. When Salinger's agents drew up the Heinemann contract in March 1962, it came with a series of demands so meticulous in their details as to have made them inconceivable when Heinemann placed its bid. The contract stipulated that no publicity was to be issued without Salinger's consent. No photograph of him was to appear on the book's jacket. All advertisements were to be submitted to Salinger for approval. And no quotes "favorable or unfavorable" were to be used.[8] William Heinemann signed the contract regardless.

When Salinger received an advance copy of the British *Franny and Zooey* in May (one can only imagine that, after the consequences of not having obtained a copy of *For Esmé* from Hamilton, this too was a stipulation), he immediately wrote to his agent at Hughes Massie. The Heinemann version of *Franny and Zooey* adhered to all of his demands but still looked cheap to him. Salinger claimed that the book reminded him of "something any of the low-budget Iron Curtain countries might have brought out as well or even better."[9] Hughes Massie conveyed Salinger's disappointment to Dorothy Olding in a response that was at once apologetic, long-suffering, and brilliantly sarcastic. Salinger's dissatisfaction, it reported, appeared to be on two counts: the size of the paper and the quality of the binding material.[10] In the end, the British edition of *Franny and Zooey* reached the public in June 1962 just as Salinger had received it in May, but when Salinger's next book appeared in England two years later, upgrades were made to both the page size and the binding material.

. . .

Salinger's fourth and, as it would turn out, final book was published by Little, Brown and Company on January 28, 1963. Like *Franny and Zooey, Raise High the Roof Beam, Carpenters and Seymour—an Introduction* was a union of two Glass stories previously published in *The New Yorker* and would simply bear the titles of those two stories. Salinger had decided to publish the book in 1960, at the same time he decided to publish *Franny and Zooey,* and arrangements were made for the production of both collections simultaneously. He had always intended that *Raise High the Roof Beam, Carpenters and Seymour—an Introduction* would follow *Franny and Zooey,* and its release was more in keeping with the publisher's itineraries than Salinger's reaction to the critical derision for *Franny and Zooey* or its enormous public success.

Like the previous collection, *Raise High and Seymour* came with Salinger's usual list of demands. There was to be no cover art, marquees, photographs, or added text other than that written by Salinger himself. There was also to be very little advance publicity. The few advertisements allowed for *Raise High and Seymour* were sober and restrained. A full-page ad appeared in *Publishers Weekly* on January 7, announcing the book's upcoming release. It contained no illustration other than a depiction of the book itself. On April 7, *The New York Times Book Review* ran an ad that portrayed a pyramid of books, similar to previous ads for *Franny and Zooey.* In fact, the release of *Raise High and Seymour* was a replica of the process undergone by the previous collection except that the ads began far closer to the release date.

At first glance, it might seem brazen of Salinger to release a new collection—especially one containing the perplexing "Seymour—an Introduction"—after the onslaught of critical reviews following *Franny and Zooey.* But by 1963, Salinger's fatalism regarding his work had grown so firm that the opinions of professional readers had lost their force with him. Indeed, his fears that he would disappear into his work had now given way to complete submission. In his dust jacket commentary for *Raise High and Seymour,* Salinger revealed the extent to which he had become enmeshed in his Glass series; and he did so without apology. Rather than confiding fears that he might bog down in his work, as he had previously, he explained to readers that he had coupled *Raise High the Roof Beam, Carpenters* and *Seymour—an Introduction* so they would not collide with forthcoming segments of the Glass se-

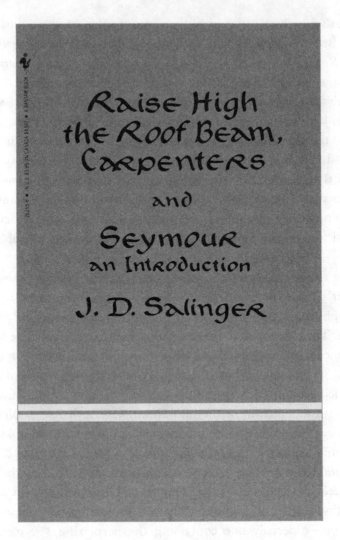

ries. He assured them that new additions to the Glass saga were in the works, currently "waxing, dilating—each in its own way," both on paper and in his mind. And if he had become entrapped by the Glass characters, Salinger revealed, he considered it a blissful imprisonment. "Oddly," he noted, "the joys and satisfactions of working on the Glass family peculiarly increase and deepen for me with the years."[11]

The year 1963, then, promised a future replete with Salinger works—books and stories that the author himself promised would continue the chronicle of the Glass family. Some of the pieces were yet developing, while others were near completion. The promise was not an empty one. When Little, Brown released *Raise High and Seymour*, it had already begun negotiations to pay Salinger an advance of $75,000 toward the publication of his next book.*

As might be expected, the critics were far less willing to suffer an extension of the Glass series—which now seemed interminable—regardless of the joys it offered the author. In general, the reviews of *Raise High and Seymour* were less antagonistic than they had been for *Franny and Zooey*, but the critics delivered a collective moan over the prospect that this book too would be followed by yet another Glass saga. They called for an end to the series in no uncertain terms. *The New York Times Book Review* accused Salinger of the "self-indulgence of a writer flirting with depths of wisdom, yet coy and embarrassed in his advances."[12] But it was *Time* magazine that boldly revealed the underlying exasperation that many critics felt but were reluctant to divulge. "The grown reader," *Time* quipped sarcastically, "is beginning to wonder whether the sphinxlike Seymour had a secret worth sharing. And if so, when Salinger is going to reveal it."[13]

The triumph of *Franny and Zooey* had taught Salinger that he could expect vindication from average readers regardless of the critics' derision. And when *Raise High and Seymour* was released, readers once again came to his defense. The book was an immediate success, quickly selling more than 100,000 copies and seizing the coveted number one spot on the *New York Times* best-seller list. The sales of *Raise High and Seymour* did not match those of *Franny and Zooey*, but the achievement of *Franny and Zooey* had been so enormous that it did not matter. *Raise High and Seymour* was still a literary sensation and the third-best-selling book of 1963.

In response, Salinger acknowledged the debt that he owed to the readers who honored his work against critical advice. In the second printing of *Raise High and Seymour*, he included a belated dedication to his readers that tenderly equated them with members of his own family. The dedication delivers appreciation to average readers as well as scorn to professional critics. Among the book's most enduring statements, it has become one of the most famous literary dedications of all time:

---

*$75,000 was an enormous sum of money in 1963. Salinger's consideration of the fee proves his intention to continue publishing and his confidence in the quality of his forthcoming projects.

If there is an amateur reader still left in the world—or anybody who just reads and runs—I ask him or her, with untellable affection and gratitude, to split the dedication of this book four ways with my wife and children.[14]

Twenty-four years after it was delivered, Salinger proved that he had learned Whit Burnett's lesson well. His respect for his readers and his faith that they would feel the inspiration of his message had once again rescued his career. With the world around him receding, his own family becoming distant, and his friends fading, it was the average reader who rose to save him: the bird-watchers, Faulkner's beloved silent readers. For the rest, Salinger's attitude was plain: damn them all.

18. Farewell

Two weeks before the release of *Raise High the Roof Beam, Carpenters and Seymour—an Introduction* in January 1963, the Ramakrishna-Vivekananda Center celebrated the centennial of Swami Vivekananda's birth with a banquet at New York City's Warwick Hotel. The keynote speaker for the occasion was U Thant, secretary-general of the United Nations, who spoke of Vivekananda's contribution to promoting understanding among diverse peoples and the center's dedication to world peace. Positioned at the foremost banquet table, almost directly in front of the podium, was J. D. Salinger, who had just approved the finishing touches to his next book. A group photo of the event shows Salinger smiling broadly with an ease and contentment not glimpsed since his photograph aboard the *Kungsholm*. And, like the 1941 image, the 1963 banquet photograph would prove to be a snapshot of a soon-to-be irretrievable world.

So much had changed for Salinger in two short years. At the beginning of 1961, the characters of the Glass family had been a faint murmur confined within the pages of *The New Yorker*. Since then, they had burst onto an international stage and brought their creator a material and professional success he had never dreamed possible. At the same time, the popularity of *The Catcher in the Rye* had exploded and the novel had established itself as a classic of American literature.

Salinger's heady position in 1963 had been recognized the previous March by Eliot Fremont-Smith of *The Village Voice* in a belated review of *Franny and Zooey*. Fremont-Smith (whose name must have inspired guffaws among fans of *Nine Stories*) stated as an incontestable fact that "J. D. Salinger is unique among contemporary authors. Relative to his tiny output . . . the attention he has received easily eclipses that given any other writer."[1]

The *Voice*'s admission of Salinger's accomplishment was high praise, but it unwittingly highlighted two private dilemmas that Salinger now faced and that together created a personal impasse. The results of success, money, admiration, and increasing attention, inescapable even within the hermitage of Cornish, played directly to Salinger's ego and reignited the great struggle he had so painfully acknowledged in "Zooey." While trying to rein in his pride, Salinger knew that he had obligated himself to future publications and recognized that they were expected to be new works. As Fremont-Smith's article had subtly pointed out, the recent books that had delivered Salinger's success were not new material but republications of old stories. In January 1963, it was nearly four years since Salinger had produced a new piece. Certainly, he possessed new works. His personal correspondence confirms that he was constantly working on fresh installments of the Glass family series. Yet he hesitated to release them.

By 1963, Salinger had clearly been absorbed by his art, and his conflicts were reflected in his characters. He shared not only the struggle of Zooey with ego but also the estrangement of Seymour Glass, who felt besieged by a world in which he no longer belonged. At his current level of fame, Salinger may have felt that another success—especially so close on the heels of two best sellers—could be the tipping point for his ego and derail him spiritually. Salinger's work was his prayer; the two had been indistinguishable for years. It was no longer success but prayer that had become Sallinger's ambition. He pursued that ambition in spite of the material rewards of publication and not in search of them. He continued to pray through his writing, and he continued to publish. For the time being, he would remain God's author and attempt to follow the teachings of Sri Ramakrishna, who had acknowledged that "There is no way of renouncing work altogether" and instructed his followers to "do your work, but surrender the result to God."[2]

Salinger walked a fine line between publishing as a spiritual obligation and resisting being seduced by the inevitable fruits of his labor. He took strength in the words of Sri Ramakrishna that it was possible to do both. In reality, his work had always been the driving force of his life and he simply knew no other way to live.

The rewards of Salinger's labor did have their place, and he was not averse to material comforts. But he developed a frugality rare for someone in his position, one who had grown up affluent and had attained an extraordinary level of professional achievement. He was never satisfied with the financial rewards he received from his publications and repeatedly cursed publishing houses for their gluttony. So he spent money sparingly—but he did spend it, most often on his family and home at Cornish.

When compared to the childhood settings of their parents, the world in which Peggy and Matthew were raised was a simple one. There was no Cornish equivalent of a Park Avenue residence or a summer home in Italy,* and the last thing the Salingers wanted was for their children to feel superior to their peers. However, Peggy and Matthew were raised with strong connections to their prosperous roots. They did not have lives of ease and privilege, as they could have, but Salinger made sure they would be able to move comfortably in upper-class circles if they ever chose to do so. Vacations in Florida became an annual February ritual for the family, with or without the author. By the mid-1960s, these trips were usually followed by long stays in Europe or the Caribbean. There were tennis and riding lessons and private school for Matthew, and Peggy learned proper table etiquette in the Oak Room of the Plaza Hotel.† The Salinger children were

---

*Claire's mother moved among three homes during the year: an apartment in Manhattan, a home in Bermuda, and another home in Italy. Although Claire's own childhood was spent in a succession of foster homes during the war, she never lost sight of her affluent upbringing.

†When it came to his children's education, Salinger defied the attitude of Holden Caulfield regarding boarding school. Matthew was enrolled at Phillips Academy Andover, one of the most renowned private schools in the nation, where he was a classmate of John F. Kennedy, Jr. (much to his grandmother's delight).

never spoiled, but their lives differed greatly from those of the children of Cornish farmers.

When royalties from *Franny and Zooey* began to fatten his income, Salinger decided to use some of them to renovate and expand the cottage. An extra room was added for Matthew, who had been quartered with his sister until age two. Peggy's room was renovated, the myriad leaks that had plagued the children's lives finally fixed. Salinger owned both a jeep and a car, which he had always stored in the Hands' garage during the winter. With the judge now gone, he needed a garage of his own and had one built with an underground passage to the house as an added comfort.

For a time these domestic renovations consumed Claire's attention. The contractors created a miniature model of the cottage for her, complete with attachable additions that she could rearrange for review. Though Salinger hated the tumult of construction, Claire was pleased and involved herself to an extent that raises an interesting question. A small apartment was erected over the new garage, complete with a kitchen and bathroom.[3] Exactly whose idea it was to add the apartment is unclear. It may have been that Claire hopefully envisioned the space to accommodate guests. But once it was completed, Salinger began to use it, signaling his increasing shift toward solitude as well as the growing strain in his marriage.

In 1966, Salinger made the most expensive addition to his property. When the neighboring farm had gone up for sale the year before, Salinger, more than satisfied with the 90 acres he already possessed, had initially shown no interest. But when he learned that a trailer park was to be built on the land, he was appalled and quickly mortgaged his own holdings in order to purchase the adjoining acreage and preserve it. The purchase devoured most of his savings. It also endeared him to the residents of Cornish, who were loath to see their village spoiled by the presence of a trailer park but lacked the means to counter the developer's bid. The event would have far-reaching results. The townspeople never forgot the rescue and quickly developed a tenacious loyalty to their most famous resident. Just as Salinger had once built a fence to protect him from his neighbors, those same neighbors now rallied around him, defending his privacy from intrusion by the outside world.

Salinger's prosperity during the opening years of the 1960s mirrored that of the nation. The static years of the 1950s, a decade of conformity and chauvinism, had given way to a social vibrancy fueled by an unprecedented economic affluence. Attitudes of self-exploration and a new questioning of traditions insinuated themselves into the American character. As they did, color and romance began to reenter American life. So did diversity and a new open-mindedness. The United States was a confident nation in 1963 when Salinger attended the centennial banquet at the Warwick Hotel. It was a nation convinced of its place in the world and secure in its vision of the future.

No symbol better represented the optimism of the era than the first family of the United States. Young, cultured, wealthy, and fashionable, the Kennedys created an image of Camelot that American society eagerly adopted as self-reflection. When President John F. Kennedy was assassinated on November 22, 1963, the entire world was stunned and America's confident poise quickly curdled into suspicion and self-doubt. The nation had lost not only its emblematic leader and its self-image but a portion of its innocence.

Salinger was devastated by Kennedy's assassination. He had respected the president, but his feelings were far more intimate than reverence: he felt he knew the Kennedy family personally. During the spring of 1962, he had received an invitation from President Kennedy to attend a White House dinner honoring popular authors. He was inclined to accept, but he wavered, having declined an attempt by the Kennedy administration to press him into public service just weeks before.

In autumn 1961, Salinger was contacted by Gordon Lish, a director of the Behavioral Research Laboratories at Palo Alto, California, a branch of the federal government's Office of Economic Opportunity. Seeking Salinger's participation in the newly formed Job Corps, the government requested that he write an inspirational essay aimed at motivating unemployed urban youths. In February 1962, Salinger called Lish on the telephone in response. According to Lish, the author sounded weary and tentative. He explained that he knew only how to write about the Caulfield and Glass families and was perhaps a poor choice for the Job Corps assignment. "Well, gee, that would be fine. Just give me some of that," Lish responded. Salinger promised nothing. "You only want me to participate in this because I'm famous," he charged. "No no, no," Lish protested, "it's because you know how to speak to children." Salinger paused and then made a startling confession. "No. I can't," he said. "I can't even speak to my own children."[4]*

So when Salinger received the White House invitation, he was wary. Though honored, he was apprehensive about attending an event where someone might try to pressure him into public service yet again. He might have dealt with Gordon Lish over the telephone, but rejecting an offer by the president at a face-to-face meeting might have proved impossible. There were other reasons too that gave him pause. The White House dinner would be an ostentatious affair where fashion took center stage and one swarmed over by the press. All eyes would have been upon him. Most likely, the dinner would have required Salinger to make a formal statement and might even have included some kind of award. In short, it was everything that he had sought to avoid and had rejected over the years.

The Kennedys were not easily denied. Having heard nothing in response to the invitation, Jacqueline Kennedy attempted to persuade the author herself. When the telephone rang at Cornish that spring, Claire answered. According to Peggy, who excitedly eavesdropped on the conversation, the first lady expressed her admiration for Salinger's talent and her hope that the Salingers would attend the dinner. Claire was in agreement and anxiously called her husband to the phone. Salinger must have been stunned when he realized that it was Jacqueline Kennedy on the line. He said little as Jackie implored him to attend the White House event, but he resisted her legendary charms nonetheless. Salinger could not bring himself to endure an ego-filled night of intense scrutiny engaging in so many of the activities that his writings had condemned. That would have been "phony."

Claire and Peggy probably never forgave him for denying them the experience of Camelot. It may be that Salinger never forgave himself. During the closing week of November 1963, Salinger spent his days like most Americans: visibly shaken, sitting silently in front of the tele-

---

*Gordon Lish's account of his 1962 telephone conversation with Salinger should be approached with caution. It was relayed to the author Paul Alexander more than three decades after it occurred and was not Lish's only encounter with Salinger. In 1973, while employed as fiction editor for *Esquire,* Lish penned a story titled "For Rupert—with No Regrets" that deliberately mimicked Salinger's style. He then published the piece in *Esquire* as "Anonymous." Widely believed to have been authored by Salinger, the story caused a sensation. When Lish finally admitted the subterfuge, it was front-page news. Furious, Salinger sent Lish a harsh scolding through Dorothy Olding, calling the deception "absurd and despicable." Lish remained unremorseful.

vision, where the mournful pageantry of President Kennedy's funeral unfolded before his eyes. As he watched the cortege's procession to Arlington National Cemetery, he was confronted with images that were hauntingly familiar and that he had not witnessed since the end of the war. Rows of military men marched before him, to the sound of somber dirges. They escorted a flag-draped coffin accompanied by a riderless horse, the sad symbol of a fallen brother in arms. The images could not help but reignite Salinger's memories of war. With old sorrows mixing with new grief, he wept openly. Remembering the event almost forty years later, Peggy recalled, still astonished, that it was the "only time I have ever seen my father cry in my whole life."[5]

. . .

Salinger is known to have worked on two projects during 1964: a new installment of the Glass family series entitled "Hapworth 16, 1924" and a piece produced for Whit Burnett as an introduction to an anthology that would become the epitaph of their relationship. Burnett set out to compile a collection of fifty short stories by various authors that had appeared in *Story* magazine over the years. He intended to entitle the collection *Story Jubilee: 33 Years of Story* and release it in 1965. He approached Salinger with yet another request to use one of his stories in the new collection. Salinger again denied Burnett's appeal, a response that probably came as little surprise to the editor. However, Salinger did offer to write the anthology's introduction. The result would be a new work that would satisfy Burnett's desire to associate Salinger with *Story* magazine while still allowing Salinger to withhold his early stories. Burnett gratefully agreed, and Salinger worked intermittently on the piece throughout 1964. Once completed, the introduction ran to 550 words, and Salinger sent it off to Story Press.

In the prologue, Salinger wrote of Burnett's lesson on Faulkner, the seminal 1939 event that had taught Salinger the importance of writing from the background and respect for the reader. It was a surprisingly touching tribute, especially considering the years of animosity that had passed between the two men. It may even have been Salinger's attempt at reconciliation with his former teacher and friend. As flattering as the tribute was, it did little to serve its intended purpose as an introduction to an anthology and was not what Burnett had in mind. He declined the submission. "The preface was embarrassing," he explained to Salinger, "because it had more about me and our Columbia class than it had about the 50 authors and I felt embarrassed to use it."[6]

Salinger's reaction to Burnett's rejection must have been incredulity and hurt. He certainly thought himself magnanimous to write the piece in the first place. It had been eighteen years since he had submitted anything to Whit Burnett, and now when he did, it was spurned as if he were still a struggling young novice. On Burnett's part, after years of being relegated to the background since *The Catcher in the Rye* and having suffered the frustration of numerous rebuffs by a former pupil, he had the final word in the end. But the episode destroyed any chance that the two men would ever come to terms. At the time, neither could have realized the irony involved: the same man who had handed back Salinger's first story in 1939 had just returned what would have been his final publication.

Whit Burnett had changed Salinger's life, arguably several times over. Salinger's tribute to him described his skills as a teacher and his love of literature. It was also an autobiographical essay far more revealing than anything offered by Salinger's fiction. By removing himself, Burnett had removed Salinger's expectations, the concepts of life and literature that stood between Salinger the student and the imaginary world of William Faulkner. By doing so, he had forced him to see Faulkner with new eyes—a vision that was uniquely Salinger's own. It had been the lesson of Salinger's life, one that had grown stronger as his career progressed. Without Whit Burnett's lesson on Faulkner, there would never have been Salinger's dedication to or appreciation for his "beloved silent reader" or one who just "reads and runs."

The story of Salinger's "Introduction to an Anthology" did not end with its rejection. Three years after the death of Whit Burnett in 1972, it was published by his widow, Hallie, as the epilogue of *Fiction Writer's Handbook*. Rightfully renamed "A Salute to Whit Burnett," it remains the only piece of nonfiction that Salinger ever approved. After the sorrow it had caused him, the 1975 release of this piece speaks poignantly of the affection and respect that Salinger would always hold for his former teacher.

. . .

In late summer 1964, Salinger and eight-year-old Peggy traveled together to New York City. Although it was not unusual for him to take the children on such a trip, where they visited their grandparents and his "family" at *The New Yorker,* Salinger carefully explained to his daughter that this trip would be special: they were going to ask William Shawn if he would honor them by being Peggy's godfather, a post that had been held by the late Learned Hand.

Salinger placed the highest importance on the request. Since Hand's death three years before, Peggy had been hospitalized twice (once during the summer of 1963 and again that winter). In addition, his marriage to Claire was in decline and he now kept almost exclusively to the small apartment above the garage. He was also anxious to honor Shawn with the request, especially after the dismal encounter with Whit Burnett.

Once in New York, Salinger and Peggy did not go directly to West 43rd Street to meet with Shawn. There was another desire on Salinger's agenda that he needed to satisfy first. Together, father and daughter walked to Central Park. There, in a moment as surreal and triumphant as any offered by the life of J. D. Salinger, he lifted his daughter onto a painted horse of the Central Park carousel and, backing away, watched joyfully as she rode round and round.[7]

. . .

In the early 1960s, most Americans connected with current events and opinions through newspapers and magazines. Television news was still in its infancy. The Kennedy assassination had proved the power of television reporting to draw a vast audience, and by decade's end, the influence of newspapers and magazines would be eclipsed by television journalism. The shift in the public's appetite from print news to television news occurred fitfully. In places such as New York City, where the number of newspapers was extraordinary, this transition was a violent one. Publications such as the *New York Post,* the *Herald Tribune, The New York Times,* and *The Wall Street Journal* vied for an ever-decreasing readership and were in a constant circulation war.

In 1963, the *New York Herald Tribune* underwent a major overhaul in a desperate attempt to revive its flagging readership. It reconstructed its Sunday supplement magazine, *Today's Living,* to resemble and challenge the city's most prestigious literary icon, *The New Yorker.* Defiantly renaming the supplement *New York,* the *Herald Tribune* then went to war with Salinger's professional family, something that no other newspaper had dared to attempt.

At first, Shawn and *The New Yorker* ignored the *Herald Tribune* affront. But the newspaper had taken on the brilliant minds of Tom Wolfe and Jimmy Breslin, and *The New Yorker*'s competition soon proved to be surprisingly successful. By late 1964, Shawn and his staff began to fight back with editorial swipes at the *Herald Tribune.* In doing so they unwittingly upped the ante against rivals whose levels of ruthlessness were out of *The New Yorker*'s gentrified league.

Tom Wolfe decided to go straight for *The New Yorker*'s jugular. William Shawn, with his collection of phobias and idiosyncrasies, was nearly as famous for his intense privacy as was J. D. Salinger, yet barely a word had ever been published about him. Wolfe not only decided to write a series of "profiles" on Shawn, two scathing parodies of the editor's management style and personal habits, but he taunted Shawn with a personal phone call asking for an interview. Shawn was mortified by Wolfe's intentions and instructed everyone he knew to shun anyone connected with the *Herald Tribune.*

Wolfe's first article on Shawn was printed four days before its scheduled release. Seeking to entice Shawn into a confrontation, he made sure that a copy of the "profile" was sitting on the editor's desk within twenty-four hours. Entitled "Tiny Mummies! The True Story of the Ruler of 43rd Street's Land of the Walking Dead!" the feature was every bit the unrestrained romp of tabloid journalism that Shawn had feared. Hysterical, he immediately wrote to the *Herald Tribune*'s publisher, John Hay "Jock" Whitney, imploring Whitney to prevent the article's release. "This is beyond libelous," he shrieked. "This is murderous. With one stroke this article will take the entire reputation of the *New York Herald Tribune* and thrust it down into the gutter."[8]

When Whitney, who had once been ambassador to Britain, presented Shawn's letter to Wolfe and Breslin, he was unsure what to do next. But the two reporters were thrilled. Without hesitation, they telephoned both *Time* and *Newsweek* and read them the letter. They then put their own spin on its contents, claiming that the mighty *New Yorker* was so fearful of Wolfe's series that it was threatening litigation to prevent its release. As a result, when "Tiny Mummies!" appeared in *New York* magazine on April 11, 1965, it was accompanied by a tumult of publicity that increased its readership many times over.*

Shawn's was not the only letter Whitney received protesting "Tiny Mummies!" John Updike, E. B. White, Muriel Spark, and others wrote to defend Shawn and express their disgust with the publication. No letter to Whitney garnered more attention than the one sent by J. D. Salinger, who was closest to Shawn and best understood what it felt like to be manipulated and maligned by the press. "With the printing of the inaccurate and sub-collegiate and gleeful and unrelievedly poisonous article on William Shawn," Salinger began, "the name of the *Herald Tribune,* and certainly your own, will very likely never again stand for anything either respect-worthy or honorable."[9]

Respect and honor were vital qualities to J. D. Salinger. They were engraved into his personality. They were solid attributes by which he measured his own life as well as the lives of those around him. He not only required duty and gentility of himself, he also expected them from others and always exhibited a surprised hurt when treated rudely or deceitfully. Much of his life had been maneuvered by events beyond his control, yet he had never lost sight of a high standard of propriety. Duty and honor had held him steadfast throughout the war, when he had forced his feelings into the background until their release would no longer endanger others. Social faux pas—bursts of ego during a lecture or hints of phoniness during dinner—embarrassed him beyond measure. Even the most scathing and dismissive of Salinger's letters adhered to a politeness that he would never dream of abandoning. And he was most hurt by the insensitivity of others: critical imperceptions, a broken promise made by a friend, a lie told to him by a child.

When it came to the *Herald Tribune,* Salinger and his friend Shawn had missed the point. It was not about respect and honor at all but about circulation, publicity, and money—the very things that Salinger most disdained. In truth, the world had moved on from concepts of duty, honor, and respectability. In 1965, such values were still given generous lip service, but they were increasingly difficult to find in daily

---

*The *Herald Tribune* died, but Wolfe's article on William Shawn saved Breslin, Wolfe, and *New York* magazine, which thrives to this day.

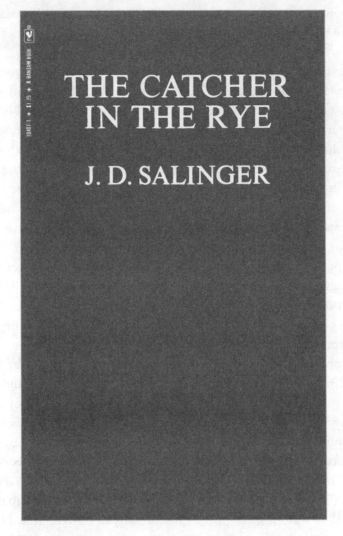

The cover of the 1964 Bantam Books edition of *The Catcher in the Rye* was designed by Salinger himself. After specifying the cover layout and selecting the fonts, Salinger mailed Bantam a swatch of the exact color to be used on the book's cover.

life. Salinger's scolding of the *Herald Tribune* was an honorable act in defense of a good friend whose innocence and sense of decorum were beyond reproach. But it did not convince Whitney, Breslin, or Wolfe, to whom such sentiments were abstract and antiquated. American society had embarked upon an era of violent change and shifting values. It was an era in which dynamic smashers of icons such as Tom Wolfe and Jimmy Breslin would find success; but it was a world in which

J. D. Salinger, an icon himself, no longer belonged, a world where the gentility and values that had formed his character were being called into question or swept away.

Salinger had at least one professional satisfaction in 1964. That year, Signet Books' contract for the paperback edition of *The Catcher in the Rye* finally expired. Salinger refused to renew the agreement and sold the rights to Bantam Books instead. He delivered his usual set of stipulations to the new publishers with the added demand that he himself design the book's cover. Bantam agreed, and Salinger sent it an austere design that featured only the title and his name. He instructed Bantam on what typeface to use, the precise size and kerning of its characters, and even mailed it a swatch of the exact color he wanted used for the book's cover. The resulting edition of *The Catcher in the Rye* was a maroon-covered edifice with its title and author in a shade somewhere between yellow and orange, the "J" and the "D" of Salinger's name of two different typefaces.[10]

To this day, Salinger's design arguably remains the most beloved and cherished book presentation in American literary history. For all of its starkness and simplicity, the sight of no other book brings on such a rush of memories or causes so many hearts to skip a beat as does the 1964 Bantam edition of *The Catcher in the Rye*. Recognizing its success, Bantam used the cover design for twenty-seven years without alteration, until the publication rights were transferred to Little, Brown and Company in 1991.

. . .

Early in January 1965, *The New Yorker* began the process of setting aside nearly an entire issue for the appearance of what would prove to be Salinger's final publication: a 28,000-word addition to the Glass family series titled "Hapworth 16, 1924." The files of *The New Yorker* are unusually silent on the details of the novella's reception by the editorial staff and its eventual acceptance by William Shawn.* It is prob-

---

*The available archives of *The New Yorker* are replete with correspondence between Salinger and the magazine's editorial staff until shortly after the death of Gus Lobrano and the publication of "Zooey" in 1957. However, when Salinger began to work primarily—and eventually solely—with William Shawn, such correspondence disappeared from *The New Yorker*'s files. Whether at Salinger's specific request or simply due to the reticence of both men to have their collaboration scrutinized by others, the unusual lack of documentation chronicling the production of these stories was probably deliberate.

able that "Hapworth" depended solely upon Shawn's inevitable approval and bypassed the usual editorial scrutiny, as had "Seymour— an Introduction." Shawn was by now accustomed to taking chances with Salinger's increasingly unorthodox work. In the past, the risk had proved to be justified and the results profitable. If the erratic nature of "Hapworth" gave the editor pause, he could soothe his misgivings with reminders of past vindications. For the same reason, if others at the magazine were aware of the structure of Salinger's new story, they would have been reluctant to speak against it. Such condemnations had proved unwise in the past, and it would have been hazardous for any employee of the magazine to attack the work of Shawn's best friend, recent defender, and father of his godchild. In a 1997 radio interview, William Maxwell refused to comment on the story's reception at *The New Yorker.* "I'd rather not talk about it, actually," he hedged. "I have been, and I hope still am, a friend of Salinger, and he doesn't really like to be talked about. So I'd just rather not do it."[11] In all probability, the acceptance of "Hapworth 16, 1924" by *The New Yorker* was a fait accompli rather than a topic of debate.

. . .

"Hapworth" begins with a preface to the reader by Buddy Glass. It is now Friday, May 28, 1965. Like Salinger himself, Buddy is forty-six. Six years have passed since he wrote "Seymour—an Introduction" and seventeen years since his brother's suicide. Buddy has just received mail from his mother, Bessie. Opening it, he discovers a letter written by Seymour to his family back in 1924. The letter is addressed from the infirmary of Camp Simon Hapworth, Maine, where Seymour and Buddy spent the summer when they were seven and five. Buddy explains that he has never seen the letter before and will transcribe it for the reader in its entirety. The same feelings of obligation that drove Buddy to write "Seymour—an Introduction" now compel him to share the exact contents of Seymour's forty-one-year-old letter.

From the beginning of Seymour's letter home, it is clear that readers are not dealing with an average child. Even those familiar with Seymour's character from previous stories cannot help but be taken aback by his vocabulary and the way he addresses his parents. He refers to his brother as "that magnificent, elusive, comical lad," explaining that

Buddy is "engaged elsewhere," much to Seymour's "eternal amusement and sorrow."[12] Such language strikes the reader as being pretentious, pedantic, and more than a bit sanctimonious—especially coming
from the pen of a seven-year-old child. Salinger quickly attempts to
counterbalance the impression by allowing Seymour to admit that he
and Buddy miss their family "like sheer hell." The disparity of tone
more than keeps readers off balance; it points to Seymour's tendency
to shift between adult sensibilities and childish reactions throughout
the novella. Nothing in "Hapworth" is absolute. For every apparent
conclusion presented by the text, readers can find a statement that calls
it into question. Salinger indirectly sums up the shifting nature of
"Hapworth" in the second paragraph when Seymour gives his opinion
on an English composition book he has been reading, calling it "alternately priceless and sheer crap."

The bulk of Seymour's letter, which seems to have been written in
installments, is a recount of events at Camp Hapworth. As he is laid up
in the camp infirmary ("forcibly abed") after suffering a leg injury, Seymour has time to write the long letter and to contemplate his position
at camp and his relationships with God, the counselors, and other
campers, as well as the members of his family.

According to Seymour, the Glass brothers don't seem to fit into
any group at camp. They have but three friends: Mrs. Happy, the pregnant wife of the head counselor; John Kolb, described as kind and
dauntless; and the bedwetting Griffith Hammersmith, who follows
Seymour and Buddy like a shadow and whose rich and pretentious
mother is disappointed to find that the brothers are her son's best
friends. Seymour complains to his family that most of the other boys,
who are otherwise "the salt of the earth," abandon their kindness
when surrounded by their friends. He compares these cliques to the
wider world, grieving that at Camp Hapworth, "as elsewhere on this
touching planet, imitation is the watchword and prestige the highest
ambition." In fact, Camp Hapworth is, to the seven-year-old poet-
saint, a microcosm of the larger world itself.

Although claiming that he and Buddy are trying their best to get
along with others at camp, the difference in their interests inevitably
causes rifts. They get into trouble for not participating with the rest of
the group. Rather than singing at "Pow Wow" or spending their time
arranging their belongings according to regulation, the brothers slip

away by themselves to meditate, read, and write—Seymour an astounding twenty-five poems in sixteen days and Buddy an equally awe-inspiring six short stories.

Consequently, like Holden Caulfield in "The Ocean Full of Bowling Balls," Seymour confesses that he and his brother are being ostracized by the other campers. At first readers are inclined to feel sympathy for the boys for being outcast by their peers, but it soon becomes apparent that their discomfort is due not to the callousness of other campers or to Seymour's sensitivity or brilliant intellect. Seymour admits his intolerance for the spiritual immaturity of those around him, and it becomes clear that his own snobbery has estranged him and Buddy from the rest of the camp. Seymour attempts to be forgiving of the other children because of their young age, but he condemns the counselors without mercy, confessing to a daily urge to smash them over the head with a shovel as punishment for their stupidity. These are shocking words for an enlightened God seeker having just entered the age of accountability, and they do nothing to endear Seymour's character to the reader.

The most definitive example of Seymour's derision for others is the incident that has exiled him to the infirmary. The morning before Seymour begins his letter, Mr. Happy took the campers on an excursion to pick wild strawberries. Along with the other boys, Seymour and Buddy piled into an ancient horse-drawn cart and drove "for miles" in search of a suitable patch of fruit. It had rained heavily the day before, and the cart soon became stuck in a muddy patch of road. Mired, the children were forced to push the cart in an attempt to free it from the mud. When the cart suddenly shot forward, a sharp piece of metal carved a two-inch gash into Seymour's thigh. Mr. Happy rushed Seymour to the camp infirmary on his motorcycle while Seymour pelted him with a torrent of abuse along the way, threatening a lawsuit were he to lose his tap-dancing leg to amputation.

At the infirmary Seymour took eleven stitches but, ashamed of his emotional outburst, refused anesthesia. His control over physical pain may appear remarkable, but the ability is diluted by five references he makes to weeping uncontrollably while writing the letter. He might have sway over his physical body, but emotional pain controls him completely.

To his mother in particular, he confides that he is oddly attracted to

Mrs. Happy, who is fifteen years his senior, married, and pregnant, describing her as having "quite perfect legs, ankles, saucy bosoms," and "very fresh, cute, hind quarters." The description of Seymour's premature sensuality is perhaps the most uncomfortable—if not shocking—portion of the letter, yet he goes on at great length to describe his sexual reaction to Mrs. Happy's charms. If readers are not astounded by the extent of young Seymour's sexual awakening (an event sure to rob him of what little innocence he still possesses), they are certainly disgusted that he conducts this conversation with his own mother, who will no doubt be appalled at her son's new preoccupation.

From past stories, readers know of Seymour's influence upon his family. His incessant lessons have molded the characters of both Franny and Zooey, and after his death, his writings continue to teach Buddy. But through "Hapworth," readers begin to understand just how oppressive Seymour's governance actually was. He dominates his family completely, instructing and ordering their daily lives even while he is away. He advises his mother, Bessie, to sing in her own natural voice while suggesting that his father, Les, conceal his Australian accent. Granting his "absolutely last word" on the subject of his mother's retirement from vaudeville, Seymour uses his precognitive powers to see into the future, warning her to wait until October at the earliest. He instructs Boo Boo to practice her reading and writing as well as her manners and etiquette. To the twins, Walt and Waker, Seymour insists that they practice their tap dancing daily, and if they do not (evidently, they gave Seymour the excuse that they are only three years old, a defense that Seymour called "frankly crap"), he orders them to wear their tap shoes at least two hours a day. He then adds that Waker should practice his juggling.

Seymour then devotes a large portion of his letter to naming an extraordinary number of books that he requests be sent to him from the library. Each title and author he mentions rests within a critique of their merits, and he reflects at length on their qualities and philosophies. Salinger himself loved to talk about literature in this way, and it is no surprise that Seymour should mimic the interests and literary tastes of his creator. Seymour's book list is so enormous that even if he were able to read them in a single summer his poor parents would never be able to acquire them all.

Seymour's book list is perhaps the most glossed-over section of the novella because it is seemingly redundant. Yet his enumeration of the books and authors that he loves are not mere requests for reading material at all; they are acknowledgments of things of beauty in the world.

As Seymour's letter progresses, it becomes increasingly internal, until, at last, he is speaking only to God. His address to God is a natural development, as he has been addressing spiritual topics throughout. In a significant section, Seymour contemplates the author John Bunyan and Bunyan's classic, *A Pilgrim's Progress.* He confesses having underestimated Bunyan in the past because he disagreed with the absoluteness of Bunyan's religious outlook. Explaining his own religious philosophy, Seymour quotes the Bible where Christ says, "Be ye therefore perfect, even as your Father which is in Heaven is perfect."

Flawlessness is a human concept, Seymour explains, while perfection is a divine condition. God is perfect, he argues, yet the world is full of famine and the death of children.* Using the logic that human beings cannot know the enormity of the nature of God or His creation, Seymour excuses the aspects of human action that Bunyan condemns as being weaknesses. He counters that Bunyan is too severe and that every aspect of human nature is part of God's design, concluding that qualities perceived by society as being deeply flawed may well be part of God's inscrutable plan and therefore perfect.

Seymour asks that his parents send a stuffed bunny to replace one that Buddy lost on the train to camp. In contrast to his own endless request for books, his brother seems to need the comfort of a stuffed animal while away from home. The request strikes the reader as being odd. If Seymour had asked for the stuffed animal at the beginning of the letter, readers would have thought nothing of it. But by the end of "Hapworth," the reader's perception of the children has changed and the desire of a five-year-old for a stuffed toy seems out of place.

Again, in "Hapworth," nothing is completely solid. No opinion is held without reservation, even Seymour's concept of God. Although he declares a "carte blanche" love for Jesus Christ, he questions the wisdom of God for allowing New Testament miracles to have taken place because, he argues, the absence of such events in the present day

---

*Seymour qualifies this example by stating that the deaths of young children were untimely "on the surface," indicating a fatalistic acceptance of the will of God as well as his belief that such children were experiencing the process of reincarnation rather than death. Salinger is known to have declared that he did not believe in death.

now fosters disbelief and encourages atheism. In the end, however, he resigns himself to the unknowable will of God and dedicates his life to God's service.

In many ways "Hapworth" is a logical progression of Salinger's work, a step in his spiritual journey. Seymour passes harsh judgment on the counselors and other campers, displaying a spiritual intolerance reminiscent of that of his sister Franny in her own story. The Glass brothers' inability to bond with other campers because their values are so vastly different is evocative of the later complaint of their brother Zooey that he and Franny had become freaks because they were weaned on too much religion. Seymour's condemnation of the adults at camp may recall the rebellion of Holden Caulfield in *The Catcher in the Rye,* but there is a significant difference between Seymour and Salinger's previous characters: Seymour, for all his holy intentions, fails to develop the level of compromise that allows Holden a measure of release. Nor does he perceive "the Fat Lady" in anyone around him. At Camp Hapworth, Seymour Glass has yet to learn the acceptance of Teddy McArdle or the lesson of indiscrimination that Buddy will in "Raise High the Roof Beam, Carpenters."

Obviously, Salinger in 1965 was still obsessed with the duality of human nature. Like the bulk of his writings, "Hapworth" examines human duality and addresses the conflict between spiritual and material forces. Salinger had clearly come to the conclusion that despite the inability of even the most enlightened and gifted of human beings to understand God's plan, the will of God must be accepted nonetheless. In fact, to Seymour in "Hapworth," although he does not understand the seemingly contrary nature of God's creation—alternately priceless and sheer crap—it nonetheless makes him revere God more because it forces him to accept the will of God without question. "My God," Seymour declares, "you are a hard one to figure out, thank God! I love you more than ever! Consider my dubious services everlastingly at your disposal!"

The camp infirmary becomes a kind of purgatory for Seymour Glass, a station where he contemplates his own dual nature and weighs the resulting choice between attempting to fit into the conventional world and abandoning it in pursuit of a solitary path to a closer union with God. Seymour possesses the mind of a genius adult and the spirit of an enlightened yogi, but he is trapped in the body of a seven-year-old boy and, despite his previous incarnations, is limited to the experiences of a child. "I am sick to death of the wide gap of embarrassing differences," he moans. "It is rotten and worrisome to have two voices." In "Hapworth," Seymour becomes the embodiment of duality and struggles to deal with the two sides of his nature: the adult and the child, the spiritual and the physical, the holy and the human.

. . .

"Hapworth 16, 1924" was published in *The New Yorker* on June 19, 1965. Professionally, it was a disaster. Not only did the novella require its readers to be familiar with Seymour's and Buddy's characters from previous stories, but it also demanded that they love them as much as Salinger did. Even then, readers were punished for their sentiments with an eighty-one-page letter that was at once pretentious, unbelievable, and taxing. Seymour himself admits to this opinion. "I am freely saddling you," he recognizes, "one and all, parent and child, with a very long, boring letter, quite filled to the brim with my stilted flow of words and thoughts." The line's location midway through the piece was unfortunate: It held the greatest truth of the novella and clearly belonged at the beginning. Of the thousands of readers who bought *The New Yorker* that June, each anticipating a fresh work from a master author, few would make it to the story's final line. By the time Seymour's embarrassed confession appeared in the text, most readers had already closed the magazine.

Salinger was spared the critics' scorn. The story was met instead by bewildered silence. It was ignored, which may actually have bothered him far more than if it had been reviled. *Time* magazine did run a disapproving review on June 25, but it was a mere single paragraph dismissively tucked away in the "People" section. Some critics were reluctant to throw stones at a famous author who had always defied their opinions. Still others felt satisfied to let "Hapworth" speak for itself, considering the story the most articulate proof that Salinger had indeed lost his way as a writer. By ignoring the story's release, they were dismissing the author himself. In "Justice to J. D. Salinger," in *The New York Review of Books,* Janet Malcolm wrote that "Hapworth" "seemed to confirm the growing critical consensus that Salinger was 'going to hell in a hand basket.' "[13] It is also possible that many critics, like many readers, were simply defeated by the text and unable to review a piece that they were incapable of reading to completion. In a strange way, the critical silence over "Hapworth 16, 1924" was an appropriate precursor of what followed next: the silence of the author himself.

Questions regarding "Hapworth" have plagued Salinger fans ever since. Did he intentionally write the story as his final publication? Why is "Hapworth" so unreadable? The story fostered a suspicion that, after alienating professional readers with "Seymour—an Introduction," Salinger attempted to release himself from the affections of average readers by feeding them a work that was completely indigestible.

"Hapworth" contains several passages that have been interpreted as gentle farewells from the author. The first is Seymour's advice to his mother to keep herself open for retirement opportunities. Less noticeable are two passages that show a creative delicacy rare for this story. In one, Seymour writes of a vision he has into the future. He describes seeing his brother Buddy in 1965. The description paints a precise portrait of J. D. Salinger, who, like Buddy, is older in Seymour's vision, his hair graying and his hands thickly veined. He is seated at his typewriter in his writing studio, complete with bookshelves and skylight. And he is happy. "It is all his youthful dreams realized to the full!" Seymour proclaims. "I would far from object if that were practically the last glimpse of my life." In this bizarre way Salinger himself makes a final appearance to readers, who are granted a parting glimpse of the author, finally with shadows removed. But it is indeed "the last glimpse."

Another passage is best understood when viewed in the context of all of Salinger's writings. At the end of "Hapworth," Salinger introduced one of his final characters to the world: a Czech woman who recommended that Seymour read the poetry of Otakar Brezina. She was a handsome woman, Seymour recalled, "in somber, costly clothes, yet with interesting, touching, dirty fingernails." Since "The Young Folks," twenty-five years earlier, Salinger's characters had primped and preened over their fingernails as a sign of self-centered phoniness. It remained one of the few symbols constant throughout Salinger's career. As he closed what would prove to be his final story, Salinger at last presented a character who ignored her nails as a signal of virtue. "God bless ladies with costly, tasteful clothes and touching, dirty fingernails," Seymour exclaims.

Passages like these, coupled with the revisionist nature of "Hapworth," which steals back from Seymour nearly every endearing quality he ever possessed, have led many readers to view the story as Salinger's final act. Many believe that through "Hapworth," J. D. Salinger completed his own transformation into his characters; he *became* Seymour Glass. Using "Hapworth" as a literary bullet, he then committed professional suicide and—as Buddy Glass once said of his brother—left the "Whole Loving Family high and dry."[14] It is easy to blame "Hapworth" for Salinger's final withdrawal. The interpretation is convenient, but it is also unlikely. There is no indication that Salinger ever intended "Hapworth" to be his final release, and he was far too tenacious a writer to throw up his hands because he had penned a bad story. "The jig is never damnable and never up," Seymour says; "when it maddeningly appears to be, it is merely time to rally one's magnificent forces again and review the issue." In 1966, defying "Hapworth" 's frigid reception, Salinger reinforced his relationship with Little, Brown and Company and formally recommitted to the publication of a new book.[15] In fact, Salinger told his friend Michael Mitchell in October 1966 that he had already completed not one but two new novels.[16]

Perhaps by 1965, Salinger had indeed "bogged down" in his own mannerisms and characters. Perhaps living twelve years in the relative seclusion of Cornish, separated from the variety of people and experiences that had always fed his creativity, had stunted his inspiration and limited the dimensions of his work. Undoubtedly, "Hapworth" is one of his weakest literary moments—a moment that became more inevitable as he took greater risks with his writing. Without the restraint of *The New Yorker,* the story mirrors the overdrawn length and aimlessness of "The Inverted Forest" or "The Children's Echelon." But to walk away from "Hapworth" with the conviction that Salinger was used up as an author sells not only J. D. Salinger short but also the resilience and adaptability of creativity itself. It was likely that, sooner or later, Salinger would discover in the solitude of rural America the same high level of inspiration he had found in the busy streets of New York.

19. The Poetry of Silence

J. D. Salinger's public life as an author ended with "Hapworth 16, 1924." In the decades to come, he would continue to write but never publish again. What followed spanned a generation of silence. To Salinger, his new life was tranquillity, a method of prayer as he exercised his faith through writing while avoiding the sin of ego. To the outside world, Salinger's withdrawal was a frustration, and it created a mysterious void that many people were determined to fill in disregard of his pleas to be left alone. Salinger's silence would prove to be a two-edged sword. It compounded the public fascination with him that had existed since the 1950s and allowed his legend to grow without contest, and as a consequence his name became synonymous with reclusion in the American psyche—something akin to an urban legend—and popular fascination with the man himself overgrew the public's appreciation for his work.

There is a certain poetic justice to the lack of information regarding Salinger's later years. The author always believed that readers' interest should be confined to his work and that information unrelated to his published books or stories belonged to his private life alone. However,

Salinger's home in Cornish, New Hampshire. Built in 1966 during his divorce, the house served as Salinger's home for forty-four years. It was here that he died in 2010. (Corbis Images)

a number of events occurred after 1965 that helped shape Salinger's professional legacy, demonstrating his personal feelings regarding his work and his decision to withdraw from the glare of public scrutiny.

. . .

Salinger's marriage to Claire Douglas officially came to an end in 1967, although in truth, it had been over for years. During the summer of 1966, Claire began to see a doctor in nearby Claremont, New Hampshire, complaining of "nervous tensions, sleeplessness, and loss of weight." The doctor could find no physical cause for the symptoms and, after analyzing Claire's account of her personal life, attributed her disorders to "marital discord."[1] Armed with this diagnosis, Claire quickly hired a local lawyer and, on September 9, filed for divorce in the Sullivan County Superior Court.

For the most part, Claire's formal complaint was indisputable. It stated that Salinger had refused to communicate with her "for long periods of time," a direct reference to his stubborn work habits, and that his "indifference" had been harmful enough "to injure her health and endanger her reason." The petition also stated that he had "declared that he does not love her and has no desire to have their marriage continue."[2] This last grievance was grounds for divorce far more pressing than Salinger's chronic absence, which had been the situation for many years. The complaint reads in such a way as to give the impression that Salinger's declaration of indifference came as a great shock to Claire. It should not have.

After purchasing the adjoining farm in 1966, Salinger had decided that the apartment above the garage had become too small, and he built a house for himself across the road from the cottage. The new structure contained a large study, and he stripped his studio bunker of its furnishings and accessories—including his venerable typewriter and car seat throne—transferring them into the new home. Claire and the children remained in the cottage, and Salinger's move was the de facto end of their marriage.

Four weeks after Claire's divorce filing, Salinger took Peggy and Matthew to New York, ostensibly for a dentist visit 250 miles from home. Rooming in Midtown's Drake Hotel, Salinger was reading in bed when he became drawn to the sight of his children sleeping next to him. Describing the evening a week later, he was still awestruck by the memory, clearly infatuated with his own children. "I loved sitting up in bed . . . watching their sleeping bodies in the same room," he recalled. "The point is, I love going anywhere with them."[3]

Salinger's divorce was not easy, a fact aggravated by his apparent unwillingness to discuss the topic with family or friends. Just as he had during his separation in 1957, he tended to ignore the subject, perhaps hoping the conflict would mend itself and go away. This time, however, the divide ran too deep for reconciliation and the history of neglect had grown too long. Salinger was forced to admit that he had lost his wife, and he began to deal with that reality. But the prospect of losing his children was unbearable.

The court granted the divorce on September 13, 1967, effective on October 3. Claire was awarded custody of the children, with Salinger given visitation rights. He was ordered to pay support in the sum of $8,000 a year with the understanding that he was obliged to pay for private school and college for the children. The cottage was also awarded to Claire, as were the original 90 acres of property with the stipulation that were Claire to sell the land, she would offer it first to Salinger for repurchase. Salinger was left with the 1966 land acquisition, his jeep, and the new house.[4]

At first glance, it might appear that the settlement stripped Salinger of much of what he had worked for over the years. Yet, had Claire not been awarded the cottage and property, it is hard to imagine that she would have remained in Cornish after the divorce. She most likely would have fled to New York City, perhaps farther; and she would have taken the children. Even with the agreement, it is still amazing that Claire remained in Cornish after so many years of apparently feeling like a prisoner there.

So, for the most part, the Salingers' lives remained the same after the divorce. J.D. and Claire were now neighbors. There was little difference between his visiting the cottage from his new home across the road and making the occasional appearance from his writing bunker or garage apartment. Most important, both did an admirable job protecting the children from the divorce process. Whatever acrimony existed between the couple was kept as far from the children as possible, and for Peggy and Matthew especially, life went on remarkably unchanged. Each saw both parents constantly. Claire indulged the children with riding and tennis lessons (which Salinger mocked incessantly but agreed to nonetheless), while Salinger taught them how to play baseball and a rural version of stoop ball, the hallmarks of his own childhood. The children attended summer camp and continued their annual vacations to Florida. Salinger continued to make frequent trips to New York to visit his parents and his friends at *The New Yorker,* frequently accompanied by at least one of the children. In 1968, he at last made the trip to England and Scotland that he had promised Claire eleven years earlier. Now, however, he took along only Peggy and Matthew.*

. . .

Salinger continued to write with unbroken devotion, even as his appetite for publication withered. Truman Capote would assert that after

---

*This trip shows the high level of accord between Claire and Salinger regarding the children, after the divorce. The settlement included a stipulation that neither could take the children out of the country without the consent of the other, and even then not for more than ten days at a time.

"Hapworth," Salinger tried to publish another story in *The New Yorker*, telling John Updike that he had overheard William Shawn on the telephone with Salinger, rejecting the submission. Shawn, Capote claimed, had been in tears while explaining to Salinger that the magazine had now abandoned him. Updike refused to believe Capote's story and cautioned him, in no uncertain terms, that he was not a reliable source. Not until 1972 did it become absolutely clear that Salinger had decided to extinguish the ambition of ever publishing again. That year, he repaid Little, Brown and Company—with 5 percent interest—the $75,000 advance toward his next book, freeing himself of his contract in the process.[5] At the same time he grew even more fixated on protecting his privacy, refusing numerous requests for anthologies of his work while maintaining complete control over those he had allowed. These had been long-standing tendencies, but a number of events would soon solidify them into obsessions.

Toward the end of 1967, none other than Whit Burnett contacted Salinger and his agent. The editor was in the process of putting together a new book, a personal anthology titled *This Is My Best*. As he had many times before, Burnett wondered if Salinger would be willing to contribute a story. That Burnett would embarrass himself with such a request, especially after having turned down Salinger's introduction to his previous anthology, is remarkable. By then Salinger had understandably lost his patience with Burnett and his persistent appeals for stories. In January 1968, he refused Burnett in no uncertain terms. "I do not have any fiction," Salinger scolded, "either published or unpublished, that I want to include in an anthology." He then went on to rebuke Burnett for his obstinacy. "We have been through this in the past many times before," he said with a scowl.[6] Whit Burnett was not alone. Salinger was receiving countless requests to republish stories, grant interviews, and release his work onto film and stage. It was usually left to Dorothy Olding to refuse such requests on Salinger's behalf, and she did so with increasing firmness. "There is no way we can authorize anthology use of Salinger's work," she warned Hughes Massie in 1972. "I'm sorry, but that's that."[7]

More distressing was an event that occurred in 1968. The chancellor of the University of Texas, Harry Ransom, had dedicated himself to elevating the school's library by acquiring enough rare books and manuscripts to rival the great collections of Princeton, Yale, and Harvard.

In securing these treasures, some of Ransom's methods were contro-versial. Competing with richer Ivy League universities, whose collec-tions were far older and better established, Ransom was not above obtaining the documents of living authors without their permission. He employed a New York agent in "the rare books and manuscripts trade" named Lew David Feldman to haunt auction houses and estate sales, and otherwise sniff out anything that could add to Ransom's trove. Feldman had reportedly been a salesman from Brooklyn who had suddenly converted to high culture and opened an office on Madi-son Avenue with the exotic but meaningless name House of El Dieff. In 1967, Feldman managed to obtain a sizable stash of Salinger man-uscripts that included more than forty personal letters written by the author to Elizabeth Murray. He sold the collection to Ransom, and on January 6, 1968, the manuscripts and letters became part of the library of the University of Texas. Appalled, Salinger quickly moved to restrict public access to Ransom's holdings, especially his personal letters to Murray.

The Ransom incident had fateful repercussions. Feeling defiled, Salinger resolved to ensure that none of his correspondence would ever fall into the hands of collectors again. He asked Dorothy Olding to destroy every letter he had ever sent to her, an invaluable correspon-dence dating back to 1941. Olding dutifully agreed and in 1970 de-stroyed more than five hundred Salinger letters, erasing a lifetime of communication and creating gaps in literary history that may never be filled.[8] Salinger may also have made similar requests to other friends and family at the same time. Also disappeared is Salinger's correspon-dence with William Shawn in its entirety, and no one has ever laid eyes upon what could arguably be the most valuable of Salinger's commu-nications: the frequent letters he sent to his family, especially to his mother.

From 1970 onward, Salinger, with the staunch support of Dorothy Olding, dedicated himself to smothering every disclosure of personal information both past and present. But Salinger's obsession with his privacy had the opposite effect. Rather than fading from public aware-ness, he became even more famous for his withdrawal. Intentionally or not, every act he employed to remove himself from the glare of public scrutiny only served to enlarge his legend. "I know I am known as a strange, aloof kind of person," Salinger admitted. "I pay for this kind of attitude."[9]

By 1970, American society had been in upheaval for years. Countless cities had suffered devastating race riots, and the war in Vietnam had so polarized society that violent street clashes were nearly commonplace. Friction between the races, the sexes, and the generations defined the era. In such an atmosphere of absolutes and opposites, it is interesting to speculate how any new Salinger writings would have been received. These were years that valued action, often reckless and even violent, rather than soft contemplation or subtle revelation. It is difficult to imagine that readers of the time would have had patience for gentle carousel epiphanies or the preaching of overly enlightened genius children.

Yet *The Catcher in the Rye* continued to gain popularity as it was handed to a new generation. This generation viewed its parents with intense suspicion and railed against "the Establishment" as vehemently as Holden rails against adult compromise and phoniness. In addition, many of Salinger's personal values, which had seemed so odd a decade before, were now embraced especially by the younger generation. The era experienced a brief return to the land with an emphasis upon simplicity as thousands of young people retreated to rural America to live and work communally. A new interest in organic foods and holistic remedies went hand in hand with a rising awareness of the environment. Zen Buddhism and various Hindu philosophies became enormously popular, and there was a general surge of spiritual exploration in a quest to deal with the uncertainty of the times. For those who embraced such trends, Salinger appeared to be something of a prophet, and his lifestyle, so curious only years before, now seemed to personify authenticity. Salinger's reaction was very much the same as ever: he simply wanted to be left alone.

Although Salinger was no longer publishing, his life continued to be driven by an unchanging routine. He awoke early and, after meditation and a light breakfast, retreated to his study to write. He enjoyed gardening and developed an intense interest in organic foods and homeopathic treatments. He kept abreast of goings-on at *The New Yorker* and continued his friendships with William Maxwell and William Shawn. His studies in Eastern philosophies were constant, and he maintained his associations with the Self-Realization Fellowship and the Ramakrishna-Vivekananda Center in New York City.

Within Salinger's routine whenever he visited New York was a pilgrimage to the Gotham Book Mart. A New York institution since 1920, the Gotham was often frequented by famous authors, and Salinger's presence met with an indifference that he found refreshing. Through their mutual interest in Eastern philosophies, Salinger had grown close to Frances Steloff, the book mart's founder. When Andreas Brown took over the Gotham upon Steloff's retirement, Salinger became close to Brown as well.*

In 1974, it had been eleven years since Salinger had released his last book and nine since his last story. It was becoming obvious to the public that the author had subsided into silence and might not publish again. Many fans were frustrated. With no new publications forthcoming, it was almost natural that they would turn to Salinger's pre–*New Yorker* stories to satisfy their appetite for his work. But reading early stories that Salinger had never collected together in book form was difficult. Most could be found only in 1940s magazines such as *Collier's, Esquire,* or *The Saturday Evening Post.* Each story had to be tracked down individually, and few libraries held them all. The magazines that could be located and that still held a story (many had been relieved of pages, torn out for "personal" collections) were often tattered and fading. So in 1974, a renegade group of Salinger fans decided to remedy the author's silence by assembling those of his short stories not already available in collections. They located twenty-one short stories, from "The Young Folks" to "Blue Melody," and transcribed and bound them together into a pirated publication called *The Complete Uncollected Short Stories of J. D. Salinger,* volumes 1 and 2. Roughly 25,000 copies of the unauthorized collection were printed. They were then hawked to bookstores in San Francisco, Chicago, and New York. When a young man, whom Brown described as being "a hippie, intellectual type," showed up at the Gotham Book Mart attempting to sell copies of the collection, Brown immediately contacted Salinger.

---

*Andreas Brown later recounted one of Salinger's visits to the Gotham Book Mart to Paul Alexander. He described Salinger entering the store with his son, Matthew. About ten years of age, Matthew rushed off to the comics section as Salinger disappeared into the books on religion. According to Brown, Matthew had the charming habit of wearing his baseball cap turned backward, many years before it became fashionable.

For Salinger, the protection of his work and the defense of his privacy had become a full-time job. He and Olding were constantly attuned to anything that might threaten his privacy or infringe what Salinger considered to be his copyright. Just a year before, he had become furious with Gordon Lish at *Esquire* for authoring the deceptively Salinger-like story "For Rupert—with No Regrets." Here was an author who demanded complete control over the tiniest aspect of his work and was determined to be the sole authority on which works would be published and how they would be presented. After having repeatedly blocked any rerelease of his early, pre–*New Yorker* stories, Salinger was incensed when he learned of the pirated collection. He contacted Dorothy Olding, and she hired a lawyer.

As angry as he was, it is likely that Salinger wanted to avoid litigation. A court case would have roused the media. Every newspaper and magazine in the nation would have covered it, anxious to reveal what the reclusive author had or had not been doing since 1965. It would have been an ordeal for Salinger. Dorothy Olding felt that there might be an alternative to a court case. If the publishers of the unauthorized collection understood how intent Salinger was on stopping its distribution, they might back down. Salinger could then avoid a trial and still prevent the release of his early stories. Olding contacted *The New York Times* and explained the situation. The newspaper, in turn, requested an interview with Salinger. So, during the last week of October 1974, Salinger did something that, for him, likely required tremendous courage: he called *Times* correspondent Lacey Fosburgh and granted the interview.

Surprisingly, Salinger's interview with *The New York Times* remains his most revealing and reflective. After warning Fosburgh that he intended to be on the phone "only for a minute," Salinger spoke for thirty. To Fosburgh, Salinger sounded "at times warm and charming, at times wary and skittish." He acknowledged that he was still writing but revealed that he had no intention of publishing. "There is a marvelous peace in not publishing," he said. "It's peaceful. Still. Publishing is a terrible invasion of my privacy. I like to write. I love to write. But I write just for myself and my own pleasure."*

*Salinger's statement "Publishing is a terrible invasion of my privacy" is a fascinating insight. It implies that he continued to embed the details of his own life and character into his works. Salinger was writing not only for himself but also of himself, to the extent that his stories amounted to personal revelations that he was uncomfortable sharing with the world.

Salinger also expounded on how he regarded his past work, explaining that he was particularly protective of it but disposed to see many of his early stories wither away. He considered them to be his personal belongings, much like socks in a drawer. "Some stories, my property, have been stolen," he explained. "Someone's appropriated them. It's an illicit act. It's unfair. Suppose you had a coat you liked and somebody went into your closet and stole it. That's how I feel."

Salinger, of course, did not contact Fosburgh to inform the world about what he had been doing since 1965 or to share his feelings about publishing or stolen clothes. He called to threaten the creators of *The Complete Uncollected Short Stories* with litigation in the hope of avoiding a trial. Fosburgh's article appeared on the front page of *The New York Times* on November 3. In it, she faithfully reported that Salinger had filed a civil suit in Federal District Court against "John Greenberg," a pseudonym for the illicit publishers, as well as against seventeen major bookstores that had dared to sell the collection. Charging Greenberg with the copyright violation, Salinger said that he was seeking $250,000 in damages and made special note that bookstores could be fined from $4,500 to $9,000 for each copy they sold. "It's really very irritating," Salinger confided. "I'm very upset about it."

As in many of Salinger's previous interviews and commentaries, the *Times* article contained a small measure of insincerity. Ignoring his years-old intention to publish the *Young Folks* anthology (an affair of which Fosburgh and readers had no knowledge), Salinger claimed that he had never intended for his early stories to appear in book form. "I wrote them a long time ago," he stated, "and I never had any intention of publishing them. I wanted them to die a perfectly natural death. I'm not trying to hide the gaucheries of my youth. I just don't think they're worthy of publishing."[10]

The *Times* article had the immediate effect that Salinger was seeking. A court injunction forbade the distribution and sale of the pirated collection. Publication stopped, the mysterious "John Greenberg" disappeared, and the lawsuit was dropped. The whole incident gave an impression of Salinger as self-absorbed and perhaps spiteful. It opened a debate on whether a work of literature, regardless of how it was perceived by the author, could ethically be taken back from the eyes of readers after having once been published.

The unauthorized story collection was far from Salinger's major concern in 1974. That year, he suffered the loss of both parents. In March, Solomon Salinger died, followed by Miriam three months later.

. . .

On December 8, 1980, a tragedy occurred that would forever stigmatize *The Catcher in the Rye* and for years associate Salinger fans with dangerous emotional instability.

John Lennon, formerly of the Beatles, his wife, Yoko Ono, and their son, Sean, were living in the Dakota, an exclusive apartment building looming over Central Park West. On the evening of December 8, as they entered the Dakota, a deranged twenty-five-year-old, Mark David Chapman, fired four hollow-pointed bullets into Lennon at close range, killing him. The assassin then calmly sat down on the sidewalk, pulled from his pocket a copy of *The Catcher in the Rye*, and began to read as if nothing had happened.

The world was stunned. An entire generation had intimately associated itself with Lennon, and his senseless death felt like a personal violation. As details of the assassination emerged, it became clear that Chapman would plead insanity. He claimed that a voice in his head had compelled him to kill Lennon. But his foremost defense was far better crafted and would have a chilling impact upon Salinger fans worldwide: he blamed his crime on *The Catcher in the Rye*.

Chapman had traveled to New York from Hawaii to commit the murder. Once in the city, he had sought out a bookstore and purchased a copy of *The Catcher in the Rye*. He had read the novel many times before and had convinced himself that he was the modern-day Holden Caulfield. Carrying the book, Chapman traced every step that Holden takes in the novel. He talked with a prostitute wearing a green dress, went to the Central Park Zoo, visited the lake and the carousel, and actually asked a policeman where the Central Park ducks go in winter. Then he made his way to the Dakota. When the police arrived to arrest Chapman, he was still reading placidly. They removed the book from his hands and took him into custody. Inside the novel, they noticed that Chapman had written a disturbing inscription: "This is my statement. Holden Caulfield, The Catcher in the Rye."

In interviews given as late as 2006, Chapman always maintained that he had killed John Lennon because he had been influenced by

Salinger's novel. He alternately explained that he felt that he was actually Holden Caulfield; was fearful that Lennon was proclaiming himself to be the new catcher in the rye; and had killed the musician to save him from descending into phoniness. Chapman later dropped the insanity ploy and pleaded guilty to the crime. Convicted, he was sentenced to twenty years to life in Attica State Prison, where he remains.

Mark David Chapman had interpreted Salinger's work in the most twisted of ways. Unfortunately, for years afterward Salinger fans were looked upon with suspicion, as if instability and appreciation of Salinger's work went hand in hand. On March 30, 1981, less than four months after Lennon's murder, an attempt was made on the life of President Ronald Reagan. A psychotic by the name of John Hinckley, Jr., shot the president, his press secretary, and his bodyguard in an attempt to capture the attention of the actress Jodie Foster. When police searched the contents of Hinckley's Washington hotel room, they found that he had brought ten books with him. Among them was a book on Shakespeare, a book on insanity pleas, and *The Catcher in the Rye*. Coming so soon after Lennon's murder, the press exploited the discovery of Salinger's novel among Hinckley's belongings. An odd speculation emerged from these crimes. Some believed that Lennon's death and Reagan's shooting were part of a complicated conspiracy, a plot reminiscent of *The Manchurian Candidate*. A number of publications and articles appeared proposing that mysterious entities within the U.S. government had diabolically infused *The Catcher in the Rye* with subliminal commands to murder. This bizarre idea was reignited in 1997 with the release of the film *Conspiracy Theory*, in which a programmed assassin compulsively collects hundreds of copies of *The Catcher in the Rye*.

. . .

Salinger's pleas to be left alone were disregarded by the media, a situation that he seems to have never completely understood. Enticed by the mystique of his self-imposed inaccessibility, newspapers and magazines hounded him in his retirement as eagerly as they had in 1961, at the height of his professional success. Perhaps the most infamous Salinger "scoop" was a rare interview that appeared on July 24, 1981, in the popular literary magazine *The Paris Review*. Entitled "What I Did Last Summer," the article was edited by George Plimpton and was bylined Betty Eppes.

Eppes had obtained the "interview" through a ruse. According to the article, Salinger had been tricked into meeting with her after reading a note left for him at the Windsor post office in which Eppes identified herself as a struggling novelist who simply wanted to meet a great author and would respect his privacy. Salinger met with Eppes but answered few questions, forcing Eppes to populate much of her article with descriptions of Salinger's reticence and her struggle to keep her tape recorder and camera concealed during the interview. She did manage to ask Salinger a significant question about the place of women in the American Dream, igniting a passionate response from the author, who was appalled by her apparent discouragement. "The American Dream is for all Americans," he protested. "Women are Americans too. It is for you too. Proceed. Claim it if you want it."[11] Then, displaying a lack of journalistic instinct, Eppes impatiently diverted Salinger from his line of conversation:

> After a while, I got to wondering if Salinger was going to bring a halt to this, which was OK by me, because the tape recorder was getting pretty close to the end where the beep was going to go off.

Eppes reported that Salinger lost his temper. She claimed that after having witnessed the meeting, which took place in a Windsor parking lot, a local resident felt free enough to strike up a conversation with Salinger, who was repelled by the approach. The incident is possible, but it is also likely that Salinger had caught on to Eppes's tactics and become indignant for that reason.

"What I Did Last Summer" was presented so unscrupulously as to elicit complete sympathy for Salinger, who appeared gentle and painfully shy. Thirty years after the article's release, Betty Eppes would come deeply to regret her participation in the episode and to charge that Plimpton, notorious for his publicity-seeking exploits, had embellished much of the article's contents. Regardless of who was responsible, the result of "What I Did Last Summer" was to do a massive disservice to future journalists and historians. The Eppes interview was Salinger's last. He would never again contribute to the telling of his own story or publicly share his point of view.

. . .

In the years immediately following the murder of John Lennon, Salinger descended into rigid isolation, as if to fulfill in reality the image long imagined by the public. It was a process that Salinger was aware of and something he acknowledged with growing sadness. Yet his fatalism prevailed.

Between 1981 and 1985, Salinger suffered frequent periods of sour depression, episodes that, like Holden Caulfield, he termed "the blues." Even his Vedantic faith seemed powerless to alleviate these moods. Seeking solace elsewhere, Salinger wandered in abstract spiritual directions, "farflung and Far-Eastern stuff" that he admitted beguiled him. Perhaps the deepest of these detours was astrology.

During the late 1970s, Salinger had written a story containing a character involved in astrology. As he researched the subject to enhance the piece, his character's interest became his own and Salinger discovered that he had become an enthusiast and an adept designer of personal horoscopes. "The thing backfired on me," he protested. When friends and family learned of his new preoccupation, they requested that he draw up their charts, and Salinger found himself constructing individual horoscopes with the same normalcy as the many fill-in crossword puzzles he worked on while riding on the train. Salinger's fascination with astrology would eventually dissolve into a convenient distraction, while his depression remained and his rancor grew.[12]

Even the seasons seemed to measure the maturing of Salinger's withdrawal. After having built his home in the hope of making it "sunny as hell," he now claimed to loathe the summer. Summer became for Salinger the time of year most likely to produce fans sneaking about his house, their tire treads leaving evidence on his driveway and lawn. After having long reveled in New Hampshire autumns, praising the season's bursts of color and invigorating chills, Salinger now found autumn depressing and began to crave only winter, explaining that frigid snows and mud enhanced his sense that his home was a fortress deterring unwelcome fans, pilgrims, and reporters.

On occasion, Salinger was forced to endure strangers even within his stronghold and regardless of the season. Years before, he had contracted for an L-shaped addition to his home that would hold a new bath, bedroom, and working studio in which to write, and where he would eventually store his unpublished manuscripts. Construction lasted for months, while Salinger became distraught over the clamor.

He complained bitterly of workmen swarming over his property, steal-ing his privacy and making it impossible for him to work. When, in the spring of 1981, Salinger resolved that he needed a new woodshed built aside the house, the thought of workers again milling about created acute feelings of dread. It took the small work crew a mere week to complete the modest structure, yet Salinger was convulsed by the ex-perience. He likened the presence of "hammerers and power tool users" to an alien invasion and admitted being shaken pale by the or-deal.[13]

Salinger made attempts to break out of isolation and venture into the world beyond Cornish, but they were usually short excursions and progressively few. In June 1981, he made an arduous journey into New York City, a rare occurrence compared with years past. Upon re-turning, he boasted to a friend that he had suffered but "was There." That summer, he managed a 258-mile drive to visit a friend on Cape Cod, but although he hated the long drive, he was back on the road to Cornish the next morning. In May 1982, he traveled to Florida to meet the actress Elaine Joyce, with whom he had been corresponding for months. But that trip was an exception. Rather than visit with friends, Salinger was more likely to repeat a 1981 day trip to Boston, where he took in a Pissarro exhibit but declined to meet a friend just a short distance away. It was safer to apologize through a letter than to chance an awkward afternoon.

The extent of Salinger's estrangement became undeniable during the summer of 1984. Peggy was pursuing graduate studies at Oxford University and Salinger decided to surprise her with a visit. He flew to England unannounced, reserved a room in a London hotel, and phoned his daughter at school. He received no answer. Taking advantage of a break in classes, Peggy was traveling abroad. Still, Salinger knew a number of people in London whom he had planned to visit during his trip. Now, however, he found it impossible to pick up the phone to contact or see anyone. Salinger instead spent the week alone in his London hotel room, staring at the telephone and trying without suc-cess to locate enough courage to dial a number. "No sound explana-tion for it," he later confessed. "I feel closed off from all general or personal conversation these years and consort with almost no one."[14] Peggy returned to England just prior to her father's flight home. They shared but a single lunch that summer, ample time for Peggy to recognize the change that had taken hold of her father: "He seemed so much less powerful than the Daddy I knew."[15]

Salinger's chronic aversion to unsolicited mail moved from dread, to scorn, to fear. By 1983, he found himself unable to face even those letters forwarded by his agent, despite knowing that Olding had sorted through those he'd received and discarded most. Salinger imagined the majority of his mail to be "fishy," consisting of appeals for favors and advice to resume publishing. After retrieving his mail from the Windsor post office—a ritual he refused to abandon—he allowed it to collect unopened on his desk, sometimes for weeks at a time. As the pile grew, it terrified him more, until he became paralyzed by the sight, claiming that it killed the last vestige of kindness his heart had been born with.[16]

That Salinger would be suspicious of fan mail after the murder of John Lennon is not irrational in itself, but, within time, he began to ignore not only mail sent by strangers but also letters from family and friends. Most of his relationships were maintained through letters, important bonds he had nurtured for years. Letters had become his primary connection with his sister, with William Maxwell, with John Keenan and Michael Mitchell. His fear of the mail now put those relationships in jeopardy.

By 1985, Salinger had rationalized his fears and self-imposed isolation. He excused himself to Michael Mitchell, whom he had increasingly ignored over the past few years. Salinger offered little regret for neglecting his friend. He instead presented a stubborn declaration of his writing philosophy entwined with a warning that his future investment in their thirty-eight-year-old friendship would be minimal. Salinger maintained that his work—what he now dubbed his "assignment"—demanded sacrifices of his personal life he was powerless to deny. Intrusions into his world had thus far been a tribulation, he explained, yet he had somehow managed to continue writing despite them. Now he was following his fiction into new territory, an exploration that left him "unable to afford the marvelous distraction of first class friendship."[17]

Since 1965, Salinger had refused to share his writings with the world. His work had since become a completely private occupation. Still, he doggedly justified his isolation as being payment for his calling, his sacrifice for his art. In truth, Salinger had now become comfortable with his seclusion, while others continued to be hurt by the exchange. Salinger no longer bore the brunt of his sacrifice. In this case, it belonged solely to Mitchell, who was required to relinquish a friendship he had cherished for years.

* * *

By the mid-1980s, Salinger had been silent for twenty years. Though he had decided against publishing his own work, he was unable to stop others from writing about him. New books on Salinger appeared on the market constantly—books over which he held no control. Frederick Gwynn had produced *The Fiction of J. D. Salinger* back in 1958. Warren French's *J. D. Salinger* followed in 1961, and 1962 saw William Belcher and James Lee's *J. D. Salinger and the Critics.* The following year a flood of Salinger-related books came out, among them Donald Fiene's annotated Salinger bibliography and works by Marvin Laser and Ihab Hassan. In subsequent years, James E. Miller, James Lundquist, and Harold Bloom added to the list, until by the mid-1980s, Salinger had been the topic of dozens of publications that served to keep his work in the public consciousness while the author himself remained silent.

Each book had been written as a critical analysis of Salinger's work. In order to support their interpretative explanations, they quoted liberally from various Salinger pieces, especially *The Catcher in the Rye.* As they were scholarly works of literary analysis, Salinger was powerless to influence their content. Aside from cursory timelines that included Salinger's birth, war service, and publication dates, no one had yet attempted an in-depth biography of the author. In 1982, W. P. Kinsella released his best seller *Shoeless Joe,* with J. D. Salinger as a main character. Yet though Salinger speaks freely of his life in Kinsella's novel, *Shoeless Joe* remains a work of fiction and Salinger's character was never intended to be a literal depiction of the author.

In May 1986, Salinger received a package from Dorothy Olding. Enclosed was a bound publisher's galley proof of an unauthorized biography entitled *J. D. Salinger: A Writing Life.* The manuscript's author was Ian Hamilton, a well-known British editor, biographer, and poet, who had been commissioned by Random House to crack the enigma of Salinger's public image. Salinger flipped through the galley's pages. They contained details of his private life never before published, generously supplemented by long excerpts from his personal letters.

After the Ransom Center had acquired his letters to Elizabeth Murray in 1968, Salinger had been successful in removing most of his personal correspondences from the archives of Ober Associates and (to a lesser extent) *The New Yorker.* But his letters to Whit Burnett could not be retrieved. The archives of Story Press had been purchased by Princeton University in 1965. Among Princeton's holdings was Salinger's communication with his former mentor. Hamilton had discovered these letters and, along with the Ransom Center collection, used them to fuel his book.

Like innumerable journalists before him, Hamilton had attempted to interview Salinger's friends, neighbors, and business colleagues. He had tracked down the author's former classmates from Ursinus and Valley Forge, requesting their opinions and memories. He had written to Ober Associates but received no reply. He had then sent a form letter to all the Salingers in the New York City phone book on the off chance they might be related to his subject. He had never traveled to Cornish and thought it useless to contact Salinger directly. In fact, he had dealt with Salinger as one might deal with a public figure long dead. "He was," Hamilton had decided, "in any real-life sense, invisible, as good as dead."[18] And though he had composed a text that was far from sympathetic, he nonetheless held out hope that it might meet with Salinger's approval. "I still rather believed," he wrote, "he might like my book."

Salinger had been aware of Hamilton's efforts months before receiving the galley. His sister, Doris, was listed in the New York City phone book and, immediately upon receiving Hamilton's form letter, had reported to her brother. Salinger had lived through such attempts before, and he dealt with Hamilton in the same way he had *Time* and *Newsweek:* He contacted friends such as William Faison and John Keenan, instructing them to ignore Hamilton's requests. He then wrote to Hamilton directly, expressing his severe disapproval of the project and the methods being used to piece together the details of his life. He accused Hamilton and Random House of breaking into his privacy as if he were "suspected of criminal activity" and was especially indignant that Hamilton had badgered members of his family with the phone book scheme. In the end, Salinger admitted that he could not prevent Hamilton and Random House from pursuing the biography if they were determined to do so. But he made it clear that he was more than displeased with the project—that it caused him pain. "I've borne all the exploitation and loss of privacy I can possibly bear in a single lifetime," he said.[19]

Hamilton wrote back to Salinger and apologized for harassing his family. He further attempted to soothe Salinger's feelings by assuring him that the biography would be respectful and that it would end at 1965 with the publication of "Hapworth." Salinger was unmoved. On May 25, 1986, Hamilton and Random House received a letter from Salinger's lawyers demanding that any quotations from unpublished letters be removed from the text. Random House instructed Hamilton to reduce the number of direct quotes taken from Salinger's personal letters. The result was a second galley, produced that September, in which Hamilton paraphrased many of the direct quotations used in the first version. A copy of the new galley was sent to Salinger, who still resented being exhibited through his own words—or what he now considered misleading versions of his words. He called the changes made by Hamilton "cosmetic" and on October 3, 1986, formally applied for an injunction against *J. D. Salinger: A Writing Life.*

Litigation would require Salinger to travel to New York and give a deposition for the court, a distasteful experience that Random House hoped might dissuade him from pursuing the lawsuit. Yet, on October 10, Salinger and his lawyer, Marcia Paul, arrived at the law offices of Satterlee Stephens in Manhattan's Helmsley Building, where they took their places at a table across from Ian Hamilton and the Random House lawyer, Robert Callagy.

At sixty-seven, Salinger appeared in fine health. He was meticulously dressed and conducted himself with what Callagy later described as an aristocratic air. But his surface polish hid the upset that he was actually feeling. Under the table, his hands shook uncontrollably, and his lawyer held them firmly throughout the proceeding.

Callagy questioned the author in a rapid-fire manner designed to break his resolve. As usual Salinger was reluctant to answer, and at times he tried to inject his own sardonic humor into his responses, but Callagy would have none of it. He barraged Salinger with question after question. How many copies of *The Catcher in the Rye* had been sold that year? Over 400,000. What was Salinger's annual income? Approximately $100,000. Had he continued to write after 1965? Yes. Had any of these writings been published in the past twenty years? No.

Callagy then produced one of Salinger's letters that had been used by Hamilton in his manuscript. Did Salinger recognize the letter? To whom was it written? When was it written? Could he explain its contents? What were its most vital lines?* The same series of questions was asked for every letter that Callagy produced, nearly a hundred. The deposition wore on for six long hours. For Salinger, it was a terrible ordeal.

Hamilton won his case in the District Court, but Salinger appealed the decision. On January 29, 1987, the U.S. Court of Appeals for the Second Circuit overturned the District Court verdict and handed down a decision in Salinger's favor. The court ruled that it was permissible for Hamilton to report on the contents and tone of Salinger's personal letters but commanded that he further remove direct quotations and close paraphrasing if he ever wanted to see his book in print. Random House attempted to challenge the decision of the Appellate Court. The case went to the Supreme Court, which refused to hear it, in essence reinforcing the decision in Salinger's favor. To this day, *Salinger v. Random House* is regarded as a building block of U.S. copyright law and is mandatory study for law students nationwide. But in truth, Salinger had done himself damage by pursuing it. In 1987, Hamilton went on to publish a version of his original Salinger biography that was only slightly altered from the second galley. He renamed the manuscript *In Search of J. D. Salinger* and incorporated his legal struggle into the story line. In the end, not only did the biography remain basically the same, but it now had a bitter tone against its subject. Even *The New York Times* observed, "Mr. Salinger would have been better served if he had allowed his letters to be quoted rather than described so vindictively."[20]

The court case had been front-page news. It enhanced the sale of *In Search of J. D. Salinger* many times over. When asked who would be

---

*When Salinger was asked about letters he had written before and during the war, he would refer to himself in the third person, as "the boy," explaining to whom "the boy" had been writing and what "the boy" had hoped to convey. Hamilton's lawyer considered this method of reference odd, as if Salinger saw his youthful self as another person completely.

the subject of his next project, Ian Hamilton replied that he was unsure but "quite certain that it won't be anyone who hasn't been dead for at least 100 years."[21]

. . .

Salinger's threats of litigation and attempts at privacy proved powerless to curtail the public's fascination with his life and seclusion. Far from being forgotten, he had become America's most famous private person. He was now a living legend—not so much for what he had written as for what he had become, or at least the public perception of what he had become. He had been somewhat successful in protecting his characters and the young man of his youth from exploitation, but the myth surrounding his adult life and retirement proved to be something he was unable to control. He became the subject of countless rumors and strange stories, myths that his silence actually reinforced because he never refuted them.

Unwilling to accept that Salinger had actually stopped publishing, many of his fans searched for similarities in other writers, hoping that Salinger was publishing under a pseudonym. In 1976, the *SoHo Weekly News* featured an article that claimed the author Thomas Pynchon was actually Salinger. The belief became widespread. Like Salinger, Pynchon was intensely private and especially averse to being photographed. In 1973, he produced his brilliant novel *Gravity's Rainbow,* a book of many voices, one of which sounded remarkably like the voice of J. D. Salinger to his fans. Even after Pynchon surfaced a number of times, proving that he was not Salinger, and the *SoHo Weekly News* had apologized for the confusion, many Salinger fans found it difficult to let go of the illusion. When in 1991 Little, Brown and Company released a new paperback design for Salinger's books, it displayed a rainbow on an otherwise plain white cover, and the Pynchon-Salinger theory was reignited.

Some Salinger myths grew out of actual events. When Salinger's wartime partner John Keenan retired in 1982, Salinger attended his farewell dinner. Almost immediately it was reported that Salinger had made a speech at the dinner announcing that he had completed a novel about the Second World War. The source of this story is unclear, and though Salinger probably did say a few words in Keenan's honor, it is unlikely that he would have upstaged his friend with a self-serving declaration about his own career.

Perhaps the most gripping legend surrounding Salinger's later life concerns the works he has produced since his retirement. There was no reason to doubt that he had written steadily since 1965 and created an enormous volume of new works. But he always worked in a way that was almost secretive. His writings became his insular private world of prayer. Even when he was publishing, no one ever saw the pieces that he was working on. There was no mention of his current stories or characters at the dinner table, no discussion of evolving plot with family and friends. Salinger's work was his alone, and he carefully separated it from that part of his life shared with others. His own daughter was unaware of her father's occupation until she went to school and her teachers informed her (with some amusement) that he was a famous author. Peggy had had no idea. Even then, she never set eyes upon much of her father's work until she was an adult. Rather than reading stories such as "A Boy in France" and "Hapworth 16, 1924" in her father's studio, she was forced to find them in the Library of Congress. So though it's clear that few people, if anyone, have actually seen Salinger's later works, stories about them abound. Most accounts placed these works in a great vault, sometimes described as large as a room, although at least one story reported that he had them buried somewhere on his property. The most hopeful of these accounts depicted these treasures as being coded by the author depending on their status: incomplete, under review, or ready for publication.

. . .

In 1996, news rippled through the literary world that after a silence of thirty years Salinger had made the stunning decision to release "Hapworth 16, 1924" in hardcover. In bestowing rights to the novella, he was said to have snubbed major publishers by selecting an obscure publishing house in Alexandria, Virginia, named Orchises Press. Critics were sent in a frantic search to find the original "Hapworth," which was now scarce, having long been razorbladed from the few July 1965 copies of *The New Yorker* that still remained. Orchises announced a tentative release of "Hapworth" for January 1997, but January came and went with no release and no comment by Orchises or Salinger. In fact, there had already been three delays in publication by early 1997, leading to a certain anxiety among Salinger fans.

The delays gave critics time to track down copies of the novella, and they were soon falling over one another in print. The result was an explosion of publicity and critical reviews of "Hapworth" that the novella had managed to avoid when it was originally published. Articles appeared in *The Washington Post, New York Newsday,* and *Chicago Tribune,* and *Newsweek, Time,* and *Esquire* magazines. CNN and other major news organizations reported on the upcoming release. Even *Saturday Night Live* poked fun at Salinger in its parody of the news. When asked to comment on why he was releasing "Hapworth" after so many years, *SNL* reported Salinger as replying "Get the hell off my lawn."

Far more serious than late-night comedy parodies, the epitome of critical reviews of "Hapworth" appeared in *The New York Times Book Review* on February 20, 1997, when *Times* critic Michiko Kakutani characterized the novella as "a sour, implausible and, sad to say, completely charmless story." She accused Salinger of pandering to his detractors by reshaping Seymour's character to defy their previous accusations of his unbelievable saintliness. Kakutani bewailed "Hapworth" 's characterization, plot, construction, and underlying motives. She produced a scathing critical assessment, not because she held any contempt for Salinger and his talents but because her critique was so thoughtfully calculated. Kakutani had done her homework and had presented a review as reverent as John Updike had years before—and just as damning. When Kakutani won the Pulitzer Prize the following year for her critical reviews, it seemed to validate her dismal assessment of "Hapworth," and the novella's prospects for hardcover publication were thrown into an uncertain limbo.* When journalists attempted to contact Orchises Press for comment that February, they received only a recorded message that remains the last word on what would have been the breach of Salinger's silence:

---

*The specter of "Hapworth" 's release in hardcover reemerged in 2007, when the publication date was reset for January 1, 2009, Salinger's ninetieth birthday. Readers and critics justifiably met the announcement with skepticism. It did, however, generate renewed interest in Orchises Press, which by 2007 had gained a reputation for the release of poetry anthologies, a cause Salinger may well have championed.

This is Orchises Press. There has been a delay in the publication of "Hapworth 16, 1924." Definite publication information is not available at this time. We apologize for the indefiniteness and the confusion.[22]

The episode scorched Salinger fans, a sensation exacerbated twelve years later when Internet booksellers replayed the feint only to deliver disappointment once again. Roger Lathbury, owner of Orchises Press, blamed himself for the failed outcome. After making extensive arrangements with Salinger to repackage "Hapworth" and actually meeting with the author in the very public restaurant of the National Gallery in Washington, D.C., Lathbury carelessly let word of the project slip to the press. Salinger's reaction was predictable. He recoiled and the book deal collapsed. However, the extent of Lathbury's resulting self-recrimination may have been undeserved. It is possible that Salinger's interest in releasing "Hapworth" was rooted in a desire for control rather than a concern for literature. In 1997, Salinger legally owned complete rights to every story and book he had ever published, with the notable exception of "Hapworth 16, 1924," the rights to which he continued to share with *The New Yorker*. Had he published "Hapworth" in book form as intended, the work would have been considered new and benefited from stricter copyright laws than it did as a 1965 story.

. . .

By the late 1990s, Salinger was nearing eighty but remained healthy, if increasingly deaf and slightly stooped with age. His hair had gone from jet black to snow white years before, but his eyes retained the same dark intensity that had mesmerized the young women of Ursinus College during his youth. The children had long grown and embarked on their own careers. In 1979, after selling the cottage and returning much of the original 90 acres to her former husband, Claire had moved from Cornish to the West Coast, where she constructed a new life.*

---

*Claire admirably reinvented herself. By the mid-1980s, she had obtained a doctorate in psychology and moved to California, where she set up a successful practice. The author of several books, Claire continues to lecture and teach. She has never exploited her marriage to Salinger.

While Salinger could look back on an impressive array of women who had been drawn to him throughout his life, he had seldom chosen wisely. Oona O'Neill had embodied everything in a woman he both despised and craved. His marriage to Sylvia Welter had been impetuous. And in Claire Douglas, Salinger had managed to find the one person whose black moods could rival his own. Salinger dated a number of women after his divorce from Claire, and he continued to make poor decisions. In 1998, one of those choices would rise to haunt him in a very public way.

In April 1972, Salinger read an essay in *The New York Times Magazine* entitled "An Eighteen-Year-Old Looks Back on Life" by a college student, Joyce Maynard. The article intrigued Salinger, as did the demure young writer herself, whose photograph was featured on the magazine's cover. He wrote to Maynard conveying his admiration. After an exchange of letters, Maynard found herself living with Salinger in Cornish, romantically involved with a man thirty-five years her senior and light-years beyond her in experience. Salinger was certainly attracted to Maynard, but he proceeded cautiously. Within a year, their bond had disintegrated and Maynard was back at home with her parents, cast away, she decided, by a man who had used her callously.

In 1998, Maynard published her memoir, *At Home in the World*, recounting her relationship with Salinger twenty-six years before. Her account was damning. It depicted Salinger as being cold and manipulative, of taking advantage of an innocent girl at an age when she was most impressionable. The book received mixed reviews and its motivation was immediately called into question, but readers pored over the text in rapt fascination. On June 23, 1999, Maynard placed her 1972 correspondence with Salinger on auction. Fourteen letters were put up for bid at Sotheby's and sold for approximately $200,000. The auction had a surprising ending. The buyer, the software entrepreneur Peter Norton, stated that he had purchased the letters in order to protect Salinger's privacy. He offered to return them to the author or to destroy them if Salinger preferred.[23] The letters have since remained in Norton's safekeeping. Their contents have never been disclosed.

Salinger remarried in 1992. He had met his new bride some years before, ironically at the Cornish Fair, a venue reminiscent of where his own parents had met in legend. She was a local woman named Colleen

Salinger accompanied by his third wife, Colleen O'Neill, on a Windsor, Vermont, shopping trip in 1998. (New York News Service)

O'Neill, a professional nurse and amateur quilter, good-natured and modest. The couple was soon spotted frequently in town, often arm in arm, grocery shopping and dining at Windsor restaurants. Since the marriage was unannounced, the exact nature of their relationship remained unclear, even to many of Salinger's neighbors. Muddying the waters further, Colleen was born in June 1959, making her forty years Salinger's junior and, perhaps, an unlikely partner.

. . .

In early December 1992, Salinger's house caught fire. The blaze roared out of control despite teams of firefighters dispatched from surrounding towns. The fire trucks were followed by news vans alerted to exactly whose house was burning. Salinger and Colleen were standing on the lawn watching their home go up in flames when reporters appeared and approached them for an interview. The couple rushed off. The incident became nationwide news, and every major newspaper described how the reclusive author had run from reporters to avoid being questioned. The papers also revealed Colleen as being Salinger's wife and emphasized her young age. Because the fire avoided his study and therefore his manuscripts, Salinger's own accounts of that night contain no mention of reporters or concern for his house and its heirlooms.[24] Salinger was upset for the well-being of his dogs, a pair of Italian greyhounds that had bolted into the woods in terror of the fire.[25]

In time, the bastion was rebuilt exactly as it had been. Incursions into Salinger's world like those invited by the 1992 fire became increasingly rare as he grew older and left home less frequently. Reinforcing his refuge, the residents of Cornish remained faithful in their shared protection of his privacy. It became a tradition—indeed, a sport—to purposely misguide strangers asking for directions to Salinger's house. Would-be trespassers were told that no one had ever heard of the author. Many found themselves directed onto meandering dead-end roads deep within the woods or sent to the driveways of the hamlet's least popular citizens. The people of Cornish relished such diversions much as they enjoyed telling Salinger stories among themselves, quips about how the aging writer had angrily demanded his salami sliced at the deli counter (thin to the point of translucence) or about the year he had forgotten the approach of Halloween, leaving him to sheepishly distribute pencils to the children in lieu of candy. Such tales and ruses bound the townspeople together, but there was also a pragmatic side to their devotion. Cornish shared in Salinger's image. It had become synonymous with hermitage, a reputation its inhabitants willingly exploited. It was extolled as an ideal location for the wealthy to escape from the world. Property values soared.

20. Coming Through the Rye

Salinger's early stories were a real technical breakthrough, and
I still hope he will emerge safe on the other side.
—John Updike, 1966[1]

On New Year's Day 2010, J. D. Salinger turned ninety-one years old.
A year earlier, on his ninetieth birthday, countless periodicals and websites had marked the occasion with an enthusiasm normally reserved
for Hollywood celebrities. Yet a close look at many of the commemo-
rations revealed them to be not genuine tributes at all but sullen re-
bukes to an author who had dared to defy the norm. Many used the
occasion to chastise him for refusing to publish, while a number went
on to rereview "Hapworth," as if it were 1965. Still, while the tone of
resentment varied among the articles, nearly all had an intensity that
confirmed the high level of emotion that Salinger's legacy continued
to ignite.

Perhaps the most bizarre—if not cruelly ironic—aspect of many of
the pieces was their depiction of the author frozen in time at the age of
thirty-two, displaying his image from the original back cover of *The*

Catcher in the Rye. In reality, Salinger was feeling the consequences of old age. Although his mind remained sharp, his thin frame had grown so fragile that he often used a cane, and the loss of hearing he had suffered during the war had degenerated into near-complete deafness. Yet Salinger at ninety had good reason to trust that his remaining years would be peaceful and free from conflict. In fact, he had taken steps to ensure that they would. Seeking to eliminate a dispute over his estate, Salinger had spent much of 2008 putting his legal and financial affairs in order. On July 24, he formally established the J. D. Salinger Literary Trust to prevent any single individual from exercising absolute control over his publications and to ensure the proper disbursement of his works' financial proceeds on his death. Salinger then renewed his copyright on a number of stories and on October 15 deposited complete rights to all of his publications into the care of the trust, thirty-nine titles in all.[2]

. . .

Salinger's expectations of tranquillity were dashed on May 14, 2009, when he was informed of an upcoming book that claimed to be a sequel to *The Catcher in the Rye*.[3] Word of the book had appeared in the British newspaper *The Guardian* and quickly rippled over the Internet and into the American news. The announcement stirred long-restrained hopes that Salinger had decided to end his seclusion by delivering a continuation of his classic novel. A search for further details led readers to the website of the sequel's publisher, the Swedish-based Nicotext, and its offshoot, Windupbird Publishing. The content there offered more questions than answers. The publication was titled *60 Years Later: Coming Through the Rye*. Although available for purchase in Britain, it was not scheduled for release in America until September. A brief description of the book's plot was vaguely familiar. *60 Years Later* featured the travels of a seventy-six-year-old character named Mr. C, who roves the streets of Manhattan after having escaped his retirement home, much the same way Holden Caulfield had wandered the streets of New York after fleeing his prep school decades before. If potential readers somehow missed the point, *60 Years Later* hailed itself as "a marvellous sequel to one of our most beloved classics."

Information on the author was even less straightforward. Identified only by the pseudonym John David California, his biography consisted of his former employment as gravedigger and Ironman triathlete and described his first encounter with Salinger's novel "in an abandoned cabin in rural Cambodia." If any hope of Salinger's involvement remained after reading California's biography, it was extinguished by a review of the publisher's Internet catalog, an array of joke books, sex dictionaries, and flip-book porn.

When, after seeing the website, the press began to speculate that the entire matter might be a hoax, the author of *60 Years Later* was compelled to reveal his true identity. John David California was actually the Swedish writer Fredrik Colting, the founder and owner of Nicotext and Windupbird Publishing. In an appeal to *The Sunday Telegraph,* Colting asked to be taken seriously. "This is no spoof," he intoned. "We are not concerned about any legal issues. We think *60 Years Later* is a very original story that complements *Catcher in the Rye.*"4

Salinger was widely considered to be gleefully litigious—especially when it came to Holden Caulfield and *The Catcher in the Rye*—and Colting's reference to legal issues seemed to reinforce the suspicion already implied by the press that he was attempting to lure Salinger into a legal battle in the hope of garnering publicity for his book. At the same time, he appeared genuinely taken aback by events, alternately perplexed and stunned by the magnitude of reaction his book was generating. After producing a number of low-profile publications in Sweden, each audacious and irreverent, he seemed to have written the sequel in complete ignorance of the emotional attachment of so many to *The Catcher in the Rye.* "I did not set out to create a bang, to upset anyone or to simply hitch a ride on the Salinger express," he protested. "All I wanted was to write a good book with some newness about it."5

The concept of "newness" was precisely at issue. When Phyllis Westberg, Salinger's longtime agent at Ober Associates, obtained a copy of Colting's book, she promised to examine it on Salinger's behalf for any creative merits that might safely place it beyond his copyright. But the outcome was inevitable.* Comparing the sequel to

---

*Dorothy Olding remained Salinger's agent until 1990, when a stroke forced her into retirement. She was then succeeded at Ober Associates by Phyllis Westberg, who acquired Salinger as a client. Salinger's affection for Olding was unshakable throughout the fifty-seven years of their friendship. She died in 1997.

Salinger's original, Westberg found many scenes and events conspicuously similar, with Holden's vernacular and psyche unchanged from 1951. The characters, too, were the same, although they had become pathetic with age (Holden can no longer control his bladder, and Phoebe has descended into a life of drug addiction). There was one major difference between *60 Years Later* and *The Catcher in the Rye*, and it may have been the difference that Westberg considered most injurious. Delving deeper into the book, she encountered the character of Salinger. In an arc now reminiscent of Mary Shelley, Holden travels to Cornish to confront his creator, who has revived his literary "monster" in order to kill him. By the end of May, Westberg had completed her assessment and consulted with Salinger. Responding to an inquiry by *The Telegraph*, their opinion was unsurprisingly steadfast. "The matter has been turned over to a lawyer," she reported.

. . .

On June 1, 2009, suit was filed in the Southern District of New York on behalf of J. D. Salinger and the J. D. Salinger Literary Trust. Plaintiffs sought a preliminary injunction against publication of *60 Years Later: Coming Through the Rye*. Salinger viewed the sequel as a clear violation of his copyright and was suing to prevent its publication and distribution in the United States. He did not appear in connection with the filing of the complaint, nor would he be present thereafter during the course of the proceedings. He was represented instead by Westberg and by his attorney, Marcia Paul, the same lawyer who had successfully defended his interests during the Ian Hamilton case twenty-two years before.

Official hearings began on Monday, June 8, and the case was assigned to Judge Deborah Batts, a fifteen-year veteran of the Federal Court. From the start, Salinger's team charged that *60 Years Later* was "a derivative work," that it consisted largely of material stolen from *The Catcher in the Rye* and should be banned as an infringement on Salinger's copyright. They summarized their point of view with a bold statement that exposed the heart of the controversy: "The right to create a sequel to *The Catcher in the Rye* or to use the character of Holden Caulfield in any other work belongs to Salinger and Salinger alone, and he has decidedly chosen not to exercise that right."[6]

With the attorney Edward Rosenthal at its head, Colting's team was no longer characterizing *60 Years Later* as a sequel. Instead, they took the position that the book was a parody, entitled to protection under the First Amendment and defensible, notwithstanding Salinger's copyright interests, under the doctrine of fair use. They attacked Salinger's claim that he owned the character of Holden Caulfield, recognizing it to be "the most fundamental issue raised."[7] "Were courts to grant the sort of protection to literary characters that plaintiff seeks for Holden Caulfield," they argued, "fiction would be frozen in time."[8]

Judge Batts was charged with considering other issues aside from Holden Caulfield: foremost, whether *60 Years Later* was "transformative" enough to avoid infringement of Salinger's copyright. Colting's lawyers held fast that the book extended enough of Salinger's original to make it a singular work, but Salinger's lawyers called it "a rip-off pure and simple." They produced a long list of marked similarities between the two books and went on to insist that Holden's voice and vernacular were also protected.

However, if Colting's side could convince the judge that his book was indeed a parody that offered sufficient and specific commentary on *The Catcher in the Rye,* Judge Batts would be inclined to afford it the latitude to borrow extensively from Salinger's original. Colting's lawyers pointed to the segments of his book where Holden confronts Salinger, holding them up as a commentary on the relationship between an author and his character. The argument had become their primary defense, but whether they had satisfied the court with enough commentary to justify the amount of material taken from *Catcher* remained unclear.

If Colting were to prevail anywhere, it should have been in regard to the judge's final consideration: the effect *60 Years Later* might have upon Salinger's future ability to market his work. Salinger's team contended that the distribution of *60 Years Later* would dampen public appetite for a genuine *Catcher* sequel if Salinger ever chose to produce one, a reasonable point if it had involved any other writer. However, few expected a new book from Salinger at ninety, and the idea of Colting's effort dissuading readers from purchasing *The Catcher in the Rye* simply made no sense.

To the media the legal arguments were a sleepy sideshow. Their interest remained fixed on Salinger himself, although the author had not been seen or heard from personally. Phyllis Westberg had submitted an affidavit clearly designed to dissuade the court from demanding Salinger's presence. In an effort to convince the judge to accept her as stand-in for the author, Westberg had openly divulged that Salinger was now totally deaf, dependent upon others, and currently recovering in a rehabilitation center after breaking his hip.[9] The press leapt upon the news, shunting aside bloodless discussions on "derivative works" in favor of headlines proclaiming the ancient author to be frail and deaf but tenaciously fighting on.

. . .

It is the ambiguity of the ending of *The Catcher in the Rye* that often draws readers back to it. As the novel ends, Holden's position is intentionally unclear because Salinger has deliberately left it to readers to insert their own selves, their own doubts, aspirations, and dissatisfactions, in order to complete his journey.

While the press concentrated on Salinger's infirmities, readers' input was revealing a very different concern. With increasing frequency, editorials and commentaries began to appear in newspapers and on the Internet that were written by people recalling the first time they had read *The Catcher in the Rye* and revealing how much Holden Caulfield had meant to them in their youth. Each memory involved Holden, yet no two Holdens were the same. There were many versions of Holden, each vivid and deeply personal, his image shifting for each individual. One man wrote that as an adolescent he could relate only to Holden and that the relationship had sustained him through a difficult time. Another recalled his admiration for Holden's rebellion and how he had carried Salinger's novel throughout college. There were also delicate memories, such as the woman who shyly admitted that Holden Caulfield had been her first crush and the young girl experiencing similar feelings even as she wrote. Within these commentaries the question arose of who actually owned Holden Caulfield and what would become of him after the trial. Few had much respect for Fredrik Colting, but a number of reactions exposed a rising disenchantment with Salinger for claiming to possess what readers plainly considered to be a part of themselves, a portion of their own self-image.

. . .

On July 1, Judge Deborah Batts delivered her decision, issuing an injunction against the U.S. release of what the court determined to be an unauthorized sequel to *The Catcher in the Rye*. She had found for Salinger on every point of argument, ruling that the character of Holden Caulfield was indeed protected by his copyright and determining Colting's book to be "a derivative work" rather than parody. She further found *60 Years Later* to be far less "transformative" than the defense had claimed, noting that the more one borrows from the original, the less innovative the result.[10]

Although her judgment was couched in the law, not all of Judge Batts's contentions were exclusively legal. She also insisted upon preserving the integrity of Salinger's novel as he had designed it and, in doing so, attempted to defend the rights of readers. "An author's artistic vision," the court asserted, "includes leaving certain portions or aspects of his character's story to the varied imaginations of his readers."[11]

At the core of the case had been the question of whether Holden Caulfield, as a character of fiction represented only through words, was legally included in Salinger's copyright of *The Catcher in the Rye*. Unlike famous images, artwork, logos, and movie characters, Holden had no physical representation. Still, he had managed to become an iconic figure, if only through the force of Salinger's text. In fact, the court had determined that Holden was as recognizable, and therefore copyrightable, as any famous image or work of art. "Holden Caulfield is quite delineated by word," the court ruled. "It is a portrait by words."[12]

During the course of the trial, Colting had become increasingly defiant and was now incredulous over Judge Batts's verdict. "If nobody gets angry you haven't done it right," he reasoned. "By all means, *Catcher* was and is a great piece of work, but so was the T-Ford. I think the ability to playfully use the old sheet of metal and from it position something that corresponds with a new time, now that's creativity."[13]

A visit to Colting's website following the trial showed the sequel claim removed, replaced instead by a white-on-red notice on the cover of *60 Years Later: Coming Through the Rye:* "BANNED IN THE USA!"

. . .

In *The Catcher in the Rye,* Holden's troubled mind is soothed by memories of the Natural History Museum, of the reassuring sameness of its diorama. He thinks longingly of the glass-encased stuffed exhibits, safely frozen in their perfection and never growing old. He remembers figures of Indians unmoving in the act of building a fire, of Eskimos eternally fishing, of motionless birds suspended in flight. "Everything always stayed right where it was," he fondly recalls. "Nobody'd be different. The only thing that would be different would be you."[14]

Since 1951, Salinger had denied many appeals to adapt Holden's character to other media. Among others, he had refused requests by Elia Kazan, Billy Wilder, and Steven Spielberg to render Holden onto stage and screen. In 2003, he threatened the BBC with litigation over a planned television dramatization of *The Catcher in the Rye.* And he had consistently fought attempts to portray Holden's image on book covers.

Salinger may have presented Holden to readers as longing to preserve a suspended world of stuffed diorama, but it had now become Salinger himself who gazed through the glass, looking on his own creation in jealous awe, desperate to preserve him unchanged. "There is no more to Holden Caulfield," Salinger told Betty Eppes in 1980. "Holden Caulfield is only a frozen moment in time."[15]

. . .

Colting promptly filed for appeal, and the case was assigned to the Second Circuit Court of Appeals. On July 23, Rosenthal submitted a brief to the court on Colting's behalf more precise than his arguments to the lower court. Although he remained adamant that *60 Years Later* had been crafted as a parody that did not infringe upon Salinger's copyright, this new appeal contained an underlying willingness to compensate Salinger for what *60 Years Later* had borrowed from *Catcher.* Home in Sweden, Colting remained hopeful but was growing increasingly resigned. "I hope we will win," he reflected. "Not only for my book, the work is done and I will not cry for what happens to it after, but for the sake of all other books the vultures will try to tear apart. I piss on them."[16]

Colting's sentiments were elevated on Friday, August 7, when the appellate court was presented with an amicus brief, a legal pleading in support of his position demanding that the decision in Salinger's favor be overturned. The document was filed by four of the nation's most powerful media giants: the New York Times Company, the Associated Press, the Gannett Company, and the Tribune Company. The brief was acute and unequivocal. It called the June 1 decision "banning" Colting's book to be in clear violation of the First Amendment, "where," the document reasoned, "the only harm appears to be to the pride of a reclusive author in not having his desires fulfilled."[17]

Salinger's attorney submitted a counterargument on August 13 rebutting Colting's appeal and countering the amicus brief. In the filing, Marcia Paul expounded the lower court's opinion that the enjoined *Catcher* sequel was in violation of Salinger's copyright. She then charged both Colting and the media moguls of attempting to set precedent by "proposing sweeping changes in the law and entirely new standards for granting a preliminary injunction."[18] Paul's argument was well structured and certainly valiant, but it could not undo the damage done by the media giants when they arrayed themselves against her client.

For Salinger and his legal team, the amicus brief was chilling. It signaled a shift in the media's portrayal of their case. The press now accused the author of attempting to ban a book while reminding readers that *The Catcher in the Rye* had itself suffered under unfair restrictions for decades—in essence calling Salinger a phony. For Salinger personally the brief contained a veiled threat far more menacing. It had been authored by media corporations that controlled hundreds of newspapers, magazines, and radio and television stations throughout the nation, as well as innumerable websites. Their ability to influence public opinion was enormous. If Salinger prevailed in Appellate Court, they might destroy his legacy in retribution.

. . .

The Appellate Court heard the case on September 3 without rendering judgment. Salinger's ninety-first birthday arrived with no indication of a decision forthcoming. Whatever the outcome, it would have far-reaching implications for American copyright law, but for Salinger, the conclusion was already apparent. Regardless of the legal verdict, he had already lost his grip on Holden Caulfield and was now struggling to retain control over his own legacy. The media's reaction to events was predictable. Confident of no response from the author, they grew weary of Salinger's arguments and were soon delivering a medley of complaints, demanding that he cease litigation and accusing him of sacrificing the First Amendment in order to protect his personal interests.

Salinger might have employed the same lawyer as when he challenged Ian Hamilton and found his case decided within the same federal courts, but the world had changed since 1987—far more than he seemed to have realized. The sequel's publication in Europe placed it beyond the reach of U.S. copyright law and therefore available for sale worldwide through the Internet. Regardless of legal conclusions, *60 Years Later* would be accessible to anyone in any nation with a mailing address and access to a computer, a situation that was not lost on the Appellate Court.

In truth, then, Salinger had lost control of Holden—not through trials or theft or carelessness but through technology—though in a deeper sense, more vital than courtroom proceedings or sterile laws, he had never truly possessed Holden Caulfield at all. His character was not a commodity to be bartered. Holden had long ago meshed with the lives of readers. He belonged to the rebel who admired him, the outcast who drew strength from him, the young girl enamored of him. And it was their affection for his character that provoked resentment against any author who refused to understand that Holden was their property, uniquely re-created each time a reader opened a copy of *The Catcher in the Rye*.

. . .

The classic film *Field of Dreams* has a famous scene in which the actor James Earl Jones enters an overgrown cornfield that holds spirits of the dead. Understanding that he is about to emerge into another realm, Jones's character is unafraid. He is instead smiling with childlike expectation. The original book version of the scene is contained in the 1982 novel *Shoeless Joe* by the Canadian author W. P. Kinsella. In Kinsella's novel, Jones's character is actually Salinger, his name changed to Terence Mann in the film. The final chapter of *Shoeless Joe* is entitled "The Rapture of J. D. Salinger," and it is Salinger who enters the cornfield to commune with the spirits of the past and of his characters.

After Salinger returned to the familiar comforts of wife and home following hip surgery in spring 2009, his health improved markedly. He and Colleen had, for years, enjoyed near-weekly trips into nearby Hartland, Vermont, to attend communal roast beef dinners held at the congregational church. When Salinger resumed the weekly ritual, continuing to make the trek even into the cold months of winter, he appeared to have mended completely. When his ninety-first birthday arrived on New Year's Day, his family was convinced that he would be with them for years to come. But as January wore on, his health began to fail. He appeared to be in no pain, but his body was slowly shutting down. In the late hours of Wednesday, January 27, 2010, J. D. Salinger died.

On January 28, Salinger's agent announced the news. Presenting a statement provided by Salinger's son, Matthew, on behalf of the family, Westberg delivered an extraordinary declaration that was in essence Salinger's final words to the world:

> Salinger had remarked that he was in this world but not of it. His body is gone but the family hopes that he is still with those he loves, whether they are religious or historical figures, personal friends or fictional characters.

That Salinger had been in the world but was no longer part of it had been obvious for decades. The reference was a biblical one and might have seemed pompous pronounced by any other writer; but for Salinger the identification was natural. It was plainly truth, and no one questioned that it had been uttered without ego. The statement provided by Salinger's family was an affirmation. In expressing their belief that he had united with those that he loved, they echoed religious convictions that Salinger had long conveyed through his writings. By equating the characters of his fiction with the souls of past friends, of religious and historical figures he had longed to know, the lines conjured up rich images worthy of Salinger himself.

In the wake of Salinger's passing, the world paused in a rare manner. Despite his age and self-imposed exile, society appeared stunned by the loss. The media tendered an eruption of tributes and recognitions perhaps not extended to an author since the death of Ernest Hemingway fifty years before. Even John Updike, whose death had occurred exactly a year before (to the day), had been granted but a distracted farewell. As with most writers, the media considered Updike's death to be a literary event, but Salinger had become part of American culture, a near-mystical figure through the allure of his tenacious reclusion, while still managing to touch the lives of everyday people through the character of Holden Caulfield and *The Catcher in the Rye*.

J. D. Salinger was unique, and many found his noble opposition comforting. Others were soothed by the simple knowledge that though most remnants of their youth had long vanished, J. D. Salinger remained. With his death, there was an immediate awareness that the world might never again see his singular mix of qualities, that a kind of terrible extinction had occurred.

The Internet exploded with the news. Within a few hours of the announcement, thousands of blogs and websites had posted tributes. Numerous authors and publishers, from Stephen King and Joyce Carol Oates to the staff of *The New Yorker* and Little, Brown, tendered testimonials of Salinger's influence. Lillian Ross, the longtime partner of William Shawn and the mother of Salinger's godson, broke years of silence to recount his virtues as a personal friend. She also shared a series of photographs taken of Salinger with her son, Erik, as a toddler— author and child playing and laughing together in magical scenes evocative of so many Salinger stories.

Television networks ran long presentations chronicling the author's life as best they could with little information, concentrating on the enduring impact of *The Catcher in the Rye*. Public television presented arrays of scholars to contemplate the longevity of Salinger's public appeal and to analyze his legacy. The subject appeared to cross borders. Salinger was as popular a topic on tabloid news programs as on scholarly broadcasts.

Salinger's death was front-page news in every American newspaper and most throughout the world. *The New York Times* delivered a lengthy tribute despite having petitioned against him in court the year before. For the first time in recent memory, the newspaper featured a black-and-white photo on its cover, a 1961 snapshot of Salinger and

William Maxwell few had ever seen. In addition to the cover article announcing the author's passing, the *Times*'s two-page spread evoked genuine grief for the loss of a favorite son. The *Times* was not alone. Its expansive coverage of what was now clearly perceived as a national loss was typical of newspapers throughout America and the world.

Unfortunately, the sudden burst of Salinger mania also lent itself to repeats of bizarre tales and misinformation. It was again reported that Salinger's mother had been Irish- or even Scotch-born, that he had been habitually infatuated with teenage girls and existed on a diet of frozen peas. Almost immediately upon Salinger's death, photographs and film of the author began to emerge, images concealed while he was alive. His short stories too suddenly appeared outside book covers, in arrangements he would never have allowed. *Esquire* reprinted "This Sandwich Has No Mayonnaise" and "Heart of a Broken Story," while *The New Yorker* provided its Internet subscribers with downloads of twelve Salinger stories it had published as "a memorial collection."

The inevitable subject that piqued the highest level of interest was the mystery surrounding the volumes of works that Salinger had reportedly produced since 1965. The secret literary contents of his safe became a constant source of speculation fueled by media allegations that he had completed at least fifteen full-length novels. Even Stephen King commented that the world might finally learn the truth of whether Salinger had been amassing great masterpieces over the years. The literary world held its breath in anticipation.

Meanwhile, from Cornish, there was only silence. Four days had passed since Salinger's death, and though memorials continued to appear in the press, nothing had been heard from the family since Westberg's initial announcement. At the time she had requested that the same level of respect and privacy afforded to Salinger now be granted to his family. Consequently, there had been no word regarding the time, place or manner of Salinger's burial or cremation, the contents of his will, or the marvels of his safe.

On February 1, America honored the author when Salinger's portrait was placed by the Smithsonian Institution on public display in the National Portrait Gallery. Such an honor would have been unthinkable in Salinger's lifetime but the admiration restrained for half of a century had now impatiently burst free.

The outpouring of grief was ironic. It is likely that Salinger would have turned his back on the honors showered on his memory, as he had shunned attention when alive. Yet his death had at least one positive effect upon the population that he doubtless would have genuinely enjoyed. In his honor, people began to read his books with newfound appreciation and in unparalleled numbers. Within two days of Salinger's passing, *The Catcher in the Rye* had become the number five best-selling book in the nation—a notch below the highest position it had attained in 1951. Amazon.com, the largest seller of books in the world, depleted its stock not only of *The Catcher in the Rye* but also of *Nine Stories, Franny and Zooey,* and *Raise High and Seymour.* It then admitted that the books were presently unobtainable. America had sold out of Salinger.

As Salinger was being laid to rest in whatever manner his family saw fit, a remarkable thing began to happen, a series of small, singular events that collectively eclipsed all other efforts to honor his memory. Slowly at first but with increasing frequency, the Internet began to populate with short impromptu home videos posted by ordinary individuals. First there was one, a single brave soul not caring how he looked through the eyes of the camera, unconcerned whether his profile was flattering or his hair disheveled. Within a day there were hundreds of such films. In two days, the number reached a thousand. All were average people—mostly young—unself-consciously aiming their faces into the camera and beginning to speak regardless of whether they would be witnessed by millions or by absolutely no one. They spoke of Salinger. They spoke of what he had meant to them, of what he had given them. They felt an overwhelming need to tell the world that his writings had touched their lives and they would miss him.

Then, as if by a conspiracy of mass intuition, the same spontaneous reaction occurred on nearly every video. Each person in front of the camera picked up a book and began to read aloud. They read from *Franny and Zooey.* They read from "Seymour—an Introduction." They read from *Nine Stories.* But above all, they read from *The Catcher in the Rye.* The result was dazzling: hundreds of readers simultaneously reading the words of Holden Caulfield, their voices often cracking, sometimes rising enthralled, but always heartfelt, and each vaguely aware that he or she was not alone.

. . .

If we choose to examine—indeed to judge—the life of J. D. Salinger, we must first accept the obligation to view his life in all its complexities: to recognize the valiant soldier within him as well as the failed husband, the creative soul that gave way to the self-protective recluse.

There is something within the human character that compels us to cast down the idols we ourselves have elevated. We insist upon exalting those we admire beyond the reality of their virtues and then, as if resentful of the heights we have forced upon them, feel it necessary to cut them down. It may be within our character to smash our own idols, but that same character is in constant longing for something to look up to.

For a time at least, Salinger may have considered himself an American prophet, a voice crying in the urban wilderness. Today he is remembered for the briefness of his witness, still reprimanded for his refusal to continue on, as if he owed more to the world than he had already given. Somehow, in a way nearly as mystical as his stories' gentle epiphanies, the passage of time may reveal that J. D. Salinger fulfilled his duty as author and perhaps even his calling as prophet long ago. The remaining obligation lies with us. In this way, Salinger's story continues on, passed from author to reader for completion. By examining the life of J. D. Salinger, with all its sadness and imperfections, together with the messages delivered through his writings, we are charged with the reevaluation of our own lives, an assessment of our own connections, and the weighing of our own integrity.

Acknowledgments

I would like to gratefully acknowledge the following institutions and individuals for their kind cooperation and for the invaluable support they have provided:

Princeton University, Department of Rare Books and Special Collections, Firestone Library:
    Archives of *Story* Magazine and Story Press
    Archives of Harold Ober Associates
    Ian Hamilton Working Papers
    Ernest Hemingway Collection

The New York Public Library, Manuscripts and Archives Division:
    Archives of *The New Yorker*
    Charles Hanson Towne Papers, 1891–1948

Harry Ransom Humanities Research Center, the University of Texas at Austin:
    J. D. Salinger Collection

The Morgan Library & Museum:
    J. D. Salinger–E. Michael Mitchell Collection

Bryn Mawr College Library Special Collections:
    Katharine Sergeant White Papers

The New York Times

San Diego Historical Society

My family
Michael Anello
Joseph Alfandre and family
Brin Friesen
W. P. Kinsella
Grzegorz Musial
Declan Kiely
Jere Call

Andy Hollis

Special thanks are extended to my editors at Random House, Susanna Porter and Benjamin Steinberg. Additional gratitude is owed to Mark Hodkinson, my long-suffering editor in the United Kingdom, who set this book in motion.

Notes

Chapter 1: Sonny

1. J. D. Salinger, *Raise High the Roof Beam, Carpenters and Seymour—an Introduction* (Boston: Little, Brown and Company, 1991), 144.

2. Ibid., 177.

3. Birth certificate of Solomon Salinger, Board of Health of the City of Cleveland, March 16, 1887. This document gives Fannie's age as twenty-two and Simon's as twenty-six. The birthplace of both parents is named as being "Polania, Russia," as Lithuania was then part of the Russian Empire. The document also provides the Salingers' address of 72 Hill Street, Cleveland, an address that no longer exists.

4. Paul Alexander, *Salinger: A Biography* (Los Angeles: Renaissance Books, 1999), 31.

5. Ibid.

6. Social Security Death Index Number 107-38-2023; Miriam Jillich Salinger. Social Security and census records give Salinger's mother's birth year as 1891, but Miriam herself often insisted that she had been born in 1882.

7. Twelfth Census of the United States, 1900.

8. Thirteenth Census of the United States, 1910.

9. Fourteenth Census of the United States, 1920.

10. Sidney Salinger to the author, December 26, 2005.

11. Fourteenth Census of the United States, 1920.

12. Selective Service Registration, Solomon Salinger, October 5, 1917. The registration was for the First World War and contained a physical description of him at age thirty.

13. *1930 Camp Wigwam Annual*, 65.

14. 1932–1933 and 1933–1934 report cards for Jerome Salinger, the McBurney School, copies in Ian Hamilton Working Papers.

15. Salinger to Jeffrey Dix, July 1993.

16. Richard Gonder to Ian Hamilton, March 1985.

17. J. D. Salinger, "Class Prophecy," *Crossed Sabres,* 1936 Valley Forge Military Academy yearbook.

18. J. D. Salinger, "A Girl I Knew," *Good Housekeeping,* February 1948, 37.

19. J. D. Salinger, "Contributors," *Story,* November–December 1944, 1.

20. William Maxwell, "J. D. Salinger," *Book-of-the-Month Club News,* July 1951.

21. Francis Glassmoyer to Ian Hamilton, February 12, 1985.

22. J. D. Salinger, "Musings of a Social Soph: The Skipped Diploma," *The Ursinus Weekly,* Monday, October 10, 1938, 2.

Chapter 2: Ambition

1. Whit Burnett to Salinger, November 7, 1959.

2. J. D. Salinger, "Early Fall in Central Park," 1939, Charles Hanson Towne Papers (1891–1948), New York Public Library, Manuscripts and Archives Division.

3. J. D. Salinger, "A Salute to Whit Burnett," *Fiction Writer's Handbook,* Hallie and Whit Burnett (New York: Harper and Row, 1975).

4. Salinger to Whit Burnett, November 21, 1939.

5. Burnett, *Fiction Writer's Handbook.*

6. Salinger to Whit Burnett, April 17, 1940.

7. Salinger to Whit Burnett, November 21, 1939.

8. Salinger to Whit Burnett, January 28, 1940.

9. Ibid.

10. Whit Burnett to Salinger, February 28, 1940.

11. Whit Burnett to Salinger, April 18, 1940.

12. Salinger to Whit Burnett, April 19, 1940.

13. Salinger to Whit Burnett, May 16, 1940.

14. Salinger to Whit Burnett, September 4, 1940.

15. Salinger to Whit Burnett, September 6, 1940.

16. Salinger to Whit Burnett, September 4, 1940.

17. Salinger to Whit Burnett, September 6, 1940.

18. Passenger list (staff), SS *Kungsholm,* March 6, 1941.

19. Salinger to Colonel Milton G. Baker, Supt. VFMA, December 12, 1941.

20. J. D. Salinger, "The Ocean Full of Bowling Balls," unpublished, 1944, 1.

21. Salinger to Whit Burnett, June 1943.

22. Gloria Murray to Ian Hamilton, 1984.

23. Jane Scovell, *Oona Living in the Shadows: A Biography of Oona O'Neill Chaplin* (New York: Warner, 1998), 87.

24. Ian Hamilton, *J. D. Salinger: A Writing Life* (unpublished October galley) (New York: Random House, 1986), 54.

25. Memo from Kurt M. Semon (editor at *Story*) to Harold Ober, August 11, 1941.

26. J. D. Salinger, "The Heart of a Broken Story," *Esquire,* September 1941, 32.

27. Salinger to Whit Burnett, January 22, 1942.

28. Ibid.

29. Ben Yagoda, *About Town: The New Yorker and the World It Made* (Cambridge, Mass.: Da Capo Press, 2001), 233.

30. John Mosher to Harold Ober, February 14, 1941.

31. Salinger to Elizabeth Murray, October 31, 1941.

32. Ibid.

33. Ibid.

34. Salinger to Herb Kauffman, July 1943.

35. J. D. Salinger, "Slight Rebellion off Madison," *The New Yorker,* December 1946, 76–79.

Chapter 3: Indecision

1. Salinger to Whit Burnett, January 11, 1942.

2. Ibid.

3. Salinger to Whit Burnett, January 2, 1942.

4. William Maxwell to Harold Ober, February 26, 1942.

5. Salinger to Whit Burnett, January 2, 1942.

6. William Maxwell to Harold Ober, ND (but after February 1942).

7. Salinger to Colonel Milton Baker, December 12, 1941.

8. U.S. National Archives and Records Administration, Enlistment Records, Jerome David Salinger, 32325200.

9. J. D. Salinger, "The Last and Best of the Peter Pans," unpublished, 1942.

10. U.S. National Archives and Records Administration, Enlistment Records, Jerome David Salinger, 32325200.

11. Salinger to Whit Burnett, June 8, 1942.

12. Colonel Milton Baker to Colonel Collins, June 5, 1942.

13. Whit Burnett to Colonel Collins, July 1, 1942.

14. Salinger to Randy Troup, December 4, 1969. Tara was the name of the plantation in *Gone with the Wind*.

15. Salinger to Whit Burnett, September 3, 1942.

16. Whit Burnett to Dorothy Olding, November 25, 1942.

17. Salinger to Whit Burnett, ND (no date) but after September 1942.

18. Truman Capote, "La Côte Basque," *Unanswered Prayers* (London: Plume, 1987). The chapter was first published in the November 1975 issue of *Esquire*.

19. Salinger to Whit Burnett, ND (but March 1943).

20. Salinger to Elizabeth Murray, December 27, 1942.

21. Salinger to Whit Burnett, ND (but after Christmas 1942 or early 1943).

22. Ibid.

23. J. D. Salinger, "The Varioni Brothers," *The Saturday Evening Post,* July 17, 1943, 12–13, 76–77.

24. Salinger to Whit Burnett, ND (but soon after Christmas 1942).

25. Salinger to Whit Burnett, ND (but March 1943).

26. Salinger to Elizabeth Murray, October 31, 1941.

27. Salinger to Elizabeth Murray, January 11, 1943.

28. Salinger to Whit Burnett, ND (but July 1943).

29. J. D. Salinger, "Soft-Boiled Sergeant," *The Saturday Evening Post,* April 15, 1944, 18, 32, 82–85.

30. J. D. Salinger, *Raise High the Roof Beam, Carpenters and Seymour—an Introduction* (Boston: Little, Brown and Company, 1991), 163.

31. Salinger to Elizabeth Murray, October 31, 1941.

32. Salinger to Whit Burnett, ND (but June 1943).

33. Ibid.

34. J. D. Salinger, "Two Lonely Men," unpublished, 1944.

35. J. D. Salinger, "Both Parties Concerned," *The Saturday Evening Post,* February 26, 1944, 14, 47–48.

36. Salinger to Whit Burnett, July 1, 1943.

37. Salinger to Whit Burnett, ND (but June 1943).

38. Salinger to Herb Kauffman, June 7, 1943.

39. Salinger to Elizabeth Murray, June 1943.

40. J. D. Salinger, "Elaine," *Story,* March–April 1945, 38–47.

41. Salinger to Herb Kauffman, ND (but late summer 1943).

42. Ibid.

43. Captain James H. Gardner to Whit Burnett, July 15, 1943.

44. Salinger to Whit Burnett, ND (but the week of October 3, 1943).

45. Ibid.

46. J. D. Salinger, "Last Day of the Last Furlough," *The Saturday Evening Post,* July 15, 1944, 26–27, 61–62, 64.

47. Ibid.

Chapter 4: Displacement

1. Salinger to Whit Burnett, October 3, 1943.

2. Story Press interoffice memo, circa late 1943 or early 1944.

3. Whit Burnett to Harold Ober, December 9, 1943.

4. Whit Burnett to Harold Ober, February 3, 1944.

5. Salinger to Whit Burnett, January 14, 1944.

6. Salinger to Wolcott Gibbs, January 20, 1944.

7. Salinger to Herb Kauffman, ND (but late summer 1943).

8. William Maxwell to Dorothy Olding, February 4, 1944.

9. Margaret Salinger, *Dream Catcher* (New York: Washington Square Press, 2000), 50, 53.

10. J. D. Salinger, "For Esmé—with Love and Squalor," *The New Yorker,* April 8, 1950, 28–36.

11. Salinger to Whit Burnett, March 13, 1944.

12. Salinger to Whit Burnett, March 19, 1944.

13. Salinger to Whit Burnett, May 2, 1944. In referring to this story, Salinger shifted between two titles, "The Children's Echelon" and "Total War Diary," and because the story was never published, it is known by both names today.

14. J. D. Salinger, "The Children's Echelon," unpublished (but spring 1944).

15. Story Press interoffice memo, 1944.

16. Salinger to Whit Burnett, April 22, 1944.

17. Whit Burnett to Salinger, April 14, 1944.

18. Salinger to Whit Burnett, March 19, 1944.

19. J. D. Salinger, "Two Lonely Men," unpublished (but spring 1944).

20. Ralph C. Greene and Oliver E. Allen, "What Happened off Devon," *American Heritage,* February 1985, 4.

21. Gordon A. Harrison, "The Sixth of June," *Cross Channel Attack* (Washington, D.C.: Center of Military History, United States Army, 2002 [1951]), 270.

22. Salinger to Whit Burnett, May 2, 1944.

23. Whit Burnett to Salinger, April 14, 1944.

24. Ibid.

25. Salinger to Whit Burnett, May 2, 1944.

26. J. D. Salinger, "I'm Crazy," *Collier's,* December 22, 1945, 36, 48.

Chapter 5: Hell

1. Margaret Salinger, *Dream Catcher* (New York: Washington Square Press, 2000), 53.

2. Richard Firstman, "Werner Kleeman's Private War," *The New York Times,* November 11, 2007.

3. Gordon A. Harrison, "The Sixth of June," *Cross Channel Attack* (Washington, D.C.: Center of Military History, United States Army, 2002 [1951]), 329.

4. Salinger, *Dream Catcher,* 45.

5. U.S. Center of Military History, Combatant Reports for the Fourth Infantry Division (hereafter USACMH), June 6, 1944–July 1945, Division Report for June 8, 1944.

6. Sergeant Jim McKee, 3rd Battalion, 12th Infantry Regiment, January 12, 2003.

7. USACMH, Fourth Infantry Division Report for June 12, 1944.

8. Salinger to Whit Burnett, June 12, 1944.

9. USACMH, Fourth Infantry Division Report for June 25, 1944.

10. Burnett to Harold Ober, June 9, 1944.

11. Ibid.

12. Salinger to Whit Burnett, June 28, 1944.

13. Salinger to Elizabeth Murray, September 25, 1945.

14. Charles R. Corbin (391 Field Artillery Battalion Third Armored Division), "100 Yards to Mortain 1944."

15. USACMH, Fourth Infantry Division Report for August 25, 1944.

16. Salinger to Whit Burnett, September 9, 1944.

17. Salinger, *Dream Catcher,* 60.

18. Salinger to Whit Burnett, September 9, 1944.

19. Salinger to Ernest Hemingway, July 27, 1945.

20. The capitalization is by Burnett.

21. Salinger to Elizabeth Murray, December 30, 1945.

22. J. D. Salinger, "The Magic Foxhole," unpublished (but 1944).

23. USACMH, June 6, 1944–July 1945.

24. Colonel Gerden E. Johnson, *History of the Twelfth Infantry Regiment in World War II* (Boston: National Fourth Division Association, 1947), 215–216.

25. Shelby W. Wood, Company I, 12th Infantry Regiment, Fourth Infantry Division, December 15, 2000.

26. Hugh M. Cole, *The Ardennes: Battle of the Bulge* (Washington, D.C.: USACMH, 2000), 238.

27. USACMH, Fourth Infantry Division Report for the end of October 1944.

28. Salinger, *Dream Catcher,* 65.

29. Marc Pitzke, "Verschollene Salinger-Briefe: Wir gingen durch die Hölle" (Unknown Salinger Letters: "We Went Through Hell"), *Der Spiegel,* March 17, 2010, www.spiegel.de/kultur/literatur/0,1518,683492,00.html.

30. Salinger to Werner Kleeman, April 25, 1945.

31. J. D. Salinger, "Contributors," *Story,* November–December 1944, 1.

32. Phoebe Hoban, "The Salinger File," *New York,* June 15, 1987, 40.

33. J. D. Salinger, "A Boy in France," *The Saturday Evening Post,* March 31, 1945, 21, 92.

34. J. D. Salinger, *Raise High the Roof Beam, Carpenters and Seymour—an Introduction* (Boston: Little, Brown and Company, 1991), 121.

35. Cole, *The Ardennes*, 238.

36. USACMH, Fourth Infantry Division Report for December 16, 1944.

37. Cole, *The Ardennes*, 242–257.

38. Whit Burnett/Story Press office memo, January 9, 1945.

39. J. D. Salinger, "This Sandwich Has No Mayonnaise," *Esquire*, October 1945, 54–56, 147–149.

40. Salinger to Elizabeth Murray, September 25, 1945.

41. J. D. Salinger, *Raise High the Roof Beam, Carpenters and Seymour—an Introduction*, 202.

42. J. D. Salinger, "The Ocean Full of Bowling Balls," unpublished, 1944.

43. Diary of Sergeant Ichiro Imamura, April 29, 1945; Pierre Moulin, *Dachau, Holocaust, and US Samurais: Nisei Solidiers First in Dachau?* (Bloomington, Ind.: Authorhouse, 2007), 125.

44. "Concentration Camp Listing," Jewish Virtual Library, American-Israeli Cooperative Enterprise, www.jewishvirtuallibrary.org, 2008.

45. Salinger, *Dream Catcher*, 156.

46. Salinger to Herb Kauffman, June 7, 1943.

47. Ian Hamilton, *J. D. Salinger: A Writing Life* (unpublished October galley, 1986).

48. Salinger to Elizabeth Murray, May 13, 1945.

49. Donald M. Fiene, *A Bibliographical Study of Salinger: Life, Work, and Reputation* (Madison: University of Wisconsin Press, 1962), 96.

50. J. D. Salinger, "Backstage with Esquire," *Esquire*, October 24, 1945, 34.

51. Salinger to Ernest Hemingway, July 27, 1945.

52. J. D. Salinger, "The Stranger," *Collier's*, December 1, 1945, 18, 77.

Chapter 6: Purgatory

1. Salinger to Ernest Hemingway, July 27, 1945.

2. Salinger to Elizabeth Murray, December 30, 1945.

3. Manifest of Alien Passengers, SS *Ethan Allen*, April 28, 1946.

4. Margaret Salinger, *Dream Catcher* (New York: Washington Square Press, 2000), 71.

5. Paul Alexander, *Salinger: A Biography* (Los Angeles: Renaissance Books, 1999), 113.

6. Salinger to Elizabeth Murray, September 25, 1945.

7. Ibid.

8. *History and Mission of the Counter Intelligence Corps in World War II* (Baltimore: Counter Intelligence Corps School [Fort Holabird]), 1959.

9. Basil Davenport to Salinger, March 28, 1946, Basil Davenport mss., Beinecke Rare Book and Manuscript Library, Yale University.

10. List of United States Citizens, SS *Ethan Allen*, May 10, 1946.

11. J. D. Salinger, "Birthday Boy," unpublished, ND (but 1946), Ransom Center, University of Texas at Austin.

12. Whit Burnett to Dorothy Olding, December 5, 1963.

13. Phoebe Hoban, "The Salinger File," *New York,* June 15, 1987, 40.

14. Salinger to Elizabeth Murray, September 25, 1945.

15. William Maxwell, "J. D. Salinger," *Book-of-the-Month Club News,* July 1951, 5–6.

16. "Backstage with Esquire," *Esquire,* October 24, 1945, 34.

17. J. D. Salinger, *Raise High the Roof Beam, Carpenters and Seymour—an Introduction* (Boston: Little, Brown and Company, 1991), 196.

18. Phoebe Hoban, "The Salinger File," 41.

19. 'Sonny: An Introduction," *Time,* September 15, 1961.

20. A. E. Hotchner, *Choice People: The Greats, Near-Greats, and Ingrates I Have Known* (New York: William Morrow & Company, 1984), 65–66.

21. Ibid.

22. J. D. Salinger, "The Inverted Forest," *Cosmopolitan,* December 1947, 73–109.

Chapter 7: Recognition

1. Salinger to Elizabeth Murray, May 13, 1945.

2. Salinger to Herb Kauffman, ND (but late summer 1943).

3. Salinger to William Maxwell, November 19, 1946.

4. Salinger to Elizabeth Murray, August 14, 1947.

5. Ben Yagoda, *About Town: The New Yorker and the World It Made* (Cambridge, Mass.: Da Capo Press, 2001), 205–206.

6. J. D. Salinger, "A Perfect Day for Bananafish," *The New Yorker,* January 31, 1948, 21–25.

7. J. D. Salinger, *Raise High the Roof Beam, Carpenters and Seymour—an Introduction* (Boston: Little, Brown and Company, 1991), 13.

8. Salinger to Elizabeth Murray, November 29, 1948.

9. Dorothy Olding to Whit Burnett, April 10, 1947.

10. J. D. Salinger, "A Girl I Knew," *Good Housekeeping,* February 1948, 37, 186–196.

11. J. D. Salinger, "Blue Melody," *Cosmopolitan,* September 1948, 50–51, 112–119.

12. J. D. Salinger, "The Inverted Forest," *Cosmopolitan,* December 1947, 73–109.

13. A. E. Hotchner, *Choice People: The Greats, Near-Greats, and Ingrates I Have Known* (New York: William Morrow & Company, 1984), 66.

14. Alec Wilkinson, *My Mentor: A Young Man's Friendship with William Maxwell* (Boston: Houghton Mifflin, 2002), 58–62.

15. Ian Hamilton, *J. D. Salinger: A Writing Life* (unpublished October galley, 1986), 102.

16. J. D. Salinger, "Uncle Wiggily in Connecticut," *The New Yorker*, March 20, 1948, 30–36.

17. J. D. Salinger, "Just Before the War with the Eskimos," *The New Yorker*, June 5, 1948, 37–40, 42, 44, 46.

Chapter 8: Reaffirmation

1. Margaret Salinger, *Dream Catcher* (New York: Washington Square Press, 2000), 17–18.

2. J. D. Salinger, *The Catcher in the Rye* (Boston: Little, Brown and Company, 1991), 139.

3. J. D. Salinger, "Notes on the Holocaust," 1948, Harry Ransom Center, University of Texas at Austin.

4. Joseph Wechsberg, "The Children of Lidice," *The New Yorker*, May 1, 1948, 51.

5. Paul Alexander, *Salinger: A Biography* (Los Angeles: Renaissance Books, 1999), 132.

6. J. D. Salinger, "Down at the Dinghy," *Harper's*, April 1949, 87–91.

7. Truman Capote, "La Côte Basque," *Unanswered Prayers* (London: Plume, 1987).

8. Salinger to Elizabeth Murray, November 29, 1948.

9. Salinger to Gus Lobrano, January 14, 1949.

10. Donald M. Fiene, *A Bibliographical Study of J. D. Salinger: Life, Work, and Reputation* (Louisville: University of Louisville, 1961), 23.

11. Gus Lobrano to Dorothy Olding, ND (but 1949).

12. Salinger to Gus Lobrano, October 12, 1948.

13. From "Conversations with John Updike," NPR, 1994.

14. Martha Foley, *Best American Short Stories, 1915–1950* (Boston: Houghton Mifflin, 1952), 449.

15. "J. D. Salinger—Biographical," *Harper's*, April 1949, 8.

16. Mary Milligan, Sarah Lawrence College Secretary, to Donald Fiene, June 7, 1971.

17. Ian Hamilton, *J. D. Salinger: A Writing Life* (unpublished October galley, 1986), 110.

18. "Backstage with Esquire," *Esquire*, October 24, 1945, 34.

19. Alexander, *Salinger: A Biography*, 142.

20. J. D. Salinger, "For Esmé—with Love and Squalor," *The New Yorker*, April 8, 1950, 28–36.

21. Salinger to Whit Burnett, March 14, 1944.

Chapter 9: Holden

1. Salinger to Gus Lobrano, April 20, 1950.

2. Jack Skow, "Sonny: An Introduction," *Time,* September 15, 1961, 84–90.

3. Ian Hamilton, *In Search of J. D. Salinger* (London: Minerva Press, 1988), 122.

4. William Maxwell, "Salinger," *Book-of-the-Month Club News,* July 1951, 5–6.

5. Salinger to the *Saturday Review,* July 14, 1951, 12–13.

6. Robert Giroux to Ian Hamilton, May 2, 1984.

7. Jamie Hamilton to Salinger, August 18, 1950.

8. Salinger to Jamie Hamilton, December 11, 1951.

9. Robert Giroux to Ian Hamilton, May 2, 1984.

10. Don Congdon to Ian Hamilton, September 1985.

11. Jamie Hamilton to John Betjeman, ND.

12. Gus Lobrano to Salinger, January 25, 1951.

13. Sarah Van Boven, "Judging a Book by Its Cover," *Princeton Alumni Weekly,* June 10, 1998.

14. Salinger to Jamie Hamilton, December 11, 1951.

15. Arthur Vanderbilt, *The Making of a Bestseller: From Author to Reader* (Jefferson, N.C.: McFarland & Company, 1999), 94.

16. Whit Burnett to the Publicity Department, Little, Brown and Company, April 6, 1951.

17. D. Angus Cameron to Whit Burnett, April 14, 1951.

18. Salinger to Gus Lobrano, June 3, 1951.

19. J. D. Salinger, *The Catcher in the Rye* (Boston: Little, Brown and Company, 1991), 117.

20. Salinger to Gus Lobrano, June 3, 1951.

21. Salinger to Jamie Hamilton (from Fort William, Scotland), June 7, 1951.

22. Passenger list, SS *Mauretania,* July 11, 1951.

23. "With Love & 20-20 Vision," *Time,* July 16, 1951, 97.

24. James Stern, "Aw, the World's a Crumby Place," *The New York Times,* July 15, 1951.

25. Maxwell, "J. D. Salinger."

26. Salinger to Dorothy Olding, September 7, 1973.

Chapter 10: Crossroads

1. Joyce Carol Oates, *First Person Singular: Writers on Their Craft* (Windsor: Ontario Review Press, 1983), 6.

2. J. D. Salinger, "A Salute to Whit Burnett," *Fiction Writer's Handbook* (New York: Harper and Row, 1975).

3. William Faulkner, *Faulkner in the University,* ed. Frederick L. Gwynn and Joseph L. Blotner (Charlottesville: University of Virginia Press, 1959).

4. J. D. Salinger, *The Catcher in the Rye* (Boston: Little, Brown and Company, 1991), 18.

5. Margaret Salinger, *Dream Catcher* (New York: Washington Square Press, 2000), 11.

6. J. D. Salinger to Eloise Perry Hazard, "Eight Fiction Finds," *Saturday Review,* February 16, 1952, 16.

7. Ian Hamilton, *In Search of J. D. Salinger* (London: Minerva Press, 1989), 127.

8. Salinger, *Dream Catcher,* 11.

9. Salinger to Jamie Hamilton, August 4, 1951.

10. Salinger to Jamie Hamilton, October 17, 1951.

11. Salinger to Jamie Hamilton, December 11, 1951.

12. Salinger to Gus Lobrano, ND (but from Westport, 1951).

13. Gus Lobrano to Salinger, November 14, 1951.

14. Salinger to Gus Lobrano, November 15, 1951.

15. J. D. Salinger, "De Daumier–Smith's Blue Period," *World Review,* May 1952, 33–48.

16. Salinger to Jamie Hamilton, December 11, 1951.

17. Thomas Wolfe, "The Virtues of Gutter Journalism," *San Francisco Chronicle,* December 17, 2000.

18. Paul Alexander, *Salinger: A Biography* (Los Angeles: Renaissance Press, 1999), 160.

19. Wolfe, "The Virtues of Gutter Journalism."

20. Whit Burnett to Salinger, February 19, 1952.

21. Ian Hamilton, *J. D. Salinger: A Writing Life* (unpublished October galley, 1986), 127.

22. Salinger to William E. Ferguson, June 25, 1952.

23. Ramakrishna-Vivekananda Center of New York, 1997.

24. Salinger, *Dream Catcher,* 80–82.

25. Salinger to Gus Lobrano, November 15, 1951.

26. J. D. Salinger, "Teddy," *The New Yorker,* January 31, 1953, 26–34, 36, 38, 40–41, 44–45.

27. J. D. Salinger, *Raise High the Roof Beam, Carpenters and Seymour—an Introduction* (Boston: Little, Brown and Company, 1991), 205.

Chapter 11: Positioning

1. Sullivan County Registry of Deeds, vol. 354, 1953, 233.

2. Ian Hamilton, *J. D. Salinger: A Writing Life* (unpublished October galley, 1986), 138.

3. Jamie Hamilton to Salinger, November 25, 1952.

4. Salinger to Jamie Hamilton, November 17, 1952.

5. Jamie Hamilton to Salinger, November 25, 1952.

6. Salinger to Gus Lobrano, April 1, 1953.

7. Charles Poore, "Books of the Times," *The New York Times,* April 9, 1953.

8. Eudora Welty, "Threads of Innocence," *The New York Times,* April 5, 1953.

9. Salinger to Gus Lobrano, April 1, 1953.

10. Ibid.

11. Margaret Salinger, *Dream Catcher* (New York: Washington Square Press, 2000), 83.

12. List of In-Bound Passengers, SS *Vulcania,* September 16, 1953.

13. J. D. Salinger, *The Catcher in the Rye* (Boston: Little, Brown and Company, 1991), 204.

Chapter 12: Franny

1. Joanna Mockler, "Life Can Begin at Any Age When You Decide to Make a Difference in the Lives of Others," *The Advisor,* Summer 2004, 3.

2. Manifest of Alien Passengers for the United States, SS *Scythia,* July 7, 1940.

3. Margaret Salinger, *Dream Catcher* (New York: Washington Square Press, 2000), 6–7.

4. Salinger to Gus Lobrano, December 15, 1951.

5. J. D. Salinger, *Franny and Zooey* (Boston: Little, Brown and Company, 1991), 41.

6. Salinger to Gus Lobrano, December 20, 1954.

Chapter 13: Two Families

1. Certificate of Marriage for Jerome D. Salinger and Claire Douglas, Office of Secretary of State, State of Vermont, February 17, 1955.

2. Ian Hamilton, *In Search of J. D. Salinger* (London: Minerva Press, 1988), 146.

3. Phoebe Hoban, "The Salinger File," *New York,* June 15, 1987, 41.

4. M., *The Gospels of Sri Ramakrishna* (New York: Ramakrishna-Vivekananda Center, 1944), chap. 1, "Master and Disciple."

5. J. D. Salinger, *Raise High the Roof Beam, Carpenters and Seymour—an Introduction* (Boston: Little, Brown and Company, 1991), 7.

6. J. D. Salinger, *Franny and Zooey* (dust jacket excerpt) (Boston: Little, Brown and Company, 1961).

Chapter 14: Zooey

1. Certificate of Live Birth, State of New Hampshire, Margaret Ann Salinger, December 17, 1955.

2. J. D. Salinger, *Raise High the Roof Beam, Carpenters and Seymour—an Introduction* (Boston: Little, Brown and Company, 1991), 91.

3. Margaret Salinger, *Dream Catcher* (New York: Washington Square Press, 2000), 115.

4. Salinger to Learned Hand, April 16, 1956.

5. Ibid.

6. Sue Publicover, "Still Growing at 91? Windsor Teacher Celebrates 65 Years of Organic Farming," *Vermont Woman,* April 2006, www.vermontwoman .com/articles/0406/organic_gardener.shtml, retrieved April 2006.

7. Salinger to Jamie Hamilton, June 19, 1957.

8. Salinger to Learned Hand, April 16, 1956.

9. Mordecai Richler, "The Road to Dyspepsia," *The New York Times,* August 9, 1987.

10. Ibid.

11. Salinger to K. S. White, March 29, 1956.

12. Salinger to Whit Burnett, February 24, 1940.

13. Salinger to "Miss Cardoza," April 16, 1956.

14. William Maxwell to Harold Ober, February 8, 1956.

15. Salinger to Jamie Hamilton, April 16, 1956.

16. Ibid.

17. Ben Yagoda, *About Town:* The New Yorker *and the World It Made* (Cambridge, Mass.: Da Capo Press, 2001), 286.

18. Salinger to "Miss Cardoza," April 16, 1956.

19. Mel Elfin, "The Mysterious J. D. Salinger," *Newsweek,* May 30, 1960, 92–94.

20. K. S. White to Salinger, November 20, 1956.

21. K. S. White to Salinger, January 2, 1957.

22. Ibid.

23. Salinger, *Dream Catcher,* 115–116.

24. Jerry Wald to H. N. Swanson, January 25, 1957.

25. J. D. Salinger, *Franny and Zooey* (Boston: Little, Brown and Company, 1991), 51.

26. "Backstage with *Esquire,*" *Esquire,* October 24, 1945, 34.

27. Salinger, *Franny and Zooey,* 169.

28. Salinger, *Franny and Zooey,* 201.

Chapter 15: Seymour

1. Paul Alexander, *Salinger: A Biography* (Los Angeles: Renaissance Books, 1999), 199.

2. Salinger to Jamie Hamilton, June 19, 1957.

3. Ibid.

4. Salinger to Roger Machell, February 1958.

5. Salinger to Learned Hand, January 10, 1958.

6. Salinger to Learned Hand, October 27, 1958.

7. Ian Hamilton, *J. D. Salinger: A Writing Life* (unpublished October galley, 1986).

8. Ben Yagoda, *About Town:* The New Yorker *and the World It Made* (Cambridge, Mass.: Da Capo Press, 2001), 287.

9. Salinger to Warner G. Rice (English Department chairman, University of Michigan), January 10, 1957.

10. Salinger to "Mr. Hammond," June 16, 1957.

11. Salinger to "Mr. Stevens," October 21, 1962.

12. J. D. Salinger, *Raise High the Roof Beam, Carpenters and Seymour—an Introduction* (Boston: Little, Brown and Company, 1991), 160.

13. Ibid., 114.

14. Salinger to Learned Hand, April 18, 1958.

Chapter 16: Dark Summit

1. Salinger to Learned Hand, April 18, 1958.

2. Letter to the editor, *New York Post,* December 9, 1959, 49.

3. Whit Burnett to Salinger, November 7, 1959.

4. Dorothy Olding to Whit Burnett, November 10, 1959.

5. State of Vermont, Certified Copy of Certificate of Birth, Matthew Robert Salinger, August 9, 1960.

6. Salinger to Learned Hand, April 18, 1960.

7. Ibid.

8. Jamie Hamilton to Ian Hamilton, June 26, 1984.

9. J. D. Salinger, *Franny and Zooey,* dedication (Boston: Little, Brown and Company, 1961).

10. Ernest Havemann, "The Mysterious J. D. Salinger," *Newsweek,* May 30, 1960, 92–94.

11. *New York Post Magazine,* April 30, 1961, 5.

12. Donald Fiene, *A Bibliographical Study of J. D. Salinger: Life, Work and Reputation,* unpublished thesis paper, August 26, 1961.

13. Frederick A. Colwell, Chief, American Specialists Branch, Bureau of Educational and Cultural Affairs, to Judge Learned Hand, September 20, 1960.

14. Learned Hand to Frederick A. Colwell, September 28, 1960.

15. Frederick A. Colwell to Learned Hand, October 5, 1960.

16. Judge Learned Hand to Frederick A. Colwell, October 11, 1960.

17. Salinger to Ned Bradford, May 13, 1961.

18. Norman Mailer, "Evaluation: Quick and Expensive Comments on the Talent in the Room," *Advertisements for Myself* (New York: Putnam, 1959), 467–468.

19. Alfred Kazin, "J. D. Salinger: Everybody's Favorite," *The Atlantic Monthly,* August 1961, 27–31.

20. Joan Didion, "Finally (Fashionably) Spurious," *National Review,* November 18, 1961, 341–342.

21. John Updike, "Anxious Days for the Glass Family," *The New York Times Book Review,* September 17, 1961, 1, 52.

22. Mary McCarthy, "J. D. Salinger's Closed Circuit," *The Observer,* June 1962.

23. Frances Kiernan, *Seeing Mary Plain: A Life of Mary McCarthy* (London: Norton, 2002), 493.

24. J. D. Salinger, *Franny and Zooey,* dust jacket excerpt (Boston: Little, Brown and Company, 1961).

25. "Sonny—an Introduction," *Time,* September 15, 1961, 84–90.

26. Ernest Havemann, "The Search for the Mysterious J. D. Salinger," *Life,* November 3, 1961, 141.

Chapter 17: Detachment

1. J. D. Salinger, *Raise High the Roof Beam, Carpenters and Seymour—an Introduction* (Boston: Little, Brown and Company, 1991), 121.

2. Salinger to Learned Hand, April 18, 1960.

3. Salinger to Roger Machell, March 22, 1960.

4. Salinger to Learned Hand, February 19, 1961.

5. Margaret Salinger, *Dream Catcher* (New York: Washington Square Press, 2000), 148.

6. J. D. Salinger, *Franny and Zooey,* dust jacket excerpt (Boston: Little, Brown and Company, 1961).

7. Salinger to Donald Fiene, September 6, 1960.

8. Heinemann Press memo, March 20, 1962.

9. Salinger to Miss Pat Cork, Hughes Massie & Co., Ltd., May 26, 1962.

10. Miss Pat Cork, Hughes Massie & Co., Ltd., to Ober Associates, May 1, 1962.

11. J. D. Salinger, *Raise High the Roof Beam, Carpenters and Seymour—an Introduction,* dust jacket commentary.

12. Irving Howe, "More Reflections in the Glass Mirror," *The New York Times Book Review,* April 7, 1963, 4–5, 34.

13. "The Glass House Gang," *Time,* February 8, 1963.

14. J. D. Salinger, *Raise High the Roof Beam, Carpenters and Seymour—an Introduction,* dedication.

Chapter 18: Farewell

1. Eliot Fremont-Smith, "Franny and Zooey," *The Village Voice,* March 8, 1962.

2. M., *The Gospels of Sri Ramakrishna* (New York: Ramakrishna-Vivekananda Center, 1944), ch. 4, "Advice to Householders."

3. Margaret Salinger, *Dream Catcher* (New York: Washington Square Press, 2000), 142.

4. Paul Alexander, *Salinger: A Biography* (Los Angeles: Renaissance Books, 1999), 221–223.

5. Salinger, *Dream Catcher,* 154.

6. Whit Burnett to Salinger, April 17, 1965.

7. Salinger, *Dream Catcher,* 185.

8. William Shawn to Jock Whitney, April 8, 1965.

9. Salinger to Jock Whitney, April 1965.

10. Kenneth C. Davis, *Two-Bit Culture: The Paperbacking of America* (Boston: Houghton Mifflin, 1984), 204.

11. William Maxwell to Susan Stamberg, *All Things Considered,* NPR, February 24, 1997.

12. J. D. Salinger, "Hapworth 16, 1924," *The New Yorker,* June 19, 1965, 32–113.

13. Janet Malcolm, "Justice to J. D. Salinger," *The New York Review of Books,* June 21, 2001, www.huffingtonpost.com/2010/01/28/jd-salinger-reviews-the-n_n_440847.html, retrieved July 27, 2010 (the Web version of the original article has expired).

14. J. D. Salinger, *Raise High the Roof Beam, Carpenters and Seymour—an Introduction* (Boston: Little, Brown and Company, 1991), 169.

15. Dorothy Olding to Hughes Massie & Company, January 14, 1972.

16. Salinger to E. Michael Mitchell, October 16, 1966.

Chapter 19: The Poetry of Silence

1. Dr. Gerard L. Gaudrault to State of New Hampshire Superior Court, filed September 28, 1967.

2. State of New Hampshire Superior Court, Libel for Divorce, *Claire Salinger v. Jerome D. Salinger,* September 14, 1967.

3. Salinger to E. Michael Mitchell, October 16, 1966.

4. State of New Hampshire Superior Court, Libel for Divorce, *Claire Salinger v. Jerome D. Salinger,* September 14, 1967.

5. Dorothy Olding to Hughes Massie & Company, January 14, 1972.

6. Salinger to Whit Burnett, January 18, 1968.

7. Olding to Hughes Massie & Company, January 14, 1972.

8. "Depositions Yield J. D. Salinger Details," *The New York Times,* December 12, 1986.

9. Lacey Fosburgh, "J. D. Salinger Speaks About His Silence," *The New York Times,* November 3, 1974.

10. Ibid.

11. Betty Eppes, "What I Did Last Summer," *The Paris Review,* July 24, 1981, 221–239.

12. Salinger to Janet Eagleson, March 2, 1981.

13. Salinger to Janet Eagleson, June 28, 1981.

14. Salinger to E. Michael Mitchell, December 25, 1984.

15. Margaret Salinger, *Dream Catcher* (New York: Washington Square Press, 2000), 388.

16. Salinger to Janet Eagleson, May 1, 1981.

17. Salinger to E. Michael Mitchell, April 6, 1985.

18. Ian Hamilton, *In Search of J. D. Salinger* (London: Minerva Press, 1988), 191.

19. Salinger to Ian Hamilton, ND (but 1986).

20. Mordecai Richler, "Summer Reading; Rises at Dawn, Writes, Then Retires," *The New York Times Book Review,* June 5, 1988.

21. Ian Hamilton, interview with Don Swain for CBS Radio, 1988.

22. *All Things Considered,* NPR, February 24, 1997, 7.

23. *The World Today,* ABC News, June 24, 1999.

24. Salinger to E. Michael Mitchell, December 16, 1992.

25. Salinger to William Dix, July 6, 1993.

Chapter 20: Coming Through the Rye

1. Jane Howard, "Can a Nice Novelist Finish First?" *Life,* November 4, 1966, 81.

2. Exhibit B, Filing 1, *Salinger et al. v. John Doe et al.,* 09civ 50951dab, F2d 31-36, June 1, 2009.

3. Filing 5, *Salinger et al. v. John Doe et al.,* 09civ 50951dab, F2d 12. June 1, 2009.

4. Fredrik Colting to *The Sunday Telegraph,* May 30, 2009.

5. Fredrik Colting to the author, January 14, 2010.

6. Filing 5, *Salinger et al. v. John Doe et al.,* 09civ 50951dab, F2d 3, June 1, 2009.

7. Filing 17, *Salinger et al. v. John Doe et al.,* 09civ 50951dab, F2d 13, June 15, 2009.

8. Ibid.

9. Filing 6, *Salinger et al. v. John Doe et al.*, 09civ 50951dab, F2d 3, June 2, 2009.

10. *Salinger et al. v. John Doe et al.*, 09civ 50951dab, F2d 22 (2d Cir. 2009).

11. *Salinger et al. v. John Doe et al.*, 09civ 50951dab, F2d 35 (2d Cir. 2009).

12. *Salinger et al. v. John Doe et al.*, 09civ 50951dab, F2d 11 (2d Cir. 2009).

13. Fredrik Colting to the author, January 14, 2010.

14. J. D. Salinger, *The Catcher in the Rye* (Little, Brown and Company, 1991), 121.

15. Betty Eppes, "What I Did Last Summer," *The Paris Review*, July 24, 1981, 221–239.

16. Fredrik Colting to the author, January 14, 2010.

17. Brief for amicus curiae filing, *Salinger v. Colting et al.*, 09 2878 cv, F. App. 2d 42, August 7, 2009.

18. Brief for plaintiff-appellee, *Salinger v. Colting et al.*, 09 2878 cv, F. App. 2d 1, August 17, 2009.

Index

Page numbers in *italics* refer to illustrations.

About the Author

KENNETH SLAWENSKI is the creator of DeadCaulfields.com, a website founded in 2004 and recommended by *The New York Times*. He has been working on this biography for eight years. Slawenski was born in New Jersey and has lived there all his life.

About the Type

This book was set in Galliard, a typeface designed by Matthew Carter for the Mergenthaler Linotype Company in 1978. Galliard is based on the sixteenth-century typefaces of Robert Granjon.